Implementing Parallel and Distributed Systems

Parallel and distributed systems (PADS) have evolved from the early days of computational science and supercomputers to a wide range of novel computing paradigms, each of which is exploited to tackle specific problems or application needs, including distributed systems, parallel computing, and cluster computing, generally called high-performance computing (HPC). Grid, Cloud, and Fog computing patterns are the most important of these PADS paradigms, which share common concepts in practice.

Many-core architectures, multi-core cluster-based supercomputers, and Cloud Computing paradigms in this era of exascale computers have tremendously influenced the way computing is applied in science and academia (e.g., scientific computing and large-scale simulations). *Implementing Parallel and Distributed Systems* presents a PADS infrastructure known as Parvicursor that can facilitate the construction of such scalable and high-performance parallel distributed systems as HPC, Grid, and Cloud Computing.

This book covers parallel programming models, techniques, tools, development frameworks, and advanced concepts of parallel computer systems used in the construction of distributed and HPC systems. It specifies a roadmap for developing high-performance client-server applications for distributed environments and supplies step-by-step procedures for constructing a native and object-oriented C++ platform.

FEATURES:

- Hardware and software perspectives on parallelism
- Parallel programming many-core processors, computer networks and storage systems
- Parvicursor.NET Framework: a partial, native, and cross-platform C++ implementation of the .NET Framework
- xThread: a distributed thread programming model by combining thread-level parallelism and distributed memory programming models
- xDFS: a native cross-platform framework for efficient file transfer
- Parallel programming for HPC systems and supercomputers using message passing interface (MPI)

Focusing on data transmission speed that exploits the computing power of multi-core processors and cutting-edge system-on-chip (SoC) architectures, it explains how to implement an energy-efficient infrastructure and examines distributing threads amongst Cloud nodes. Taking a solid approach to design and implementation, this book is a complete reference for designing, implementing, and deploying these very complicated systems.

Implementing Parallel and Distributed Systems

Alireza Poshtkohi
M. B. Ghaznavi-Ghoushchi

CRC Press
Taylor & Francis Group
Boca Raton London New York

CRC Press is an imprint of the
Taylor & Francis Group, an **informa** business

AN AUERBACH BOOK

Cover Image Credit: Mr. Amir Sadeghian

First Edition published 2023
by CRC Press
6000 Broken Sound Parkway NW, Suite 300, Boca Raton, FL 33487-2742

and by CRC Press
4 Park Square, Milton Park, Abingdon, Oxon, OX14 4RN

CRC Press is an imprint of Taylor & Francis Group, LLC

ISBN: 978-1-032-45867-0 (hbk)
ISBN: 978-1-032-15122-9 (pbk)
ISBN: 978-1-003-37904-1 (ebk)

DOI: 10.1201/9781003379041

Typeset in Garamond
by SPi Technologies India Pvt Ltd (Straive)

Please access the Instructor and Student Resources: https://routledge.com/9781032151229.

"If I have seen further than others, it is by standing upon the shoulders of giants."

Isaac Newton

The first author would like to dedicate this book to his parents,
Effat *and* **Abdollah**,
Also for all leading pioneers in
computer science,
particularly
Dennis M. Ritchie, Ian T. Foster *and* **Charles Babbage**

The second author wishes to thank his parents, family, teachers and professors.

Contents

Preface

This book arrives at a critical time when Moore's Law is fading, and the development of distributed systems and high-performance computing is of unprecedented demand and importance. The book aims to convey necessary knowledge, principles, and software practices that underly the development of a vast majority of parallel and distributed systems, particularly Grid/Cloud Computing and supercomputers. Advanced topics relevant to computer architecture, operating systems, and parallel programming techniques and models for many-core processors, supercomputers, and computer networks are provided to allow readers in order to gain incremental experience to implement their own platforms from scratch. The text helps you gradually think parallel through a programming language that had been primarily intended to model distributed systems!

Over the past seven decades, computers have created a dramatic revolution in civilisation. Parallel and distributed systems (PADS) have evolved from their first uses in the early days of computational science and supercomputers into a wide range of novel computing paradigms, each of which is exploited to tackle particular problems or application needs, including distributed systems, parallel computing and cluster computing generally called high-performance computing (HPC). The simultaneous growth in the availability of scientific demands, big data, and the number of simultaneous users on the Internet places particular pressure on the need to carry out computing tasks in parallel, distributed fashion or simultaneously both. PADS takes place across many different topic areas in computer science and applied mathematics, including algorithms, computer architecture, networks, operating systems, software engineering, and scientific computing. Since the year 2007, all the commercial processors have been multi/many-core processors, each core operates in parallel with others. This enables the era of computer networks just inside a tiny computer chip. This is the third revolution in human society after the industrial and agricultural revolutions. This revolution is considerably influencing on our life, science, and technology trends. Commodity clusters revolutionised HPC when they first appeared three decades ago. As scale and complexity have grown, new challenges such as energy efficiency and optimisation and software complexity have emerged. Petascale clusters are increasingly common and dominate the Top500 list of the world's most powerful computers. Recently, the world's fastest supercomputers are emerging as exascale systems. The push towards exascale computing has enabled science applications to run complex simulations. However, the gap between computation and I/O has grown wider, even as applications seek to generate and persist increasing amounts of data. Optimising I/O is challenging and remains a bottleneck at scale.

Additionally, the results of academic research and industrial applications have turned into new generations of distributed computing paradigms. Grid, Cloud, and Fog computing patterns are the most important of them. All of these PADS paradigms have practically many concepts in common. Parallelism on different levels is becoming ubiquitous in today and tomorrow's computers. Programmers are facing with hundreds of hardware threads per processor chip to leverage thread-level parallelism. The trend in many-core architectures, multi-core cluster-based supercomputers, and Cloud Computing paradigms altogether towards the era of exascale computers has tremendously influenced on the way that the application of computing is being used in science and academia, such as scientific computing and large-scale simulations. In this book, we present our experiences to build a PADS infrastructure referred to as Parvicursor from the ground up that can facilitate the construction of scalable and high-performance parallel distributed systems such as HPC, Grid, and Cloud Computing. With computers and computer networks getting cheaper and cheaper, our lives are under continual change more and more.

The authors of the current book have realised the lack of a complete reference for designing, implementing, and deploying these types of systems that have very complicated structures. In other words, to create a distributed environment or each of the expressed technologies above, a developer, a student, or a researcher, to create customised software or participate in a large design project, has to spend several years learning about many practical and research results and a variety of references towards getting familiar with available development methods. By recognising this need for the scientific community, we decided to publish our experiences in the context of a technical, academic book. The present book attempts to express the experiences of its authors from different angles to the reader.

The book covers parallel programming models, techniques, tools, development frameworks, and advanced concepts of parallel computer systems used in the construction of distributed and HPC systems. It describes how to specify a roadmap for developing high-performance client-server applications for distributed environments and supplies step-by-step procedures for constructing a native and object-oriented C++ platform. Focusing on data transmission speed that exploits the computing power of multi-core processors and cutting-edge System-on-Chip (SoC) architectures, it explains how to implement an energy-efficient infrastructure and examines distributing threads amongst Cloud nodes. We take a solid approach to describe what we have carried out to design and implement a large number of research projects for PADS. It is worthwhile to note that such a book is unique in its own right because scholars do not usually provide a precise and detailed guideline on how they have implemented their platforms at the source-code level and only present a high-level structure of their work. There is almost no reference not only how to develop distributed systems from an architectural point of view but rather from the ground-up. The text will strive to give the opportunity to the readers to gradually practise what they are learning through the several chapters of the book as a series of case studies. What will be published by the authors in this book is the result of 15 years of learning, researching, and implementing a wide array of distributed applications ranging from HPC to complex realistic systems such as Grid and Cloud computing.

There is no single best sequence in which to approach the chapters of this book, except that all readers are supposed to start with Chapter 1. If you do not want to read everything and have basic knowledge of computer science, you may skip reading Chapters 1 through 3. It is worth noting that many chapters of the current book have been successfully taught to both undergraduate and postgraduate students in computer science and electrical engineering over years by the first author.

The authors also provide a comprehensive package for rapid application development using the frameworks introduced in this book, including a Linux image, a Windows development package, the latest source codes, etc. The readers are strongly recommended to benefit from this package that can be found on the GitHub page below: `https://github.com/poshtkohi/pads`

Additionally, the book structure is given as follows:

Chapter No.	Chapter Title	Chapter Description
1.	Introduction	This chapter presents a historical overview of the development of computing from its origins in analogue computers to digital computers. Current and future status of computing in distributed systems and high-performance computing (HPC) paradigms are discussed. Some theoretical aspects of computing are also provided.
2.	IoT and Distributed Systems	This chapter attempts at giving the necessity and a high-level overview of the current status of distributed systems.
3.	Advanced Operating System Concepts in Distributed Systems Design	Operating systems have been at the heart of parallel and distributed systems for more than half a century. This chapter first lays a conceptual framework for operating systems. Then, a comprehensive classification of operating systems is given, which plays major roles in the future of exascale computers; to name a few, exokernel OSes and language-based OSes. A number of hardware and software aspects of optimal design concerns in operating systems are also presented.
4.	Parallelism for the Many-Core Era: Hardware and Software Perspectives	Many-core processor architectures are now an integral part of modern computing systems ranging from embedded systems to supercomputers. This chapter lays the foundation of the book in order to define parallelism at different levels of abstraction from instruction-level parallelism and thread-level parallelism to heterogenous hardware accelerators and transactional memory. Software aspects underlying the hardware concepts are also given, including many-core OSs, synchronisation, deadlocks, graph theory, and so on. The emphasis here is on many-core processors. The chapter concludes by instructing the reader to set up a Linux-based Code::Blocks environment needed to develop parallel programs throughout the next chapters.

Chapter No.	Chapter Title	Chapter Description
5.	Parallelism for the the Many-Core Era: A Programming Perspective	Parallel programming is a non-trivial task and is often much more complex compared to standard sequential programming models. This chapter prepares the reader to take his long journey into the world of parallel programming through thread-level parallelism for many-core machines. The reader gradually becomes familiar with a C++ library for parallel programming which is part of the Parvicursor.NET Framework explained in Chapter 8. Since the Parvicursor.NET Framework is a partial C++ implementation of the Microsoft.NET standard, a programmer having minimal knowledge of the C# programming language can quickly dive into the chapter. Parvicursor.NET applications seamlessly run on many operating systems including Windows, Linux, and Android! Threads, mutual exclusion primitives, barriers, condition variables, fibres, implementation aspects of thread pools and lock-free data structures, and several other parallel programming constructs are introduced through several examples. The chapter concludes with an introduction to programming transactional memory systems.
6.	Storage Systems: A Parallel Programming Perspective	Although parallel computers have enabled science applications to run complex simulations, the gap between computation and I/O has grown wider. Optimising I/O is challenging and remains a bottleneck at scale. This chapter deals with storage systems. First, a hardware view of the underlying storage systems and their profiling is described. Then, programming interfaces from the Parvicursor.NET Framework, which are widely used to manipulate files and directories in Chapter 10, are discussed. The chapter shows several examples of concurrent file/ directory operations whose underlying procedures are implemented using threads, condition variables, and thread pools. The examples aim to combine I/O with concurrency that is heavily employed in the Parvicursor infrastructure (e.g., Chapter 10).
7.	Computer Networks: A Parallel Programming Approach	Complex network architectures are an integral part of distributed systems. This chapter begins with an introduction to principles used in network layers. Major network protocols and network architectures are elaborated, including TCP/IP stack, InfiniBand hardware and HTTP protocol. A major part of the chapter is devoted to developing optimal network programming strategies, where parallelism is made explicit to the developer. Multi-threaded client-server examples are aimed at preparing the reader for advanced network programming concepts. Next, the chapter takes an asynchronous parallel approach

Chapter No.	Chapter Title	Chapter Description
		to network programming. An asynchronous event-driven I/O library based on the ECAM.NET standard is designed and implemented in the native C++ code. The framework makes heavy use of thread pools and asynchronous sockets from the Linux kernel. We give several practical examples of using its powerful programming interface. The asynchronous framework comes up with several many-core programming constructs that allow the programmer to efficiently manage the execution of network sessions across processor cores. The chapter closes by developing a fully-fledged concurrent HTTP proxy server that supports hundreds of thousands of network requests.
8.	Parvicursor.NET Framework: A Partial, Native, and Cross-Platform C++ Implementation of the .NET Framework	This chapter explains step-by-step procedures that guide the reader towards constructing an object-oriented C++ platform called Parvicursor.NET Framework. In fact, the Parvicursor.NET Framework is a native and cross-platform implementation of the standard .NET CLI (Common Language Infrastructure) profiles and libraries relied upon the standard ISO C++. It provides fundamental framework libraries and classes easily to develop/port .NET-based applications in/into native C++ on most contemporary platforms, including Microsoft Windows operating systems and POSIX-compliant operating systems like Linux.
9.	Parvicursor Infrastructure to Facilitate the Design of Grid/Cloud Computing and HPC Systems	In this chapter, we present the Parvicursor infrastructure, a low-level middleware system grounded on a specialised concept of distributed objects and native ECMA.NET-compliant execution for highly concurrent distributed systems, to make writing middleware easier on heterogeneous platforms. It takes care of low-level network programming interfaces for Grid/Cloud-specific platforms and allows the middleware architects to focus their efforts on their middleware logic with the help of the integrated, scalable, Parvicursor Execution System. Specifically, the xThread parallel programming model is introduced that provides the capability of remote code execution, dynamic distributed object registration and activation, transparent communication on the underlying transport protocols, data marshalling and unmarshalling, distributed operation dispatching, checkpoint/restore, etc.

Chapter No.	Chapter Title	Chapter Description
10.	xDFS: A Native Cross-Platform Framework for Efficient File Transfers in Dynamic Cloud/Internet Environments	This chapter describes a highly concurrent file transfer protocol on top of the Parvicursor infrastructure. We introduce multi-threaded event-driven pipelined server architecture for the protocol. The position of the xDFS protocol is detailed amongst existing file transfer protocols widely used in Cloud environments. High-performance client-server design plays a key role in satisfying the performance needs of different applications in distributed systems. In this chapter, we specify a roadmap to performantly program client-server applications.
11.	Parallel Programming Languages for High-Performance Computing	This chapter reviews the state-of-the-art parallel programming languages, models, and frameworks to develop large-scale parallel systems in high-performance computing and supercomputers. Subsequently, it provides a brief introduction to advanced features in the latest version of the Message Passing Interface (MPI) standard. We will implement several interesting example problems using MPI such as scalability of parallel programs and parallel applications for scientific computing systems. The necessary mathematical background is likewise given.

Acknowledgement

The authors wish to give special thanks to Mr. Amir Sadeghian for providing the book cover image, which was taken from the world-renowned building of Nasir-ol-Molk located in the ancient city of Shiraz, Iran.

Authors

Alireza Poshtkohi applies computer science and mathematics to tackle grand research challenges in engineering, physics, and medicine. He has worked internationally in both academia and industry in many different roles ranging from computer scientist, neuroscientist, university lecturer, electronics engineer, software engineer, IT consultant and data centre architect, to full-stack developer. He holds BSc and MSc degrees and a PhD in electrical and electronics engineering and computational neuroscience, respectively. To date, he has taught 17 courses—such as parallel algorithms, advanced algorithms, operating systems, and computer networks, to name just a few—in electrical and computer engineering departments at different universities. His current research interests include applied mathematics, biophysics, high-performance computing, and theoretical physics.

M. B. Ghaznavi-Ghoushchi holds a BSc degree from Shiraz University, Shiraz, Iran (1993), and MSc and PhD both from Tarbiat Modares University (TMU), Tehran, Iran, in 1997 and 2003, respectively. During 2003–2004, he was a researcher at TMU Institute of Information Technology. He is the founder and director of High-Performance and Cloud Computing (HPCC) and Integrated Circuits and Systems (ICS) laboratories at Shahed University. He is currently an associate professor at Shahed University, Tehran, Iran. His interests include VLSI Design; Low Power and Energy-Efficient circuits and systems; Computer-Aided Design Automation for Mixed Signal; and UML-based designs for SoC and Mixed-Signal.

Chapter 1

Introduction

Computers are incredibly fast, accurate and stupid; humans are incredibly slow, inaccurate and brilliant; together they are powerful beyond imagination.

Albert Einstein

1.1 Introduction

We welcome you to this book and are delighted to have the opportunity to share our experiences from different perspectives on the world of computer systems (particularly the *de facto* distributed systems). This branch of science is rapidly changing. In this book, we try to focus on the systems that allow us to take advantage of the available hardware to solve problems in science that cannot be easily tackled based on traditional computation techniques. This broad scientific field is called *parallel and distributed systems*, which we will define in the most general form with its sub-branches relied on our experiences. We believe that all new generations of computing, such as Grid and Cloud Computing, are a subset of distributed systems.

Computers have created the third revolution in humanity after agricultural and industrial ones. In this chapter, we attempt to encourage readers to follow our book by describing a brief history of computing and computers and their impact on the human life. This text is the outcome of our 15-year development of distributed software infrastructures ranging from simple networked programs to complex real-world Grid and Cloud applications.

Computers are transforming societies, and time is collapsing. Distance is no longer an obstacle. We can navigate oceans with a click of a mouse. Computers are almost considered the most important technological achievement of humankind in the twentieth and twenty-first centuries. Using computers, we can solve problems without which they are impossible to cope. Due to the broad effects of computer capabilities, they are constantly making significant achievements in different societies, particularly in medicine, education, astronomy, engineering, and our daily lives.

It is undeniable that computers have revolutionised medical services and sciences in recent decades. Computers can go halves with the heavy tasks of a medical

DOI: 10.1201/9781003379041-1

doctor and save lives. Ever since computers were invented, computer-aided therapies have been progressively advancing to cure millions of patients. Also, computers with other medical peripheral devices can detect diseases in a short amount of time. In addition, computers have found excellent applications in gene analysis. Nowadays, scientists have many tools in their hands to investigate organic structures for new drug discoveries. Moreover, understanding information processing and storage in the human nervous system depends on an accurate view of the structure and function of neurons. Since the brain possesses both properties of digital and analogue computers, the complete understanding of its computational structures for medical scientists can shed light on the way for discovering the human mind.

Over the recent decades, the use of computers in education has increased dramatically, and many educational computer programs have been designed and implemented for classroom and individual use. Virtual universities are one of the specific applications of computers in recent years.

Computers have tremendously contributed to astronomy by which astronomers unravel the underpinnings of our universe. From their use to store and analyse big data to control spacecrafts outside of the Earth's atmosphere, our knowledge relative to the universe has broadened. There are billions of galaxies in the universe, every of which has ten million to one trillion stars. For example, the machine learning code models relying on the human brain are employed to accurately and effectively classify galaxies [1]. Although the human eye is very efficient in identifying patterns, intelligent computational methods that produce this behaviour are vital as astronomers strive to pull the frontiers aside until they can discover farther galaxies through a more visible universe.

Computers have entered almost all families and have effectively influenced our lives. Families can use computers to talk to each other via email or other services like online chat and Voice over IP[1]. Social networks like Facebook and Twitter have enabled us to keep in touch online. Cloud services like Gmail and online spreadsheets are another view of the pervasive power of computers.

Obviously, the advances in this technology have more or less affected all aspects of human societies. Hardware advances have allowed computer programmers to design powerful software to tell us that computers are extraordinary. Future computers can be fallen into three major classes based on recent technological advancements. Quantum computing depends on the strange and highly mathematical calculations of quantum mechanics for information processing. DNA[2] computers will make use of DNA to encode and store information. Optical (or photonic) computers are of other generations of computing devices that will use the motion of electrons into and out of transistors based on semiconductor technologies for performing logic operations.

In the next section, we will take a brief look at the history of computing. We will also shortly examine distributed systems from a software's point of view. The chapter closes with a conclusion.

1.2 History of Computing

We do not intend to comprehensively touch on the history of computing because it requires a book with several hundred pages by itself. This history can be divided into two: classical and modern times. Computing is principally related to the presentation of numbers. However, abstracts, such as numbers, had been created before that. Mathematical concepts existed in different civilisations.

1.2.1 Analogue Computers

The first device discovered to perform computations was the abacus, which is believed to emerge about 2400 BC in the ancient city of Babylon in Iraq. The method of employing an abacus was by using lines drawn on sand and marking them. Advances in numerical systems and mathematical symbols ultimately resulted in the discovery of mathematical operations such as addition, subtraction, multiplication, division, square, square root, and so on.

In the fourteenth century, the engineering ruler was invented and used as a manual computing instrument consisting of a simplified form of a ruler and an intermediate movable piece calibrated by logarithmic scales. In 1642, Blasé Pascal invented the mechanical machine, for which the Pascal programming language was named after him in his respect. Analogue computing in two mechanical and electronic forms became two influential classes of computing throughout the period before the emergence of digital computers.

For more than 40 years, early mechanical analogue computers were being employed in the US Navy along with fire control systems for missile launches and fuse adjustment on bullets to destroy ground and aerial targets. The history of mechanical analogue devices dates back at least to Vitruvius's time, who described using a wheel to measure the length along a curve. Of other analogue devices, differential gears were notably employed to add and subtract two variables. The discovery of the device is usually accredited to Leonardo da Vinci, but Gottfried Wilhelm Leibniz is also cited for the idea of this device in the late seventeenth century relative to a similar triangular device to solve the root equation.

The first mechanical analogue device was built by B. H. Hermann for calculating an integral under a curve or a closed area inside a closed curve in 1841. Hermann integrator was essentially a pressed wheel in front of a disc shown in Figure 1.1. There was a secondary disc on the first one, which compressed the wheel between them. The wheel rotation rate is dependent on the product of the disc rotation rate and the radial position of the wheel's contact point on the disc.

The angular displacement rate of the wheel z is given by Equation (1.1). In this equation, z is the integral of y variable multiplied by a constant number. x is the angular disc position, and k is a scaling coefficient. It is necessary to note that variables are linear and angular positions in this device. The initial application of such integrators was the integral of force along the length to measure work. Mechanical analogue computers were referred to also as differential analysers.

$$\frac{dz}{dt} = ky\frac{dx}{dt} \tag{1.1}$$

The decline of mechanical analogue computers as computers used in fire control systems began before World War II.

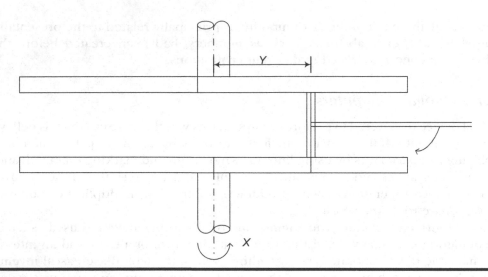

Figure 1.1 Hermann integrator.

Shrinking the price of electrical devices, increasing their accuracy, reducing their weight, and their resilience against noise and blow were of those major players that made mechanical analogue computers completely obsolete for ten years between the 1950s and 1960s.

The similarity between linear mechanical components, such as springs and dash-pots, and electrical components, such as capacitors, inductors, and resistors, is remarkable in mathematics. Modern analogue computers get built by electronic operational amplifier circuits. Early operational amplifiers (often abbreviated as *opamp*) were enjoyed from vacuum tubes. Modern opamps depend on semiconductor integrated circuits. Those circuits that use these opamps can precisely carry out mathematical operations such as integration, multiplication, subtraction, and inversion employed in systems described by differential equations. This technology was embedded into the research and development of military, aerospace, economics, and engineering sectors in the 1950s.

In this section, to help the reader understand how an electronic analogue computer works, the solution of a simple linear ordinary differential equation is considered in Equation (1.2).

$$a\frac{d^2 y}{dt^2} + b\frac{dy}{dt} + y = x(t) \tag{1.2}$$

Suppose that x and y are two signals as functions of time, where x and y are input and output signals, respectively. Also, let's require that, for the analogue computer in question, the following three assumptions apply:

- They have an infinite voltage gain ($A = \dfrac{V_{out}}{V_{in}}$, where V_{in} and V_{out} are input and output voltages, respectively).
- They have an infinite input resistance (or, in other words, a zero-input current).
- They have a zero-output resistance (or infinite output current property).

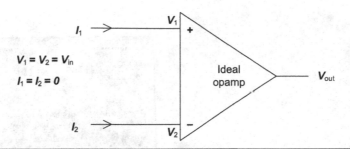

Figure 1.2 Scheme of an ideal opamp.

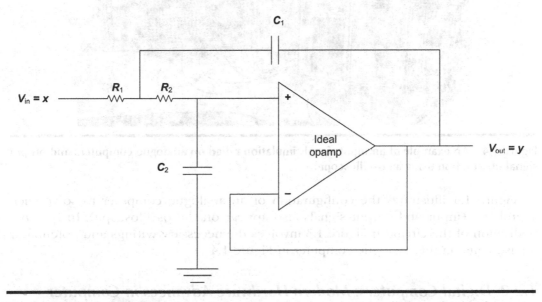

Figure 1.3 The realisation of an electronic analogue computer relied on the ideal opamp, capacitors, and resistors.

According to these assumptions, an ideal opamp appears in Figure 1.2.

For deriving the transfer function (or network function), we take the Laplace transform of Equation (1.2) to arrive at Equation (1.3). From $T(s)$, a network of linear electrical components can be constructed by using an ideal opamp. For example, using the Sallen-Key topology, this network function can be realised relied on the filter and synthesis circuit theory in Figure 1.3.

$$as^2Y + bsY + Y = X(s) \rightarrow T(S) = \frac{Y(S)}{X(S)} = \frac{1}{as^2 + bs + 1} \tag{1.3}$$

By solving this circuit according to Kirchhoff's laws of voltage and current (and replacing all the capacitance values by the values of their respective Laplace transforms, namely, $\frac{1}{Cs}$), and deriving $T(s)$ and comparing it with Equation (1.3), we can calculate a and b coefficients based on Equation (1.4).

$$a = R_1R_2C_1C_2, b = C_2(R_1 + R_2) \tag{1.4}$$

Figure 1.4   An example of an input signal simulation relied on analogue computers and output signal observation using an oscilloscope.

Figure 1.4 illustrates the configuration of an analogue computer to solve such a problem (input and output signals also appear on the oscilloscope). In fact, the realisation of the circuit in Figure 1.3 involves the necessary wirings and potentiator adjustments on the analogue computer in Figure 1.4.

1.2.2 Digital Computers: Modern Hardware Advances in Computer Architectures

In the late 1940s, the first generation of digital computers using electronic components emerged. The developers of these systems were unaware that the conceptual and functional traits of these electronic computers had been constructed virtually a hundred years earlier, principally developed by Charles Babbage, an English mathematician. Charles Babbage, in 1821, was intrigued to automate the printing and computation of mathematical formulas. He managed to build a small apparatus called the difference engine, thereby capable of calculating consecutive values of simple mathematical functions by applying finite differences to them. After the invention of modern electronic systems, electric currents replaced mechanical moving components of primitive computers. The developers of the first-generation computers hardwired them, and the underlying circuits were their computer programs. Through the years, computer architectures have made incremental progress.

After 1956, vacuum tubes, which had formed the basis of Eniac computers, were replaced by semiconductor transistors, and therefore the second generation of digital computers arose. The discovery of transistors had an impact on the third generation of computers because it was a more reliable technology. The life of the transistor era was short until 1964 when integrated circuits (ICs) became the de facto development in the semiconductor industry. The evolution of computers accelerated as computers got faster and more energy efficient. The advent of IC technology with operating systems created the third-generation computer technology allowing the average person to buy affordable computer machines. The fourth generation began with the advent of microprocessors in 1971 and still is the current generation of computers in use. Thousands of ICs come with microprocessors on a silicon chip comprising of central processing unit (CPU), random access memory (RAM), and input/output (I/O) control subsystems. The rising widespread of computer networks (followed by the invention of distributed systems) led to the age of the Internet. It is surprising to contemplate how a flat-filled computer transformed into a small machine, which is still used today at home and in the workplace!

Computers have changed scientific research on how data compiles and is then analysed. Computers can evaluate a large amount of data at speeds impossible to be traced with a scientist's naked eye. As a highly beneficial example use of modern computers, complex mathematical equations are solved by computers numerically to find whether data is valid or not. Large-scale mathematical models run on supercomputers to model how experimental data expressed by mathematical equations can manifest itself in the future. These predictions in a wide range of fields of science, such as computational biology and climate modelling, are practical to letting us understand the nature of the problems in question.

Figure 1.5(a) shows a modern single-processor system which relies on the stored program concept. In this conceptual framework, data and executable programs are stored in individual areas of memory, of course, treated similarly. This simple but powerful architecture makes developing computers much easier by reprogramming. In this idea, there are three basic structural units. The control unit (CU) is responsible for handling all the control signals issued by the processor. It manages the flow of input and output transactions, fetches instruction codes, and, finally, takes control of how data circulates the entire system. An arithmetic logic unit (ALU) handles all basic calculations, such as addition and comparisons, and performs logical operations and

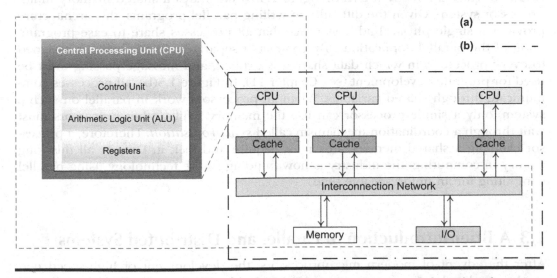

Figure 1.5 The classic organisation of (a) a single-processor system and (b) a shared-memory multi-processor system.

bit shifting. Registers store results calculated by the ALU, keep track of the address of the next instruction needed to fetch from memory, and so on.

On one side of the coin, classically, the number of transistors on ICs doubles every two months based on Moore's law. However, it is difficult to shrink silicon-based transistors below 1 nm because critical physical problems governed by quantum mechanical phenomena emerge. On the other side of the coin, another principle called Dennard scaling states that the energy required to run transistors stays nearly constant in a specific unit of volume as the transistor count rises. Transistors have shrunk such that Dennard scaling is no longer valid. Therefore, the power at which transistors operate is increasing. Thermal problems are also a big challenge in IC design. When billions of transistors are rapidly switched on and off on a single chip, it creates a large amount of heat. This heat can quickly deteriorate the precision and speed of the underlying silicon wafers. Sophisticated cooling systems are needed when more transistors accumulate on the chip. Due to all such hurdles, the processor technology has been founded on adding more cores on the chip since 2007 instead of increasing the CPU clock frequency in order to manage the power-related issues. Manufacturers are dramatically adding more processor cores to computing systems. As Moore's law is fading and scientific and industrial compute-bound applications demand unprecedented compute cycles, software design still has not accustomed itself adequately to this trend. The following chapters try to familiarise the reader to engage with software-based parallel design principles.

Figure 1.5(a) shows a simple architecture of a single processor made up of an arithmetic logic unit (ALU), a control unit (CU), and registers. The CU manages all processor-relevant control signals by handling input/output (I/O) operations, fetching machine code for instructions and taking care of how data moves in the entire system hardware. The ALU is the heart of the processor for performing arithmetic and logical operations such as multiplication and comparison. Registers are small temporary memory units to store and retrieve data from the main memory and the results of calculations by the ALU. Figure 1.5(b) illustrates a shared memory multiprocessor system. Given the difficulty in writing parallel programs, this architecture provides a single physical address space that all processes share to ease programming of the parallel applications. By contrast, a separate address space is assigned to every processor, in which data sharing is explicit, and message passing must be used for program development (see Chapter 11). In Figure 1.5(b), all processes communicate through shared variables. When all processors work in parallel on such a system, only a single processor can use the memory whilst other processors must wait through a coordination mechanism called *synchronisation*. Therefore, a processor claiming a shared memory area must acquire and lock it. Despite all this long history in computing, the industry is now building future technology using parallel computing for an unforeseeable time.

1.3 A Brief Introduction to Parallel and Distributed Systems

After the advent of modern microprocessors, the development of high-speed networks—such as local-area networks (LANs) and wide-area networks (WANs)—allowed the construction of highly scalable computing systems by connecting thousands of machines. These results enable computers to operate across geographically dispersed deployments to form the so-called *distributed system*. The scale of a distributed system can range from a few nodes to thousands or millions of computers. The underlying connection network can be wired and/or wireless. Therefore, a distributed system is a collection of autonomous computers by which we aim to solve a large-scale problem or support massive collaboration over the Internet. In such a system, there is no shared memory, but computers communicate with one another through explicit message exchanges. On the contrary, in parallel systems, multiple processes execute multiple tasks concurrently. Of course, a parallel computer might be thought as a particular type of distributed systems, where exploiting distributed system principles with a high-speed interconnection network can increase the system capacity (parallel and distributed systems share many intertwined fundamental characteristics). A trait of distributed systems is that their nodes can interact independently; therefore, there is no global notion of time called a *global clock* (namely, each node sees its own local clock). This fundamental principle regarding time leads to critical issues of coordinating actions between multiple nodes of a distributed system (which is studied by synchronisation algorithms). Due to the complex nature of distributed systems, they are constructed by a concept known as *middleware*. A middleware is a set of software layers to assist in developing highly complex distributed applications. The layers are placed on top of an intended operating system and encapsulate many features which are in common with distributed system principles. Comparatively, an operating system takes care of low-level hardware, whilst a middleware takes over sharing and managing resources across a computer network.

Several design features make a distributed system worthwhile to use. The facilitation of a distributed system must simplify access to heterogeneous resources, whatever they are (a file, service, network, etc.). Distributed systems export their resources to users that may reside across geographically different areas on heterogeneous computers. On the other hand, a primary duty of a distributed system is to hide the underlying details to end users; that is, they can transparently access distributed entities. With the rising number of services hosted by different types of distributed systems, such as the cloud and devices connected to such computer networks, scalable distributed systems are becoming a critical issue for developers and service providers. A distributed system should be scalable to service on-demand requests, including computational and storage capacity and network resources/infrastructure. Organisations enjoy computers for communicating their needs through a network, in which programs operate on behalf of their users. Therefore, an essential aim of distributed systems is to be open to a broad spectrum of services and operating systems. It means that components of a distributed application must comply with a set of pre-agreed and standard rules by which they can reach one another without paying attention to the internal details of other components. One of the popular methods is to define the interaction points via *interfaces* described by an interface definition language (IDL). In this regard, only the way components call each other is specified by a collection of interface functions, whilst the internal detail is hidden. Interoperability and portability are two significant features of *open distributed systems*. The former indicates that two implementations of a single service can interoperate as specified by an agreed standard. In fact, the extent to which a distributed application can be either compiled or executed on another distributed platform is referred to by the latter.

There are various types of distributed systems; however, a complete treatment of all of them is beyond the scope of this book. A prominent class of distributed systems used ubiquitously is high-performance distributed computing systems, including Cluster Computing, Grid Computing, and Cloud Computing.

Cluster Computing is an arrangement of computers connected through a high-speed communication fabric, in which every processing element is called a node. Figure 1.6 presents a simplified architecture of a typical cluster. A node can consist of simple or advanced multi-processor systems that function on top of an operating system and connects to other nodes through a LAN interconnect. Clusters usually offer incredible computing power and storage capacity to solve complicated computational problems. The whole computers try to provide a uniform execution system whose program operations appear to reside on a single virtual machine. This kind of transparency is reached by leveraging networking technologies and distributed system principles. Cluster Computing systems are cost-effective (concerning their performance), highly available (fault tolerant), and expandible/flexible (easily extensible to additional nodes). Although Cluster Computing facilities are widely employed to run challenging problems, they are classified relying on their use. High-performance computing (HPC) clusters exploit high-end clusters and supercomputers to tackle problems whose size is interactable on a single node or requires enormous cycles of processing power. On the other side, load-balancing clusters are leveraged to distribute incoming requests evenly for resources on a farm of cluster nodes, each of which runs similar programs. This strategy removes the burden on a single node

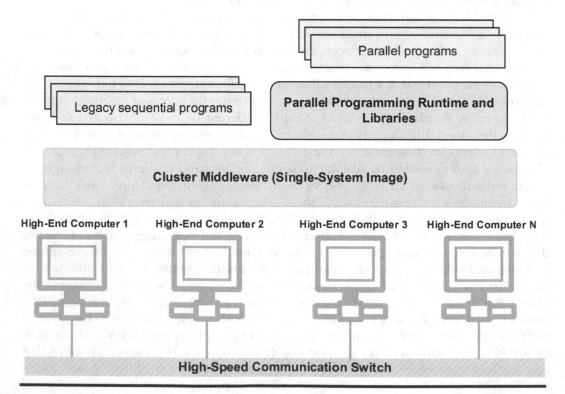

Figure 1.6   A typical cluster architecture.

by dispatching a proportionate amount of tasks to several nodes. Web hosting environments often employ load-balancing clusters to increase their uptime. The third cluster class introduces redundant nodes for high availability (HA) when a failure occurs. Critical services benefit from HA clusters, such as complex relational databases and networked file systems. Therefore, uninterrupted access to data is offered to the end-users.

A key feature of conventional Cluster Computing platforms is that they are composed of homogenous hardware in the specification and almost usually host the same operating system through the same network. Nevertheless, we have observed an inclination towards heterogeneous architectures emerging from the fact that the Internet paradigm is changing the notion of computing. These needs led to a new type of distributed architecture known as *Grid Computing*, by which different administrative domains seamlessly work together with no assumption on the underlying hardware, operating systems, security policies, etc. A grid infrastructure brings computers (clusters, supercomputers, servers, etc.) together to create a massive resource capacity of computation, storage, and network. Grids are employed to solve large-scale computational problems. Despite the enormous processing power delivered by HPC clusters, Grid Computing harnesses internationally or nationally scattered compute and storage resources for aggregating more performance and throughput. Figure 1.7 portrays a layered grid architecture. The user applications run on the top layer of the grid platform. These applications require a group of collective services such as collective computing and communication. The next layer in this architecture corresponds to hardware and software resources that sit under the collection layer. Beneath the resource layer, the connectivity layer supports connecting the resources through establishing direct physical links or virtual networks. Note that this layer must precisely take care of the fabric layer, such as virtual private channels and physical network links. The fabric accommodates all aspects of hardware resources or their software-based management components, such as operating systems, storage systems, and network connections. This layered grid architecture closely corresponds to the layered Internet protocol stack (which includes application, transport, Internet, and network access layers). An essential issue in Grid Computing is that

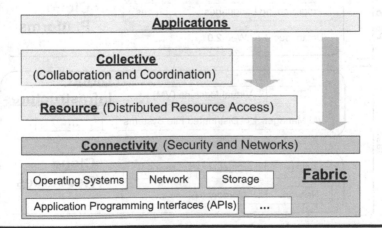

Figure 1.7   A layered grid architecture.

individual organisations take part in sharing their resources in pursuit of collaboration and solving problems. This coordination is achieved by *virtual organisations*, each of which defines its own access rights to resources.

Whilst computational grids got restructured to be easily accessible, vendors and IT companies were dealing with strategies to outsource their resources to their customers. As a result, these endeavours gave rise to forming the basis of *Cloud Computing*. In fact, Cloud Computing is defined as on-demand access to resources, especially over the Internet, without the direct involvement of end-users in managing the behind-the-scenes preparations of the cloud service provider. Major cloud solutions often own powerful data centres scattered over the globe, and their customers benefit from their services using a *pay-as-you-go* model.

Clouds are, in practice, arranged in a four-layer model shown in Figure 1.8. The lowest layer, the *Cloud Resources* layer, includes all the necessary hardware utilities (such as processors, routers, storage systems, etc.) to form the fabric of the cloud data centre. The key next layer is *Cloud Infrastructure*, which provides the foundation of most cloud platforms by deploying virtualisation technologies, namely virtual machines (VMs). A VM is the virtualisation of a computer system grouped into several virtual entities composed of a limited amount of CPU usage, memory, storage, and so on. The platform layer provides the developers with vendor-specific APIs to build their own applications. In a similar approach to operating systems, the platform layer presents a comprehensive set of tools and libraries that enable the programmers to write code easier for cloud platforms. Finally, the *Cloud Application Layer* is where the end-users receive a myriad of software services. It is necessary to note that most of these applications are vendor-specific, and thus, interoperability between vendors is hard to obtain.

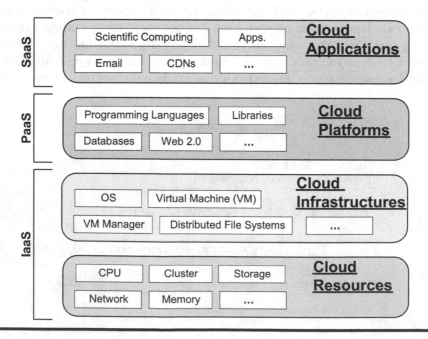

Figure 1.8   A typical cloud architecture.

Based on the layers introduced above, cloud providers often classify their services into three primary models: (a) infrastructure-as-a-service (IaaS), which incorporates resource and infrastructure layers; (b) platform-as-a-service (PaaS), which covers the platform layer; and (c) software-as-a-service (SaaS), which offers real applications. Cloud is still an area of intense research and is no longer a hype. On the one hand, strategists and big IT companies are looking for the exploitation of cloud technology in minimising their costs and risk of service outages. On the other hand, local enterprises are looking at the cloud paradigm as a profound option to outsource their computing infrastructures. Despite the maturity of Cloud Computing, several significant obstacles remain, such as security and privacy issues.

1.4 Conclusion

In this chapter, we briefly introduced a journey in computing towards the recent advancements in distributed systems. Without a doubt, we are at the beginning stage of a paradigm shift in computing that allows complex industrial, societal, and scientific applications to emerge or evolve. Most importantly, semiconductor technology is finding an unprecedented role in the future of energy-efficient computing systems. New computer technologies, such as quantum and neuromorphic computers coupled with existing parallel and distributed systems, will lead to the ability of humankind to experience unseen applications and cope with previously unsolved problems. We expect the traditional computer architectures will coexist and instead continue to help us with advanced hybrid computers. The following chapters will lay the foundation for developers and researchers who want to get involved in the research and construction of next-generation distributed systems in the coming years.

Notes

1 Internet protocol.
2 Deoxyribonucleic acid.

Reference

[1] Computers Automatically Classify Galaxy Shapes. 2010; Available from: https://astronomy.com/news-observing/news/2010/06/computers%20automatically%20classify%20galaxy%20shapes.

Chapter 2

IoT and Distributed Systems

If you think that the internet has changed your life, think again. The IoT is about to change it all over again!

Brendan O'Brien

2.1 Introduction

In the traditional viewpoint, the Internet was designated for Internetworking of homogenous and heterogeneous computers, servers, hosts, applications, and services. But the surge of tiny smart device production and diverse scope of applications directed to a new paradigm in connectivity of smart devices. Thanks to Moore's law, the advancements in the semiconductor industry led to electronic devices with a form factor of a coin at the capabilities of one-decade-ago computers. This really is a revolutionised, rather than evolved, achievement.

On the other side, the orchestra of tiny connected devices embraced the era of smart distributed systems. Now, we consider that the ease of access, open protocols, and higher-speed data transfer rates to face the actual problems gain many interesting application scopes.

The term Cybernetics, or control and communication between animal and machine, is then virtually revised to interact with a physical system as an environment or information exchange. This led to the term Cyber-Physical Systems (CPS). The extension of connectivity amongst tiny devices as new connected "Things" also led to the term Internet of Things (IoT). IoT is a term to represent CPS with engineering-like details and approaches.

Finally, merging all the above items, a new topic is resulted with the name "Distributed Systems and Internet of Things." This new term represents an insight into where the Internet is extended into real-world entities and objects. Distributed systems are tightly related to distributed computing.

DOI: 10.1201/9781003379041-2

2.2 CPS and IoT

In the system modelling approach and considering the universe as an ensemble of systems with a set of specified subset as corporative systems, any CPS is a superset for a target IoT. Figure 2.1 depicts a hierarchical aspect in this regard. Whilst the theoretical basis for CPS has very good support for technical issues in IoT, in practice we are more interested in IoT implementation aspects than the CPS concepts in engineering fields. This selection enables us to have very clear application scenarios.

For example, as shown in Figures 2.2 and 2.3 [1], it seems that an unseen event for an observer (sensor) is a seen event for another connected observer (sensor) that may be corporate to enable its visibility to the unseen ones. This is a very good system-level anticipated-like application.

2.3 Internet of Things (IoT)

Although IoT is stacked on top of many individual factors, including open protocols, device communication standards, and systems-level modelling in electronic devices and tools, it is projected to have automated integration into almost all fields and environments. In this case, various types of centralised, decentralised, and distributed systems are the subject of influence.

This means more efforts are required to engage with modelling, programming, and management. Whilst in distributed computing groups of networked computers

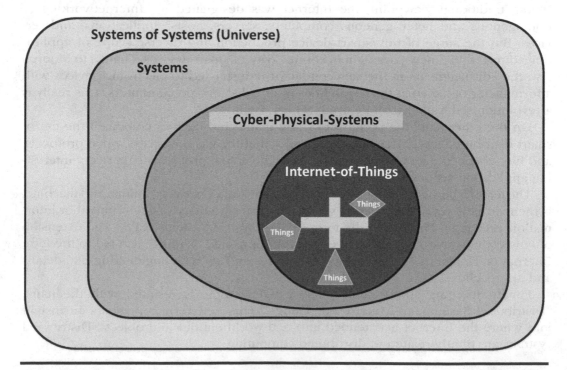

Figure 2.1 Internet of Things is an actual subsystem of Cyber-Physical-Systems in modelling perspectives.

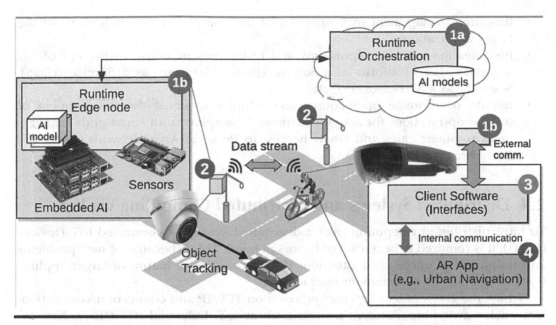

Figure 2.2   A scenario of connected devices and sensors   (Picture adopted from [1].)

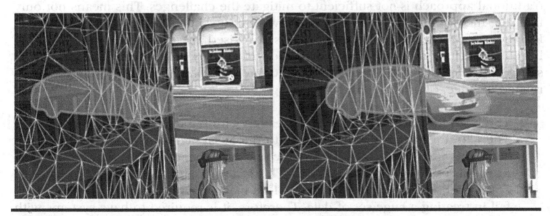

Figure 2.3   An interesting application scenario on the benefits of connected devices and cooperate sensing augmentation [1].

are used for a predefined computational goal, in distributed computing it deals with and treats major concerns with concurrent and parallel computing mostly dominated in scientific areas.

In this way, normally different technologies related to distributed computing are utilised. Some of the most important utilisations amongst them are the following:

- Cross-hardware and cross-operating system migration with hardware virtualisation.
- Complexity and platform-insensitive open-access or service-oriented architectures.

- Resource management by inspection of the complexity and behaviour of the target application.
- Investigation of novel algorithms and techniques to utilise in the era of "as a service" (i.e., Platform as a Service (PaaS), Hardware as a Service (HaaS), Software as a Service (SaaS), etc.
- Initiate or promote open-source technologies to boost the development of diverse applications for actual situations. This spans from smart-grids management to smart cities and smart homes, to Personal Area Network (PAN) and Body Area Network (BAN).

2.4 Distributed Systems and Distributed Computing via IoT

To have distributed computing over a distributed system of connected IoT Devices (IoTD), it is required to bear a set of factors in mind. This is because of new problems and unknown or unspecified situations due to the diverse nature of target applications or systems or environment interactions.

Whilst the conventional Internet is based on TCP/IP and connection/connectionless packet switching, different aspects such as IoT, Industrial IOT (IIoT), Narrow-Band IoT (NBIoT) and other technologies like LoRA, LoRAWAN, Zigbee, IEEE 802.15.4, and many others are also considered, and they are the reasons why the traditional approach is not sufficient to mitigate the challenges. This means not only that one must consider software and hardware issues but also that the conventional Internet requires to have new architectures or revised and modified architectures. To have a good look and consider the situation in more detail, it is required to understand and take into account the newly adopted factors. Most of these factors are related to Edge, Cloud, and Fog Computing.

1. The need to have scalable systems dealing with big data:
   The nature of IoT is directly related to the ecosystem of connected smart sensors. This implies that the sensors are not only connected but also transferring a sort of reasonable volume of data. This is not the main problem; the main one is the high volume of sensor count. This means conventional approaches may fail in treating a huge set of data. Therefore, it is required to have systems with the real meaning of being scalable. This system needs to store/process not only current time data but also its historical footprints of data. This is a key feature for future investigation, which later showed its effectiveness in emerging fields of Industrial IoT for predictive maintenance and conditional monitoring.

2. Need to have online/offline processing with real-time answer capability:
   In most diverse situations in IoT-related applications, there is an urgent need for real-time operations to handle events in progress to produce an on-time response. One of the obvious samples of this scenario one may call the multimedia stream processing in audio/video. Another one is the security checking and packet inspection in video/audio or TCP/IP ICMP packets.

3. High-performance Edge/Fog/Cloud Computing:
   The basic hierarchy of Edge/Fog/Cloud Computing with annotated major decisive factors annotation is depicted in Figure 2.4 as a simple stacked layer and in

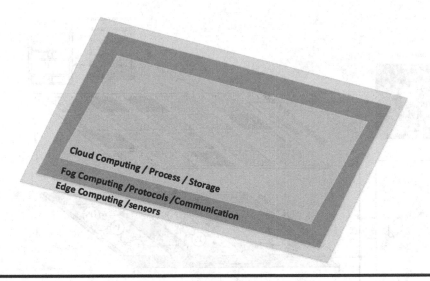

Figure 2.4   The main hierarchy of Edge/Fog/Cloud Computing.

Figure 2.5 with more details and inner layers. As shown in Figure 2.5 detailed layers map, in the Edge layer the main issues are the sensors and their different types of data conversion, local storage, and local processing. In the Fog layer, data transfer, protocols, and communication issues are the major factors. Interestingly, in the newly coming 6G mobile communication basis, the core network, which roughly could be considered as the virtual Fog is to be considered with mobility support. This is a very attractive point from the basics of Edge/Fog/Cloud computing for 6G. Therefore, it will require many innovations in this regard. In the third layer or the topmost layer of Cloud Computing, the main issues are heavy process, extra storage, information retrieval, data modelling, and application of recent development of machine learning to apply stored data to have value-added services.

4. Non-uniform distributed systems:
   IoT systems come with two distinct properties: One is the ensemble of nodes, sensors, and actuators with different and diverse goals of sensing and actuating. This means that we must not only be engaged with different resolutions, bit width, power consumptions, signal, and noise conditions for a huge set of scenarios but also interact with different communication protocols and generations. On the other side, handling the different data types and satisfying the timing for real-time and offline situations must also be issued. The complexity in hardware and software at the edge is dictating the storage and processing boundaries from fog and cloud.

   Moreover, the heterogeneous structure needs to have gateways to control in/out data transfer amongst them. This not only impacts the uniformity but also implies additional complexity on software and hardware in turn.

5. Data integrity/data security/data privacy/data availability:
   The elements of IoT are considered alive as long as they are connected. It means they are net-worked if connected and not-worked if not connected. The main soul in this point is the unique interpretation of data for a subject.

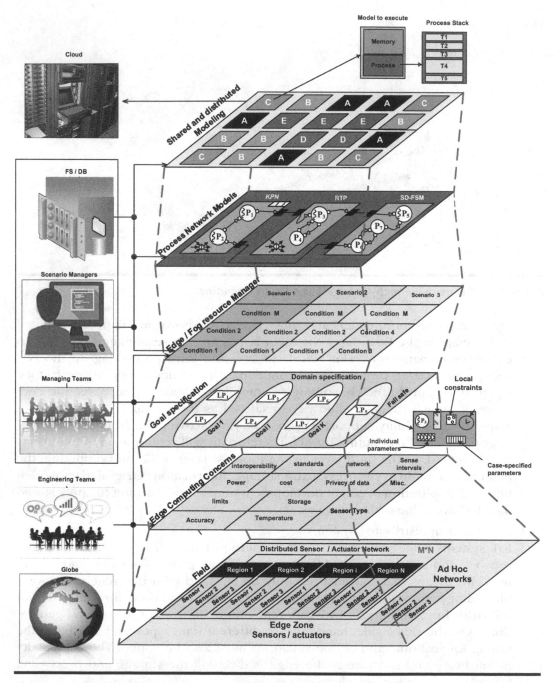

Figure 2.5   A detailed layered stack model Edge/Fog/Cloud Computing.

It means the update/modify must be handled with care and data integrity is a key concept.

Integrity must be ensured with the confidence of data security and privacy. The insecure or non-trusted elements in a trusted network must be identified and labelled or reduced in critical situations.

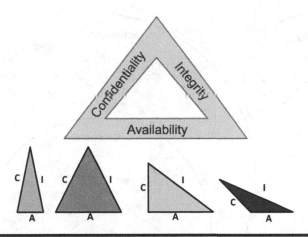

Figure 2.6   The CIA Triangle and different aspects of biased elements.

The rise of a huge set of data, its live stream, and higher speeds in transfer may violate data privacy even in unintended situations. Privacy is also a must for value-added services and the protection of individuals.

All of these concerns must be considered but not at the cost of availability. Availability must be addressed as a key performance index. It is the final goal of connected systems and services, and the goal must be supported by privacy, integration, etc.

Considering the basic items of security/privacy as confidentiality, to have a sustainable system, one must encounter three items at once. This is usually called CIA. Triangle. Sometimes, the share and impact of each item may not be equal as the others. This is artificially illustrated in Figure 2.6, which shows that there are different aspects of biased elements arrangement with less or more gained factor (shown as the different side sizes).

6. Centralised, distributed, decentralised, and peer-to-peer networks

To have a clear look at the different types of networks, a hierarchical viewpoint is the best suited. This is illustrated in Figure 2.7. Semantically speaking, the networks may be divided into two main categories of centralised and other networks.

The former, or centralised, is a widely used model with direct management and control of its sub-units via a central agent or unit. In this structure, all of the connected elements directly rely on star-like centric node connectivity.

In a centralised system, the single control node is mainly responsible for failures and heavy-duty storage and processing.

The latter one or other networks are divided into three subsets of classifications: distributed, decentralised, and peer-to-peer networks.

The main specifications in the characterisation of these three networks are physical location of the nodes, Inter-Intra organisation sub-networking, different ownership policies, hardware and software, anonymous and private access, communication layers and protocols, and many other individual factors.

There are other forms of networking, such as ad hoc networks that may be considered for a special area of applications and situations.

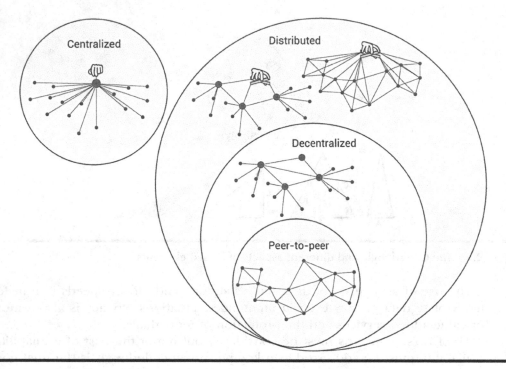

Figure 2.7 The hierarchical perspective of centralised, distributed, decentralised, and peer-to-peer networks.   (Adopted from pngwing.)

In all of the above-mentioned networks, there is a process and resource-hungry situation that needs to be overcome. The more the diversity and complexity in the networking and processing, the more there is difficulty in rapid and efficient code development. The main aim of this book is to deal with this problem.

In the present book, we introduce Parvicursor infrastructure, a low-level middleware system grounded on a specialised concept of distributed objects and native ECMA. NET-compliant execution for highly concurrent distributed systems, to make writing middleware easier on heterogeneous platforms. It takes care of low-level network programming interfaces for Grid/Cloud-specific platforms and allows the middleware architects to focus their efforts on their middleware logic with the help of the integrated, scalable Parvicursor Execution System. xThread provides the capability of remote code execution, dynamic distributed object registration and activation, transparent communication on the underlying transport protocols, data marshalling and unmarshalling, distributed operation dispatching, checkpoint/restore, etc. xSec introduces techniques for authentication of users and secure communication. xDFS proposes utilities and libraries for transmitting, storing, and managing massive data sets. Parvicursor Concurrent Asynchronous Sockets (PCAS) presents interfaces for designing optimised and highly concurrent network services.

Reference

[1] CPS/IoT Ecosystem. 2022; Available from: https://cpsiot.at

Chapter 3

Advanced Operating System Concepts in Distributed Systems Design

UNIX is basically a simple operating system, but you have to be a genius to understand the simplicity.

Dennis M. Ritchie

WHO WAS DENNIS RITCHIE?

When I (Alireza Poshtkohi) started working on this book, unfortunately I heard of a late scientist's death, so I decided to write a short memoir to thank him for his impact on my scholarly life. After being admitted to the university as an electrical engineering student in 2001, I took a module on the C programming language, towards which I developed hatred after a while and thought to withdraw from that module. One day, the module lecturer spoke about one of the C language's creators, a man called Dennis M. Ritchie. After the class, I researched Dennis's life, and in the following weeks I was fascinated by his scientific personality. This event led me to step into the world of software and operating systems, and after ten years, the idea of developing this book emerged in 2011. The C language changed my scientific life somehow.

DOI: 10.1201/9781003379041-3

Ritchie was born on 9 September 1941 in the Brownsville neighbourhood of New York City. His name is associated with great works such as the C programming language and Unix operating system. Currently, the C programming language plays a fundamental role in many famous programs and big projects worldwide: operating systems such as Linux, Solaris, BSD, Mac OS, Windows, and other variants, and programming languages such as C++, C#, Java, JavaScript, and many more. It can be said that operating systems, such as Windows and Linux that would become too controversial, could not have been created without the C language. The world of open-source software certainly is familiar with its fathers.

3.1 Introduction

Since the input interface to work with hardware is operating systems (OSs), this abstraction is the lowest level with which every software (such as a distributed system) must interact. As we are aware, all distributed systems and their middleware are implemented based on OS interfaces through application programming interfaces (APIs). This book aims to teach you how a distributed system and its middleware are built. So, you are supposed to take advantage of OS capabilities in your favourite programming language. In this chapter, we try our best to draw an image of OS concepts, which mainly affect the design and implementation of distributed systems. Familiarity with these essential concepts helps the reader from two different points of view. First, learning these concepts makes programming styles relied on the OS APIs easier to understand. It can improve the learning process and ease the combination of concepts at different abstraction levels for problem-solving and coming up with new ideas for unapproachable areas through conventional methods. Second, a milestone that paved the way for the emergence of distributed computing was to tackle problems unsolvable on a single processor. Instead, we must have harnessed the processing power of many systems within a network of computers to solve a computationally hard problem. Therefore, how optimal a system is designed for improving the performance and throughput of applications is studied in distributed systems. It is a fact that when we do not know about advanced concepts in operating systems, a poorly designed system either incurs a lot of overhead or even fails to achieve the performance of a single processor. Designing such systems requires several years of study and direct involvement in systems software development with a background in distributed applications.

In this chapter, we make an effort to briefly discuss the key concepts in operating systems that we encountered over the years in designing systems and distributed software.

3.2 An Introduction to Modern Operating Systems

A computer system is a collection of hardware and software components that work together to run a computer program. System implementations at different abstraction levels change over time, but basic concepts do not. All computer systems have similar hardware and software components that perform similar tasks. An operating system (OS) is a collection of programs that manage computer hardware resources and provides shared services for application software. The operating system is by far the most critical type of systems software in a computer system. Especially in distributed systems, middleware, or composition of OS services, based on the definitions and requirements of distributed environments, supply developers in order to hide the complexity of low-level OS from the developer's sight.

OS executes programs and makes a computer system more optimal and suitable for use. In this section, we briefly look at a modern operating system's concepts and functions. Figure 3.1 shows the holistic view of a modern computer system consisting of software and hardware components.

Busses are a set of electrical wires that transfer bytes of information back and forth between components of a computer system. They are usually designed to transfer data fragments with a fixed size of bytes known as words. The number of bytes in a word is a basic system-wide parameter which varies in different systems. For instance, this number can be 8 bytes for 64-bit processors.

Input/output (I/O) devices are connections of the system to the external world. Each I/O device connects to the I/O buss by either a controller or an adaptor. The difference between these two is mainly due to their packaging method. Controllers are

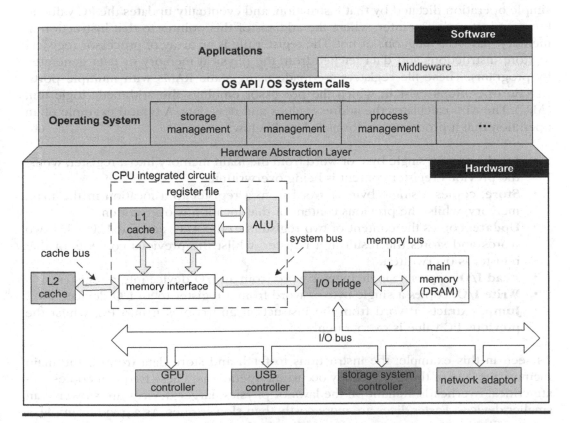

Figure 3.1   The software/hardware view of a modern computer system.

a collection of chips in the device itself or placed on the main printed circuit board of the system (often called the mainboard). An adaptor is a card plugged into a slot on the mainboard. Each of these devices is used to transfer information back and forth between the I/O bus and an I/O device. Of course, research has recently been conducted on moving the adaptor into the network-on-chip (NoC) in the processor design cycle in order to eliminate the communication overheads of I/O busses.

Main memory is a volatile storage device which holds a program with the data it manipulates, whilst the processor is running the program. Physically, the main memory is made up of a set of dynamic random-access memory (DRAM) chips. Logically speaking, the main memory is organised as a linear array of bytes, each of which owns its unique address (array index) that starts from the index zero. Each machine instruction that forms a program could be composed of a variable number of bytes.

The central processing unit (CPU), or the processor, is an integrated device that executes instructions stored in physical memory. Within each processor, there is a storage device with the size of words (or registers) called the program counter (PC). At any moment of time, the PC points to the address of the next machine instruction. From the time at which the electrical power is connected to the systems until it is disconnected, the processor frequently repeats this basic operation blindly and automatically. The processor reads the instruction from the memory location to which the program counter points. Then, it interprets the instruction bits, executes the simple operation dictated by that instruction, and eventually updates the PC value to the next instruction pointer, where the address of this pointer to that instruction in memory may be contiguous or not. The register file is an array of processor registers to store instructions and data fetched from the physical memory or data generated by programs. These file registers are made using static RAMs with multiple ports. Certain operations exist in which the processor employs the arithmetic logic unit (ALU). The ALU calculates the address values and new data. A typical example of an operation that a processor performs is listed below:

- **Load**: copies a single byte or word from the main memory into a register, whilst the previous register content is being overwritten.
- **Store**: copies a single byte or word from a register to a location in the main memory, whilst the previous content of that location is overwritten.
- **Update**: copies the content of two registers to the ALU, and the ALU adds two words and stores the result in a register, whilst the previous contents of that register is overwritten.
- **Read I/O**: copies a single byte or word from an I/O device into a register.
- **Write I/O**: copies a single byte or word from a register to an I/O device.
- **Jump**: extracts a word from the instruction and copies it into PC, whilst the previous PC value is overwritten.

As seen in this example, the instructions to fetch and store data from/to the main memory are one of those frequently occurring operations. These frequent copies create critical overheads. Reliant on the laws of physics, larger devices are slower than smaller devices. Faster dices are more costly than slower ones. As a good example, a register file that can store up to several hundred bytes of information, as compared to the main memory for millions of bytes, is almost a hundred times faster than the main memory. The more semiconductor technology progresses, the more and more this gap widens. Processors are equipped with small faster devices referred to as caches to address this problem. Cache memory is a component that transparently stores data in order for future requests to be delivered faster. The data stored within a cache may be values that were calculated previously or a repetition of the original values stored elsewhere. If the requested data is in the cache (cache hit), this request can be serviced immediately simply by reading from the cache, which is also often very fast. Otherwise (cache miss), data has to be recomputed or fetched from their original storage location, which is relatively a slow operation (i.e., the more requests delivered from the cache, the better is the overall system performance). Several factors, such as software transactional memory (STM), multi-core architectures like non-uniform memory access (NUMA), symmetric multi-processor (SMP) architectures, and concurrent programming (which will also take up much of this book), will affect the future of cache-based platforms. In distributed systems, particularly Cloud and Grid Computing, software-based caching plays a vital role in implementing distributed systems.

Having founded the hardware framework of modern computer systems, we now pay closer attention to a number of essential concepts in operating systems that you will encounter throughout this book. In the following, we consider the software part shown in Figure 3.1.

3.2.1 Process Management

A process is an instance of a computer program that runs. A process can consist of multiple threads of execution that execute the instructions simultaneously. In this book, we only make use of the multi-threaded abstraction to build a distributed system and creating processes frequently is highly avoided; consequently, the reader will understand the reason behind this strategy, which is due to the heavy overhead of using processes. However, since the concepts of processes and threads are very similar, a concise overview of process management is thus given.

A process involves more things than the program code, known as a text section. Every process involves current activity expressed by the PC value and the contents of processor registers. Also, every process contains a process stack, which stores temporary information (such as function parameters, return addresses and local variables) and a data section. A process also often has a heap memory dynamically allocated to at runtime.

An operating system keeps track of all information of a process for execution, as stated earlier. This information is known as a context. At any moment in time, each processor core just has a running process. When the operating system decides to transfer the processor control from a process to another, at this time a context switch is issued by storing the context of the current process, the context of the new process is loaded, and the execution control is finally transferred to the new process. Context switching the processes often poses a lot of overhead, because the system does not perform any useful work in completing this operation. This overhead depends on various metrics, including the memory speed, the number of registers that must be copied, and the presence of specific instructions (e.g., a single instruction for loading and storing all registers).

Concurrent programming and multi-core systems aim to achieve maximum CPU utilisation by keeping all programs running. Since there are many processes on processors, scheduling techniques should be used to allocate processor time to different processes. This method is called a process scheduler. Whilst processes run for the first time, they are placed inside a work queue which has a list of all OS processes. The process residing in the main memory waiting to run is kept in a linked list known as the ready queue. The status of the processes that are in sleep mode is changed to runnable state by the OS on some occasions, such as the occurrence of an interrupt or a specific event like the completion of an I/O request.

A wide range of scheduling algorithms have been proposed, including first in first out (FIFO), shortest job first (SJF), fixed priority pre-emptive scheduling (FPPS), round-robin scheduling (RRS), and multi-level queue scheduling. Three major metrics are taken into account in the design and use of process schedulers. The first is throughput, which is the number of processes that complete their execution for each unit of time. The second is latency, which depends on two quantities, turnaround time and response time. The former is the total time between the submission of a process and its completion. The latter is the amount of time that is taken in order for a submitted request to generate a response for the first time. The third is fairness, which is the equal amount of time of a processor that is allocated to each process.

Practically, these goals (e.g., throughput against latency) are in conflict with each other, and so a scheduler must consider a trade-off between them at the implementation time. Given the user's needs and the OS's goals, a preference is given to each of these three metrics.

3.2.2 Memory Management

Memory management is the function of handling the memory of a computer system and is very critical. In a general schema, this unit of OS provides methods to allocate parts of the memory for programs if requested. Virtual memory is an abstraction pretending to each process that is exclusively using the main memory. Each process sees a memory from its own point of view which is referred to as the virtual address space or logical address space; this address is generated by the processor. By contrast, physical address space is the address of the real location of memory hardware that is owned by the memory management unit (MMU). The quality of the virtual memory manager has a significant impact on the overall system performance. The memory management subsystem is responsible for several main tasks as follows:

- **Large address spaces**: OS changes the system in such a way that programs think the system really has a large amount of memory.
- **Memory mapping**: is used to map files and other storage systems onto the address space of processes. In this manner, the contents of a file are directly mapped onto a process's address space.
- **Protection**: each process in the system has its own virtual address space. These address spaces are completely separate, and therefore a running process cannot affect other processes. Hardware mechanisms implemented for virtual memory

enable the OS to protect any arbitrary segments of the memory against writes made by other processes. This procedure gives rise to the protection of code and data that are likely to be overwritten by malicious programs.

- **Fair physical memory allocation**: The MMU allows each running process in the system to use a fair share of the system's physical memory.
- **Shared virtual memory**: although virtual memory makes processes own separate virtual address spaces, there are some cases in which processes must share a part of the memory. Applications of this method include dynamic libraries (which let an executable code be shared between several processes) and interprocess communication (IPC) (where two or more processes have a privilege to exchange information through a shared segment of memory).

3.2.3 Storage Management (SM)

Often, not only is the main memory small to store all data of programs, but it is also volatile. Computer systems make secondary storage systems such as hard discs accessible to programs for coping with this issue. A file system, as the most essential abstraction of an SM, provides the ability to access and store data and programs on hard discs. The essence of a file consists of a collection of information relevant to it. OS maps files into physical devices. A set of files are organised as a hierarchical structure referred to as folders. Storage systems ground different specifications on hardware and network technologies. Some of them can only be accessed sequentially or randomly. Some of these systems transmit data synchronously and others asynchronously. A storage system managed through an OS stores the security of its data by exploiting software techniques in file metadata in the form of file permissions (i.e., permission bits) and access control lists (ACLs).

In addition to conventional physical disc-based storage systems, distributed storage technologies are of significance, including network attached storage (NAS), storage area network (SAN), clustered NAS, and parallel network file system (pNFS).

3.2.4 Userspace and Kernel Space

Userspace is part of the system memory in which user processes run. Contrary to this definition, kernel space is a part of memory in that OS kernel processes run. A primary duty of the OS kernel is to manage these two spaces and prevent them from interfering with each other. The kernel is a program that constitutes the central heart of an operating system. A kernel is not a process but rather a process controller, which has complete control over everything that happens in the system. In the kernel's address space, we can directly access all addresses that belong to the threads of execution by using C language pointers.

Kernel space features are accessible to user processes through system calls. A system call is a request by which an active process can receive services as a unit of execution from the kernel, such as I/O and creation of a new process. An active process is a process that is moving ahead on the processor, as compared with a process waiting for its processing on the processor. The program I/O is an operation or a device that transmits data to/from the processor and to/from an auxiliary device (such as discs and network cards).

3.3 Memory Hierarchy Models

What is stated up to here was a model of a computer system that has different processors for executing instructions and a memory system that keeps data and instructions for processors. So far, we have assumed that the memory system is a linear array of bytes, and the CPU is able to access every memory location within a constant value of time. However, this is not a model used in practice. In essence, a memory system is a hierarchy of storage devices with a broad range of capacities, costs, and access times. A key method to increase system efficiency is to minimise data manipulation time. In the era of many-core processors, this issue becomes more complicated for programmers because of memory contention between processors. Processor registers keep frequently used data. Fast, small caches near the CPU act relatively slower as a settling region for a collection of data and instructions stored in the main memory. Main memory hosts the data stored on large and slow discs, which, in place of discs, act as the settling regions for the data stored on discs or other machines connected by networks.

As a programmer, we need to be able to understand the memory hierarchy because it has a significant impact on the performance of our programs. For example, if our program data has been stored in the CPU registers, then they can be accessed in zero cycles during the execution of that instruction. If stored in the cache, they can be accessed from 1 to 30 cycles, and if stored in the main memory, their access time is between 50 and 200 cycles; however, this number can be tens of millions of cycles. If we can know how the system transfers data up and down the memory hierarchy, we will be able to write programs that always strive to store their data at the highest level of the hierarchy, where processors can access them much faster. This idea in programming principles is known as the locality of reference. Programs with good locality incline to access the same set of data items repeatedly, or they tend to access sets of data items close to themselves. Programs with good locality tend to have more access to data items from higher levels of the hierarchy and, thus, run faster. For instance, the execution time of various matrix multiplication kernels that perform the same number of mathematical operations, but have different degrees of locality, is highly likely non-identical.

In Section 3.2 of this chapter, caches were discussed (particularly in multiprocessor systems). In the following section, main memory is examined, and in the next chapters, we will introduce storage systems based on disc drives.

3.3.1 Main Memory

Integrated circuits are utilised to make the main memory of modern computer systems. The most general form of the main memory of a computer system is random access memory (RAM). RAMs exist normally in two variants: static (SRAM) and dynamic (DRAM). SRAM is faster and significantly more expensive than DRAM. SRAM is used as caches inside or outside CPUs and buffers in disc drive devices. DRAM is used as the main memory in the system as well as the frame buffer of a graphics system.

SRAM stores every bit in a bistable cell. Every cell is implemented as an electronic circuit made up of six transistors. This circuit has a feature that can indefinitely stay in two voltages or states. Every other state will be unstable and causes the circuit to move quickly towards its stable states. Due to such a bistability, an SRAM memory cell will maintain its value until it is supplied electrically. Even when chaos, such as electrical noise, occurs, the circuit returns to a stable value if the chaos is removed. Figure 3.2 shows the structure of a typical SRAM cell. Each bit is stored in four transistors (M1 to M4), which consist of two inverters. Two extra transistors (M5 and M6) control access to a storage cell during read and write operations. Access to every cell is activated through a word line (WL) that controls these two transistors. Bit line (BL) and its negated line ($\overline{BL}$) are used to transfer data for both read and write operations. During read accesses, BLs are actively pulled up and down by the inverters in the SRAM cell.

DRAM has a very simpler structure than SRAM. The basic structure of a DRAM cell for modern computers is illustrated in Figure 3.3. It only consists of a transistor and a capacitor. This big difference in complexity shows that DRAM functions very different from SRAM. A DRAM cell holds its state in the capacitor C. The transistor M is in charge of guarding access to that state. To read the cell state, the access line (AL) is raised, which results in either a current flow over the data line (DL) or nothing, depending on the capacitor charge. For writing to a cell, the DL is properly adjusted, and then AL is pulled up for a long enough time to charge or discharge the capacitor. The use of a capacitor means that reading a cell discharges its capacitor. This procedure cannot be repeated indefinitely because the capacitor must recharge at some points. Various sources of leakage currents bring a cell about losing its charge. In a quest to resolve this problem in modem computers, each cell is usually refreshed

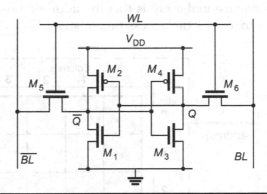

Figure 3.2   An SRAM cell comprising of six transistors for storing a single bit.

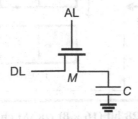

Figure 3.3   A DRAM memory cell is made up of a transistor and a capacitor to store a single bit.

every 64ms by the memory subsystem. In the refreshing cycle, the memory is not accessible. Reading a cell makes a capacitor discharge. It, in turn, signifies that reading the contents of the memory requires extra power and, most importantly, additional time. In a DRAM cell, since every capacitor charges and discharges with an RC time constant, unlike SRAMs, we must wait for the cell contents to become available (prepared). This delay always limits how fast a DRAM can perform. Because DRAMs are much cheaper than SRAMs, programmers must try figuring out how to cope with this type of main memory and write optimal programs.

To sum up this section's subject matter, we explain the high-level view of a DRAM chip. Figure 3.4 shows the high-level view of a 128-bit (16 × 8) DRAM chip. Cells (bits) in the DRAM chip are divided into supercells. Every supercell has the respective number of bits equal to the number of a word. In this example, an 8-bit DL is shown, which is indicative of every DRAM cell being 8 bits. Each DRAM is connected to a circuit referred to as the memory controller that can transfer the bits of a supercell at a time to/from the DRAM chip. To read the contents of (i, j) supercell, the memory controller first sends the address of row i, and then the address of column j to DRAM. DRAM finally responds by sending the contents of (i, j) supercell to the controller. The address of the i row and j column is usually called a row memory strobe (RAS) request and a column access strobe (CAS) request, respectively. Generally, as presented in this example, DRAM circuit designers organise it as a two-dimensional array instead of a linear array to reduce the number of address bases needed on the chip. For this purpose, in this example, a 2-bit address line that addresses at most a value between 0 and 3 is used. As long as a linear array was employed, we would have to avail of a 4-bit address line for addressing the locations of 0 to 15. The difficulty of using a two-dimensional array is that the address must be sent within two individual steps, which increases the access time instead.

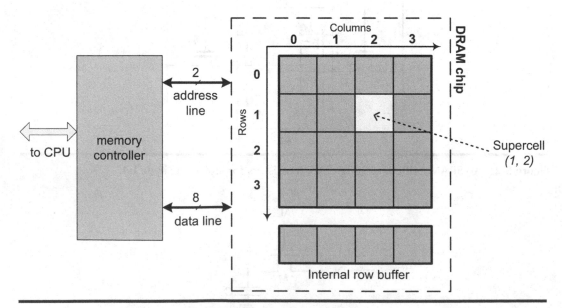

Figure 3.4 A high-level view of a 128-bit (16 × 8) DRAM chip.

3.4 A Brief Review on Modern OS Kernels

This book does not aim to teach the design of a modern operating system, but rather we try to assist the reader on how to efficiently use common programming interfaces of the existing operating systems to build a distributed software infrastructure. Hence, having some insight into the OS classification will aid the reader to implement a distributed framework, middleware, or software optimally by exploiting common OS APIs such as POSIX and Win32/64 in their place. In the computer systems literature, operating systems are generally fallen into six major families: microkernel, monolithic kernel (like Unix and Linux), hybrid kernel (like Windows), exokernel, objected-oriented kernel, and language-based kernel.

3.4.1 Microkernel Operating System

This type of operating systems contains the minimum amount of code necessary to implement fundamental OS services in the kernel space. As shown in Figure 3.5, these services include low-level address space management, thread management, and inter-process communication. OSs provide hierarchical protection domains, called *protection rings*, for different levels of access to hardware resources. This protective enforcement is usually satisfied by those processor architectures that provide CPU modes at the microcode level. In ring 0, the kernel code runs with the highest privilege and is in direct interaction with physical hardware through this method. Device drives execute in rings 1 and 2 based on access-level privileges, which have a lower level of security than ring 0 of execution. Userspace programs run in ring 3. A microkernel is the only software code that runs in ring 0. In a microkernel, some operations, such as device drivers, protocol stacks, and file systems, are moved to the kernel space from userspace.

In microkernels, IPC mechanisms are used to send messages to different processes to establish communication between them. IPC allows an operating system to get made up of a number of small programs referred to as servers. Since IPCs are employed in microkernels by defining message sends instead of shared memory,

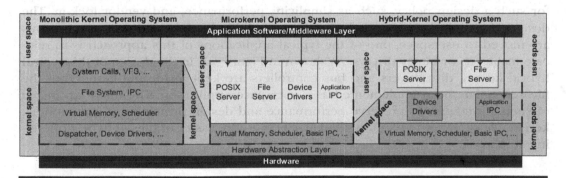

Figure 3.5   Comparison of three types of the OS classification: monolithic kernel, microkernel, and hybrid kernel.

sensitive applications that frequently execute IPC operations can experience critical overheads. In microkernels, an intended service is requested by sending an IPC message to a server program in userspace (which implements that service like a file server), and the result generates another IPC message for a new response. In this manner, if the intended drivers have been implemented as processes in userspace, it requires a context switch or system call (so long as these drivers have been programmed as procedures). Likewise, transferring actual data to a server (i.e., reading/writing a file or sending/receiving over a network socket) and receiving the response can incur extra copy overheads. Performance is a vital issue in microkernel operating systems. QNX and L4, to name a few, are amongst microkernel OSs.

3.4.2 Monolithic Operating System

In this classification of operating systems, all OS functions run merely in userspace and ring 0 through 2. A monolithic operating system is different from a microkernel and defines only a high-level virtual interface on top of computer hardware. System calls are used to access all implemented OS services in the kernel space (such as process, memory and concurrency management, and device drivers). One of the benefits of monolithic kernels is to establish high efficiency during the implementation, as compared to microkernels, because all OS services are managed within the uniform kernel address space. Of course, putting most of the basic services in monolithic kernels has three major drawbacks: kernel size, lack of extensibility, and poor maintainability. Fixing bugs or adding new features means recompiling the entire kernel. However, using loadable kernel modules in operating systems like Linux and Unix can highly alleviate this shortcoming. These modules can be dynamically loaded (and unloaded) in kernel space at runtime.

3.4.3 Hybrid Operating System

A hybrid operating system as pronounced by its name is an admixture of a monolithic kernel and a microkernel. Unlike a microkernel where everything happens in servers and userspace drivers, the designers of a hybrid kernel may decide to keep many components inside the kernel and a few others outside. Several factors exist for such a design policy, such as simplicity, performance, and vendor lock-in. The design of most hybrid kernels begins as monolithic kernels, and then components are moved to userspace, one of the typical applications of this approach is to relocate malicious or buggy drivers. As shown in Figure 3.1, in the design of this typical hybrid kernel, disc drivers and bus controllers are kept inside the kernel, but the file server has been implemented as a userspace application. The main advantage of such a system is to preserve performance and design principles of a monolithic kernel. We can refer to Windows and Mac OS X (XNU) as examples of hybrid operating systems.

3.4.4 Exokernel Operating System

Exokernels are an attempt to separate security from abstraction. The goal is to avoid forcing any specific abstraction on applications; instead, applications are allowed to

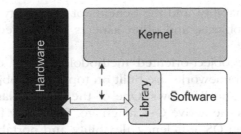

Figure 3.6   A graphical view of an exokernel.

use or implement whatever abstractions that have the best fit for their work without layering them on top of other abstractions, which may impose limitations or extra overheads. This is achieved by moving abstractions into untrusted userspace libraries, called library operating systems, which are linked to applications and invoke the operating system on their behalf. The graphical view of an exokernel is portrayed in Figure 3.6.

Let us consider the typical abstraction of a file. Files, as application programs see them, do not exist on the disc. There are sectors only on the disc. The operating system abstracts the reality of the disc to create a better image of files. Security is also often provided at this level. ACLs and permissions are applied to files. Security combines with abstraction.

In exokernels, security is provided on an unabstracted hardware level, in this example, to disc sectors. Library operating systems provide the requested abstractions on this interface. Non-overridable security is placed inside the microkernel, and overridable abstractions are implemented in a library operating system. Security is separated from abstraction.

The main strength of exokernels is to allow userspace applications to implement operations like access to files (by directly accessing the raw disc) and optimal memory management (by having direct memory access) by themselves. This method can lead to a dramatic increase in the performance of the network and distributed applications. The design of exokernel interfaces is very difficult. Designers must develop adequate and suitable interfaces for low-level hardware.

3.4.5 Object-Oriented Operating System (O3S)

Objected-oriented technology eliminates a major part of the complexity in traditional and procedure-oriented programming. Most traditional operating systems are procedure oriented (such as Unix, Linux, and Windows) and present native procedural interfaces. Therefore, the services provided by these operating systems can only be accessed through procedures defined by their respective procedural interfaces. If a program requires to access one of the services provided by these procedural operating systems, that program must execute a command to reach the service by calling an appropriate OS procedure. This is the path that the intended software must take, whether objected-oriented or procedure-oriented. Thus, the benefits of objected-oriented technology disappear when an object-oriented program is developed in a procedure-oriented environment. This is because all classes in an object-oriented environment must warp their native procedural interfaces. Hence, some of the features of maintainability, and the benefits of reusability and modularity in the expression of classes, objects, and other aspects of objected-oriented systems are destroyed.

O3Ss internally use object-oriented methodologies. In contrast, some object-oriented languages or frameworks are built on top of non-objected-oriented operating systems like Linux and Windows. One of the optimal languages for designing this type of language is the native C++ language. Three key factors justify the need to use an object-oriented OS: efficiency, flexibility and portability. An O3S provides resources through objects. H/W tools, and entities such as processes, files, system data structures, resource allocation management, policies, etc., are encapsulated by an O3S.

3.4.6 Language-Based Operating System (LOS)

LOSs take advantage of language features to stratify security rather than hardware mechanisms. In these systems, the code referenced as a trusted base is responsible for agreeing to run programs, ensuring that they cannot perform operations harmful to the stability of the system without first being detected and dealt with. One common way to provide such a mechanism is to use high-level languages (HLLs) such as C# and Java. LOSs prevent dangerous structures; most of their code is written in an HLL, and a small amount of low-level code is likely used. Because LOSs make use of ahead-of-time (AOT) techniques in the compilation phase that cannot harm the system (such as dangling pointers in the C language that do not point to a valid object of an appropriate type; for example, when in C language a memory allocated to a pointer is not set to a null value after being freed), in addition to maintaining executable code security, expensive address space switching can be avoided to increase performance.

One of the most important recent experimental LOSs is the Singularity operating system developed by the Microsoft research department. Singularity is a highly dependable operating system in which the kernel, device drivers, and applications are entirely written in managed code. One of the key aspects of this OS is to propose a model based on software-isolated processes (SIPs). SIPs encapsulate components of an application or a system and provide information hiding. SIPs are actually OS processes in Singularity. Singularity is a microkernel operating system that runs SIPs in a uniform address space. Figure 3.7 demonstrates the Singularity OS architecture.

The lowest level of interrupt dispatch in x86 architecture is written directly in assembly and C languages. This code invokes the kernel. The kernel runs the runtime and garbage collector (GC) written in Sing# language (Sing# is an extended version of the Spec# programming language, which is itself an extension of the C# language). The hardware abstraction layer (HAL), as shown in Figure 3.1 at the beginning of this chapter, is a set of software routines that simulate platform-specific details and allow applications to access hardware resources directly. Since HAL operates at a level between hardware and operating system, applications and device drivers do not require to have knowledge about hardware-specific information. HALs hide hardware-dependent details, such as I/O interfaces, interrupt controllers, and multiprocessor communication mechanisms. Singularity's HAL is written in C++ language and runs in protected mode. During the process of OS installation, opcodes (operand

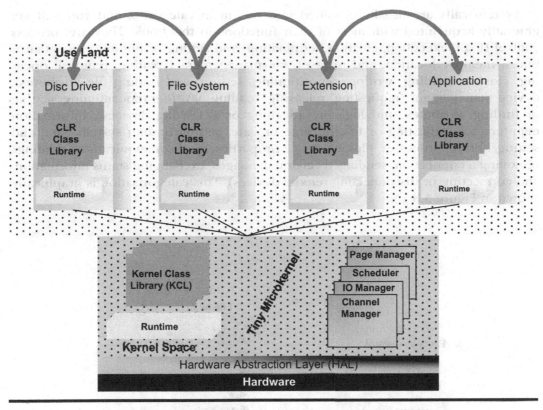

Figure 3.7   The architecture of an LOS operating system is called singularity.

codes) of the common intermediate language (CIL) are translated directly into the code of native ×86 architecture operators using the Bartok compiler.

3.4.7 System Calls to Request Linux and Windows OS Services

System calls are the *de facto* standard interfaces to the operating system kernel. They are used to request services offered and implemented by the operating system kernel. Whilst different operating systems present a variety of services, the underlying mechanism of basic system calls has been common in all multi-processor operating systems for decades.

System call invocation typically involves writing arguments to proper registers and then issuing a machine-specific instruction that raises a synchronous exception. This exception immediately transfers the execution of an user-mode code to a kernel-mode exception handler. Two important properties in designing a conventional system call are as follows: (1) a processor exception to make a communication with the kernel is used and (2) a model of synchronous execution is exerted, whilst the application is waiting for the completion of the system call before recovering from the user-mode execution. Both effects give rise to performance degradation, which is elaborated in this section. The main purpose of this book is to develop distributed systems on top of the Linux and Windows operating systems (and those that comply with the POSIX standard); therefore, system calls in these OSs are examined.

System calls are usually classified into five main categories, and you will get gradually acquainted with most of their functions in this book. They are: process control (load, execution, creation, termination, and setting or finding process attributes, memory location, and release), file management (creating, removal, opening, closing, reading, writing, repositioning, setting, and finding file attributes), device management (requesting, releasing, reading, writing, repositioning, setting or finding attributes, and logically attaching or detaching devices), information maintenance (adjusting or finding time or date, setting/finding system data, and setting/finding processes, files, or device properties), and communication (creating/removing a connection, sending/receiving messages, exchanging status information, and connecting or disconnecting remote devices). This categorisation is graphically shown in Figure 3.8.

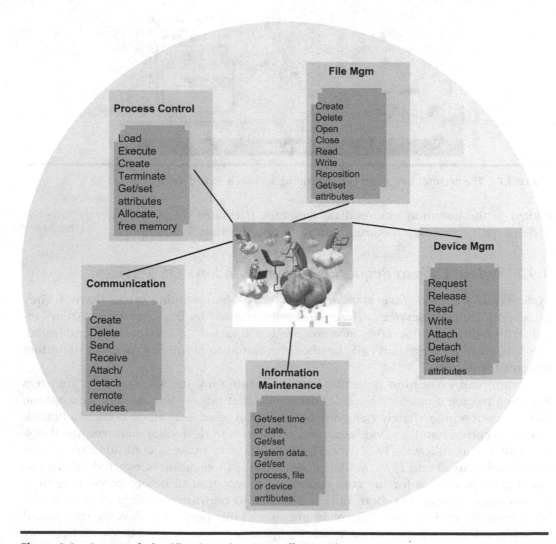

Figure 3.8   A general classification of system-call operations.

3.4.8 System Calls in the Linux Operating System

Implementation of system calls in Linux can be different for distinct architectures. For instance, the older x86 processors use an interrupt mechanism to migrate from userland to kernel, but new Intel and AMD processors provide instructions that optimise this transition to protect ring 0 (sysenter/sysexit and syscalls are used respectively in Intel and AMD processor lines). In this section, we will only look at interrupt-based system calls to avoid the complexity of different underlying mechanisms.

A hardware interrupt forces the processor to store its current state of execution and start executing an interrupt handler. Software interrupts are usually implemented as instructions in the instruction set, which lead to context switches to software handlers similar to hardware interrupts. The function of interrupting is referred to as interrupt request (IRQ). Part of a program that deals with interrupts are known as interrupt service routine (ISR). Interrupts provide low overhead and good latencies in low offered load, but severely reduce at high interrupt rates unless several pathologies take place. Under critical conditions, a large number of interrupts may completely stall the system.

Figure 3.9 illustrates the steps involved in the execution of a system call to read from a userspace function inside the *main()* function. Every arrow in this figure represents a jump in the CPU instruction flow. In the Linux operating system, every system call is multiplexed into the kernel through a single-entry point. The *eax* register is used to identify a specific system call that should be invoked; this routine is located in the C library (for each call from the userspace). When the C library loads the system call index and its arguments, a software interrupt is invoked (interrupt 0x80), which makes the function *syscall* execute through the interrupt handler. This function handles all system calls, as detected by *eax* contents. After a few simple tests, the actual system call is invoked by using *syscall_table* and the index available in *eax*. The file object must first be looked up, reliant on the file descriptor that the user program has passed to the system call. The method *read()* for the file object

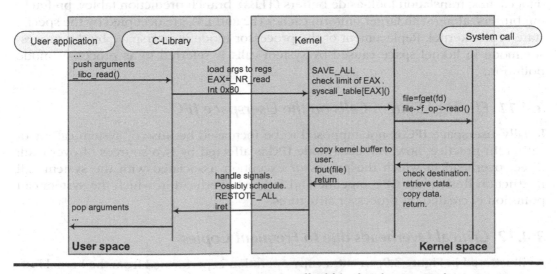

Figure 3.9 The steps involved in a *read()* system call within the Linux operating system.

ultimately executes, and the data transfer from the storage system to the kernel buffer completes. After copying the kernel buffer into the user buffer, in the end the execution within the C library is resumed, and the execution flow returns to the user mode. Every jump in this diagram may require flushing the prefetch queue and probably a cache miss event.

Transitions between user and kernel spaces are very important, whilst they are the most expensive in terms of processing time and prefetching behaviour. As seen, a system call is processed in the kernel, which is carried out by changing the mode of CPU execution to a more privileged ring, but in this transition, a context switch is unnecessary. Hardware views the world in terms of execution mode according to the processor status register, and processes are just an abstraction provided by the operating system. A system call does not mandate a context switch to another process, but rather is processed in the context of the process that has invoked it. Consequently, the overheads caused by a system call have to be sought in other sources. Here we look at four noticeable sources of overhead in system calls.

3.4.9 Costs Due to the Mode Switch of System Calls

Traditionally, the performance cost attributed to systems calls is the time taken by mode switches. This time consists of the time required to execute the system call instruction in user mode, resume execution in the protective ring 0 (kernel space), and return control to user mode. Modern processors implement this mode switch as a CPU exception: clearing the user mode pipeline, storing a few numbers of registers into the process stack, changing the protection domain, and redirecting the execution to an exception handler. Consequently, returning from the exception is necessary for the execution resumption in user mode.

3.4.10 Costs Due to the Footprints of System Calls

During execution in kernel space, processor structures, including instruction and L1 data caches, translation look-aside buffers (TLBs), branch prediction tables, prefetching buffers, along with larger uniform caches (L2 and L3), are occupied by the special state of the kernel. Replacement of the processor mode in userspace by the processor mode in kernel space caused by system calls is referred to as processor mode pollution.

3.4.11 Effect of System Calls on the Userspace IPC

Ideally, userspace IPC is not supposed to be increased because of system call invocation. In practice, however, user-mode IPC is affected by two sources of overhead: direct overhead in which the processor exception associated with the system call instruction flushes the CPU pipeline and indirect overhead in which the system call pollution is created on processor structures.

3.4.12 Critical Overheads due to Frequent Copies

As illustrated in Figure 3.9, an extra copy operation is performed from the kernel buffer to the user buffer during the completion of the *read()* system call. Each time the data crosses the boundary of kernel and user spaces, it must be copied, which consumes many CPU cycles and too much memory bandwidth. Even a simple analysis of data processing paths in the kernel indicates that data is repeatedly transferred from one buffer to another. Measurements reveal that memory operations are responsible for a significant amount of processing costs. Therefore, these system-call overheads in distributed environments can have much more negative impacts on applications compared to the former three sources explained above. In the userspace, the so-called zero-copy methods can be used in that the processor does not perform the task of data copy from one memory region to another. These methods are often employed to save computing power and use memory when sending files over a network.

3.4.13 System Calls in the Windows Operating System

System calls are also present in Windows OS but have strictly been hidden from users. Windows has a set of hidden APIs that are used by the OS internally. This API is known as Native API. The Native API reveals nuances that have not been documented by Microsoft. This API follows one goal: as means of invoking OS services in kernel mode in a controlled way. Native API is equivalent to system calls on a Linux operating system. The main language of Windows API is Win32, and the Win32 architecture illustrates this well. The Win32 execution environment is split into a processor server—CSRSS.EXE (Client/Server Runtime SubSystem)—and client-side dynamic-link libraries (DLLs) linked to programs that use the Win32 API.

When a Win32 program calls a Win32 API, control is transferred into the address space of one of these client-side Win32 DLLs. This DLL can perform one or more of the following operations:

- Immediately returns to the caller.
- Sends a message to the Win32 server requesting for help.
- Invokes the Native APIs to do that operation.

The latter is usually employed for system calls. The KERNEL32.DLL file has functions that directly invoke Native APIs. This file includes I/O functions (such as *CreateFile()*, *ReadFile()*, and *WriteFile()*), synchronisation routines (such as *WaitForSingleObject()* and *SetEvent()*), and memory management functions (such as *VirtualAlloc()* and *VirtualProtect()*). Figure 3.10 shows the control flow from a Win32 application running system calls through the KERNEL32 and NTDLL files into kernel mode, where system service execution control (like *NtCreateFile*) is transferred.

The Native API is presented to user-mode programs by the NTDLL.DLL library, which also contains user-mode entry points of Native API. The control transfer to the kernel mode is achieved by executing a software exception. If we take a close look at a piece of code for Native API in NTDLL inside a debugger on x86 architecture, the information shown in Figure 3.11 can be obtained. The first instruction is to load a register with the index number of the Native API. Every Native API has a unique index number, which is automatically generated by a script that runs a part of the Windows build process. Therefore, the index number for a particular function can vary from one build of Windows to another, whilst Native APIs are added or removed incrementally.

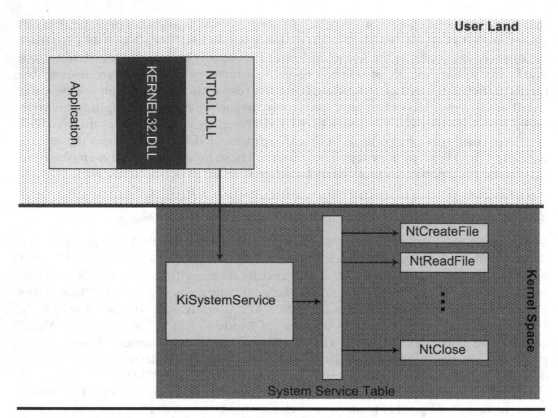

Figure 3.10 Execution flow of system calls in Windows operating system.

```
NtCreateFile:
  mov   eax, 0x0000001A
  lea   edx, [esp + 04]
  int   0x2E
  ret   0x2C
```

Figure 3.11 Assembly code in debug mode for *NtCreateFile()* function.

The second instruction loads a register with a pointer to the call parameters. The next instruction is related to software exceptions. Windows registers a kernel-mode exception handler to handle Native API exceptions. In x86, this exception is the number 0x2E. The last instruction pops off parameters from the call stack. All Native APIs begin with *Nt*. The export table in NTDLL.DLL also makes the Native API accessible through an auxiliary naming convention, in which instruction names start with *Zw* instead of *Nt*. So, *ZwCreateFile()* is an alias for *NtCrteateFile()*.

3.4.14 Timeline of Operating System Evolution

Over the course of five decades, the evolution of three major types of operating systems (including Unix, Linux, and Windows) has created a revolution in the computer industry and humankind. Figure 3.12 shows a timeline for the evolution of operating systems in the period from 1969 to 2021.

In 1969, Unix emerged on a DEC PDP-7 at AT&T Bell Labs. When AT&T decided to withdraw Multics (Multiplexed Information and Computing Service) operating system, Ken Thompson and Dennis M. Ritchie cobbled together an operating system to play a space travel game developed by Thompson. One of their colleagues gave the operating system a jockey name, UNICS, which was later changed to UNIX. Between 1969 and 1973, Ritchie developed the general-purpose C language for the Unix operating system. In 1973, Unix was rewritten in the C language. Computer Systems Research Group at the University of UC Berkeley released an open-source version of Unix called BSD in 1977.

In 1983, Richard Stallman announced his plan to support GNU free software, as a Unix-like operating system that did not contain any propriety software. In 1985, version 1 of Windows went on sale just for $99. This version of Windows was marketed as a graphical user interface that extended the DOS operating system. Andrew Tenenbaum created the MINIX operating system in 1987 for educational purposes, which was a Unix-like OS with a microkernel architecture. In 1991, Linus Benedict Torvalds curious about operating systems, whilst attending the University of Helsinki, was frustrated by the MINIX copyright, which limited it to educational use only. Linus started working on his own operating system, which eventually turned into the Linux kernel.

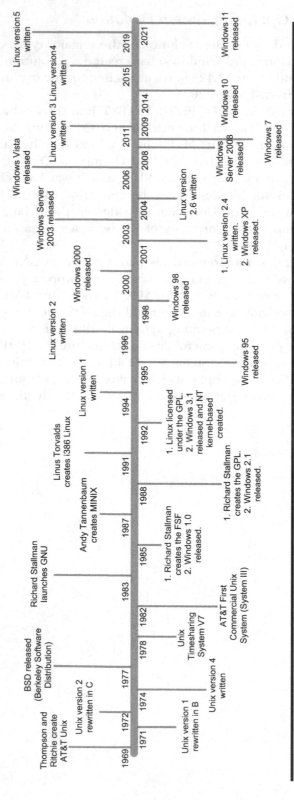

Figure 3.12 Timeline of the evolution of Unix, Linux, and Windows operating systems.

Chapter 4

Parallelism for the Many-Core Era: Hardware and Software Perspectives

Scientifically, happiness is a choice. It is a choice about where your single-processor brain will devote its finite resources as you process the world.

Shawn Achor

4.1 Introduction

In this chapter, we will gradually prepare you to step into the real world of parallelism that forms the basis of today's computing, such as Grid and Cloud Computing. By combining the hardware and software perspectives of single-processor architectures in Section 4.2, we attempt to give the reader a deeper understanding of the current generation of multi-core processing in Section 4.3.

4.2 Exploiting Instruction-Level Parallelism (ILP) by Hardware and Software Approaches

It is important to note that a complete survey on all ILP approaches is beyond the scope of this book, as our sole purpose in this chapter is to acquaint the reader with the basic concepts of ILP. All processors have been benefitting from pipelining techniques since 1985 to overlap the execution of multiple instructions and improve the overall system performance. A pipeline is like an assembly line. In a car assembly production line, there are many steps, every of which is dedicated to constructing part of the car. Every step is performed in parallel with the other steps on a different car. In a processor pipeline, every step of the pipeline completes part of an

DOI: 10.1201/9781003379041-4

instruction. In this method, different steps complete different parts of the instructions in parallel. Each of these steps is called a pipeline stage. The stages are connected consecutively to form a pipeline. Instructions enter from one side and exit from the other end after passing through the stages.

The time it takes to move an instruction from one step to another in the pipeline is called the processor cycle. The pipelining approach reduces the average execution time per instruction. This reduction can be thought of an increase in the number of clock cycles per instruction (CPI) or a decrease in the clock cycle time. A pipeline is an implementation method in which parallelism between instructions is exploited in a sequential instruction stream. One of the most significant advantages of the pipelining technique is that it is not visible to the programmer.

The basic idea of the pipelining method is to split the processing of an instruction into a series of steps along with storage at the end of each step. To better understand this approach, we take the classic pipeline of Reduced Instruction Set Computer (RISC) processors into account. This pipeline is broken into five stages:

- **Instruction Fetch (IF)**: The program counter is sent to memory and the current instruction is fetched from memory. The PC value is updated to the next PC that points to the next instruction.
- **Instruction Decode and Register Fetch (ID)**: The instruction is decoded and the registers corresponding to the registers referring to source registers are read from the register file. Whilst the registers are being read, they are examined for a probable branch. Decoding is done in parallel with reading the registers.
- **Execution (EX)**: ALU operates on operands prepared in the previous cycle and operations such as memory referral, register-register ALU instruction, and register-immediate ALU instruction.
- **Memory Access (MEM)**: If the instruction is a load (from memory to a register), the memory performs a read operation using the effective address calculated in the previous cycle. If the instruction is a store, the memory writes the data of registers into memory.
- **Write-back (WB)**: In register-to-register ALU instructions or the load instruction, the following operation is carried out: the calculation result is written into the register files, whether from the system memory (for one load) or the ALU (for one ALU instruction).

Figure 4.1 shows a five-stage pipeline of classic RISC machines. In the fourth clock cycle, the first instruction is in the MEM stage, and the last instruction has not yet

Instruction Number	Pipeline Stages								
1	IF	ID	EX	MEM	WB				
2		IF	ID	EX	MEM	WB			
3			IF	ID	EX	MEM	WB		
4				IF	ID	EX	MEM	WB	
5					IF	ID	EX	MEM	WB
Clock Cycle	1	2	3	4	5	6	7	8	9

Figure 4.1   The basic five-stage pipeline of a classic RISC machine.

entered the pipeline. As can be seen in this figure, in pipeline architecture, operations related to five instructions are somewhat overlapping in nine clock cycles. The chequered story of parallelism begins with this very simple pipeline architecture.

When a programmer (or compiler) writes assembly code, he assumes that each instruction is executed before the execution of the next instruction begins. This assumption is invalidated by the pipeline. This factor causes a program to behave incorrectly and is usually referred to as a hazard. Hazards are divided into three general categories of structural hazards, data hazards, and control hazards, which can be resolved by adding possible data paths at the hardware level.

A structural hazard is a situation in which the hardware cannot support a combination of instructions that must be executed in the same clock cycle. For example, if two instructions attempt to use a single source at the same time, a structural hazard occurs. Data hazards take place when a pipeline must be stalled because one stage must wait for another to complete. Data hazards are created due to the dependency of an instruction on another preceding one. Control hazards happen because of conditional and unconditional branches. Hazards can lead to many stalls occurring in the pipeline. Avoiding a hazard often requires that some instructions in the pipeline are allowed to continue whilst other instructions are delayed. These stalls will deteriorate the pipeline performance from its ideal state.

Such a potential overlapping in pipeline architecture is known as *instruction-level parallelism* because instructions can be evaluated in parallel. There are two completely different ways to exploit ILP. One is a hardware-dependent method that helps to dynamically discover and harness parallelism. Another approach relies on software methodologies that find parallelism statically at compile time. The degree of parallelism available inside a basic block, like a sequence of straightforward code with no jumps, is small. To achieve maximum efficiency, ILP must be applied between multiple basic blocks.

Instruction scheduling in loops is one of the most important methods of ILP because many programs spend most of their execution time within loops. One widely used technique for enlarging the basic blocks is loop unrolling. The iterative operations of an algorithm are usually expressed as a loop to obtain a compact and elegant form of code. Nevertheless, the same algorithm could be expressed equivalently by explicitly repeating a number of loop bodies. Figure 4.2 demonstrates an example of loop unrolling to exploit ILP in accordance with the classic five-stage RISC architecture.

In this example, it can be seen that a single instruction of a loop is broken into five instructions, and this state is executed in parallel for the converted loop in a five-stage pipeline. When the assembly code of a loop is generated, branch instructions are used to implement the loop iteration mode; so, if loop unrolling is not performed, frequent control hazards can introduce many stalls into the pipeline and performance is seriously degraded. Other ways exist to transform loop codes such as loop peeling, loop fusion, loop distribution, and software pipelining. Since instruction scheduling is of paramount importance in the ILP method, we describe an example at the assembly code level to examine how scheduling can eliminate hazards to a large extent by removing stalls and helping increase ILP parallelism. First, for a better picture of the three hazards stated in this section, we consider them in three different examples in the context of a RISC processor, as shown in Figure 4.3.

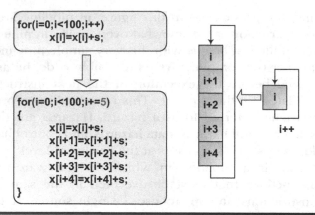

Figure 4.2 **Unrolling a loop for ILP exploitation corresponding to the five-stage architecture explained in the text.**

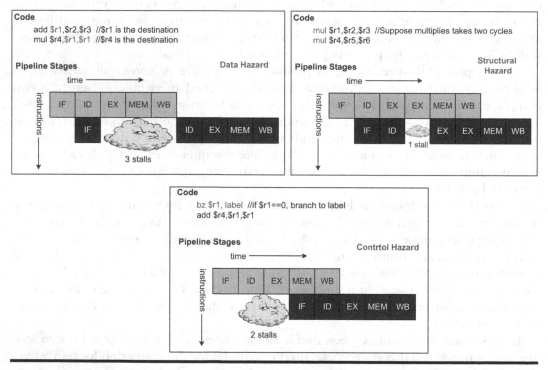

Figure 4.3 **Three examples of data, structural and control hazards in the pipeline model of the RISC processor.**

In the data hazard case, since the MUL instruction requires ADD instruction, three stalls must be inserted in the pipeline so that in the WB stage the data calculated in the ADD instruction is prepared for the next instruction. In a structural hazard, because two instructions have to use a single ALU, a stall must be inserted in the EX stage. In the control hazard, since there is no store register for the branch instruction, two stalls have been introduced, but the first instruction that uses ALU in this architecture to calculate the PC cannot be used by ADD instruction.

Now that we have gained some insight about hazards, a practical example is given to see how code scheduling at the assembly language level (statically at compile time by software) or native machine language (dynamically at runtime by hardware) can reduce the number of stalls by code motion or transformation and make use of the maximum parallelism within the pipeline structure. Suppose in the intended pipeline, hazards are created in two other cases: load instruction (ld) is immediately followed by an ALU operation; a store instruction (st) is immediately followed by a load instruction. Figure 4.4 illustrates a piece of assembly code for the RISC architecture. With the assumptions taken, hazards are marked with a square. As seen, for example, the first instruction has a data dependence with the seventh instruction in the $r2 register. To display all data dependencies of this example, we compare each line of code with others and then draw a directional graph known as a dependence graph.

This graph is a directional tree whose nodes represent instructions and edges (x_1, x_2) represent a dependency between two x_1 and x_2 instructions, where x_1 must be executed before x_2. This graph is usually called a *data dependence graph* or *data flow graph*. As shown on the left side of this figure, this code has four hazards. Consequently, our goal is to schedule the code to reduce the number of stalls that must be inserted by hardware or software in the code incurred by these hazards. Different scheduling algorithms exist to solve this problem. Figure 4.5 demonstrates a typical instruction scheduling algorithm to reduce stalls in a pipeline architecture. If we apply this algorithm to the graph in Figure 4.4, the scheduling code in Figure 4.6 is generated that has only a single hazard.

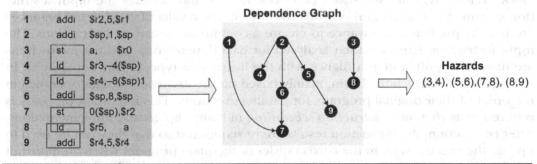

Figure 4.4 An example of the topological dependence graph to examine the pipeline stalls of the RISC architecture before scheduling.

```
Build dependence graph G
Candidates ← set of all roots (nodes with no in-edges) in G
while Candidates ≠ ∅
    Select instruction s from Candidates
    Schedule s
    Candidates ← Candidates – s
    Candidates ← Candidates ∪ "exposed" nodes
```

Figure 4.5 A typical instruction scheduling algorithm to reduce stalls in pipeline architecture.

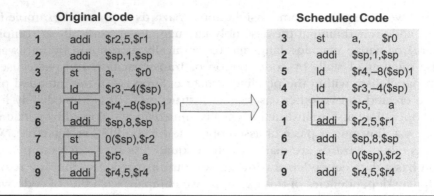

Figure 4.6   A scheduling code that only has a hazard in (8,1).

In the literature on optimal compiler design, scheduling algorithms are split into two local and global types. Algorithms that only schedule single acyclic basic blocks are known as *local schedulers*. Algorithms that jointly schedule multiple basic blocks are called *general scheduling algorithms*. Acyclic global scheduling algorithms (like the given example) usually deal with control flow graphs that do not include any cycles.

4.2.1 Superscalar Processors

Superscalar processing is the ability to initiate multiple instructions during the same clock cycle. A typical superscalar processor fetches and decodes the input instruction stream at a time. As part of instruction fetch, the results of conditional branches are usually predicted in advance to ensure a continuous stream of instructions. The input instruction stream is then analysed for data dependence, and the instructions are dispatched, often in accordance with the instruction type, to functional units. In the next step, instructions begin, mainly based on the existence of data operands in the order of their original program, for parallel execution. This important property is referred to as *dynamic instruction scheduling* in many superscalar implementations. After completion, the instruction results are re-sequenced so that they can be used to update the process state in the correct order of the main program when an interrupt condition occurs. Because single instructions are entities running in parallel, superscalar processors make the maximum exploitation of IPL methods.

Figure 4.7 shows the method used in most superscalar processors. Instructions are initiated in a static program. After fetch operation and branch prediction, instructions are dispatched into the window of execution. Other instructions in the window of execution are not expressed in sequential order, but rather are sorted partially relied on their data dependence. Instructions are issued from the window in a certain order by correct data dependencies and the existence of hardware resources. Finally, after execution, instructions are conceptually placed into the order of the sequential program (whilst they are removed from execution) and their results update the state of the constructed process.

With the exception of processors used for low-power applications, embedded systems, and battery-powered devices, all general-purpose processors have been built

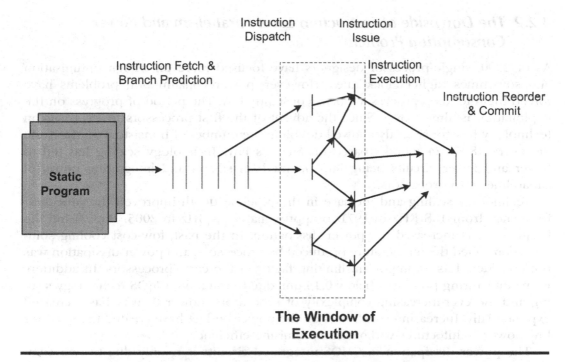

Figure 4.7   A view of superscalar execution. Processing phases are listed above in the figure.

Instruction Number	Pipeline Stages								
1 (ALU)	IF	ID	EX	MEM	WB				
2 (FPU)	IF	ID	EX	MEM	WB				
3 (SIMD)		IF	ID	EX	MEM	WB			
4 (FPU)		IF	ID	EX	MEM	WB			
5 (ALU)			IF	ID	EX	MEM	WB		
6 (SIMD)			IF	ID	EX	MEM	WB		
7 (ALU)				IF	ID	EX	MEM	WB	
8 (FPU)				IF	ID	EX	MEM	WB	
9 (ALU)					IF	ID	EX	MEM	WB
10 (ALU)					IF	ID	EX	MEM	WB
Clock Cycle	1	2	3	4	5	6	7	8	9

Figure 4.8   A simple pipeline for a RISC superscalar architecture.

in a form of superscalars as of 1998. These processors have several functional units, such as ALUs, FPUs, and SIMDs, for the maximum leverage of ILP. Figure 4.8 portrays a simple example of a superscalar processor. In this example, two instructions (with different types such as FPU, ALU, and SIMD) are fetched and dispatched at the same time, so a maximum of two instructions can be completed per cycle. Here, ten instructions are completed in nine clock cycles.

4.2.2 The Downside of Instruction-Level Parallelism and Power Consumption Problem

As of 2000, single-processor designers have focused more on design optimisation and sometimes higher clock rates. However, power consumption problems have forced them to keep processor clocks constantly low. The period of progress on ILP exploitation is almost over. Since the advent of the first processors in 1971, silicon technology has consistently allowed doubling the number of transistors on the same die every 18 or 24 months based on Moore's law. Technology scaling has led to larger and faster circuits being implemented on silicon and integrating powerful capabilities into processors.

Technology scaling and increase in the pipeline depth improved the processor frequency from 108 KHz in 1971 to approximately 4 GHz in 2005. But raising the frequency has increased the power dissipation. In the past, low-cost cooling solutions controlled the temperature produced by processors, and power dissipation was not considered as an important limiting factor in the early processors. In addition, in manufacturing processes below 0.13 µm, due to the more CMOS technology scaling and the ever-increasing complexity of processors, power density has increased exponentially. Increasing constraints on the power budget have created the need for low-power architectures without compromising efficiency.

The power dissipation in CMOS integrated circuits is mainly due to two components of dynamic (switching) power and static power. The total power is shown in Equation (4.1). Equation (4.2) shows the dynamic power in which C parameter is the switching capacitance in every clock cycle, V is the applied voltage, and f is the switching frequency. As the frequency changes, dynamic power varies linearly. Dynamic power does not constitute the total chip power, but in the manufacturing process of recent years with very small dismissions it exhibits static power in itself, which is mainly due to different leakage current components—including subthreshold leakage current, gate-induced leakage (GIDL) current, punchthrough leakage current, and band-to-band and reverse bias p-n junction leakage currents. The smaller the feature size and the lower the threshold voltage of transistors, the more important the leakage current has become in recent years. In the latest advances in deep submicron technology, two-thirds of power consumption is related to the dynamic power and the rest has been reported arising from the leakage power. Therefore, increasing the frequency to improve the pipeline performance of single processors has faced an ultimate limitation in terms of power consumption.

$$P_{total} \approx P_{switching} + P_{static} \tag{4.1}$$

$$P_{switching} = V_{dd}^{2} . f . C_L \tag{4.2}$$

To achieve a low CPI and a high clock rate, a processor must switch more transistors faster, which significantly increases the dynamic power. Issuing multiple instructions in superscalar processors is an important source of overhead that grows faster than the issue growth rate. The number of transistor switching is proportional to the maximum issue rate. Consequently, the energy consumed per unit of efficiency increases. On the other hand, since increasing the frequency elevates power consumption, deep pipelines cause extra overheads with higher switching rates.

Besides these hardware inefficiencies, code compilation has become too complex to exploit the high ILP of processors. Not only does a compiler have to support a wide range of complex transformations, but also it is very difficult to set up a compiler to achieve optimal performance for a vast array of applications.

These technical issues have led to instead focusing on multi-core and thread-level parallelism, and in the coming years, multi-core processors will move the computer industry revolution ahead. We will comprehensively deal with this issue in the next section.

4.3 Thread-Level Parallelism (TLP) and Multi-Processor and Multi-Core Parallelism

4.3.1 Introduction

As stated in the previous sections, over the past decades, general-purpose single-core processors evolved to exploit a low degree of instruction-level parallelism in sequential programs. Whilst clock frequencies rose, wire delays in these processors restricted scalability. At a higher clock frequency, the chip area that a signal can reach in a single clock cycle becomes smaller. In addition to these problems, the power consumption constraint has brought a new trend about seamlessly concentrating on instruction-level multi-processor and multi-core computing.

Besides these technical issues which have grounds in electronically manufactured processors, other intrinsic trends further the TLP revolution, some of which we point out herein. Many of the phenomena happening in the universe, and a variety of branches in science own inherent parallelism that cannot be described on the basis of ILP, like the simulation of brain neurons in a living creature, or the simulation of electronic devices through hardware description languages (HDLs) such as Verilog and SystemC. There has always been a strong interest in TLP in servers and server applications and increasing their performance, particularly data centre energy consumption is accounted as a growing challenge in the server industry. In the Cloud Computer industry, virtualisation has recently been of great importance; virtualisation platforms provide a virtual version of anything in the computing world, such as an operating system, a hardware platform, a storage device, and network resources. One of the other fundamental advantages of TLP is a cost-effective design for replication versus a unique design. Another trend originates from the system-on-chip (SoC) industry, SoC is a technology that allows a variety of digital devices to be integrated into a single chip; multi-core architectures in the mobile industry based on SoCs that have low-power, high-performance characteristics are vital.

As it is clear from all the previous paragraphs, the main motivation behind TLP is to reduce power consumption. Here, we look at a simple example to examine how a multi-processor system can significantly reduce the power consumption of an application program in tandem with maintaining its performance. Suppose that a task requires the time with a T window to complete as demonstrated in Figure 4.9. The single-processor system in Figure 4.9(a) works with F frequency. By this assumption

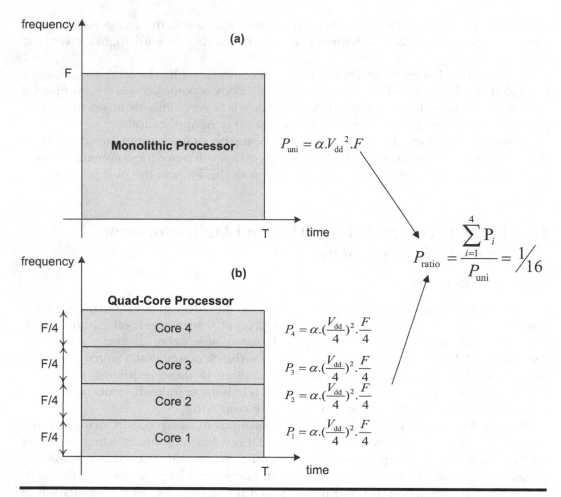

Figure 4.9 **Calculation of the reduced amount of power consumption in a quad-core processor (a) with respect to a single-processor system (b) for a task with *T* size of the execution time.**

that this work can be made parallel, in Figure 4.9(a) with a quad-core processor, the frequency of each core must be equal to $f/4$, whilst its applied voltage is also reduced by the same amount. The reason for this ¼ coefficient is due to Figure 4.9(b) becoming smaller compared to Figure 4.9(a); in the semiconductor industry, this dimension reduction is known as a *scaling factor*, in which frequencies and voltages are scaled with a $1/k$ coefficient. Of course, this coefficient leads to a continual increase in the circuit speed and complexity per unit area of the chip.

Accordingly, the multi-core system in this example consumes 1/16 less power than a single-core processor for this processing task. As a result, the overall system performance can be improved by parallel processing mechanisms without increasing the clock frequency, whilst a significant reduction in power consumption is made. One of the main challenges in parallel computing is to design optimal algorithms that can apply parallelism to the code of a sequential or inherently parallel program. This simple example has established the foundation for the processor industry revolution.

In the rest of this section, we introduce general concepts of ILP, multi-processors, and multi-core processors.

4.3.2 Thread-Level Parallelism

In this section, the concept of a multi-threaded model is first introduced from a software perspective, and with the description of a specific type of TLP which is implementable using functional ILP hardware components, we prepare the reader to delve into the fascinating topic of current processor revolution.

A thread is a path of execution through a program. It is a runnable entity that belongs to one and only one process. Each process has at least one thread of execution, which is automatically formed when that process is created. The original program runs in the first thread. In certain conditions, a particular application may require performing several tasks. For instance, a file server accepts client requests for various files. If this server, which simultaneously serves many clients, ran traditionally with a single-threaded process, it would be only able to service a single client at a time. A fundamental solution for this problem could be to create a process for every input connection. However, as you will see during this book, the creation of processes is time-consuming and resource intensive. Generally, it is optimal to use a single process having multiple threads.

Figure 4.10 shows the structure and data in a heavyweight process consisting of multiple threads of execution. All threads of a process share information, such as shared variables, files, and open sockets, with one another. Of course, in order to have simultaneous access to this shared information, special mechanisms like locks must be introduced. Each thread has its own activation records and a copy of its own CPU registers, including a stack pointer and a program counter, which totally describe the execution state of that thread.

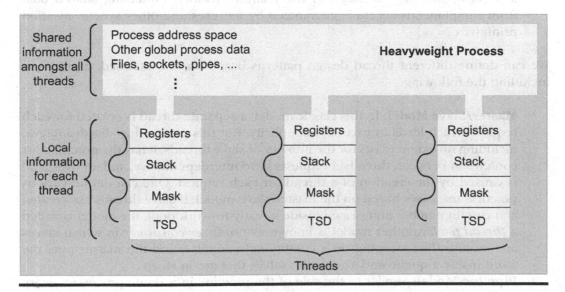

Figure 4.10   Structure of a multi-threaded process.

In single-core processors, the multi-threaded mode is done by time-division multiplexing, where the processor switches between different threads. These context switches are repeatedly performed as if the user feels all threads or tasks are running concurrently. In multi-processor or multi-core systems, threads or tasks really run at a time, whilst each processor or core runs a certain thread or task. An operating system usually supports a mixture of time-sliced threading and multi-processing through a process scheduler. Operating system kernels provide system call interfaces that allow programmers to work with threads. In Chapter 5, we will introduce POSIX multi-threading for this purpose. The main advantages of thread abstraction can be noted as follows:

- **Thread Management**: Creating and managing the execution of threads require lower system resources than processes. For example, creating a thread just needs allocation of a private thread area which is usually a constant value, such as 64 KB, and two system calls. The creation of a process is much more expensive because the entire address space of the parent process must be duplicated. Context switches between threads of a process are much cheaper and faster than context switching of multiple processes.
- **Multi-Processor and Multi-Core Systems**: As stated earlier, threads in multi-processor or multi-core systems are executed simultaneously on processors or multiple cores. Therefore, multi-threaded programs can run much faster than on a single processor. They can also be faster than programs using multiple processors because threads require fewer system resources and create less overhead. One major benefit of threads is that a single multi-threaded program will work on a single-processor system but can naturally avail of a multi-processor system without recompilation.
- **Inter-thread Communication (ITC)**: ITC is much more efficient and easier to use relative to IPC because all threads share the same address space within a process; they do not need to use shared memory. Protecting shared data from simultaneous access is guaranteed by mutexes and other synchronisation primitives.

We can define different thread design patterns based on the intended application, including the following:

- **Master/Slave Model**: In this classic model, a separate thread is created for each request which leads to excessive simplicity. But this pattern has disadvantages, including no extent exists for the number of slave threads, it has the potential for contention between threads if requests have interdependency, and an overhead is caused by the creation of a thread for each request. One can define various practical use cases based on the master/slave model. If slave threads are created at a certain number and placed inside a ready-to-work pool, the model is called a *thread pool*. Another model is known as *producer/consumer* in which slaves are waiting (like sleeping on a conditional variable), and the master puts the work inside a queue and signals the salves that are in sleep.
- **Pipeline Model**: Similar to the role of the pipeline in a single processor, every thread is part of a long chain in a processing factory. Each thread works on the

data processed by the preceding thread and hands the data over to the next stage thread. In designing this model, sufficient care must be taken to evenly distribute works and perform additional steps to ensure non-blocking behaviour in order for the model to avoid stalls. The overall throughput in this model is limited by the slowest stage. A pipeline model can be very well suited for sensitive applications that need to be spread over a network and to communicate with each other. Since network I/O and storage systems exist in such an environment, blocking I/O mechanisms cannot be used in the threaded pipeline stages. In Figure 4.11, we propose a novel architecture to solve this problem for I/O-bound tasks. In this model, a stream of data with the operations defined for them (through a finite state machine implementation inside every pipeline thread) is performed one after the other with a sequence of stages of $S_1, S_2,..., S_n$; if a stage requires I/O operation, the state offloads it to the thread pool below for further management. If the relevant task is only CPU bound, its processing is completed, and its generated data along with the operation that must be performed by the next stage is placed inside an intermediate queue (such as a circular buffer). In this mode, if the queue is full, the thread of the current stage has to create a stall to wait until there is an adequate place in the intermediate queue. Adjusting the size of this intermediate queue along with the number of pipeline stages can be somewhat challenging, and profiling methods may be used to set this number. However, the existence of an intermediate queue between the pipeline stages can significantly increase or balance the throughput and performance of this architecture logically in comparison with a case in where there is no such a queue. At the lowest level of this architecture, OS's asynchronous I/O methods, which are non-blocking, are used. In Chapters 7 and 10, event-driven and asynchronous approaches are discussed in detail.

- **Work Crew Model**: In this model, multiple threads work together on a single task. The task is broken horizontally into pieces that run in parallel, and each thread operates on one piece.

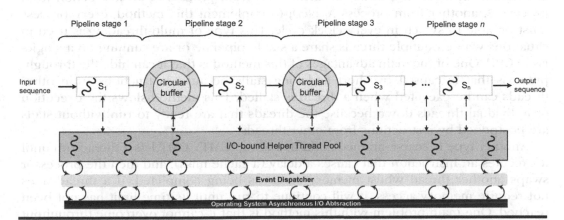

Figure 4.11 A novel architecture proposed for the threaded pipeline model, in which using a thread pool and event-driven techniques tries to avoid possible stalls in the pipeline for I/O-bound components.

- **Role-Specific Models**: These models can be used as customised for a specific design. For example, in services utilising network sockets, either a thread per connection or a dedicated thread to accept the incoming connections, and a thread pool to service them, may be used.
- **Upcall Model**: This model is a way in which we organise an application in such a way that calls can be made from the bottom-up. There is a thread pool in each layer. This model is especially used in the implementation of transport protocols and the open systems interconnection (OSI) model in operating systems. Asynchronous network events must be handled by a mechanism that can initiate an independent control flow in an ordered sequence of procedural invocations upwards through the protocol stack. The upcall programming methodology requires a language mechanism that allows the upper layer to bind local routines that are components of the upcall sequence to the adjacent lower layer. The conventional method to access this binding is based on language support for defining higher-order functions. In C language, one can make use of the possibility to pass functions as arguments to other functions (function pointers). In the network protocol stack, the upper layers are clients of the services provided by the lower layers. In a layered file system, the hierarchy layer is created on the *vnode*, which is built on the *inode* and the disc block layers instead. In the upcall method, higher levels of handler functions are passed into lower layers. These handler functions are called when a lower layer needs to inform the higher level of something. Upcalls can be used for synchronous control flow transfer mechanisms as well as a tool for organising programs. A major drawback of this approach is that it complicates programming, for instance, in synchronisation when a lower layer is invoked.

In single processors, special techniques have been used to realise TLP at the instruction level by employing multiple functional units on a single core. From this point of view, there are two main multi-threading methods.

In fine-grained multi-threading (FMT), threads are context-switched on every instruction (in a rotating form—an instruction from process A, an instruction from process B, another from process A, etc.); to implement this method, every process must be able to switch in every clock cycle. This type of multi-threading is used in situations where multiple threads share a single pipeline or are running on a single-issue CPU. One of the main advantages of this method is that it can hide the throughput loss that is caused by short and long stalls because instructions from other threads can be executed when a thread is stalled. This method slows the execution of individual threads down because the threads that are ready to run without stalls are postponed by instructions from other threads.

Another type is coarse-grained multi-threading (CMT). CMT lets a thread run until it executes an instruction that causes a delay (a cache miss), and then the processor swaps another thread whilst memory access is being completed. If a thread does not require memory access, it will continue to run until its time limit has not been reached. One main problem with this method is that it cannot overcome throughput losses well. This may be due to the costs of initiating the CMT pipeline. Because a CMT processor issues instructions from a single thread, when a stall occurs, the pipeline must be flushed or frozen.

One of the practical processors that use the above two methods is the simultaneous multi-threading (SMT) processor. SMT is a technique to improve the overall performance of superscalar processors by exploiting hardware multi-threading approaches. In SMT, instructions from more than one thread can be executed in each given pipeline at a time. This is done by a few tweaks to the base processor architecture, which requires the ability to fetch instructions from multiple threads in a single cycle, and a larger register file to hold the data of multiple threads. During every clock cycle, all threads are allowed to have access to all resources (probably except the fetch unit). A potential disadvantage of this design type is that it leaves contention of threads free, and, as a result, it may lead to contention for undesirable resources or interference.

On the other hand, single-threaded performance is an important criterion that must not be overlooked. Although modern operating systems eminently help with the widespread use of multi-threading, an application must often be executed with maximum priority without being affected by other processes. The hardware must provide mechanisms so that the operating system can achieve its desired behaviour in every specific scenario. If certain priority schemes are made accessible by an SMT processor, all of these requirements must be handled effectively. Since a dynamically scheduled superscalar processor is likely to have a deep pipeline, SMT is unlikely to be able to benefit greatly from performance if the CMT method is used in its design base.

4.3.3 Multi-Processor Parallelism

As mentioned in the previous sections, the most key factor, namely power consumption, has made the microprocessor architecture shift towards multi-processors. An attempt is made in this section to examine the general concepts of multi-processors.

In multi-processor systems, all processors may become identical, or some of them are utilised for specific purposes. For example, a processor in a system may respond to all hardware interrupts, whereas all other tasks of the system are distributed between the remaining processors. The execution of the kernel mode code is restricted to a single processor, and the userspace code is distributed between all processors. If such restrictions apply, the design of these systems becomes easier, but in the meantime, they will take advantage of less-efficient systems than systems that are using all processors evenly. Systems that deal with all processors equally are called *symmetric multi-processing* (SMP) systems. In systems where all processors are not identical, system resources may be divided in different ways, such as asymmetric multi-processing (ASMP) or non-uniform memory access (NUMA) multi-processing.

The main idea of using multi-processors dates back to the first electronic computers. In 1966, Flynn introduced a simple way to classify all computers that are still in widely use today. Flynn's taxonomy is based on a stream of information, two types of information flow into a processor: instructions and data. The instruction stream is defined as a sequence of instructions run by the processing unit. The data stream is expressed as a sequence of data traffic between the memory and the processing unit. Based on this classification, each of the instructions or data streams can be single or multiple.

- **Single Instruction Stream, Single Data Stream (SISD)**: All single processors are within this classification.
- **Single Instruction Stream, Multiple Data Streams (SIMD)**: In this category, an instruction is executed by multiple processors using different data streams. These computers exploit data-level parallelism by applying the same operation to multiple items of data in parallel. Every processor has its own data memory, but there is a single instruction memory and control processor, which fetches and broadcasts instructions. SIMD architecture can be very efficient for applications that exhibit data-level parallelism. One of the downsides of this method is that a large part of the system stays idle when running programs or system tasks are unable to be divided into units so as to be processed in parallel. This architecture has found a wide range of use cases in a wide spectrum of applications, such as computer simulations, vector processors, and graphic applications, but has had little use in general-purpose computing environments like desktop computers.
- **Multiple Instruction Streams, Single Data Stream (MISD)**: This architecture is employed to achieve high redundancy, in which multiple processing units perform unit works on single data. This method reduces wrong results in the event of a failure of a functional unit. This architecture is very costly, and so far its commercial version has not been made. MISDs are used in array processors and implemented in machines resistant to faults. For instance, the processing units inside critical controllers of missiles where single data is handled by different processors to prevent faults created at runtime by processing elements. This structure is also beneficial to computations in that input must be placed under different operations.
- **Multiple Instruction Streams, Multiple Data Streams (MIMD)**: In this model, every processor fetches its own data and functions on its own data. MIMD processors leverage TLP techniques and multiple threads run in parallel within them. For this sake and ease of implementation, MIMD dominates the multi-processor industry. This architecture introduces issues like deadlock and resource contention. MIMD requires special coding approaches in the operating system but does not consider any requirements for changing applications unless the programs themselves use multiple threads through the operating system APIs.

Multi-processors are usually built based on a combination of these four classifications. Existing MIMD multi-processors are fallen into two general families relied on the count of their processors, which in turn this count dedicates a memory architecture and an interconnection policy.

The *first category* is *shared-memory architectures* that deploy a modest number of processors (let's say, less than 200 cores). A typical architecture of this type is shown in Figure 4.12. With larger caches, a single memory can account for a small number of memory requests from processors. Since there is a single main memory that has a symmetric correspondence to all processors, and this system has a uniform access time to the memory from every processor, these multi-processors are often called *symmetric multi-processors* (SMPs). Processors are connected to the main memory by a system bus or a crossbar system (a crossbar switch is a device that connects multiple

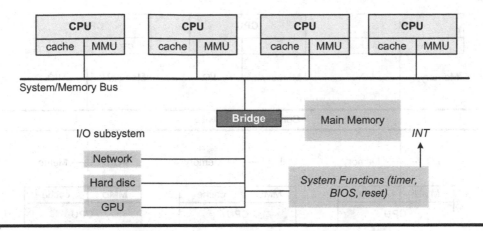

Figure 4.12   An architecture of a shared-memory multi-processor.

inputs to multiple outputs in a matrix form). Every processor has a high-speed cache that accelerates access to the main memory and reduces system bus traffic.

Therefore, the use of multi-level caches can vitally decrease memory bandwidth requests and significantly increase performance. SMP machines usually support two private and shared caches. Private data is used by a single processor, whilst shared data is utilised by multiple processors. The latter usually operates to provide inter-processor communication through reading and writing from/to shared data. Shared data caching creates a technical issue, which is referred to as *cache coherence*. When a cache is updated with the information that may be used by other processors, this change must also be notified to other processors, otherwise they will work on incoherent data. Several coherence protocols can mitigate this problem for highly efficient access to shared information between multiple processors. Two general classes of coherence protocols are as follows:

- **Snooping Protocols**: In this technique, any cache that has a copy of a cache block, as well as its shared status, but there is no centralised status, is kept. The snooping protocol broadcasts a message across the bus whenever a word is modified in the cache. This technique also intercepts the bus to detect such messages from other processors. When a processor learns that another processor has changed a value in an existing address within its cache, the snooping protocol invalidates that entry in its cache. This invalidation reminds the processor of the invalid state of the value in the cache in order to look for the true value somewhere else (in the main memory or another processor cache). As the number of processors in a multi-processor system or the memory requests of each processor grows, system resources can turn into a bottleneck. Because this invalidation method increases cache misses and the snooping protocol contributes to bus traffic, solving the coherency protocol reduces the performance and scalability of SMP systems. As processors become faster and the count of cores per processor increases, designers are steadily trying to abandon these protocols due to broadcast limitations.
- **Directory-based Protocols**: In this method, a directory state of a block that may be cached is kept. The available information in this directory includes

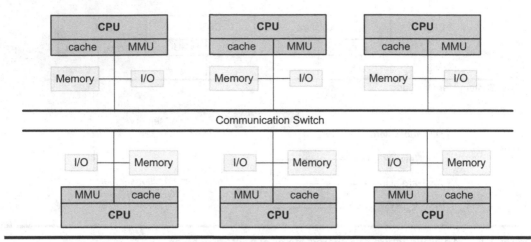

Figure 4.13 An architecture of a distributed shared-memory multi-processor.

which cache has copies of that block, whether it is dirty, and so on. A directory-based protocol can be used to decrease bandwidth requests in an SMP system. This variant is mostly employed in distributed shared-memory multi-processor systems, which are discussed as follows.

The major issues with SMP machines can be pointed out as memory contention, limited bus bandwidth, I/O contention, and cache coherency.

The *second category* is *distributed shared-memory multi-processors* in that every processor has its own cache, main memory and I/O subsystem. The architecture of this classification is illustrated in Figure 4.13. In this architecture, in order to realise a large number of processors, memory must be distributed separately amongst all processors. In this type of processor, a communication switch connects all components of the system, so high-bandwidth inter-communication mechanisms are highly influential in increasing or decreasing the efficiency of this class of multi-processors. This architecture can significantly reduce latencies in accessing local memory. One of the downsides of this structure is that due to the use of a distributed memory architecture, data communication between processors becomes very complex, which even requires making use of software layers for reducing the complexity.

4.3.4 Multi-Core Parallelism

Chip multi-processor (CMP), also known as multicore processor in the computer industry, has recently become the only way to build high-performance, cost-effective microprocessors, which solve many of the problems stated for single processors. In CMPs, a processor die is filled with multiple, relatively simpler processor cores instead of a large core. The full size of cores of a CMP can vary from very simple pipelines to relatively complex superscalar processors, but once a core is selected for the intended performance of a CMP, we can easily reach more cores in generations of the silicon manufacturing process by simply copying that core. The low-latency inter-processor communication (because all cores are built on a silicon wafer) between cores in a CMP leads to making a wider range of practical applications for parallel

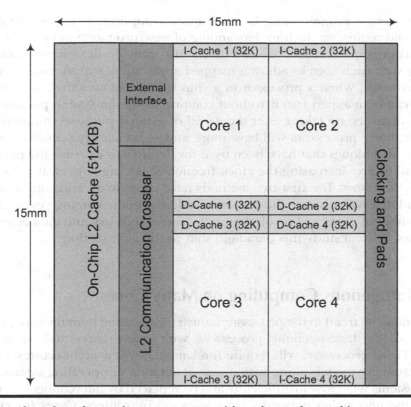

Figure 4.14 Floorplan of a quad-core processor with cache on the L2 chip.

execution with respect to traditional multi-processor multi-chips. Furthermore, the possibility to change the number and clock frequencies of processors allows the same hardware to operate at very different price points.

Figure 4.14 shows a floorplan of a quad-core processor in its microelectronic design. Every core is made of a superscalar processor that is connected to other cores by a crossbar switch, which allows the cores to share the cache on the L2 chip. On the die, four cores are arranged in a grid. Each of the cores has data caches, and single-port and single-bank caches of 32 KB. In this architecture, since four cores share a single L2 cache, the cache requires additional latency to allow the time for inter-processor operations and crossbar switch delay.

In CMP processors, identical cores on the die let the cache coherence circuits operate at much higher clock rates than in multi-processors, where signals must travel outside the chip. These processors allow snooping protocols to be capable of increasing performance dramatically because signals travel much shorter distances and therefore their strength is not reduced (so that they need to be amplified and dissipate a lot of energy). CMP chips can deliver higher performance at lower power consumption. This key factor makes them very suitable for mobile devices that run on batteries. One of the key issues in designing applications for CMP processor generations is that new algorithms and methods must be devised to make the use of threads highly beneficial, which will be the only tool available to new generations of processors, and to increase the performance of an application program. The art of multi-processor programming is much more complicated than single-processor machines and requires a deep understanding of new programming paradigms, algorithms, and principles. Multi-core processors also provide flexible ways for dealing differently with each core to adjust a mapped application, supply voltage and clock rate. For instance, when a processor in a chip is much slower than the rest, a slow workload can be mapped into it without compromising the system performance.

CMP processors are taking over the world of general-purpose computing. In the near future, these processors will have more impact on latency-sensitive computing. Three basic techniques that have been used for decades to increase the performance of applications are: increasing the clock frequency, issuing superscalar instructions, and multi-processors. The first two methods have come to an end, and it is only the last method that will advance the processor industry in the coming years. CMPs with a large number of cores will revolutionise the server industry and data centres in the future years. We will study this paradigm shift in the next section.

4.4 Heterogenous Computing on Many Cores

As mentioned, the trend in the processor industry has shifted to multi-core processors. Homogenous or heterogenous processors with many cores will soon become available. These processors will require fundamentally new architectures, compilers, and programming models along with a new generation of operating systems. Busses in these systems will grow insufficiently and be replaced by interconnection networks in which the underlying networks are connected by routers. Cores (or clusters of cores) will have their own clocks, which will be synchronised by protocols running along the interconnections. Figure 4.15 portrays a possible architecture of thousands of heterogenous cores in future processors. For example, in this architecture, a core

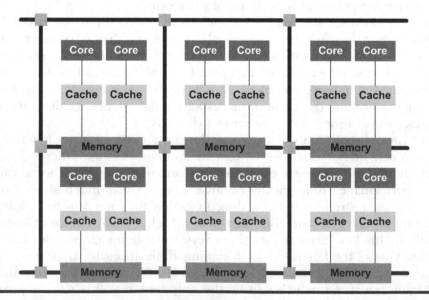

Figure 4.15   A probable schematic of thousands of heterogenous cores in future processors.

could be a superscalar processor, another a GPU, an SMT processor, and so forth. As seen, interconnection topologies play a major role in this model.

The most advanced multi-core chips available benefit from two methods to deal with interconnection costs. Multi-core chips with a small number of cores exploit a single bus. Another scalable approach used by some multicores is to employ a peer-to-peer network architecture where software takes control of communication. No matter which existing network topology is used, dynamic communication patterns that lead to network contention make these architectures very difficult in order to coordinate hundreds or thousands of processors in an ordered structure. Even simple functions such as issuing instructions to all cores are very challenging. A promising method, that the industry is moving towards, is to use optical communication channels on the chip instead of electrical channels. Compared to electrons, optical photons are much faster and give more bandwidth, for example light traverses a direct distance of 30 cm in just 1 ns. Optical devices can be fabricated using standard CMOS manufacturing techniques, and in the near future silicon wires will be replaced by optical busses. The use of optical interconnect technology in chips will solve many of the existing grand challenges in processors with a large count of cores.

One of the current realised methods in the revolution of many-core processors is *accelerated processing units* (APUs), which provide additional processing capabilities to accelerate computations with different types outside of a CPU. An APU can be composed of a combination of a *graphics processing unit* (GPU) used for general-purpose processing, a *field-programmable gate array* (FPGA), or other special-purpose processing systems. Recently, APUs are described as processing units that integrate a CPU and a GPU on a shared die, where data transmission rates between components reduce power consumption in addition to improving efficiency.

A GPU is a dedicated circuit designed to quickly manipulate and change memory in a way to speed up making images in a frame buffer intended for output to the screen. Today's GPUs are very efficient to manipulate computer graphics, and their very parallel structure makes them much more effective than general-purpose CPUs for algorithms, where the processing of large blocks of data is carried out in parallel. General-Purpose GPU (GPGPU) is a method in which a GPU that is usually used for graphic tasks is exploited to perform computations in application programs conventionally handled only by CPUs. Also, the use of graphics cards or a lot of graphics chips adds to the parallelism of GPUs. Like the vector processor architecture, GPUs can only work well with data-level parallelism. Both have scatter/gather transfer operations and mask registers, and GPUs even have many more registers than vector processors. Unlike many vector architectures, GPUs are only based on multi-threading inside a multi-threaded SIMD processor to hide memory latency. GPGPU applications have to adhere to an intensely high operating capacity, otherwise the latency of memory access (e.g., copy from a GPU memory to the main memory of the system and vice versa) will greatly limit any computational speedup.

Figure 4.16 shows the GPU architecture of NVIDIA GTX580. This device has 16 cores, each of which has 2 SIMD arrays with 16 lanes (processing elements) in every core. Every core has a shared memory, an L1 cache, and a separate array of specific functional units to perform complex operations. The fine-grained scheduler selects the hardware threads to map to each SIMD array whilst they get ready to run. To achieve a high memory bandwidth, a large number of pins are allocated to memory

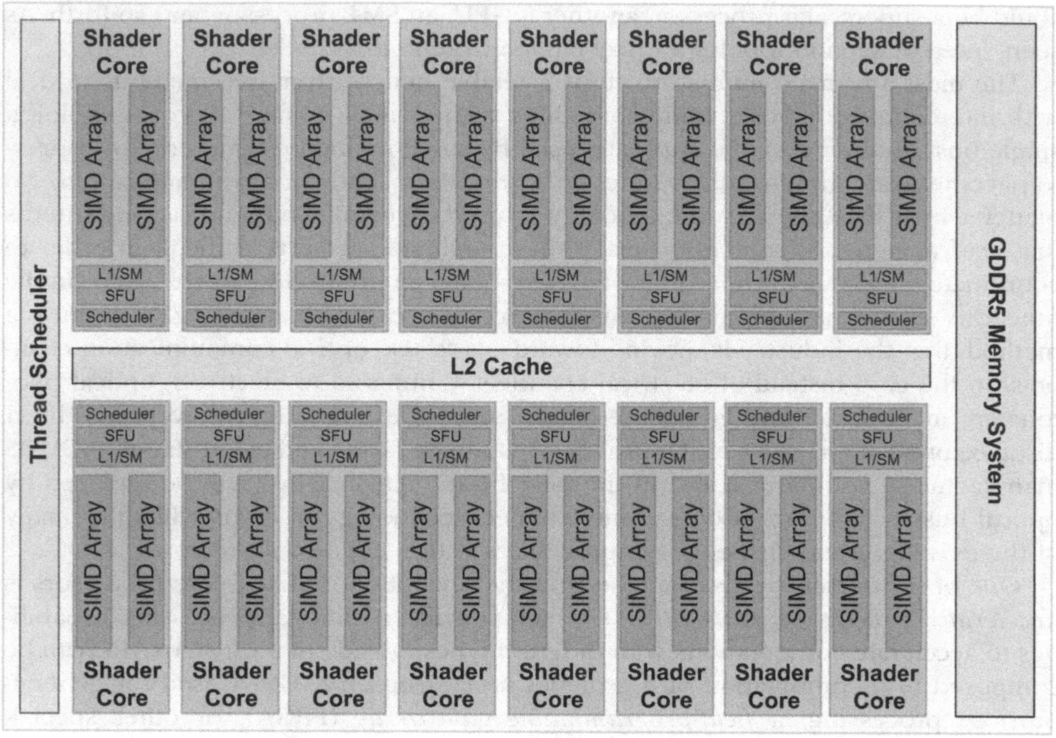

Figure 4.16 The architecture of the NVIDIA GTX580 graphics processing unit.

traffic, and Graphics Double Data Rate 5 (GDDR5) memory (this type of memory is a DRAM memory of a graphics card that is used for computer applications that require high bandwidth) is used to increase the memory bandwidth per pin at a higher latency cost.

These processors use SIMD arrays to maximise the throughput of mathematical operations for a number of issued instructions. It also executes a vector with a length of 32 over two cycles. Unlike most system processors, the aim of the NVIDIA compiler's instruction set is an abstraction of the hardware instruction set. Parallel thread execution (PTX) provides a stable instruction set for compilers with compatibility amongst GPU generations. This instruction set architecture (ISA) is hidden from programmer. The NVIDIA GPU programming language is an extension of the ISO C99 language standard, called compute unified device architecture (CUDA). CUDA allows developers to access the virtual instruction set and processing elements in GPUs.

To further understand this description, we consider a simple example in which an operation on two arrays is performed in two ways: traditionally on a CPU, and on a GPU using the CUDA language. Figures 4.17 and 4.18 illustrate this example. As seen in the traditional method, after filling two arrays a and b, addition is carried out in a loop by traversing the array elements one by one, and its value is printed on the output screen at the end. In this case, no apparent TLP technique has been applied by the programmer and ILP parallelisation is likely to be done by the compiler and the hardware in a single-processor pipeline. However, the CUDA example shows an inherently different parallel coding style. First, the desired memory on the GPU

```
 1: #define N 10
 2: #include <stdio.h>
 3:
 4: void FillArrays(int *a, int *b){
 5:     // fill the arrays 'a' and 'b' on the CPU
 6:     for (int i=0; i<N; i++) {
 7:         a[i] = i;
 8:         b[i] = i * (i - 10);
 9:     }
10: }
11:
12: void DisplayArrays(int *a, int *b, int *c){
13:     for (int i = 0; i < N; i++) {
14:         printf( "%d + %d = %d\n", a[i], b[i], c[i]);
15:     }
16: }
17:
18: void add(int *a, int *b, int *c) {
19:     int tid = 0; // this is array index
20:     while (tid < N) {
21:         c[tid] = a[tid] + b[tid];
22:         tid += 1; // we have one CPU, so we increment by one
23:     }
24: }
25:
26: int main(void) {
27:     int a[N], b[N], c[N];
28:
29:     // fill the arrays 'a' and 'b' on the CPU
30:     FillArrays(a, b);
31:
32:     add(a, b, c);
33:
34:     // display the results
35:     DisplayArrays(a, b, c);
36:
37:     return 0;
38: }
```

Figure 4.17   A simple C program to add two arrays stored on a traditional processor.

is allocated by the cudaMalloc function, and then the values of the two arrays are copied into the GPU memory by the cudaMemcpy function. In the literature on CUDA language, a GPU is called a device and a local system with its host processor. In line 7, the keyword __global__ is used to denote that ADD function must be translated by the CUDA compiler and executed on the device. In CUDA language, data are divided into N blocks (each block runs in one of the SIMD processors), each of which has M threads that perform operations on the data of each block. The block and thread

```
1: #define N 10
2: #include <stdio.h>
3:
4: void FillArrays(int *a, int *b);
5: void DisplayArrays(int *a, int *b, int *c);
6:
7: __global__ void add(int *a, int *b, int *c) {
8:    int tid = blockIdx.x;    // this thread handles the data at its thread id
9:    if (tid < N)
10:       c[tid] = a[tid] + b[tid];
11: }
12:
13: int main(void) {
14:    int a[N], b[N], c[N];
15:    int *dev_a, *dev_b, *dev_c;
16:
17:    // allocate the memory on the GPU
18:    cudaMalloc((void**)&dev_a, N * sizeof(int));
19:    cudaMalloc((void**)&dev_b, N * sizeof(int));
20:    cudaMalloc((void**)&dev_c, N * sizeof(int));
21:
22:    // fill the arrays 'a' and 'b' on the CPU
23:    FillArrays(a, b);
24:
25:    // copy the arrays 'a' and 'b' to the GPU
26:    cudaMemcpy(dev_a, a, N * sizeof(int), cudaMemcpyHostToDevice);
27:    cudaMemcpy(dev_b, b, N * sizeof(int), cudaMemcpyHostToDevice);
28:
29:    add<<<N,1>>>(dev_a, dev_b, dev_c);
30:
31:    // copy the array 'c' back from the GPU to the CPU
32:    cudaMemcpy(c, dev_c, N * sizeof(int), cudaMemcpyDeviceToHost);
33:
34:    // display the results
35:    DisplayArrays(a, b, c);
36:
37:    // free the memory allocated on the GPU
38:    cudaFree(dev_a);
39:    cudaFree(dev_b);
40:    cudaFree(dev_c);
41:
42:    return 0;
43: }
```

Figure 4.18 Modified program of adding two arrays to run on a GPU using the CUDA programming language.

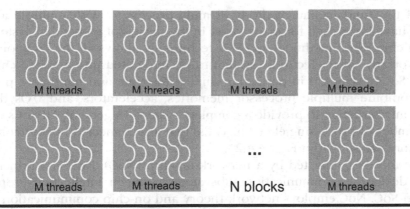

Figure 4.19   Structure of blocks and threads in CUDA language.

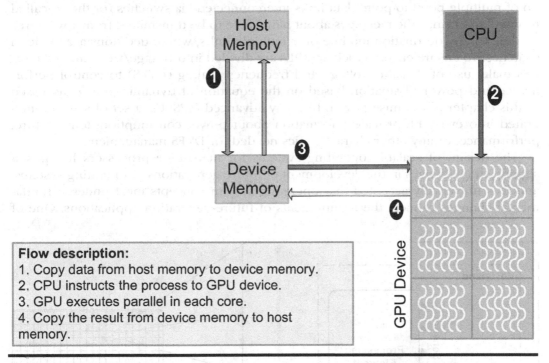

Flow description:
1. Copy data from host memory to device memory.
2. CPU instructs the process to GPU device.
3. GPU executes parallel in each core.
4. Copy the result from device memory to host memory.

Figure 4.20   An example of execution of a CUDA flow for an off-chip GPU.

structure are shown in Figure 4.19. As shown in line 29 of the CUDA code, there are N blocks in this example, of which a single thread operates on the data. In this example, since each cell in the array is assigned to a block, in add function in line 7, the current location of each block that in fact operates on the i'th index of the array is obtained from blockIdx.x instruction. After performing the calculations, the result is copied from the device memory into the host memory by using the cudaMemcpy function, and, finally, the allocated memory on the device is released by calling the cudaFree function. An example of running a CUDA flow is demonstrated in Figure 4.20 for an off-chip GPU for the explained case.

One of the fundamental methods in multi-processors with multiple and many cores that have been used for many years in the design of embedded systems is the system on chip (SoC) methodology. This technology allows all the components of a computer or any other electronic system to be integrated into a single chip. Multi-processor SoCs (MPSoCs) in particular employ multiple and multi-core processors. MPSoCs combine multiple processor memories, accelerators, and I/Os through a dedicated infrastructure to provide a complete system. In general, MPSoCs consist of a large number of processing elements (PEs) that are connected by intercommunication structures as shown in Figure 4.21.

PEs are mostly connected by a network-on-chip (NoC). NoC is a principal technique for designing communication subsystems between Intellectual Property (IP) cores in an SoC. NoC employs network theory and on-chip communication methods and provides significant improvements with respect to crossbar and bus intercommunication strategies. Research has also been done on optical NoCs. An SoC is made up of multiple point-to-point data links interconnected via switches (or the so-called routers) and brings the messages about being able to be transmitted from any source module to any destination module over multiple links, where decisions are made in switches. To ensure energy efficiency, PEs are divided into voltage/frequency islands. PEs make use of dynamic voltage and frequency scaling (DVFS) to control performance and power dissipation based on the equation of dynamic power discussed in this chapter to optimise power. In many advanced MPSoCs, a set of sensors integrated into every PE provide information about power consumption, temperature, performance, or any other characteristics needed for DVFS management.

The design of scalable operating systems for many-core processors has posed significant challenges in the development of future generations of operating systems, and it is universally accepted that operating system concepts must undergo fundamental changes to meet the requirements of future-generation applications. One of

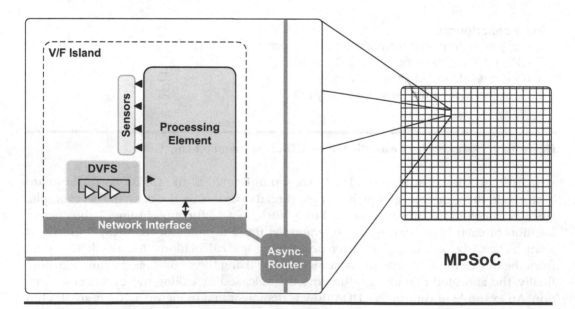

Figure 4.21 A general MPSoC architecture.

the main hurdles for new generations of processors stems from the basic structure of the shared-memory operating system kernel along with data structures protected by locks. Moreover, kernel heterogeneity indicates that kernels can no longer share a single OS kernel instance because there are different performance conditions for these kernels and each kernel has a different ISA.

Task scheduling and load balancing have become challenging for such devices. The scheduler must take care of the heterogeneity issue, such as different ISAs, the performance of cores, and the characteristics of cache hierarchy. For example, it could assign and schedule sequential parts of application programs demanding critical performance to more powerful, higher-clocked cores and parallel tasks to weaker cores. Furthermore, the operating system must play a more fundamental role in power management. In the future, thermal power limitation issues in processor design will likely prevent us from using all the cores at the same time with maximum speed. For instance, non-critical tasks in terms of performance (or tasks with memory-bound performance) could be performed at lower frequencies with higher energy efficiency. To deal with these dilemmas, the operating system should be aware of hardware features such as cores, caches, interconnects, and static and dynamic power consumption. Additionally, the operating system must look after the behaviour of tasks at runtime, estimate and measure power in finer granulations, and control finer power stages in core granulation through new interfaces. We believe that, besides these issues, the separation of the two user and kernel spaces that were created in single-processor operating systems can lead to many overheads in future systems. To give an instance, frequent context switches and invalidation of TLB entries can be accounted as cases of these overheads. We suggest that future operating systems make use of the architecture of a single address space OS and languages such as Java and C# for the implementation of applications in pursuit of secure execution (because these languages lack pointers, and the security of applications is satisfied by the underlying intermediate language and runtime). In the following, we review five types of research projects for designing many-core operating systems; it is worth noting that, despite rapid advances in processor hardware, the number of these research operating systems is very small:

- **Barrelfish**: This operating system uses a multi-kernel model where instances of multiple independent OSs communicate with others via explicit messages [1]. Its architecture is shown in Figure 4.22. Barrelfish distributes the OS instance on each core into a privileged CPU driver and differentiated userspace monitor process. CPU drivers are all on a single local core, and all coordinations between kernels is done by monitors. The distributed system of monitors and their dependent CPUs encapsulate the functions found in a typical monolithic kernel, such as scheduling, communication, and low-level resource allocation. The rest of Barrelfish is made up of driver tools and system services (such as network stacks, memory allocators, etc.), which run in user-mode processes as a microkernel. Hardware interrupts are sent to appropriate kernels, demultiplexed by the CPU driver of that kernel, and delivered to the process driver as a message.
- **Factored Operating System (FOS)**: FOS is a new operating system that considers many-core systems with scalability as a primary design parameter, where space sharing replaces time sharing to increase scalability [2]. FOS is built on a message exchange scheme and is inspired by a set of Internet services. Each OS

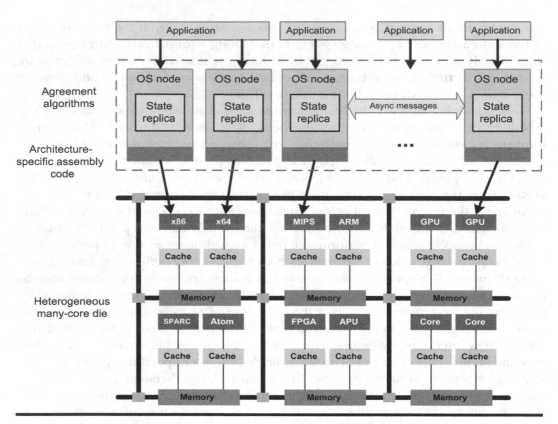

Figure 4.22 Architecture of the Barrellfish operating system.

service is factorised into a set of communication servers that collectively implement a system service. These servers are mostly designed in the way that distributed Internet services are designed, but instead of providing high-level Internet services, these servers provide traditional kernel services and replace traditional kernel data structures in a factorised fashion and spatially distributed. In other words, FOS servers bind to individual processing kernels and do not fight with end-user applications for implicit resources such as TLBs and caches.

- **Helios**: It is an operating system designed to simplify the writing, deployment and configuration of applications for heterogeneous platforms [3]. Helios introduces satellite kernels which export a single uniform set of OS abstractions across CPU architectures and inhomogeneous performance features. Access to I/O services, like file systems, is made transparent by remote message exchange, which extends a standard microkernel message passing abstraction to a satellite kernel architecture. Helios retargets applications to existing ISAs by compiling from an intermediate language.
- **Corey**: In this operating system, applications should control sharing and the kernel should organise every data structure so that only a single processor needs to be updated [4]. Based on this research work, three OS abstractions are proposed (address boards, kernel cores, and subscriptions) that let applications control cross-kernel sharing and benefit from the abundance of cores by assigning cores to specific functions of the operating system. Hardware event counters

confirm that the improvements made by the Corey architecture are due to the avoidance of operations that are expensive on multi-core machines.

- **Tessellation**: This operating system is based on two fundamental ideas: space-time partitioning (STP) and bilevel scheduling [5]. STP provides performance separation and robust segregation of resources between interactive software components called *cells*. Bilevel scheduling separates general decisions about resource allocation to cells from special-use resource scheduling within cells.

4.5 Latest Optimal Approaches in Synchronisation

A cooperative process can either influence other processes running on the system or be affected by them. They either can share a logical address space (code and data) directly or are allowed to share data only through messages or files. Concurrent access to shared data may lead to data inconsistency. In this section, we discuss a variety of techniques that fulfil the correct and fair execution of cooperative processes, which share a logical address space, thus maintaining consistency. Synchronisation is a cooperative action of two or more threads guaranteeing that each thread reaches a known point of operations in relation to other threads before continuation. An attempt for resource sharing without a proper use of synchronisation is one of the most common causes of damage to program data. In the rest of this chapter, the two terms *process* and *thread* are used interchangeably from a conceptual point of view, unless their dissection is explicitly stated.

An atomic operation is the one that appears to the remainder of the system to happen instantly. Atomicity is to guarantee separation from concurrent processors. This operation is effectively performed as a single step and is a very important feature in algorithms that deal with multiple processors, both in synchronisation and in algorithms that update shared data without requiring synchronisation. This type of hardware operation ensures that at any moment of time only one thread can access a memory location without interference of any other threads.

The most key hardware capability to build primitive synchronisation instructions (and then higher-level software routines) is to use uninterruptible instructions or a sequence of instructions that are able to atomically retrieve and change a value. Software synchronisation mechanisms are subsequently constructed on top of these primitive structures. In many-core systems or high-contentious situations, synchronisation turns into a performance bottleneck because contention creates redundant latency which is much higher in multi-processors. The key ability to implement synchronisation in multi-processors is a set of hardware primitives that can atomically read and modify a memory location. Without having such a mechanism, the construction of basic synchronisation primitives will give rise to heavy overheads, whilst the number of processors increases these overheads become much higher. We succinctly refer to a number of these approaches (these primitives are usually utilised to make non-blocking locks):

- **Atomic Exchange**: This instruction exchanges a value in a register with the value of a location in memory. This exchange is *indivisible*, and two simultaneous exchanges are ordered by write serialisation mechanisms (through hardware queues). A spin lock is designed in this section using this primitive. One of the x86 assembly instructions is XCHG for this purpose. If two processes use this instruction to set a synchronisation variable, it is impossible for both the processes to concurrently set the location as if it appears to both of them that they are simultaneously performing this operation.

- **Test-and-Set**: This instruction, which is available on old processors, is used to write to a memory location and return its old value as an atomic operation. tsl is one of the x86 assembly instructions for this objective.
- **Fetch-and-Add**: This instruction returns the value of a memory location and atomically adds a value to it.
- **Compare-and-Swap (CAS)**: This operation atomically compares the value of the first operand's pointer with the value of the second operand's pointer. If they are equal, the value of the swap operand's pointer is stored in the second location of the compare operand, otherwise the value of the second compare operand's pointer is stored in the location of the first compare operand. Figure 4.23 shows the idea of a typical pseudocode for this operation in the C language: note that the structure in line 3 means the code block between lines 4 and 10 is performed atomically. A widely used x86 assembly instruction is cmpxchg, which implements this mechanism.
- **Load-Linked/Store-Conditional (LL/SC)**: The implementation of a single atomic memory operation leads to obstacles because it requires writing and reading to/from memory in a linearisable (atomic, indivisible, or uninterruptible) instruction. As a matter of course, this issue complicates the implementation of coherence protocols because hardware cannot allow performing any other operation between a read and a write. A solution is to take advantage of a pair of LL/SC instructions. LL returns the current value of a memory location. An SC instruction will subsequently store a new value to the same memory location if no update has taken place since the execution of the LL instruction. Also, if the processor performs a context switch between these two instructions, the SC instruction will fail.

```
1: bool compare_and_swap(int *accum, int *dest, int newval)
2: {
3:    atomic {
4:       if (*accum == *dest) {
5:          *dest = newval;
6:          return true;
7:       } else {
8:          *accum = *dest;
9:          return false;
10:      }
11:   }
12: }
```

Figure 4.23   A pseudocode implementation of CAS operation in the C language.

Concurrency control is the activity of coordinating concurrent access to shared objects, that is, controlling the relative order of conflicting operations from different threads. Synchronisation techniques are algorithms that perform such a concurrency control based on the hardware primitives mentioned. In the following, we examine high-level methods in software-based synchronisation.

Suppose there is a set of asynchronous processes, each of which alternately executes a critical section and a non-critical part. These processes must be synchronised so that two processes never run their critical sections simultaneously. Mutual exclusion ensures that two processes or threads cannot be in each other's critical section at the same time. A critical section is the time interval during which a thread accesses a shared resource. Since a critical section is a subjective model for reasoning about concurrency, it is one of the most popular methods for coordinating correct access to shared data and has been widely studied over the years. Almost all formal concurrent processing models are based on the hardware assumption of mutually exclusive atomic operations.

Lock-based synchronisation algorithms are the use of a software variable, referred to as a lock, to protect the right to enter a critical section of the code. The lock guarantees that only a single thread in the critical section has access to the shared data within that critical section. A lock is a software structure that depends on a shared object and determines whether that shared object is recently available or not. Once a process acquires the lock, no other process will be able to continue its execution until the current lock owner releases that lock. The process that tends to run the critical section must first acquire the corresponding lock. After handling the lock, the current lock owner is guaranteed that no other process will have access to the locations used inside the critical section. When the lock owner completes its own critical section, it releases the lock and allows other processes to see the updates made by the current committed critical section.

One of the simplest locks but widely used inside OS kernels is the *spin lock*. In this locking technique, a thread waits in a loop and repeatedly checks to see if a lock exists or not; at this time, the thread is currently waiting and does not do any useful work. Therefore, spin locks are only useful when they need to be blocked for a short period of time, and they also prevent context switching overheads and involving OS process rescheduling. Proper implementation of spin locks is possible through the hardware primitives stated earlier. Figure 4.24 illustrates a typical implementation of a spin lock in assembly language. As can be seen, the use of `xchg` instruction is required to create an indivisible operation. The `spin_lock` label is for the code of lock operation and the `spin_unlock` label is associated with the code for unlock operation. Spin locks without the requirement for an OS scheduler using hardware primitives make the process go to sleep if the indented resource is busy.

In the following, we first discuss the problems that arise from using threads and their synchronisation and then introduce common high-level software approaches to satisfy mutual exclusion.

4.5.1 Deadlock

A computer resource is any type of physical or virtual component with limited availability within a computer system. Each piece of device equipment connected to

```
lock:                            ; The lock variable. 1 = locked, 0 = unlocked.
    dd      0

spin_lock:
    mov     eax, 1               ; Set the EAX register to 1.

    xchg    eax, [lock]          ; Atomically swap the EAX register with the lock variable.
                                 ; This will always store 1 to the lock, leaving the previous value in the EAX register.

    test    eax, eax             ; Test EAX with itself. Amongst other things, this will
                                 ; set the processor's Zero Flag if EAX is 0.
                                 ; If EAX is 0, then the lock was unlocked and
                                 ; we just locked it. Otherwise, EAX is 1 and we didn't acquire the lock.

    jnz     spin_lock            ; Jump back to the XCHG instruction if the Zero Flag is
                                 ; not set; the lock was previously locked, and so
                                 ; we need to spin until it becomes unlocked.

    ret                          ; The lock has been acquired, return to the calling function.

spin_unlock:
    mov     eax, 0               ; Set the EAX register to 0.

    xchg    eax, [lock]          ; Atomically swap the EAX register with the lock variable.

    ret                          ; The lock has been released.
```

Figure 4.24   Implementation of a spin lock based on ×86 assembly code.

a computer system is a resource. Each component of the internal system is also a resource. Virtual system resources include files, network connections, and memory regions. Deadlocks arise when the members of a group of processes that hold resources are indefinitely blocked from accessing resources held by other processes within the group. When no member of the group relinquishes control over its resources after it has completed its acquisition, a deadlock is inevitable and can only be broken by involving an external force. A set of processes comes to a deadlock as an outcome of exclusive access and circular wait. The simplest picture of this circumstance involves only two processes, each of which holds a different resource for exclusive access and requests access to the resource held by the other. The result is a circular wait that cannot be broken until one of these processes abandons its resource or cancels its request.

An example of a deadlock may occur in a database system. Client applications using the database may require exclusive access to a table and request a lock to take advantage of their exclusive access. If a client application holds a lock on a table and tries to acquire the lock on a second table that was previously held by a second client application, this situation may lead to a deadlock if the second application attempts to acquire the lock held by the first lock.

We show this example more clearly in the code snippet of Figure 4.25. Here, Process P tries to acquire the locks M and N respectively, whilst Process Q tries to acquire the N and M locks respectively. In line 4, both processes have a critical section. In this state, Process P acquires the M lock, whilst Process Q acquires the M lock. Even though a deadlock is possible in this example, a deadlock does not happen if

1: // Code for Process P 2: Lock(M); 3: Lock(N); 4: CriticalSection(); 5: Unlock(N); 6: Unlock(M);	1: // Code for Process Q 2: Lock(N); 3: Lock(M); 4: CriticalSection(); 5: Unlock(M); 6: Unlock(N);

Figure 4.25 An example of a deadlock based on using an improper lock sequence to access a critical section of code.

Process P can acquire and release the M and N locks before Process Q tries to acquire the locks. This matter shows that it is difficult to identify and test the deadlocks that may occur under certain conditions.

In a state of deadlock, processes never finish their execution, and system resources become busy, which will prevent other tasks on the system from starting. In the most general state, deadlocks occur if any of the following conditions are met, so the best way to avoid deadlocks is to consider these parameters when programming concurrent systems. These conditions are referred to as *deadlock prevention parameters*:

- **Mutual Exclusion**: At least one resource must be kept in a non-shared mode, only one process at a time can use the resource. If another process requests that resource, the requesting process must be postponed until the resource is released.
- **Hold and Wait**: A process must be holding at least one resource and waiting to acquire additional resources that are currently being held by other processes.
- **No Pre-emption**: Resources cannot be pre-empted; a resource can only be released voluntarily by its holding process after that process has finished its work.
- **Circular Wait**: Two or more processes form a circular chain in where each process waits for a resource that the next process holds in the chain.

By guaranteeing that at least one of these conditions cannot be maintained, we are able to prevent a deadlock from happening. So, we have the following:

- Elimination of the mutual exclusion means that no process may have exclusive access to a resource. Algorithms that avoid mutual exclusion are called non-blocking synchronisation algorithms, which will be discussed in this section.
- The hold-and-wait condition may be prevented before it starts by forcing processes to request all the resources they will need.
- This prognosis is often difficult to satisfy due to inefficient use of resources. Another way is to require processes to release all their resources before requesting all the resources before that they will need. Of course, this method is also often impractical.
- The no-pre-emption condition may be difficult or impossible to avoid whilst a process has to be able to have a resource for a certain amount of time, or the processing result may be inconsistent or thrashing happens (this refers to two or more processes for frequent access to a shared resource, in which state system

performance degradation occurs because the system spends a disproportionate amount of time to access the shared resource). However, the inability to force pre-emption may interfere with a priority algorithm. Algorithms that allow pre-emption include lock-free and wait-free algorithms, and optimistic concurrency control.

- Algorithms that avoid circular waits include disabling interrupts during critical sections, using hierarchy to specify an incomplete sequence of resources, and Dijkstra's solution.

Deadlock prevention is one of the main ways to develop concurrent systems. Providing that a system has been already designed, another set of methods called *deadlock avoidance* can be used. Deadlocks can be avoided if certain information about the process is available before resources are allocated. For each resource request, the system examines whether granting the request would mean that the system enters an unsafe state that leads to a deadlock. The system then only grants those requests that will lead to safe states. In order for the system to be able to determine whether the next state will be safe or unsafe, the system must always be aware in advance of the number of types of all resources in existence, available, and requested. One of the well-known algorithms used for deadlock avoidance is Banker's algorithm, which requires knowing the resource usage limit beforehand. However, it is impossible for many systems to know earlier what each processor will request. This also means that it is often impossible to avoid a deadlock. To better understand this description, we consider a two-dimensional Cartesian projection example for two threads T_1 and T_2 shown in Figure 4.26.

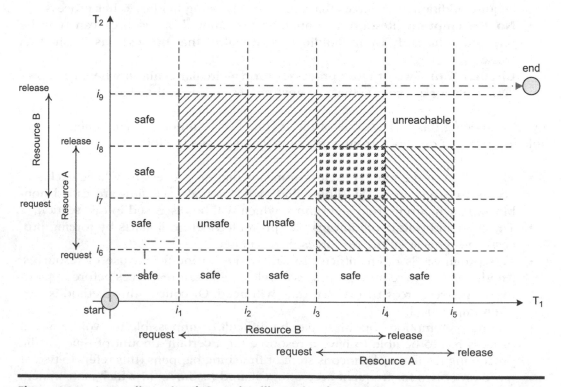

Figure 4.26   A two-dimensional Cartesian illustration for a better understanding of deadlock avoidance.

These two threads deal with two resources. The horizontal and vertical axes represent the execution sequence of instructions in both threads T_1 and T_2. For example, thread T_1 in instruction i_3 requests resource A and in i_5 releases it. Boxes displayed as hatched are overlapped areas that are being used by both threads from two resources A or B. If we suppose that these two threads run on at least a dual-core processor, then the existence of two horizontal and vertical axes is necessary. Since processes cannot go back in time, the trajectory in this two-dimensional diagram is only possible towards the north and east. Two unsafe regions exist in this diagram, and if we travel the path in this diagram and enter these two regions, then the occurrence of a deadlock is definite because we can only move in the north and east directions; if we move in these two areas, then the state of both processes transitions to the hatched, forbidden regions. A possible and safe route is shown as a dotted zigzag path from start to end.

The difference between deadlock prevention and deadlock avoidance strategies can be summarised as follows:

- **Deadlock Prevention**: Preventing deadlocks is achieved by constraining how requests can be made for resources in the system and how they are handled (system design). The goal is to ensure that at least one of the requirements for a deadlock is never met.
- **Deadlock Avoidance**: The system dynamically takes the request into account and decides whether it is safe to grant at this point. The system requires extra a priori information about the overall potential use of each resource for each process. Also, deadlock avoidance makes more concurrency possible.

Deadlock detection and prevention are widely recognised as the best practices for precisely engineered concurrent software. But these two methods cannot always be used. For example, these methods are not applicable to those systems that are highly complex and dynamically composed (composition is the ability to put two entities alongside in order to form a larger and complex entity, which in turn is abstracted into a single composite entity), especially those that are not equipped to deal with deadlocks (such as transaction processing systems including databases and transactional memory synchronisation and hosted or plug-in software). In such systems, deadlock detection techniques and process restart are used by an algorithm that keeps track of resource allocations and process states. In this approach, one or more processes are rolled back and restarted for eliminating the deadlock. It is easy to detect a deadlock that has already occurred because the resources that have been locked by each process or recently requested are known to resource scheduler or operating system.

For a practical description of how a deadlock detection system works, we introduce a dynamic deadlock detection system in which deadlocks are identified from a specific resource, namely locks, because locks are the most key element in synchronised access to resources and variables or shared objects. This method is particularly useful for problems in previously developed codes and fixing parts of the lock hierarchy that are causing a deadlock. First, a graph model is described for modelling deadlocks.

Deadlocks can be modelled based on directed graphs. These graphs have two types of nodes in which processes are represented as circles and resources as squares. A directed edge from a resource node to a process node means that the resource has already been requested by the process and the system has granted it, and so the process has held the resource. A directed edge from a process side to a resource indicates that the process is recently waiting for the resource. These two modes are shown in Figure 4.27(a) and (b). In Figure 4.27(c), which represents a deadlock that has occurred in Figure 4.25, the Q process is for the resource N (in this example, a lock), which is recently held by the P process. The P process cannot abandon the resource N because it is waiting for the resource M, which is held by Q. Both processes will be waiting indefinitely. In this example, a cycle is formed. This shows that there is a deadlock comprised of processes and resources; of course, in this section for simplicity, we assume that only one resource (lock) exists per type. Here, the cycle formed is M-Q-N-P-M.

Following this section, we describe a method for dynamically identifying deadlocks based on the concepts of resource graphs and cycles indicating deadlocks within the graph. In a concurrent system where locks are used to synchronise the access of threads to shared objects, the existing lock routines such as lock() and unlock() functions must be placed inside new routines (e.g., new_lock and new_lock). Each time that a request arrives for lock operation through the invocation of the new_lock routine, the code checks at runtime whether this lock has previously been held or not. If the intended lock is not held, this lock along with the thread identifier requesting the lock is added to a linked list data structure, which keeps the lock graph information. If this lock is already held by a thread, the code inside the new_lock routine first forms a lock graph at runtime and then checks if there is a cycle in the graph. If there is no cycle, nothing has happened and the execution of the new_lock routine completes successfully. Otherwise, it is dynamically notified to the application program, usually by throwing an exception in its address space if the last thread has caused a cycle in the lock graph, and a deadlock has happened, and the thread must manage the circumstance through a particular way.

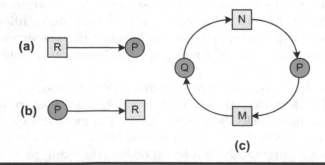

Figure 4.27 Resource allocation graphs: (a) keeping a resource, (b) requesting a resource, and (c) deadlock.

This management can be handled comprehensively by a deadlock detection system. Therefore, such a system must provide two basic functions:

- An optimal algorithm to reduce overheads created at runtime that checks the system state to determine if a deadlock has occurred (for instance, by forming a resource graph). If the resource graph-based detection method is used in this case, existing algorithms in graph theory can be exploited to find cycles.
- An algorithm for deadlock recovery.

In this section, we examine how to find a cycle in a graph dynamically and then briefly describe deadlock recovery strategies. Figure 4.28 illustrates an undirected graph and a directed graph (digraph). A graph is a pair of $G = (V, E)$ consisting of a V set of vertices and an E set of edges. The sets of vertices and edges of G_1 and G_2 graphs are shown in Figure 4.28. As seen, for the G_2 digraph, a pair (U, v) reparents the presence of an edge exiting from vertex U and entering vertex V.

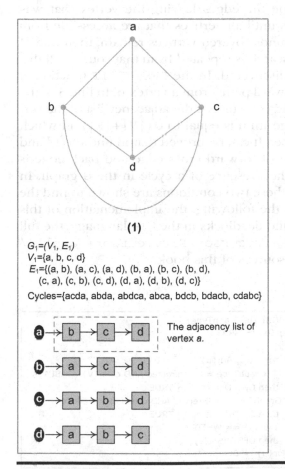

(1)

$G_1=(V_1, E_1)$
$V_1=\{a, b, c, d\}$
$E_1=\{(a, b), (a, c), (a, d), (b, a), (b, c), (b, d),$
$(c, a), (c, b), (c, d), (d, a), (d, b), (d, c)\}$

Cycles=\{acda, abda, abdca, abca, bdcb, bdacb, cdabc\}

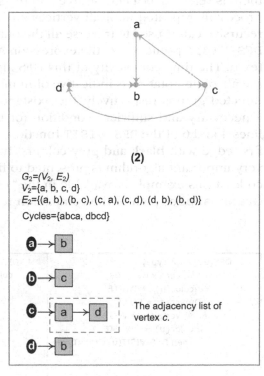

(2)

$G_2=(V_2, E_2)$
$V_2=\{a, b, c, d\}$
$E_2=\{(a, b), (b, c), (c, a), (c, d), (d, b), (b, d)\}$

Cycles=\{abca, dbcd\}

Figure 4.28 **Two graphs containing cycles along with their adjacency lists: (1) an undirected graph and (2) a directed graph.**

A cycle is referred to as a closed path in a graph. If repeated edges are allowed, this cycle is usually known as a *closed walk*. If the path is a simple path along with no repeated vertices or edges except the starting and ending vertices, this path is called a *simple cycle, circuit, circle*, or *polygon*. A cycle in a digraph is called a *directed cycle*. In this example, G_1 and G_2 have seven and two cycles, respectively. In order to find an algorithmic approach to identifying cycles, we must be able to traverse them deeply and completely. One of the algorithms that helps to find cycles is the *depth-first search algorithm* (DFS). In this algorithm, a graph must be represented as an adjacency list. This dynamic list (like a link list) stores the vertices in that colours are used to keep track of search progress in each vertex. All vertices start with white and later probably become grey and then black. A vertex that is discovered for the first time during a visit gets a non-white colour; hence, the grey and black vertices have already been discovered. Figure 4.29 show a typical DFS algorithm for finding cycles in directed and undirected graphs. This algorithm applies to the definitions shown in the graphs in Figure 4.28.

In this algorithm, the outward edges of the last discovered edge v, which still has its leaves, unexplored edges, are examined. When all edges of v are explored, the search process is repeated to examine the edges leaving the vertex that was discovered from v. This process continues until all vertices that are accessible from the main source vertex are discovered. If undiscovered vertices remain, then one of them is selected as a new source and the search is repeated from that source. All this process is repeated until all vertices are discovered. In the DFS-VISIT function, a recursive call is used to traverse all the outward paths from a vertex u. In line 3 of the DFS-VISIT pseudocode, the expression Adj{u} means the adjacency list of the vertex u. The time complexity of this DFS algorithm is equal to $O(|V|+|E|)$ in which the absolute notation is indicative of number. It can be proved that in undirected and directed graphs respectively, the existence of forward/cross edge and back edge is a necessary and sufficient condition for the presence of a cycle in the G graph. In lines 4 and 6 of the DFS-VISIT function, these two conditions are shown to find the first edge with black and grey colours. In the following, the implementation of this very important algorithm is presented to find deadlocks in the C++ language, the full code of this example is available in the "/Parvicursor/Parvicursor/Samples/GraphSample" path of the companion resources of this book.

1: DFS(G, GraphType)
2:　for each vertex u in V{G}
3:　　do color{u} := WHITE
4:　CycleDetected := FALSE
5:　for each vertex u in V{G}
6:　　do if color{u} == WHITE
7:　　　then DFS-VISIT(u, GraphType)

1: DFS-VISIT(u, GraphType)
2:　color{u} := GRAY　//White vertex u has just been discovered.
3:　for each v in Adj{u}　//Explore edge(u, v).
4:　　do if GraphType == Undirected AND color{v} == BLACK
5:　　　then CycleDetected := TRUE
6:　　if GraphType == Directed AND color{v} == GRAY
7:　　　then CycleDetected := TRUE
8:　　if color{v} == WHITE
9:　　　then DFS-VISIT(v)
10:　color{u} := BLACK /*Blacken u, it is finished.*/

Figure 4.29　DFS algorithm to find cycles in directed and undirected graphs.

```
1: class Vertex : public Object
2: {
3:    /*--------------------fields---------------*/
4:    private: ArrayList *adjacency_list; // The adjacency list of the current vertex.
5:    private: VertexColor color; // The colour of the current vertex that represents the recently explored status of
this vertex.
6:    /*--------------------methods---------------*/
7:    public: Vertex();
8:    public: ~Vertex();
9:    public: void set_Color(VertexColor color); // Set the vertex color.
10:   public: VertexColor get_Color(); // Get the vertex colour.
11:   public: void Add_AdjacentVertex(Vertex *vertex); // Add a vertex instance to the current vertex.
12:   public: void Remove_AdjacentVertex(Vertex *vertex); // Remove a vertex instance to current vertex.
13:   public: Int32 get_AdjacencyList_Count(); // Get the number of available slots in the adjacency_list.
14:   public: Vertex *get_AdjacentVertexAt(Int32 index); // Get an adjacent vertex at the specified index.
15: };


1: class Graph : public Object
2: {
3:    /*--------------------fields---------------*/
4:    private: ArrayList *vertices; // The vertices of the graph.
5:    private: bool has_cycle;
6:    private: GraphType type; // The type of the graph instance.
7:    /*--------------------methods---------------*/
8:    public: Graph(GraphType type); // Graph constructor.
9:    public: ~Graph();// Graph destructor.
10:   public: void Add_Vertex(Vertex *vertex); // Add a vertex to the graph.
11:   public: void Remove_Vertex(Vertex *vertex); // Remove a vertex from the graph.
12:   public: void DFS(); // Do the depth-first search algorithm.
13:   private: void DFS_visit(Vertex *u); // Perform the recursive traversal of the graph from the vertex u.
14:   public: bool has_Cycle(); // Get whether the graph contains at least one cycle.
15: };
```

Figure 4.30 **The** Vertex **and** Graph **C++ classes.**

It is necessary to make a note on the understandability of the programming examples in this book. The reader is supposed to have adequate and previous acquaintance with the C++ language, and the Parvicrusor.NET Framework and its programming environment, which are presented in Chapter 8 and in Section 4.6 at the end of this chapter.

Figure 4.30 shows the class implementation for the two vertex and graph data structures in the C++ programming language. Each vertex has its own adjacency list (as a dynamic array list used from the Parvicursor.NET Framework's classes) and colour. The explanation of all fields and methods come directly in the code. The graph class has an array list to store the vertices associated with the graph. The implementation of DFS() and DFS_visit() methods is shown in Figure 4.31, which is related to the algorithm implementation of Figure 4.29 to find cycles in undirected and directed graphs.

Let's take a look at how to benefit from the class above and its methods for finding cycles in G_1 and G_2 graphs as shown in Figure 4.28. The implementation of this example inside two main() functions is presented in Figure 4.32. For instance, in the directed graph case, after instantiating four vertices a, b, c and d using the Add_AdjacentVertex() method, we add the vertices v_i, which has a common edge with a vertex u, to the linked list of the vertex u. As an example, lines 12 through

```
1: void Graph::DFS()
2: {
3:     if(this->vertices != null)
4:     {
5:         this->has_cycle = false;
6:         for(Int32 i = 0 ; i < this->vertices->get_Count() ; i++)
7:         {
8:             Vertex *u = (Vertex *)this->vertices->get_Value(i);
9:             u->set_Color(WHITE);
10:        }
11:        for(Int32 i = 0 ; i < this->vertices->get_Count() ; i++)
12:        {
13:            Vertex *u = (Vertex *)this->vertices->get_Value(i);
14:          if(u->get_Color() == WHITE)
15:              this->DFS_visit(u);
16:        }
17:    }
18: }


1: void Graph::DFS_visit(Vertex *u)
2: {
3:     u->set_Color(GRAY);
4:     for(Int32 i = 0 ; i < u->get_AdjacencyList_Count() ; i++)
5:     {
6:         Vertex *v = u->get_AdjacentVertexAt(i);
7:
8:         if(this->type == Undirected && v->get_Color() == BLACK) // for undirected graph
9:             this->has_cycle = true;
10:        if(this->type == Directed && v->get_Color() == GRAY) // for directed graph (digraph)
11:            this->has_cycle = true;
12:        if(v->get_Color() == WHITE)
13:            DFS_visit(v);
14:    }
15:    u->set_Color(BLACK);
16: }
```

Figure 4.31   Implementation of DFS () **and** DFS_visit () **methods.**

25 add three vertices a, d and c to the adjacency list of the vertex b. In line 30, the DFS () method must be called at first from the graph object to determine if the graph has a cycle after traversing it. In line 37, those objects that had been instantiated are freed by using the new operator.

Once the existence of a deadlock is attained based on the theory outlined above, procedures must be provided to restore the system to its state before the deadlock. One of the easiest ways to come up with an approach to deadlock detection due to improper programming of locks is to report it to the programmer as saving a log which contains the topology of graph G, for code modification and process termination.

Another approach is to use checkpoint and rollback mechanisms. Checkpointing a thread means that its state is periodically saved in physical memory or on hard

```
 1: int main(int argc, char* argv[])              1: int main(int argc, char* argv[])
 2: {  // for the undirected graph G₁.            2: {  // for the directed graph G₂.
 3:     Vertex *a = new Vertex();                  3:     Vertex *a = new Vertex();
 4:     Vertex *b = new Vertex();                  4:     Vertex *b = new Vertex();
 5:     Vertex *c = new Vertex();                  5:     Vertex *c = new Vertex();
 6:     Vertex *d = new Vertex();                  6:     Vertex *d = new Vertex();
 7:                                                7:
 8:     a->Add_AdjacentVertex(b);                  8:     a->Add_AdjacentVertex(b);
 9:     a->Add_AdjacentVertex(c);                  9:
10:     a->Add_AdjacentVertex(d);               10:     b->Add_AdjacentVertex(c);
11:                                              11:
12:     b->Add_AdjacentVertex(a);               12:     c->Add_AdjacentVertex(a);
13:     b->Add_AdjacentVertex(d);               13:     c->Add_AdjacentVertex(d);
14:     b->Add_AdjacentVertex(c);               14:
15:                                              15:     d->Add_AdjacentVertex(b);
16:     c->Add_AdjacentVertex(a);               16:
17:     c->Add_AdjacentVertex(b);               17:     Graph *graph = new Graph(Directed);
18:     c->Add_AdjacentVertex(d);               18:     graph->Add_Vertex(a);
19:                                              19:     graph->Add_Vertex(b);
20:     d->Add_AdjacentVertex(a);               20:     graph->Add_Vertex(c);
21:     d->Add_AdjacentVertex(b);               21:     graph->Add_Vertex(d);
22:     d->Add_AdjacentVertex(c);               22:
23:                                              23:     graph->DFS();
24:     Graph *graph = new Graph(Undirected);    24:
25:     graph->Add_Vertex(a);                   25:     if(graph->has_Cycle())
26:     graph->Add_Vertex(b);                   26:         cout << "Cycle detected." << endl;
27:     graph->Add_Vertex(c);                   27:     else
28:     graph->Add_Vertex(d);                   28:         cout << "No cycle detected." << endl;
29:                                              29:
30:     graph->DFS();                           30:     delete a; delete b; delete c; delete d;
31:                                             delete graph;
32:     if(graph->has_Cycle())                  31:
33:         cout << "Cycle detected." << endl;  32:     return 0;
34:     else                                    33: }
35:         cout << "No cycle detected." << endl;
36:
37:     delete a; delete b; delete c; delete d;
delete graph;
38:
39:     return 0;
40: }
```

Figure 4.32 The way to use two vertex and graph classes to find cycles in G_1 and G_2 graphs.

disc. As mentioned in this chapter, the state of a multi-threaded program is divided into a private state (such as stack pointer, registers, and program counter) and a shared state (anything common to all threads in a process). Therefore, a checkpoint mechanism must store and retrieve both shared and private states. There are three forms of checkpointing: kernel level (where modifications to the kernel threads are carried out), userspace level (where no kernel mode modification is required), and the third type of application level that requires the programmers to make modifications to their code. In Chapter 9, whilst describing the xThread component of Parvicursor infrastructure, we will refer to a very flexible sample of this level in a distributed environment like Grid). When a deadlock is detected, it is easy to determine which resources are needed based on resource graph information. In the rollback operation, a thread or process that owns a required resource is rolled back to a point in time before it acquired that resource by starting one of its previous checkpoints. If the restarted process tries to retake the resource, it will have to wait until the resource becomes available.

4.5.2 Race Condition

In concurrent systems and multi-threaded programs, time-dependent failures known as race conditions can occur if access to shared memory is not properly synchronised. Race conditions take place when different processes access shared data without explicit synchronisation. Because these races can cause the program to behave unexpectedly from a programmer's point of view, finding them is an important aspect of debugging tools. Two different types of race can occur. General races lead to nondeterministic execution and are failures in a program intended to run deterministically. A general race exists in the execution of a P program if two events a and b have data conflicts and their access order is not guaranteed by the synchronisation of that execution. Data races cause the atomic execution of critical sections and are failures in nondeterministic programs in that critical sections access and update shared data. General races are much less common to happen but much harder to find. Race circumstances are usually symptoms that result from careless code design such as bad logic or bad coding style. The challenging nature of general race conditions and deadlocks have encouraged many researchers to study an alternative approach called transactional memory, which is examined at the end of Chapter 5.

Let us now consider an example of when a general race condition occurs and how it can be resolved. Figure 4.33 shows this example. A function is used that can be executed by threads simultaneously. An obj variable is removed from the src array list and added to the dest array list. The left function has no data race because it locks two shared variables src and dest by two critical sections using two different

```
1: // A data-race-free but general-race non-free method.
2: void thread_fucnction(ArrayList *src, ArrayList *dest, Object *obj) {
3:     // Remove obj from src.
4:     Lock(M);
5:     src->Remove(obj);
6:     Unlock(M);
7:
8:     /* Here is a transitory state which may cause a general race condition */
9:
10:    // Add obj to dest.
11:    Lock(M);
12:    dest->Add(obj);
13:    Unlock(M);
14: }
```

```
1: // A general and data race-free method.
2: void thread_fucnction(ArrayList *src, ArrayList *dest, Object *obj) {
3:     // The expensive lock M.
4:     Lock(M);
5:     {
6:         // Remove obj from src.
7:         src->Remove(obj);
8:
9:         /* Here is the secure code section to execute. */
10:
11:        // Add obj to dest.
12:        dest->Add(obj);
13:    }
14:    Unlock(M);
15: }
```

Figure 4.33 An example of a method in which a general race condition might occur. The left-hand-side function has a general race condition. The function on the right lacks any general race because of using a single lock for two separate operations on two shared variables.

locks. Consequently, to eliminate a data race, synchronisation mechanisms like locks must be employed.

If there is some code in line 8 that is a transition between the two critical sections, a general race condition may take place. If another thread exists working on the obj variable, the thread may lose the obj object because the object is homeless at that critical time. For example, if the address of the obj variable is changed by the first thread in line 8 of the right code whilst the second thread is reading from this variable, the first thread will find a wrong value of obj. In the worst case, if the first thread changes the value of obj to null, the second thread, when accessing the variable obj, causes a segmentation fault, resulting in the termination of the process. To solve this problem, we have to put the whole body of the function inside a lock, as shown in the code on the right. However, this lock will be very expensive because, as we know, critical sections must not take much in terms of execution time, and if an operation is done in line 9 of the code on the right that consumes a lot of time, then the M lock will become too expensive.

4.5.3 Priority Inversion

This phenomenon occurs when a lock or a critical section held by a lower priority thread delays the execution of a higher priority thread whilst both are contending for the same resource. We consider an example of how priority inversion can severely impair system performance. Figure 4.34 shows time transition diagram for this example. Suppose a system has three threads: a high-priority thread (HPT thread), a medium-priority thread (MPT thread), and a low-priority thread (LPT thread). The HPT and MPT threads are in sleep or blocked in the time before t_1. At time t_1, the LPT thread executes and enters a critical section. At time t_2, the MPT thread starts its execution and pre-empts the MPT thread. Therefore, the LPT thread continues to own the critical section. At time t_3, the HPT thread starts its execution and pre-empts the MPT thread. The HPT thread tries to enter the critical section that is in possession of the LPT thread, but because it is owned by another thread, the MPT thread is blocked and waits for that critical section. At time t_4, the MPT thread starts to execute because it has a higher priority than the LPT thread and the HPT thread is not also running. The LPT thread never leaves the critical section for which the HPT thread is waiting because the MPT thread continues executing.

Therefore, the highest-priority thread, the HPT thread, is blocked in the time interval $[t_4, \infty]$ and waits forever for the lower-priority thread to run. In $[t_4, \infty]$, a negative phenomenon known as *priority inversion* occurs.

Contrary to the unfavourable state of deadlocks, no complete proof has yet been given to fully predict priority inversion occurrences. Since this phenomenon usually happens in real-time operating systems (RTOSs), methods that prevent priority inversion mostly are implemented and used in such systems. An RTOS is used to service the requests of real-time applications such as embedded systems. One of the key features of an RTOS is its level of consistency with the amount of time it takes to accept and complete a task. Therefore, one of the vital issues in designing RTOSs is the use of appropriate process scheduling algorithms that are able to prevent priority inversion.

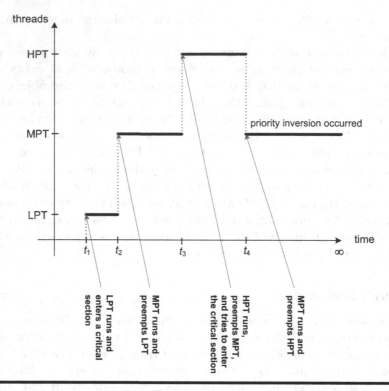

Figure 4.34 Time transient diagram for three threads: high-priority thread (HPT), middle-priority thread (MPT), and low-priority thread (LPT). The priority inversion phenomenon has occurred in the time interval $[t_4, \infty]$.

One of the most common ways to prevent this phenomenon in RTOSs is priority inheritance. Here, the problem is resolved by dynamically modifying the priorities of threads that cause a blocking state. In particular, when the T_1 thread is blocked on a shared resource, it conveys its priority to the T_2 thread that is holding the resource. In this method, T_2 will execute its critical section with the priority of the T_1 thread. Overall, T_2 inherits the highest priority amongst the threads that block it. Additionally, priority inheritance is transferrable, so if thread T_3 blocks thread T_2, which in turn blocks T_1, then T_3 inherits the priority of T_1 and T_2. There are other methods, such as the priority ceiling, that are beyond the scope of this book.

4.5.4 Starvation

If a thread is not granted CPU time because other threads gain this time, this state is called *starvation*. That thread is left to starve to death because other threads are instead allowed to use the CPU time. The solution to starvation is called *fairness*. Most operating system schedulers have the concept of thread priority. High-priority threads always swallow the whole CPU time from low-priority threads. To solve this issue in a simple manner, the priority can be assumed to be equal by default. Starvation can also occur by synchronised methods or functions based on hardware synchronisation primitives. Assume an object provides a synchronised primitive method that often takes a long time to return from its call point. If a thread invokes this method repeatedly, other threads that also need to have synchronised repeated access to the object are often blocked and a starvation state is created for them as a result. To solve this problem, rather than placing the entire body of the method inside a hardware synchronisation primitive block, we must use ready-made operating system locks through system calls or APIs so that the responsibility to schedule and synchronise threads is allotted to the OS process scheduler. In the most general case, starvation can be avoided by using a first-come, first-served resource allocation policy.

4.5.5 Livelock

Assume a lock or a routine to acquire a critical section is built solely based on hardware primitives without the help of an operating system scheduler. Consider the example in Figure 4.25. Suppose the two locks M and N are of the type of a spin lock shown in Figure 4.24. If the process P is executed first and acquires the lock M and then the process Q is executed and acquires the lock N, none of the processes progresses further and neither is blocked. They use their processor quantum over and over again without any progress and being blocked. In this case, there is no deadlock because no process is blocked, such a negative incident is called a *livelock*.

4.5.6 Convoying

A lock convoy occurs when multiple threads with equal priority repeatedly compete for a single lock. Unlike deadlocks and livelocks, threads make progress in very close tandem, but each time a thread attempts to acquire a lock and fails, it relinquishes the rest of its scheduling quantum and exerts a context switch. Frequent context switching overheads and underutilisation of quanta scheduling impair overall efficiency. This destructive situation does not exist in non-blocking systems such as lock-free algorithms, which are discussed in Chapter 5.

4.6 Installation Steps of the Integrated Development Environment (IDE) Code::Blocks on Unix-Like Operating Systems Such as Linux

Code::Blocks is a free, open-source and cross-platform IDE environment that allows programmers to compile C or C++ codes based on a wide range of compilers. You can always get the latest version of this environment at http://www.codeblocks.org for Windows, Linux and Unix operating systems. Because the codes in this book are based on Code::Blocks in Linux and Microsoft Visual Studio in Windows, Linux users can take advantage of Code::Blocks to develop, modify, and deploy their codes. Figure 4.35 illustrates a shell file that, according to its description, you can easily compile and run this environment from source code on a Linux operating system. Note that in order for Code::Blocks to work properly, all installation tasks must be taken step by step and carefully. Figure 4.36 shows a screenshot of the execution of this IDE in Linux.

```bash
#!/bin/bash

#All rights reserved to Alireza Poshtkohi. (C) 2001-2023.
#Contact: arp@poshtkohi.info

# As a first step, create this directory for our installation process.
mkdir ~/devel

# Because codeblocks makes use of wxWidgets for its graphical user
#interface GUI), we first must also install it. Download it from
# wxWidgets website at http://www.wxwidgets.org/.
# Copy the wxWidgets source code into ~/devel.
cp wxWidgets-2.8.12.tar.gz ~/devel/wxWidgets-2.8.12.tar.gz

# Next, download codeblocks source codes at http://www.codeblocks.org.
# Copy the codeblocks source code into ~/devel.
cp codeblocks-10.05-src.tar.bz2 ~/devel/codeblocks-10.05-src.tar.bz2

# Change your current directory to ~/devel.
cd ~/devel

# Now we unzip the copied files at directory ~/devel contained above.
tar zxf wxWidgets-2.8.12.tar.gz
tar jxf codeblocks-10.05-src.tar.bz2

# Here, we build the wxWidgets.
# Change directory to wxWidgets source.
cd wxWidgets-2.8.12
# Here we will create a separate build directory instead of building from
the src
# directory, so that we can easily rebuild with different options (unicode
/ ansi,
# monolithic / many libs, etc). The documentation says the default is for
gtk2 to
# use unicode and wx > 2.5 to build as a monolithic library. This doesn't
appear
#to be the case, so these flags are passed to configure
# Bulid wxWidgets libraries with the following commands.
mkdir build_gtk2_shared_monolithic_unicode
cd build_gtk2_shared_monolithic_unicode
../configure --prefix=/opt/wx/2.8 --enable-xrc --enable-monolithic --
enable-unicode
make
make install

# Add /opt/wx/2.8/bin to the PATH to ~/.bashrc (if this file does not
exist create it
# with a text editor or vi command in the shell)
# Add the following line to the ~/.bashrc file
# export PATH=/usr/bin:/opt/wx/2.8/bin:$PATH

# Add /opt/wx/2.8/lib to /etc/ld.so.conf (nano /etc/ld.so.conf) then run:
ldconfig
source /etc/profile

# That's it. Now the linker will look at /opt/wx/2.8/lib for wx libraries
and you will
```

Figure 4.35 A shell file with full instructions for installing a cross-platform integrated development environment (IDE) known as Code::Blocks in Unix-like operating systems such as Linux.

(Continued)

```
# have a monolithic shared library unicode build.
# To check that things are working, type:
wx-config --prefix
# which should give you /opt/wx/2.8
wx-config --libs
# which should have at least -L/opt/wx/2.8/lib -lwx_gtk2-2.8 but can
contain other flags as well.
which wx-config

# Finally, we build the codeblocks.
cd ~/devel/codeblocks-10.05-release
./configure
make
make install

# Add the following line to the file /etc/ld.so.conf:
# /usr/local/lib
# and then run:
ldconfig
```

Figure 4.35 (Continued) A shell file with full instructions for installing a cross-platform integrated development environment (IDE) known as Code::Blocks in Unix-like operating systems such as Linux.

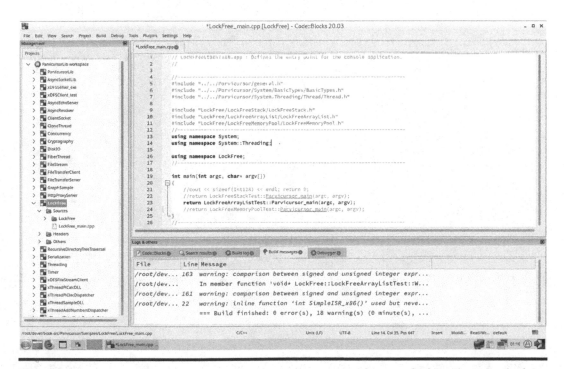

Figure 4.36 A screenshot of the Code::Blocks environment within a typical Parvicursor platform project in the OpenSUSE Linux operating system.

References

[1] A. Baumann, P. Barham, P.E. Dagand, T. Harris, R. Isaacs, S. Peter, T. Roscoe, A. Schupbach, and A. Singhania, The multikernel: A new OS architecture for scalable multicore systems, In *Proceedings of the 22nd ACM Symposium on OS Principles*, Big Sky, MT, USA, October 2009.

[2] D. Wentzlaff, and A. Agarwal, Factored operating systems (FOS): The case for a scalable operating system for multicores. *SIGOPS Oper. Syst. Rev.*, 43(2):76–85, 2009.

[3] E.B. Nightingale, O. Hodson, R. McIlroy, C. Hawblitzel, and G. Hunt, *Helios: Heterogeneous Multiprocessing with Satellite Kernels*, In *ACM, SOSP"09*, Big Sky, Montana, USA, October 11–14, 2009.

[4] O. Mao, F. Kaashoek, R. Morris, A. Pesterev, L. Stein, M. Wu, Y. Dai, Y. Zhang, and Z. Zhang, Corey: An operating system for many cores, In *Proceedings of the 8th USENIX Symposium on Operating Systems Design and Implementation OSDI '08*, San Diego, California, 2008.

[5] J.A. Colmenares, S. Bird, H. Cook, P. Pearce, D. Zhu, J. Shalf, S. Hofmeyr, K. Asanovic, and J. Kubiatowicz, Resource management in the tessellation manycore OS, In *Proceedings of 2nd USENIX Workshop on Hot Topics in Parallelism (HotPar'10)*, Berkeley, CA, USA, 2010.

Chapter 5

Parallelisation for the Many-Core Era: A Programming Perspective

> The way the processor industry is going, is to add more and more cores, but nobody knows how to program those things. I mean, two, yeah; four, not really; eight, forget it.
>
> **Steve Jobs**

5.1 Introduction

This chapter focuses on software aspects of parallel programming for many-core systems, as discussed in Chapter 4. Several examples are also given such as multithreaded programming, concurrent systems, parallel algorithms and lock-free data structures.

5.2 Building Cross-Platform Concurrent Systems Utilising Multi-Threaded Programming on Top of the Parvicursor.NET Framework for Distributed Systems

5.2.1 Introduction

In the previous chapters, the theory of concurrent systems was examined. Abstractions such as thread, synchronisation, and concurrency were frequently discussed without a deep dive at software and code levels. In this and the next sections, we will teach the reader how to design and program concurrent systems. A rich set of examples given will help the reader to have thorough experience in designing concurrent systems and have a better understanding of the principles of concurrency and parallel processing for use in distributed systems. As mentioned earlier, this chapter assumes that the reader is relatively familiar with programming based on the Parvicursor.NET Framework; otherwise, please refer to Chapter 8 before continuing to study this chapter.

In this section, we first introduce the details of classes in the `System::Threading` namespace. This namespace provides several classes and utilities for multi-threaded programming. The implemented classes are responsible for synchronising thread activity and accessing data (such as mutex, barriers, and conditional variables). This namespace also includes a `ThreadPool` class that allows using a pool of threads and a `Timer` class that executes a callback on a given thread. All of these classes are implemented on a cross-platform basis and allow to run target applications on the most recent operating systems. These native C++ classes, in the background, are based on the POSIX Thread standard in Unix/Linux operating systems and Win32 APIs on Windows operating systems. The implementation of these classes is tightly close to the ECMA.NET standards as much as possible. For example, we designed the `Resume()` and `Suspend()` methods of the `Threading` class, which unlike the Windows APIs are not directly presented in the POSIX-compliant Thread standard.

The interested reader can refer to the "`/Parvicursor/Parvicursor/System.Threading`" path from the companion resources of the book to look at the full implementation of these classes. Numerous examples given are designed in such a way that the reader can easily generalise them to distributed systems. For example, this section will present a concurrent producer/consumer model, which we will generalise in Chapter 6 to utilise an asynchronous file copy concept. In addition, based on the content presented in Chapter 7, we will take benefit of this generalised example to design a concurrent architecture to support high-speed InfiniBand-based network transfers for xDFS file transfer framework in Chapter 10.

5.2.2 *Thread Creation and Management in the Parvicursor.NET Framework*

Creating and managing threads in the Parvicursor.NET Framework is done directly through the `Thread` class. Threads take pointers to arbitrary functions and their corresponding input arguments and execute them. Table 5.1 describes the methods and the constructor of this class.

Given the description of the `Thread` class, as the first sample, we provide an example in which the `main()` function of the program spawns two threads and repeatedly suspends and resumes them. Each thread also prints a message to the output at the same time. Figure 5.1 shows our first example in this section.

The code for this example is located in the "`/Parvicursor/Parvicursor/Samples/Threading`" path. Line 2 provides the program with the `System::Threading` namespace. The `Display()` method of the `TestThread` class repeatedly prints `threadID` of the thread which is executing it in an infinite loop to the output. In line 13, the current thread execution is suspended for 1 millisecond, because otherwise the CPU utilisation will eventually reach 100% pointlessly. Since a native C-type function pointer must be specified in the `Thread` class constructor, we cannot give the address of the C++ non-static `Display()` member function as the start argument. The static function `Wrapper_To_Call_Display()` (treated by the compiler as a native C language function) solves this problem. The `pt2Object`

Table 5.1   Methods and Constructor of the `Thread` Class in Parvicursor.NET Framework

Name	Description
`Thread(void *(*start) (void *), void *arg)`	The `Thread` class constructor initialises an instance of this class. The `start` variable specifies a function pointer that will be executed by this thread. The `arg` pointer fills the input arguments of the `start` pointer function.
`void Start()`	Causes the operating system to change the state of the current thread instance to a running state.
`bool get_IsAlive()`	Returns a value indicative of the current thread execution status.
`void Abort()`	Raises an abnormal thread termination request in the thread on which it is invoked, and the termination process of that thread begins. This is a dangerous method because the clean-up handler is not performed on the thread. If the target thread locks a mutex, that thread ends with the locked mutex. Because a mutex cannot be unlocked on another thread, the application must be fully prepared to release the mutex. This means that any other threads that might be waiting for the released mutex will continue to wait for the mutex indefinitely unless they are also terminated by calling the `Abort()` method. It is strongly recommended not to use this method in applications as much as possible.
`void Join()`	Blocks the caller (parent) thread until a running thread (child) terminates.
`void SetDetached()`	Sets the thread mode to detached. If you already know that a thread never needs to join another thread, call this method after invoking the `Start()` method right away. In fact, by invoking this method, the caller thread will never wait for the execution of the thread to end.
`void Resume()`	Resumes a suspended thread.
`void Suspend()`	Either suspends the thread or, if the thread has already been suspended, it has no effect.
`static void Sleep(Int32 ms)`	This static method suspends the current thread for a specified time in milliseconds.

pointer in line 17 as the input argument contains the address of the `TestThread` class's instance whose `Display()` method must be called, and in line 19 is converted to the type of the `TestThread` class. In line 21, the `Display()` method is invoked indirectly through the `myself` object.

In the `main()` function, threads are initialised. The `test1` and `test2` objects are instantiated in lines 27 and 28, and in lines 29 and 30 their `Wrapper_To_Call_Display()` method's addresses are passed to the `Thread` class constructor along with the addresses of these objects. In lines 31 through 34, these two threads are executed, and their state is set as detached. This operation causes the `main()` function not to be blocked, and the flow of the `main()` function reaches the `while` loop

```
 1: using namespace System;
 2: using namespace System::Threading;
 3:
 4: class TestThread : public Object {
 5:    private: Int32 threadID;
 6:    public: TestThread(Int32 threadID) {
 7:       this->threadID = threadID;
 8:    }
 9:    public: void Display(const char *message) {
10:       Int32 i = 0;
11:       while(true) {
12:          printf("I'm thread %d. Message: %s. i: %d\n", threadID, message, i);
13:          Thread::Sleep(1); // Suspends the current thread for 1ms.
14:          i++;
15:       }
16:    }
17:    public: static void *Wrapper_To_Call_Display(void *pt2Object) {
18:       // explicitly cast to a pointer to TestThread
19:       TestThread *mySelf = (TestThread *)pt2Object;
20:       // call member
21:       mySelf->Display("Hello World");
22:       return pt2Object;
23:    }
24: };
25:
26: int main(int argc, char* argv[]) {
27:    TestThread test1 = TestThread(0);
28:    TestThread test2 = TestThread(1);
29:    Thread t1 = Thread(test1.Wrapper_To_Call_Display, (void *)&test1);
30:    Thread t2 = Thread(test2.Wrapper_To_Call_Display, (void *)&test2);
31:    t1.Start();
32:    t2.Start();
33:    t1.SetDetached();
34:    t2.SetDetached();
35:    Thread::Sleep(1);
36:    while(true) {
37:       t1.Suspend();
38:       t2.Resume();
39:       Thread::Sleep(2000); // Suspends the main() thread for 2 seconds.
40:       t1.Resume();
41:       t2.Suspend();
42:       Thread::Sleep(2000);
43:    }
44:    return 0;
45: }
```

Figure 5.1 The way to create threads in the Parvicursor.NET Framework and to use the `Thread` class methods. In this example, the execution of two threads is repeatedly suspended and resumed.

in line 36 (this would never have happened if the two threads had been joined). In this loop, the first thread is suspended, and the second thread is resumed, and after a two-second delay in line 39 (by calling the Sleep() method) the first thread is resumed, and the second thread is suspended. According to this scenario, only one thread displays its message on the output screen every two seconds. It is important to note that in this simple example the Suspend() and Resume() methods are repeatedly used, despite the correct operation of the example, but should not be used for thread synchronisation purposes. Calling the Suspend() method on a thread that holds a synchronisation object, such as a mutex, can lead to a deadlock if the calling thread tries to acquire a synchronisation object possessed by a suspended thread. These two methods are commonly used in debuggers. In addition, as noted in Chapter 9, we will benefit from the unique feature of these two methods for implementing a new checkpoint and rollback (restore) mechanism in distributed environments such as grid and cloud for Parvicursor infrastructure. In such an application, to activate this mechanism for simplification in favour of the developers, it will be assumed that the developed applications consist of fine-grained threads that do not hold any locks (this assumption is not mandatory and is only for simplification). However, to avoid such a deadlock state, a thread within an application should signal another thread to suspend itself. The target thread should be designed to monitor and respond appropriately to this signal. For this purpose, conditional variables that are discussed later in this chapter can be used.

5.2.3 Implementing the System::Threading::Timer Class of the ECMA Standard Based on the Thread Class in the Parvicursor. NET Framework

Timers often play an important role in both client applications and server-based components. A timer invokes a specific code regularly. It executes a method every few seconds or minutes. This feature is especially powerful for monitoring the health of an important application along with diagnostics. Another example of using this class is to report the throughput of file and data transfers on the client side of the xDFS framework in Chapter 10. In this use case, a timer calculates the amount of transmitted data during a one-second interval in order to find the resultant throughput in terms of megabits per second.

Timers are usually made up of two objects, a TimerCallback and a Timer. TimerCallback defines an action that executes at a specified interval, whilst Timer object performs a counting mechanism. Figure 5.2 shows a typical prototype for defining the TimerCallback and Timer objects and implementing a number of the Timer class members. Line 2 defines the Callback function pointer using the typedef keyword. The TimerCallback class stores a variable of the type of Callback. The Timer class constructor in line 33 takes a TimerCallback variable as an argument. In this constructor, the state variable represents the object that will be passed to the TimerCallback callback class when getting invoked. The dueTime variable indicates the amount of time delay after which a callback is called. The period variable specifies the time interval between callback invocations in milliseconds. Inside the timer class constructor, after assigning variables, a thread of the Thread class is created for the worker variable, and after starting it, its state

```
1: // The Callback definition.
2: typedef Object *(*Callback)(Object *);
3:
4: class TimerCallback : public Object {
5:     private: Callback callback;
6:     public: TimerCallback(Callback &callback);
7:     public: TimerCallback();
8:     public: Callback &get_BaseCallback();
9: };
10:
11: class Timer : public Object {
12:     // A TimerCallback delegate representing a method to be executed.
13:     private: TimerCallback callback;
14:     // An object containing information to be used by the callback method, or null.
15:     private: Object *state;
16:     // The amount of time to delay before callback is invoked, in milliseconds. Specify Timeout::Infinite to prevent
the timer from starting.
17:     private: Int32 dueTime;
18:     // The time interval between invocations of callback, in milliseconds. Specify Timeout::Infinite to disable
periodic signalling.
19:     private: Int32 period;
20:     private: Thread worker;
21:     // Initialises a new instance of the Timer class, using a 32-bit signed integer to specify the time interval.
22:     public: Timer(const TimerCallback &callback, Object *state, Int32 dueTime, Int32 period);
23:     // Class destructor.
24:     public: ~Timer();
25:     // A static method that will be executed by the worker thread.
26:     private: protected: static void *Wrapper_To_Call_Worker(void* timer);
27:     // Changes the start time and the interval between method invocations for a timer.
28:     public: bool Change(Int32 dueTime, Int32 period);
29:     // Releases all resources used by the current instance of Timer.
30:     public: void Dispose();
31: };
32:
33: Timer::Timer(const TimerCallback &callback, Object *state, Int32 dueTime, Int32 period) {
34:     // ...
35:     worker = Thread(Wrapper_To_Call_Worker, (void *)this);
36:     worker.Start();
37:     worker.SetDetached();
38: }
39:
40: void *Timer::Wrapper_To_Call_Worker(void *timer) {
41:     // explicitly cast to a pointer to Timer
42:     Timer *_timer = (Timer*) timer;
43:     while(true) {
44:         _timer->callback.get_BaseCallback()(_timer->state); // Executes the timer callback.
45:         Thread::Sleep(_timer->period); // Suspends the Timer based on period.
46:     }
47:     return timer;
48: }
```

Figure 5.2   The prototype for defining TimerCallback and Timer objects and implementing several members of the Timer class.

```
1: static Int32 counter = 0; // Our counter.
2: // Our timer callback.
3: Object *test(Object *obj) {
4:     printf("%s, %d\n", ((String *)obj)->get_BaseStream(), counter);
5:     counter++;
6:     return obj;
7: }
8:
9: int main(int argc, char *argv[]) {
10:     String s = "Alireza Poshtkohi";
11:     Callback callback = test;
12:     TimerCallback timerDelegate(callback);
13:     Timer timer(timerDelegate, &s, 0, 1000);
14:     while(true)
15:         Thread::Sleep(10); // Sleeps for 10ms.
16:     return 0;
18: }
```

Figure 5.3 An example of using the `Timer` class.

is changed to a detached type. This thread executes the static method `Wrapper_To_Call_Worker()`, which itself repeatedly executes the callback of the passed `Timer` object in an infinite loop. To realise the periodic execution mode in defining functionality of the timer class, this method suspends the execution of the worker thread after the execution of each callback equal to `period` by calling the `Sleep()` method in line 45. For brevity's sake, parts of this code have been removed from the implementation shown in Figure 5.2. To take a closer look at the full implementation of these classes, refer to "/Parvicursor/Parvicursor/System.Threading/Timer" from the companion resources of the book.

Figure 5.3 shows a simple way to use the designed timer. In this example, a callback named `test` prints the string passed to the output. `TimerCallback` is prepared in lines 11 and 12, and the `timer` object is instantiated in line 13. This timer invokes a callback every second. The `while` loop allows the program to run forever. The full code for this example can be found in the "/Parvicursor/Parvicursor/Samples/Timer" path.

5.2.4 Synchronisation in the Parvicursor.NET Framework

Chapter 4 stated that when data is shared in a multi-threaded environment, a synchronisation issue may arise. Furthermore, threads in a concurrent system are often interdependent or interact with other threads to achieve a practical task. In this section, we discuss how to program synchronisation techniques in the Parvicursor.NET Framework. In the next section, examples are provided that teach how to use C++ classes for this section. This section forms the basis for the following sections of this chapter. Before going into the main discussion, let us distinguish between two different, but very related, classifications of synchronisation:

- *Data Synchronisation*: Shared resources, including memory, must be protected so that threads using the same resource do not interfere with each other in parallel. Such interferences can give rise to problems ranging from crashes to data corruptions, and worse, to the production of random results (a program may produce correct results once but not again). Using mutual exclusion, such as a mutex in the Parvicursor.NET Framework, and lock-free methods given in Section 5.3, these requirements are met.
- *Control Synchronisation*: Threads can depend on one another's progress through control flow and program state space. A thread often needs to wait until another thread, or a set of threads, has reached a certain point in the execution of the program. Control synchronisation in the Parvicursor. NET Framework is performed by conditional variables and barriers. Also, the Join() method of the Thread class is another provider of this type of synchronisation.

Data synchronisation is necessarily performed through the Mutex class. Mutex is a synchronisation primitive that grants exclusive access to shared resources to only one thread at a time. If a thread acquires a mutex, the second thread that wants to get that mutex is suspended until the first thread releases the mutex. Table 5.2 describes the methods and the constructor of this class.

The most basic mechanism for supporting control synchronisation within the Parvicursor.NET Framework is the conditional variable class. Consider this conundrum: How does a thread deal with a situation in which it is waiting for a condition to become true. The thread could lock and unlock a mutex sequentially and check a shared data structure for a certain value each time. But this method is a waste of time and resources, and this form of busy polling is very inefficient. The best way to cope with this is to call the Wait() method of the conditional variable class. Conditional variables allow threads to be synchronised to a single value from a shared resource. Typically speaking, conditional variables serve as a

Table 5.2 Methods and Constructor of the Mutex Class in the Parvicursor.NET Framework

Name	Description
Mutex()	The constructor of the Mutex class initialises a new instance.
void Lock()	Locks the mutex instance.
bool TryLock()	This method does the same as the Lock() method, except that if the mutex object is already locked, it returns immediately.
void UnLock()	Unlocks the mutex instance.
void Close()	Releases all resources held by the mutex object.

Table 5.3 Methods and Constructor of the `ConditionVariable` Class in the Parvicursor.NET Framework

Name	Description
`ConditionVariable(Mutex *mutex)`	The constructor of the `ConditionVariable` class initialises a new instance of this class; to specify this constructor, we must pass a pre-created mutex object to it.
`void Wait()`	This method blocks the conditional variable on the current instance.
`void TimedWait(Long seconds, Long nanoseconds)`	This method is the same as the `Wait()` method, except that it blocks the conditional variable only on the current instance based on the time specified.
`void Signal()`	This method unblocks at least one of the threads that are blocked on the current conditional variable instance.
`void Broadcast()`	This method unblocks all recently blocked threads on the current instance of the conditional variable.

notification system between threads. Table 5.3 describes the methods and constructor of the `ConditionVariable` class. To use the constructor of this class when being instantiated, we must pass an instance object instantiated from the `Mutex` class to it. Understanding how the `Wait()` method works is crucial, as it is at the heart of the conditional variable signalling system and is the most difficult part of multi-threaded programming to comprehend. When using conditional variables, we must always place part of the code they use inside the critical section of the mutex object.

Let's consider a scenario in which a thread locks a mutex object to inspect a linked list, and this list accidentally becomes empty. This particular thread can do nothing because it has been designated to remove a node from the list whilst there is no node. Whilst the mutex lock is still being held, our thread invokes the `Wait()` method. Calling `Wait()` is somewhat complicated, so we follow this scenario step by step to better understand it. The first thing that `Wait()` does is to simultaneously unlock the mutex and wait for the conditional variable object (until `Wait()` wakes up when it is signalled by another thread). Now that the mutex is unlocked, other threads can access and modify the linked list, possibly to add items to it. At this point, the `Wait()` call has not yet returned. Mutex unlocking occurs immediately, but waiting on the conditional variable object is normally a blocking operation, meaning that our thread will go to sleep, and no CPU cycle will be consumed when the thread wakes up. This is exactly what we want to happen. The thread is asleep and waits for a certain condition to become `true`, without doing any busy polling that wastes CPU time. From our thread's point of view, it is simply waiting for the `Wait()` call to be returned. Now, let's assume that another thread with an ID of 2 locks the mutex and adds an item to our linked list. Immediately after unlocking the mutex, Thread 2 calls the `Broadcast()` method. With this operation, Thread 2 will cause all threads waiting on the conditional variable object to wake up immediately. This signifies that our first thread that is in the middle of a `Wait()` call will now wake up.

Now, let's look at what happens to our first thread. After Thread 2 calls the `Broadcast()` method, we may think that it will return the `Wait()` of Thread 1 immediately. But this does not take place; instead, `Wait()` will perform a final operation: it will lock the mutex object again. Once `Wait()` has the lock, it will then return it, allowing Thread 1 to continue running. At this point, it can check the list for any changes. The operation of conditional variables is very similar to the way an operating system serves I/O requests to programs. An I/O request from a user application due to a system call may complete immediately. If this happens, the operating system may delay the I/O service and serve another user until the I/O operation completes. The operating system then resumes the I/O service.

The last synchronisation class we are willing to examine in this section is the `Barrier` class of the Parvicursor.NET Framework. This synchronisation structure allows many threads to meet at one point in time. In many applications and especially numerical applications, whilst part of the algorithm can be paralleled, the other parts are inherently sequential. That algorithm can use barriers to synchronise parallel and sequential segments. For example, we might generate a set of matrices with a strictly linear computation and perform operations on those matrices that use a parallel algorithm. We then use the results of these operations to generate another set of matrices, operate in parallel on these matrices, and so on. The nature of parallel algorithms for such computations requires very little synchronisation, which is required during the computations. However, the synchronisation of all threads is required to ensure that sequential computations occur before parallel computations begin. The barrier forces all threads that are doing parallel computations to wait until all the threads involved reach that barrier.

Table 5.4 shows the methods and constructor of the `Barrier` class. When instantiating this class, we must pass the number of threads that are intended to take part in the barrier-based synchronisation. In Figure 5.4, a `Barrier` object with a value of 3 causes the `SignalAndWait()` method to be blocked until that method is called three times. This feature allows multiple threads to be held in step with each other as they process a series of tasks. Note that the barrier object cannot be used again after all threads have reached it, but, if necessary, the barrier object must be re-instantiated for later uses.

Table 5.4 Methods and Constructor of the `Barrier` Class in the Parvicursor.NET Framework

Name	Description
Barrier(Int32 count)	The constructor of the `Barrier` class initialises a new instance of this class; the count value specifies the number of participating threads.
void SignalAndWait()	Informs that one participant has reached the barrier object and is also waiting for all other participants to reach the barrier.

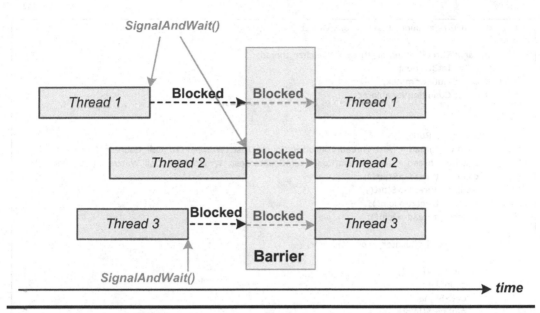

Figure 5.4   An example of three threads reaching a barrier object. Execution of every thread is blocked when reaching the barrier. When all threads arrive at the barrier, the execution of all of them is restored.

5.2.5 Two Concurrency Examples Relied on Synchronisation Classes in the Parvicursor.NET Framework

In this section, we present two examples, a concurrent counter and a multiple producer/consumer system, to prepare the reader for the development of concurrent systems in later sections. These examples use the synchronisation classes described in the previous section.

First, let's design a concurrent counter in which multiple threads may change the value of the counter simultaneously. We tend to have an observer thread always aware of any change in the counter. Figure 5.5 shows part of the implementation code for this concurrent counter. In this example, two threads are created in the Run() method. The counter_thread thread increments the count value, and the watcher_thread thread is used to asynchronously inform us of changing the count variable by the first thread. Both threads are joined after starting, and this program will always run. Consider the Counter_proc() method, in which the count variable is incremented in line 20, and this is done in an infinite while loop. Since the variable count is a shared data between threads, it is placed in a critical section created by the mutex object between lines 19 through 22 of the code. In line 21, since the count value has been updated, we will notify the watcher_thread thread by invoking the Signal() method from the conditional variable object cv. As mentioned earlier, a conditional variable object always depends on an object of the type of the Mutex class, so, as can be seen, the object cv is placed between the protected critical section according to the Lock() and Unlock() methods of the mutex object. In the Watcher_proc method within the while loop, every time after calling the Lock() method we must wait for the cv object through the Wait()

```
 1: class ConcurrentCounterTest : public Object {
 2:    /*---------------------fields---------------*/
 3:    private: Thread *counter_thread, *watcher_thread;
 4:    private: Int32 count;
 5:    private: Mutex *mutex;
 6:    private: ConditionVariable *cv;
 7:    /*---------------------methods--------------*/
 8:    //...
 9:    public: void Run() {
10:       counter_thread = new Thread(ConcurrentCounterTest::Wrapper_To_Call_Counter, (void *)this);
11:       watcher_thread = new Thread(ConcurrentCounterTest::Wrapper_To_Call_Watcher, (void *)this);
12:       counter_thread->Start();
13:       watcher_thread->Start();
14:       counter_thread->Join();
15:       watcher_thread->Join();
16:    }
17:    private: void *Counter_proc(void *ptr) {
18:       while(true) {
19:          mutex->Lock();
20:          count++;
21:          cv->Signal();
22:          mutex->Unlock();
23:          Thread::Sleep(1);
24:       }
25:       return ptr;
26:    }
27:    private: void *Watcher_proc(void *ptr) {
28:       while(true) {
29:          mutex->Lock();
30:          cv->Wait();
31:          printf("%d\n", count);
32:          mutex->Unlock();
33:       }
34:       return ptr;
35:    }
36:    //...
37: };
```

Figure 5.5 A concurrent counter based on mutex and conditional variables.

method in line 31; whenever this method returns, it indicates that the value of the variable count has been changed by another thread. Ultimately, after getting notified of this change, the current value of count is printed in line 31. Note that in the Watcher_proc() method the conditional variable and the read operation of the count variable are protected by a critical section created by the mutex object, as explained for the Counter_proc() method.

Our second example is a producer/consumer system with support for multiple threads but limited to only two threads because it is also used in Chapters 6 and 10 for concurrently copying files, respectively, locally, and locally/remotely. The producer/consumer problem, also known as the bounded-buffer problem, consists of two classes of threads: (1) producer threads, which generate data items and insert them into a buffer, and (2) consumer threads, which remove data items from the buffer and consume them one by one. Producer and consumer threads are constantly in need of accessing shared buffers, and both classes of threads operate at their own individual speeds. The main issue here is to synchronise the activity between all threads.

In this example, the shared buffer has n slots and is a circular buffer of constant size. A circular buffer is a data structure that uses a buffer as if it was connected from end to end. Figure 5.6 shows a multiple producer/consumer architecture with a fixed-length circular buffer and its full and empty slots. The simplest implementation of a circular buffer requires two integer numbers `start` and `end`. The `start` value represents the valid starting point of the data, and the `end` value represents the valid data end point. A circular buffer can be very conveniently used as a queue or FIFO buffer. This example has two limitations: (a) producer threads cannot insert a data item into the buffer when the buffer is full, and (b) consumer threads cannot remove a data item from the buffer when the buffer is empty. The synchronisation operation to insert/remove a data item into/from a slot in the buffer must be made atomic and protected by a mutual exclusion mechanism due to synchronising the threads.

To solve the stated two problems, we will make use of a mutex object when threads want to concurrently access the circular buffer and of two conditional variable objects to inform the producer and consumer threads of whether the buffer is full or empty. Figure 5.7 shows the implementation of this circular buffer as a `ConcurrentCircularBuffer` class. This class has two threads, `producer_thread` and `consumer_thread`. Our circular buffer is allocated as an array of characters with n holes set to `BUFFER_SIZE` in line 7. In this example, a character with a length of one byte is stored and retrieved in each buffer hole. The `bufferNotFull` and `bufferNotEmpty` conditional variables are respectively used by producers and consumers. In the `Run()` method, threads are joined after getting created and started by the `Join()` method.

In the `producer()` method, in lines 28–31, the `Wait()` method is called using the `bufferNotFull` conditional variable until the buffer is full. The condition inside the `while` loop in line 28 holds until the buffer is full. In line 33, since the buffer is

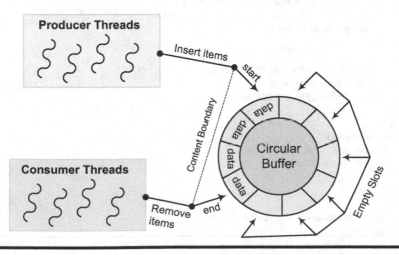

Figure 5.6 A multi-producer/multi-consumer architecture around a circular buffer for concurrent data storage and retrieval.

half full or empty, a random character is created and in line 34 is inserted at the end of the buffer; in line 35, the new end of the circular buffer is stored in the end variable. In line 40, since data was recently inserted into the buffer, the `Signal()` method is invoked from the `bufferNotEmpty` object to wake it up if the previous thread is asleep. In this example, the `System::Random` class uses the Parvicursor.NET

```
1: class ConcurrentCircularBuffer : public Object {
2:    /*--------------------fields----------------*/
3:    private: Thread *producer_thread;
4:    private: Thread *consumer_thread;
5:    private: Mutex *mutex;
6:    private: ConditionVariable *bufferNotEmpty, *bufferNotFull;
7:    private: char circular_buffer[BUFFER_SIZE]; // A buffer with BUFFER_SIZE slots.
8:    private: Int32 start, end; // Integers to index circular_buffer.
9:    /*--------------------methods---------------*/
10:   // ...
11:   public: void Run() {
12:       producer_thread = new Thread(ConcurrentCircularBuffer::Wrapper_To_Call_producer, (void *)this);
13:       consumer_thread = new Thread(ConcurrentCircularBuffer::Wrapper_To_Call_consumer, (void *)this);
14:       producer_thread->Start();
15:       consumer_thread->Start();
16:       producer_thread->Join();
17:       consumer_thread->Join();
18:   }
19:   private: void *producer(void *ptr) {
20:       static const char *str = "abcdefghiklmnopqrstvxyzABCDEFGHIKLMNOPQRSTVXYZ0123456789";
21:       static Random rnd = Random();
22:       while(true) {
23:          Thread::Sleep(1); // Simulates some work.
24:          mutex->Lock();
25:          {
26:             // Use modulo as a trick to wrap around the end of the buffer back to the beginning
27:             // Wait until the buffer is full
28:             while((end + 1) % BUFFER_SIZE == start) {
29:                // Buffer is full - sleep so consumers can get items.
30:                bufferNotFull->Wait();
31:             }
32:
33:             char c = str[rnd.Next(0, 55)]; // strlen(str) - 1 = 56 - 1 = 55
34:             circular_buffer[end] = c;
35:             end = (end + 1) % BUFFER_SIZE;
36:
37:          }
38:          mutex->Unlock();
39:          // If a consumer is waiting, wake it.
40:          bufferNotEmpty->Signal(); //
41:       }
42:       return ptr;
43:   }
44:   private: void *consumer(void *ptr) {
45:       while(true) {
```

Figure 5.7 **An implementation of the concurrent circular buffer with the use of a mutex and conditional variables for the multiple producers/consumers problem.**

(Continued)

```
46:        mutex->Lock();
47:        {
48:            // Wait until the buffer is empty
49:            while(end == start) {
50:                // Buffer is empty - sleep so producers can create items.
51:                bufferNotEmpty->Wait();
52:            }
53:            char temp = circular_buffer[start];
54:            start = (start + 1) % BUFFER_SIZE;
55:            printf("c: %c\n", temp);
56:        }
57:        mutex->Unlock();
58:        // If a producer is waiting, wake it.
59:        bufferNotFull->Signal();
60:        // Simulate processing of the item.
61:        Thread::Sleep(1);
62:    }
63:    return ptr;
64:  }
65:  // ...
66: };
```

Figure 5.7   (Continued) An implementation of the concurrent circular buffer with the use of a mutex and conditional variables for the multiple producers/consumers problem.

Framework to generate random characters; the values of these characters are stored in line 20 in a static string variable.

In the `consumer()` method, we wait by invoking the `Wait()` method of the `bufferNotEmpty` object until the buffer is empty. The `while` loop condition holds in line 49 as long as the buffer is empty. When the loop is half full or full, the code execution reaches line 53 by ending the loop execution in line 49. At this time, we take our data out of the beginning of the buffer, which marks the beginning of it, and changes the new value of the `start` variable in line 54. In line 59, if the producer thread is already waiting, we wake it up. This example runs forever because both producer and consumer methods are embedded in two infinite `while` loops. In this example, the `mutex` object satisfies the task of protecting the beginning and end of the circular buffer when simultaneously being accessed by multiple threads.

5.2.6 *Thread Pools: Design and Implementation of the* `System::Threading::ThreadPool` *Class of the ECMA .NET Standard Based on the Parvicursor.NET Framework*

Simultaneous work units are often relatively short, mostly independent, and often for a short period of time before results are produced and the execution cycle ends. For example, many server applications, such as web and file servers, are oriented towards a wide range of short-term tasks that come from a remote source. Creating a dedicated thread for each piece of code is a very bad idea, as it pays significant execution time costs (both in time and space) for each thread that is created and destroyed. In addition to these performance overhead pressures, other overheads include more time spent in the scheduler to perform context switches when the number of threads exceeds the processor count, pressure on cache locality due to the threads that have to be moved from one processor to another, and the increase in the work set resulting from multiple threads to discretely access to virtual memory pages actively at the same time. Whilst thread pools have turned into a powerful mechanism for organising multi-threaded applications, they are not without risks. Programs built on thread pools are also vulnerable to all the risks that any multi-threaded program is exposed to, such as synchronisation errors and deadlocks. There are a number of risks specifically associated with thread pools, such as thread pool deadlocks, displacement status (thrashing), and thread leakage:

- *Deadlock*: Whilst deadlocks have become a major drawback of multi-threaded programs, thread pools offer another opportunity to create deadlocks, where all pool's threads are performing tasks that, due to waiting for the results of another task, are blocked on the task queue, but another task cannot be executed because there is no unoccupied thread space. This can happen when thread pools are used to implement simulations in that many interactive objects are involved, and the simulated objects can send queries to each other and then these queries are executed as enqueued tasks, and the querying object waits for a response at the same time.
- *Displacement Status*: An advantage associated with thread pools is that they generally work well against alternative scheduling mechanisms. But this is true when the size of the thread pool is properly adjusted. Threads consume a variety of resources, including memory and other system resources. If the thread pool was too large, the resources consumed by those threads could put a lot of pressure on system performance. Time is wasted whilst switching between threads, and having more threads than necessary may lead to resource starvation problems, as the pool's threads are consuming resources that could have been more efficiently exploited by other tasks.
- *Thread Leakage*: An important hazard in all types of thread pools is thread leakage, which occurs when a thread is removed from the pool to perform a task but is not returned to the pool when the task is complete. One way in which this problem occurs is when a task throws an exception (note that within the Parvicursor.NET Framework all exceptions inherit from the base System::Exception class). If the thread pool class or the return function specified by the program code written by the developer does not catch these exceptions, then the thread is simply removed, and the thread pool size decrements by one. When this happens often enough, the thread pool is eventually empty, and the system will stop because there are no threads to process tasks. Permanently stopped tasks can also cause an equivalent thread leakage. If a thread is consumed permanently with such a task, it is definitely removed from the thread pool. Such tasks should either be given a separate thread from the pool's threads or just wait for a limited time.

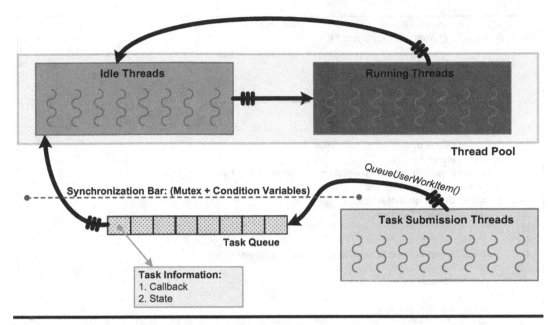

Figure 5.8 The `ThreadPool` class architecture implemented in the Parvicursor.NET Framework.

The following is an implementation of the `System::Threading::ThreadPool` class of the ECMA .NET standard based on the Parvicursor.NET Framework, and at the end, we come up with guidelines for more efficient use of thread pools. Figure 5.8 shows the implementation architecture of our `ThreadPool` class. We will first describe this abstraction and then its implementation in C++ on top of the Parvicursor.NET Framework. The task submission threads employ the `QueueUserWorkItem()` method to place their tasks at the end of the task queue (it is a type of FIFO queue). Each task, which is executed by a thread from the thread pool, has two attributes that are passed to this method: a callback method that will be invoked by a worker thread from the thread pool and a state object reference that contains information used by the callback method. The thread pool contains running and idle threads. Idle threads always take a task out of the task queue and execute its callback method, at which time an idle thread becomes an executable thread. Since multiple threads have access to this shared queue at once, and they must be waiting or waking up depending on whether the task queue is empty or full, synchronisation techniques must be leveraged in this architecture. The synchronisation bar in Figure 5.8 provides these two features through a mutex and two conditional variables.

Figure 5.9 shows the prototype for defining our thread pool class. Callback declaration is carried out using function pointers in line 1. In the `TaskInfo` structure, the state and callback passed are defined as an argument to the `QueueUserWorkItem()` method. In line 10, the variable q indicates the task queue. The two conditional variables `poolNotEmpty` and `poolNotFull` are employed by threads to fall asleep or wake up other threads when the queue is full or empty. In this implementation for simplicity, we statically create the threads, where their count is equal to `numThreads`, and store their reference in the array `workers` when the thread pool class is instantiated. The `queueMaxSize` variable dictates the maximum number of tasks that can

```
 1: // Represents a callback method to be executed by a ThreadPool thread.
 2: typedef void (*WaitCallback)(Object *);
 3:
 4: class ThreadPool : public Object {
 5:    /*--------------------fields---------------*/
 6:    private: struct TaskInfo : public Object {
 7:       Object *state;
 8:       WaitCallback callback;
 9:    };
10:    private: Queue q; // The ThreadPool task queue.
11:    private: Mutex *mutex;
12:    private: ConditionVariable *poolNotEmpty, *poolNotFull, *waitcv;
13:    private: UInt32 numThreads;
14:    private: UInt32 queueMaxSize;
15:    private: Thread **workers;
16:    /*--------------------methods---------------*/
17:    // ThreadPool Class constructor.
18:    public: ThreadPool(UInt32 numThreads, UInt32 queueMaxSize);
19:    // ThreadPool Class destructor.
20:    public: ~ThreadPool();
21:    // Gets the number of elements available in the ThreadPool.
22:    public: Int32 get_Count();
23:    // Queues a method for execution, and specifies an object containing data to be used by the method.
24:    // The method executes when a thread pool thread becomes available.
25:    // If the method is successfully queued, true will be returned.
26:    public: bool QueueUserWorkItem(WaitCallback callBack, Object *state);
27:    // Waits on the ThreadPool task queue until the queue is empty.
28:    public: void WaitOnTaskQueue();
29:    private: void *Worker(void *ptr);
30: };
```

Figure 5.9   **The prototype of the `ThreadPool` class definition.**

be stored and retrieved in the task queue. The Worker() method is executed in the ThreadPool class constructor after the threads are instantiated by them. The WaitOnTaskQueue() method allows the caller thread to wait until the task queue is empty. This method is used to synchronise applications that use the ThreadPool class and require it. It takes advantage of the waitcv object to achieve this function.

Figure 5.10 illustrates the implementation of a number of thread pool class methods. Refer to path "/Parvicursor/Parvicursor/System.Threading/ThreadPool" for full implementation. All threads in the constructor of this class are created as detached. The QueueUserWorkItem() method's body is placed between the critical section of the mutex object. In line 4, we have to wait for the poolNotFull object until the task queue is full. Otherwise, in lines 6 through 8, the task object is prepared and placed inside the queue. If the queue is empty, in line 10 we must invoke the Signal() method of the poolNotEmpty object to wake up the threads if they are sleeping because of an empty task queue. The Worker() method is a pointer to a function that is executed by all the pool's threads. All threads run in an infinite while loop. Inside the Worker() method, we wait on the poolNotEmpty object in lines 25 and 26 until the task queue is empty. In line 27, we dequeue a task from the queue and execute a callback in line 32 by passing its state

```
1: bool ThreadPool::QueueUserWorkItem(WaitCallback callBack, Object *state) {
2:     mutex->Lock();
3:     {
4:         while(q.get_Count() == queueMaxSize)
5:             poolNotFull->Wait();
6:         TaskInfo *task = new TaskInfo();
7:         task->callback = callBack;
8:         task->state = state;
9:         if(q.get_Count() == 0) {
10:             q.Enqueue(task);
11:             poolNotEmpty->Signal();
12:         }
13:         else
14:             q.Enqueue(task);
15:     }
16:     mutex->Unlock();
17:     return true;
18: }
19:
20: void *ThreadPool::Worker(void *ptr) {
21:     TaskInfo *task;
22:     while(true) {
23:         mutex->Lock();
24:         {
25:             while(q.get_Count() == 0)
26:                 poolNotEmpty->Wait();
27:             task = (TaskInfo *)q.Dequeue();
28:             if(q.get_Count() == queueMaxSize - 1)
29:                 poolNotFull->Broadcast();
30:         }
31:         mutex->Unlock();
32:         task->callback(task->state);
33:         waitcv->Broadcast();
34:         delete task;
35:     }
36:     return ptr;
37: }
38:
39: void ThreadPool::WaitOnTaskQueue() {
40:     mutex->Lock();
41:     {
42:         while (q.get_Count() != 0)
43:             waitcv->Wait();
44:     }
45:     mutex->Unlock();
46: }
```

Figure 5.10 Implementation of the `ThreadPool` class's methods.

object. This region shows the main role of the thread pool class in executing the tasks. In line 28, if the queue is full, we will notify all the task submission threads (which have called the `QueueUserWorkItem()` method) by invoking the `Broadcast()` method of the `poolNotFull` object (because the number of these threads can be more than one, the `Broadcast()` method is used instead of `Signal()`). In line 33, since the work of a task taken out of the task queue is complete, we need to invoke the `Broadcast()` method from the `waitcv` object, this will cause the threads that have fallen asleep on the `WaitOnTaskQueue()` method to be informed of this change. In the `WaitOnTaskQueue()` method, the `Wait()` method is called from the `waitcv` object until the task queue is empty. As seen in this implementation, all three conditional variables `poolNotEmpty`, `poolNotFull`, and `waitcv` use a single shared mutex object.

Finally, here are some important guidelines to keep in mind when working with the `ThreadPool` class:

- Whilst thread pools are usually the best way to add multi-threading to programs for performance purposes, there are some situations where they are not appropriate. The thread pool scheduler used is non-pre-emptive. Thread pools are therefore intended for high-performance algorithms that are non-blocking. They still work well if tasks are rarely blocked. However, if tasks are blocked repeatedly, there is a severe loss of performance because one task is blocked. Blocking typically occurs whilst waiting for I/O or mutexes for long periods of time. If your tasks are waiting for a resource, such as completion of an I/O, use a maximum waiting time (or asynchronous I/O methods), then fail and re-queue the task to run at another time (the `TimedWait()` method of the `Mutex` class makes this property possible).
- To effectively adjust the size of your thread pool, you need to understand the tasks that are being queued and what they are doing. You should check if they are CPU or I/O bound.
- Do not queue tasks that are waiting synchronously for results from other tasks. This can lead to a type of deadlock described at the beginning of this section, where all threads are occupied with tasks that they instead cannot be executed for the results of other enqueued tasks because all threads are busy.

5.2.7 *Four Examples of Concurrency and Parallel Processing Based on the* `ThreadPool` *Class*

In this section, we describe several examples of using the introduced thread pool to give the reader a better understanding of its power to implement concurrent applications and parallel processing algorithms. The first example is the traditional "Hello World" program, but simultaneously. The second and third examples describe matrix multiplication and prime number calculation atop parallel processing algorithms. Finally, the fourth example will implement a scenario to combine the use of the `Barrier` class and conditional variables with the implemented thread pool. The code for these examples is available in the path "`/Parvicursor/`

`Parvicursor/Samples/Concurrency/Concurrency/ThreadPool`" from the companion resources of the book.

In the first example, we want a certain number of threads within a thread pool to output the phrase "Hello world", n times at the same time. We will wait in the `main()` function of the program until this time is over to terminate the program. Figure 5.11 demonstrates this flow. The `MethodInfo` structure shows the state object that is passed to the `Print()` callback method via the `state` argument. In the `Print()` method, after converting the type of `state` variable from `Object` to `MethodInfo` in line 14, the message and ID of the callback, which has already been placed in the thread pool's task queue by the caller thread, are printed in the output. In the `main()` function, the `pool` object is instantiated in line 25. The static `get_ProcessorCount()` method, a member of the `Environment` class, finds the number of cores (or processors) of the current machine; in this example, the number of pool's threads is four times this value. In lines 26–39, 1,000 dummy methods are instantiated to print the phrase "Hello World" in a `for` loop, the callback of these methods along with their state objects are placed in the thread pool's task queue in line 38. A conditional variable and a mutex are used to wait in line 42 on the `cv` object until all methods execute. Between lines 16 and 20 in the callback method, a value of one is always added to the counter, and if its value is equal to `methodNum`, the `Broadcast()` method is called from the `cv` object to inform other threads of this matter, especially the `main()` function's thread. Here, the `mutex`, `cv`, and `counter` variables (via its address in the `counter_addr` pointer, which is a member of the `MethodInfo` structure) are shared between the pool's threads and the `main()` function's thread.

In the second example, we perform multiplication of two square matrices (n×n) based on the thread pool in parallel. Figure 5.12 shows this multiplication for two typical 4-by-4 matrices. Suppose here that the multiplication operation is performed by two threads. The matrix A is divided into two rows. Each segment divided by a thread is multiplied by matrix B and placed in the corresponding row segment in matrix C. This algorithm then can be generalised to n threads for multiplying square matrices.

Figure 5.13 shows the algorithm and implementation for multiplying the two matrices A and B, which are taught to students in traditional C programming textbooks. n denotes the number of rows and columns of the input and output square matrices. The only difference between this algorithm and those in the textbooks is that rather than using a two-dimensional array, it is allocated as a one-dimensional array for the purpose of increasing efficiency due to contiguous memory allocation. Thus, the element $A[i][j]$ (a two-dimensional array) in this example is expressed as $A[i \times n + j]$ (a one-dimensional array). Now, based on this simple algorithm and the method discussed in Figure 5.12, we implement a parallel algorithm for multiplying two square matrices reliant on a thread pool.

Figure 5.14 shows the parallel multiplication of two matrices A and B based on the thread pool. The `MatrixMultiplyCallback()` callback method is the same as the sequential multiplication algorithm of two matrices, except that the range of the split row block of the matrix A for parallel multiplication is passed to the `MethodInfo` structure through the `slice` variable. Lines 19 and 20 calculate this

```
 1: class ThreadPoolExample1 : public Object {
 2:     /*--------------------fields----------------*/
 3:     private: struct MethodInfo : public Object {
 4:         Int32 methodID;
 5:         char *message;
 6:         Int32 methodNum;
 7:         Int32 *counter_addr;
 8:         Mutex *mutex;
 9:         ConditionVariable *cv;
10:     };
11:     /*--------------------methods----------------*/
12:     private: static void Print(Object *state) {
13:         MethodInfo *info = (MethodInfo *)state;
14:         printf("I'm method %d. Method Message: %s\n", info->methodID, info->message);
15:
16:         info->mutex->Lock();
17:         (*info->counter_addr)++; // Increment the counter value by its address
18:         if(*info->counter_addr == info->methodNum)
19:             info->cv->Broadcast(); // Signals the main thread of all methods' completion.
20:         info->mutex->Unlock();
21:     }
22:     /*--------------------------------------------*/
23:     public: static int Parvicrursor_main(int argc, char *argv[]) {
24:         // Initialises the thread pool instance.
25:         ThreadPool pool = ThreadPool(Environment::get_ProcessorCount()*4, 10000);
26:         const Int32 methodNum = 1000;
27:         MethodInfo methods[methodNum];
28:         Int32 counter = 0;
29:         Mutex *mutex = new Mutex();
30:         ConditionVariable *cv = new ConditionVariable(mutex);
31:         for(Int32 i = 0 ; i < methodNum ; i++) {
32:             methods[i].methodID = i;
33:             methods[i].message = "Hello World";
34:             methods[i].methodNum = methodNum;
35:             methods[i].counter_addr = &counter;
36:             methods[i].mutex = mutex;
37:             methods[i].cv = cv;
38:             pool.QueueUserWorkItem(Print, &methods[i]);
39:         }
40:
41:         // Waits on counter until all methods complete.
42:         mutex->Lock();
43:         cv->Wait();
44:         mutex->Unlock();
45:
46:         // Releases the mutex and cv objects.
47:         delete mutex;
48:         delete cv;
49:         return 0;
50:     }
51: };
```

Figure 5.11   Concurrent "Hello World" example utilising the ThreadPool class.

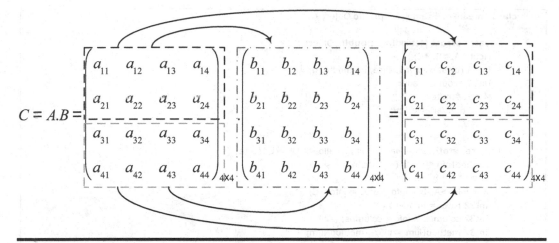

Figure 5.12 Parallel multiplication of two matrices A and B by two threads of control.

```
1: void MatrixMultiplySequential(Float *A, Float *B , Float *C, Int32 n) {
2:    register Int32 i, j, k;
3:    Float temp;
4:    for(i = 0 ; i < n ; i++) {
5:       for(j = 0 ; j < n ; j++) {
6:          temp = 0;
7:          for(k = 0 ; k < n ; k++)
8:             temp += A[I*n + k]*B[k*n + j];
9:          C[i*n + j] = temp;
10:      }
11:   }
12: }
```

Figure 5.13 Sequential multiplication of two matrices A and B.

range, and this method, which is executed by one of the pool's underlying threads, calculates the corresponding block and stores the result in the C matrix. In the main() function, after allocating the memory of the matrices in lines 43–45, the cells of the matrices A and B are randomly filled by the MatrixFillRandom() method. In the for loop, all the tasks are prepared, in line 55 the slice variable of each task is filled with index i, which is actually the desired thread of execution's ID. In lines 65–68, we wait for the conditional variable cv until all the threads are done, and after printing the values of the matrices to the output, the allocated memory regions are freed.

In the third example of this section, we calculate prime numbers in parallel. A first number is a natural number that is not divisible by any number except itself and 1. The only exception is the number 1, which is not included in these numbers. If a number is not natural and greater than 1, it is a compound. The abbreviation for these numbers is n. Sieve of Eratosthenes is a simple algorithm that can be used to find prime numbers between different integers. The discovery of this method is

```
 1: class ThreadPoolExample2 : public Object {
 2:    /*---------------------fields---------------*/
 3:    private: struct MethodInfo : public Object {
 4:       Float *A, *B, *C;
 5:       Int32 rows, columns, slice, methodNum;
 6:       Int32 *counter_addr;
 7:       Mutex *mutex;
 8:       ConditionVariable *cv;
 9:    };
10:    /*--------------------methods---------------*/
11:    private: static void MatrixMultiplyCallback(Object *state) {
12:       MethodInfo *info = (MethodInfo *)state;
13:       Float *A, *B ,*C;
14:       A = info->A; B = info->B; C = info->C;
15:       Int32 rows = info->rows;
16:       Int32 columns = info->columns;
17:       Int32 methodNum = info->methodNum;
18:       Int32 s = (Int32)info->slice;
19:       Int32 from = (s * rows)/methodNum;    // note that this 'slicing' works fine
20:       Int32 to = ((s + 1) * rows)/methodNum;  // even if rows(n) is not divisible by methodNum
21:       register Int32 i , j, k; Float temp;
22:       printf("computing slice %d (from row %d to %d)\n", s, from, to - 1);
23:       for(i = from ; i < to ; i++) {
24:          for(j = 0 ; j < rows ; j++) {
25:             temp = 0.0;
26:             for(k = 0 ; k < rows ; k++)
27:                temp += A[i*rows + k]*B[k*rows + j];
28:             C[i*rows + j] = temp;
29:          }
30:       }
31:       printf("finished slice %d\n", s);
32:       info->mutex->Lock();
33:       (*info->counter_addr)++; // Increment the counter value by its address
34:       if(*info->counter_addr == methodNum)
35:          info->cv->Signal(); // Singnal the main thread of all methods's completion.
36:       info->mutex->Unlock();
37:    }
38:    public: static int Parvicrursor_main(int argc, char *argv[]) {
39:       const Int32 methodNum = 10;
40:       ThreadPool pool = ThreadPool(methodNum, 10000); // Intilizes the thread pool instance.
41:       const Int32 rows = 2000, columns = 2000; // This example only works on square matrices, i.e., the n*n
matrices.
42:       MethodInfo methods[methodNum];
43:       Float *A = new Float[rows*columns];
44:       Float *B = new Float[rows*columns];
45:       Float *C = new Float[rows*columns];
46:       MatrixFillRandom(A, rows, columns);
47:       MatrixFillRandom(B, rows, columns);
48:       Mutex *mutex = new Mutex();
49:       ConditionVariable *cv = new ConditionVariable(mutex);
50:       Int32 counter = 0; // The main thread waits on the value of this shared counter.
```

Figure 5.14 Implementing the parallel multiplication of two matrices A and B based on the thread pools.

(Continued)

```
51:        for(register Int32 i = 0 ; i < methodNum ; i++) {
52:            methods[i].A = A;
53:            methods[i].B = B;
54:            methods[i].C = C;
55:            methods[i].slice = i;
56:            methods[i].rows = rows;
57:            methods[i].columns = columns;
58:            methods[i].methodNum = methodNum;
59:            methods[i].counter_addr = &counter;
60:            methods[i].mutex = mutex;
61:            methods[i].cv = cv;
62:            pool.QueueUserWorkItem(MatrixMultiplyCallback, &methods[i]);
63:        }
64:
65:        // Waits on counter until all methods complete.
66:        mutex->Lock();
67:        cv->Wait();
68:        mutex->Unlock();
69:
70:        MatrixPrint("A", A, rows, columns);
71:        MatrixPrint("B", B, rows, columns);
72:        MatrixPrint("C", C, rows, columns);
73:        delete A; delete B; delete C; delete mutex; delete cv;
74:        return 0;
75:    }
76: };
```

Figure 5.14 **(Continued) Implementing the parallel multiplication of two matrices A and B based on the thread pools.**

attributed to the ancient Greek scientist Eratosthenes. Let's assume that we want to look for prime numbers between 2 and an integer number n. First, we write integers from 2 to n in a row. The first prime number is equal to 2; below the number 2, we draw a line on all multiples of 2 (even numbers). The first number that remains is 3. Below it, we draw a line as a prime number and cross multiples of 3 out. The first remaining number is 5 (the number 4 has already been crossed out.). Below this number, we draw a line as a prime number and cross the rest of every other four out (numbers that are multiples of 5), and so on, until the end. All numbers that are not crossed out are prime. We use this simple mechanism to calculate prime numbers in parallel.

Figure 5.15 shows the parallel implementation of Eratosthenes sieve for calculating prime numbers based on a thread pool. To find all prime numbers from 2 to n, we must first list all the numbers in the prime array, then delete multiples of 2, then 3, and so on. Whatever is left at the end are prime numbers. The SieveCallback() method uses three main items stored in the MethodInfo structure as input arguments: the variable n, which indicates the upper range; the shared variable nextbase (this variable is shared via its address), which specifies the next

```
 1: class ThreadPoolExample3 : public Object {
 2:    /*--------------------fields----------------*/
 3:    private: struct MethodInfo : public Object {
 4:       Int32 n, methodNum;
 5:       Int32 *prime;
 6:       Int32 *nextbase;
 7:       Mutex *nextbaselock, *mutex;
 8:       Int32 *counter_addr;
 9:       ConditionVariable *cv;
10:    };
11:    /*--------------------methods---------------*/
12:    private: static void crossout(Int32 *prime, Int32 k, Int32 n) {
13:       for (Int32 i = k ; i*k <= n ; i++)
14:          prime[i*k] = 0;
15:    }
16:    private: static void SieveCallback(Object *state) {
17:       MethodInfo *info = (MethodInfo *)state;
18:       register Int32 lim, base;
19:       lim = Math::Sqrt(info->n); // no need to check multipliers bigger than sqrt(n)
20:       while(true) {
21:          info->nextbaselock->Lock();
22:          (*info->nextbase) += 2; // Increment two units to the counter value by its address.
23:          base = (*info->nextbase);
24:          info->nextbaselock->Unlock();
25:          if (base <= lim)  {
26:             // don't bother with crossing out if base is known to be
27:             // composite
28:             if (info->prime[base])
29:                crossout(info->prime, base, info->n);
30:          }
31:          else
32:             break;
33:       }
34:
35:       info->mutex->Lock();
36:       (*info->counter_addr)++; // Increment the counter value by its address
37:       if(*info->counter_addr == info->methodNum)
38:          info->cv->Signal(); // Singnal the main thread of all methods's completion.
39:       info->mutex->Unlock();
40:    }
41:    public: static int Parvicrursor_main(int argc, char *argv[]) {
42:       // Shared variables
43:       const Int32 methodNum = 100;
44:       const Int32 n = 100000000; // upper bound of range in which to find primes
45:       Int32 *prime = new Int32[n + 1];  // in the end, prime[i] = 1 if i prime, else 0
46:       Int32 nextbase = 1;  // next sieve multiplier to be used
47:       Mutex *nextbaselock = new Mutex();
48:
49:       for(Int32 i = 2 ; i <= n; i++)
50:          prime[i] = 1;
```

Figure 5.15 Parallel implementation of the Eratosthenes sieve for calculating prime numbers based on a thread pool.

(Continued)

```
51:        crossout(prime, 2, n);
52:
53:        // Intilises the thread pool instance.
54:        ThreadPool pool = ThreadPool(methodNum, 10000);
55:        MethodInfo methods[methodNum];
56:        Mutex *mutex = new Mutex();
57:        ConditionVariable *cv = new ConditionVariable(mutex);
58:        Int32 counter = 0; // The main thread waits on the value of this shared counter.
59:        for(register Int32 i = 0 ; i < methodNum ; i++) {
60:            methods[i].n = n;
61:            methods[i].prime = prime;
62:            methods[i].nextbaselock = nextbaselock;
63:            methods[i].methodNum = methodNum;
64:            methods[i].nextbase = &nextbase;
65:            methods[i].counter_addr = &counter;
66:            methods[i].mutex = mutex;
67:            methods[i].cv = cv;
68:            pool.QueueUserWorkItem(SieveCallback, &methods[i]);
69:        }
70:        // Waits on counter until all methods complete.
71:        mutex->Lock();
72:        cv->Wait();
73:        mutex->Unlock();
74:
75:        // Report results
76:        Int32 nprimes = 0;  // number of primes found
77:        for(Int32 i = 2 ; i <= n ; i++)
78:            if(prime[i])
79:                nprimes++;
80:        printf("the number of primes found was %d\n",nprimes);
81:        delete prime; delete nextbaselock; delete mutex; delete cv;
82:        return 0;
83:    }
84: };
```

Figure 5.15   (Continued) Parallel implementation of the Eratosthenes sieve for calculating prime numbers based on a thread pool.

number from where the coefficients must be eliminated; and the array pointer prime, which denotes whether the number has been eliminated or not. In every iteration of the while loop, a deletion multiplier is fetched for processing in the base variable, and then all base coefficients from the range 2 to n are removed. Updating the value of the nextbase shared variable is protected inside a Mutex object block.

The fourth and final example in this section is how to use the Barrier class coupled with the thread pool. In Figure 5.16, in line 32, the barrier object is instantiated with the desired number of threads, and in line 38, its reference is inserted into the thread pool's task queue within the for loop for all thread pool functions. In the MethodCallback() method, when the code execution reaches line 16 because the SignalAndWait() method has been invoked from the barrier object, the

```
 1: class ThreadPoolExample4 : public Object {
 2:     /*---------------------fields----------------*/
 3:     private: struct MethodInfo : public Object {
 4:         Int32 methodID, methodNum;
 5:         Barrier *barrier;
 6:         Int32 *counter_addr;
 7:         Mutex *mutex;
 8:         ConditionVariable *cv;
 9:     };
10:     /*--------------------methods---------------*/
11:     private: static void MethodCallback(Object *state) {
12:         MethodInfo *info = (MethodInfo *)state;
13:         printf("I'm thread %d at phase 1\n", info->methodID);
14:         Thread::Sleep(1000);
15:
16:         info->barrier->SignalAndWait();
17:
18:         printf("I'm thread %d at phase 2\n", info->methodID);
19:
20:         info->mutex->Lock();
21:         (*info->counter_addr)++; // Increments the counter value by its address
22:         if(*info->counter_addr == info->methodNum)
23:             info->cv->Signal(); // Signals the main thread of all methods' completion.
24:         info->mutex->Unlock();
25:     }
26:     public: static int Parvicrursor_main(int argc, char *argv[]) {
27:         const Int32 methodNum = 2;
28:         ThreadPool pool = ThreadPool(Environment::get_ProcessorCount()*4, 1000); // Initialises the thread
pool instance.
29:         MethodInfo methods[methodNum];
30:         Mutex *mutex = new Mutex();
31:         ConditionVariable *cv = new ConditionVariable(mutex);
32:         Barrier *barrier = new Barrier(methodNum);
33:         Int32 counter = 0; // The main thread waits on the value of this shared counter.
34:         for(Int32 i = 0 ; i < methodNum ; i++) {
35:             methods[i].methodID = i;
36:             methods[i].methodNum = methodNum;
37:             methods[i].counter_addr = &counter;
38:             methods[i].barrier = barrier;
39:             methods[i].mutex = mutex;
40:             methods[i].cv = cv;
41:             pool.QueueUserWorkItem(MethodCallback, &methods[i]);
42:         }
43:
44:         // Waits on counter until all methods complete.
45:         mutex->Lock();
46:         cv->Wait();
47:         mutex->Unlock();
48:
49:         delete mutex; delete cv; delete barrier;
50:         return 0;
51:     }
52: };
```

Figure 5.16   Using the `Barrier` class synchronisation in thread pools.

execution of the thread that runs this method stops. When all the threads reach this point, the execution of all the threads that were previously fallen asleep at this point (in line 16) is restored, and at this time the expression of phase 2 is printed in the output.

5.2.8 Low-Level Implementation of Threads in the Linux Operating System: Userspace Fibres

In the previous sections, we used the Thread class as the most essential structure for implementing concurrency and parallel processing algorithms on multi-processor systems based on the Parvicursor.NET Framework. This class itself has been implemented according to the POSIX multi-threading standard. In this section, we will take a brief look at how threads are implemented in the Linux operating system by using a multi-threading system call, as this abstraction provides powerful possibilities for designing higher-level multi-threading standards. In Linux, threads and processes are treated almost identically. Both are considered as tasks. The only difference is that the threads share the same memory space. In Linux, kernel threads are created by calling the clone() system. Figure 5.17 shows the prototype of the clone() system call definition. fn is a function pointer that is executed by clone(). The arg argument is passed to the fn function. When the function fn(arg) returns, the child process terminates. The child_stack argument specifies the location of stack used by the child process. The least significant byte of flags contains the termination signal number sent to the parent when the child dies. The flags argument may also get bitwise with zero or more constants to specify what is between the calling process and the child process. For example, if CLONE_VM is set, the calling process and the child process run in the same memory space. The best way to allocate stack memory is to use the system function mmap(), but for simplicity in this book we only use the malloc() function.

Figure 5.18 shows an example in which ten threads are created by the clone() function and the main() function waits until all of them complete their execution. The stack size of each thread is 64 KB, which is allocated to all threads by the malloc() function in lines 19–30. Threads are created in lines 33–39, this way of coding to create threads is very similar to how to use the Thread class. Because in most processors the stack grows downwards, adding a constant value of THREAD_STACK to the stack pointer of each thread in line 34 causes the stack in each thread to point to the highest address in the memory space. CLONE_SIGHAND tells the kernel that signals are shared between the child and parent process. In lines 43–50, we wait for the completion of each thread, the waitpid() system function here plays the same role as the Join() method of the Thread class. In the end, in lines 53–54, the space allocated by the malloc() function for each thread is freed by calling the free() function. Each thread performs the thread_proc() function. Line 14

```
1: int clone(int (*fn)(void *), void *child_stack, int flags, void *arg);
```

Figure 5.17   Prototype of the `clone()` system call definition.

```
 1: #include <malloc.h>
 2: #include <sys/types.h>
 3: #include <sys/wait.h>
 4: #include <signal.h>
 5: #include <sched.h>
 6: #include <stdio.h>
 7: #include <stdlib.h>
 8: #include <unistd.h>
 9: // 64kB stack
10: #define THREAD_STACK 1024*64
11: #define Thread_Num 10
12: // The child thread will execute this function
13: int thread_proc(void *arg) {
14:       printf("I'm child thread %d with pid %d\n", (int)arg, getpid());
15:       return 0;
16: }
17:
18: int main(int argc, char *argv[]) {
19:     void *stack[Thread_Num];
20:     pid_t pid[Thread_Num];
21:     int i;
22:
23:     // Allocate the stack
24:     for(i = 0 ; i < Thread_Num ; i++) {
25:        stack[i] = malloc(THREAD_STACK);
26:        if(stack[i] == NULL) {
27:           perror("malloc: could not allocate stack");
28:           exit(1);
29:        }
30:     }
31:
32:     printf("Creating children threads\n");
33:     for(i = 0 ; i < Thread_Num ; i++) {
34:       pid[i]= clone(&thread_proc, (char *)stack[i] + THREAD_STACK,
35:                  SIGCHLD | CLONE_FS | CLONE_FILES | CLONE_SIGHAND | CLONE_VM, (void *)i);
36:       if(pid[i] == -1) {
37:          perror("clone");
38:          exit(2);
39:       }
40:
41:     }
42:
43:     for(i = 0 ; i < Thread_Num ; i++) {
44:        // Wait for the child thread to exit
45:        pid[i] = waitpid(pid[i], 0, 0);
46:        if(pid[i] == -1) {
47:           perror("waitpid");
48:           exit(3);
49:        }
50:     }
51:
52:     // Wait for the children threads to exit
53:     for(i = 0 ; i < Thread_Num ; i++)
54:        free(stack[i]);
55:     printf("Child threads returned and stack was freed.\n");
56:
57:     return 0;
58: }
```

Figure 5.18   Creating threads based on the `clone()` system function.

uses the getpid() system function to print the current thread's ID to the output. The code for this example can be found in the "/Parvicursor/Parvicursor/ Samples/CloneThread" path.

What we have used so far for multi-threaded programming is based on pre-emptive scheduling and kernel threads. In pre-emptive multi-tasking, the operating system kernel can create an interrupt for one task and force it to switch its context to another task, the current task state is saved before the new task starts. Not only does this mechanism allow the scheduler to assign an active time slot reliably, but also the system to deal quickly with important external events such as input data, which may require immediate attention by one or more processes.

Contrary to the above is cooperative multi-tasking in which one thread voluntarily gives its execution to another thread. In this mechanism, the term *fibre* refers to threads. Fibre is a unit of execution that must be manually scheduled by the application. Fibres run in the contexts of the kernel threads that schedule them. Fibres are not scheduled exclusively. We must schedule a fibre by means of switching from one to another. Like threads, each fibre has a set of execution modes that can be run on the hardware: a user mode stack and a context (which includes the state of CPU registers when a fibre is switched).

Besides, fibres are lightweight. The operation for switching from one fibre to another is performed by several instructions to load and save the processor state without involving the operating system kernel. This means that if you have a lot of small tasks to do, fibres may be a better choice, as threads involve kernel calls and scheduler invocations. Fibres run in the time slot of the thread in which they are running, thereby avoiding context switches between a large number of threads with short blocking computations in the kernel. Eliminating synchronisation structures (such as spin locks and atomic operations) in in most cases eliminates the need for involving operating system scheduler and synchronisation primitives and increases efficiency. Simplicity in using fibres closely resembles using threads. Instead of having to write intricate code that tries to do multiple things at once, we write simple code that does just one thing and takes advantage of multiple fibres to do different works. Fibres are used in conjunction with non-blocking I/O methods. Fibres cannot employ multi-core processors without the use of pre-emptive threads; of course, N:M threading models can provide an alternative solution to this issue, which is discussed below.

By using fibres, we can implement highly customised algorithms for our domain-specific applications and operational needs. For example, we can have a pool of threads with the number of processors in our machine, each of which will be responsible for switching and scheduling between fibres. This approach leads to giving a lot of complexity and scheduling responsibilities to the programmer, which is called M:N threading. Finally, fibres can be used to implement dynamically scalable schedulers (especially for service-oriented network applications) and useful abstractions such as coroutines and agent-based simulators. Table 5.5 demonstrates the methods and constructor of the designed fibre class in the Parvicursor.NET Framework. The constructor of this class is very similar to the constructor of the Thread class. The start_routine function pointer specifies the address of the function that will be executed by the fibre object; the arg pointer specifies the input of this function when it is called.

Table 5.5 Methods and Constructor of the `Fibre` Class in Parvicursor.NET Framework

Name	Description
`Fibre(Long stackSize, void *(*start_routine) (void *), void *arg)`	Allocates a fibre object, assigns a stack, and sets the execution up to start at the address of the function specified by `start_routine`. This pointer does not schedule a fibre function.
`static void SwitchToFibre(const Fibre &from, const Fibre &to)`	This static method stores the `from` fibre's state information and restores the `to` fibre's state. This method can be called with a fibre created by a different thread. To perform this operation, you must use an appropriate synchronisation.
`static Fibre ConvertThreadToFibre()`	This static method converts the current thread into a fibre. We have to convert a thread into a fibre before we can schedule other fibres. Only fibres can run other fibres.
`static void ConvertFibreToThread()`	This static method converts the current fibre into a thread. It frees up resources allocated by the `ConvertThreadToFibre()` method. After invoking this method, fibre functions cannot be called from inside that thread.

At the end of this section, we take a look at two examples of using fibres. The code for these examples is available in the "/Parvicursor/Parvicursor/Samples/ Concurrency/Concurrency/Fibre" path. Figure 5.19 shows a simple example of creating two fibres and using a single function pointer by them. In the main() function in lines 26 and 27, two fibre objects are instantiated, the identifier of each fibre is specified as a number in the input argument of its function pointer, and also the value of zero for the stack size tells the Parvicursor.NET Framework that the default value should be used to allocate the stack space. Both fibres run the static fibre_ proc() method. By calling the ConvertThreadToFibre() method, in addition to storing the current state in a fibre (fib object), we provide the ability to change the main() function's fibre to fib1 by calling the SwitchToFibre() method from in line 30 (i.e., to jump to fib1 that executes the fibre_proc() method). The flow of code execution is now transferred to line 8. After converting the arg pointer to a fibreID variable type, we make an intended decision for which the fibre is currently running. For example, if the first fibre is running inside the infinite while loop, after printing a message to the output, we switch the context to the second fibre using the SwitchToFibre() method, so if fibreID is equal to 2, then we are in the second fibre and we issue a context switch to the first fibre in line 19.

In the second example, we describe the implementation of a finite state machine (FSM) in terms of fibres. An FSM is a mathematical model for designing computer programs, transmission protocols, and digital logic circuits. This computational model is composed of a set of states, a set of inputs, and a function that maps the ordered pair (input, state) to a new state, and the operations executed in each state. Suppose that we want to write a program that has three states. The program takes a character from the input and determines the next FSM state based on a

```
 1: static Fibre *fib;
 2: static Fibre *fib1;
 3: static Fibre *fib2;
 4:
 5: class FibreExample1 : public Object {
 6:     /*-------------------methods----------------*/
 7:     private: static void *fibre_proc(void *arg) {
 8:         Int32 fibreID = (Int32)arg;
 9:         if(fibreID == 1) {
10:             while(true) {
11:                 printf("I'm fibre %d\n", fibreID);
12:                 Fibre::SwitchToFibre(*fib1, *fib2);
13:                 Thread::Sleep(1000);
14:             }
15:         }
16:         if(fibreID == 2) {
17:             while(true) {
18:                 printf("I'm fibre %d\n", fibreID);
19:                 Fibre::SwitchToFibre(*fib2, *fib1);
20:                 Thread::Sleep(1000);
21:             }
22:         }
23:         return arg;
24:     }
25:     public: static int Parvicrursor_main(int argc, char *argv[]) {
26:         fib1 = new Fibre(0, fibre_proc, (void *)1);
27:         fib2 = new Fibre(0, fibre_proc, (void *)2);
28:
29:         fib = &Fibre::ConvertThreadToFibre();
30:         Fibre::SwitchToFibre(*fib, *fib1);
31:         Fibre::ConvertFibreToThread();
32:
33:         delete fib1;
34:         delete fib2;
35:         return 0;
36:     }
37: };
```

Figure 5.19   A simple example of two fibres running a shared function pointer.

lowercase letter (state 0), an uppercase letter (state 1) or a number (state 2). Figure 5.20 illustrates the FSM of this scenario. In the first run of the program, the program state is set to 0. For example, if in state 0 a character with a lowercase letter has been entered in the input, the next state will be zero, if the input is of a capital character, the next state will transition to state 1, and so forth. In either case, if the input character is @, the next state is Exit and the program terminates.

The implementation of this FSM comes in Figure 5.21 based on fibres. The FibreInfo structure stores global information accessible by all fibres as well as

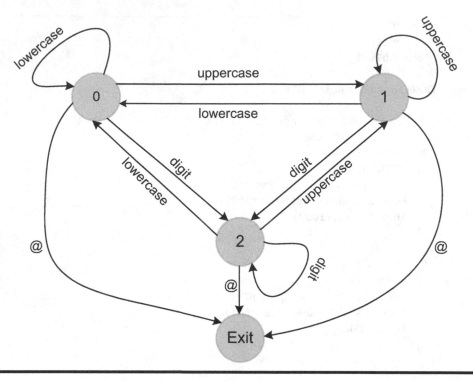

Figure 5.20   A sample finite state machine that is implemented using fibres.

specific fields (such as identifiers) of every fibre. In the main() function and lines 36–45, all fibres are instantiated. The stack size of every fibre (of which represents a state of the FSM) in this example is set to 4 KB. The mainFib object stores the fibre corresponding to the main() function; if the @ character is entered in the program, the execution of the program is transferred to line 49 (Exit state from FSM) and the program terminates. In line 46, by calling the SwitchToFibre() method, the program state is transferred to state 0 in line 13, which is executed by the fibre 0 via the fibre_proc() method. After reading a character using the getch() function and specifying the type of the entered character through the islower(), isupper(), or isdigit() functions, we decide what the next FSM state will be. For example, if we assume that an uppercase character is entered in the current state, we change the execution context in line 21 by calling the SwitchToFibre() method from the current fibre (whose identifier is fibreID) to the fibre 1 (which represents state 1).

5.2.9 A Practical Implementation of Synchronisation: Linux Futexes

In the previous sections, different synchronisation techniques were introduced through several classes such as Mutex, ConditionVariable, and Barrier. Since synchronisation is one of the most important topics in concurrent systems and operating systems for modern multi-core processors and has occupied a major part of this chapter, in this section we make an attempt to examine a real implementation

```
1: class FibreExample2 : public Object {
2:     /*-------------------fields---------------*/
3:     private: struct FibreInfo {
4:         Int32 fibreID;
5:         Fibre *mainFib;
6:         Fibre **fibs;
7:     };
8:     /*-------------------methods---------------*/
9:     private: static void *fibre_proc(void *arg) {
10:        FibreInfo *info = (FibreInfo *)arg;
11:        Int32 c;
12:        while(true) {
13:            printf("\n------\nCurrent state: %d\nEnter a charachter: ", info->fibreID);
14:            c = getch();
15:            printf("%c", c);
16:            if(islower(c)) {
17:                Fibre::SwitchToFibre(*info->fibs[info->fibreID], *info->fibs[0]);
18:                continue;
19:            }
20:            if(isupper(c)) {
21:                Fibre::SwitchToFibre(*info->fibs[info->fibreID], *info->fibs[1]);
22:                continue;
23:            }
24:            if(isdigit(c)) {
25:                Fibre::SwitchToFibre(*info->fibs[info->fibreID], *info->fibs[2]);
26:                continue;
27:            }
28:            if(c == '@')
29:                Fibre::SwitchToFibre(*info->fibs[info->fibreID], *info->mainFib);
30:            else
31:                printf("\nInvalid charachter");
32:        }
33:        return arg;
34:    }
35:    public: static int Parvicrursor_main(int argc, char *argv[]) {
36:        const Int32 FibNum = 3;
37:        FibreInfo infos[FibNum];
38:        Fibre **fibs = new Fibre*[FibNum];
39:        Fibre *mainFib = &Fibre::ConvertThreadToFibre();
40:        for(Int32 i = 0 ; i < FibNum ; i++) {
41:            infos[i].fibreID = i;
42:            infos[i].mainFib = mainFib;
43:            infos[i].fibs = fibs;
44:            fibs[i] = new Fibre(4*1024, fibre_proc, (void *)&infos[i]);
45:        }
46:        Fibre::SwitchToFibre(*mainFib, *fibs[0]);
47:        Fibre::ConvertFibreToThread();
48:
49:        printf("\nThe program is to terminate ...\n");
50:
51:        for(Int32 i = 0 ; i < FibNum ; i++)
52:            delete fibs[i];
53:        delete fibs;
54:        return 0;
55:    }
56: };
```

Figure 5.21 An implementation of a finite state machine relied upon fibres.

of synchronisation constructs briefly. For this purpose, we describe synchronisation in the Linux operating system based on the futex() system function. As a typical example, an implementation of the mutex abstraction through this function is detailed. The main purpose is to prepare the reader to design high-level synchronisation constructs with high flexibility, efficiency, and scalability. A very small number of programmers directly use this method for synchronisation in their programs.

A futex is made up of a kernel space wait queue that is connected to an aligned integer number. Multiple threads on the integer operate perfectly in userspace (with atomic primitives) and resort to relatively expensive system calls only to request operations on the wait queue. A futex-based programmed mutex (lock) will not use system calls unless when the mutex is contended. The implementation and operation of futexes are similar to the critical sections in the Windows operating system. Figure 5.22 defines the futex() system function's prototype. The uaddr argument must point to an aligned integer that holds the counter. The operation on this value is passed by the op argument to be executed. The state of a lock can be defined as 0 (unlocked) and 1 (locked). To acquire the lock, an atomic test-and-set instruction (like CAS) can be used to test 0 and set 1. In this case, the locking thread acquires the lock without contention. When the next thread tries to take over the lock, the test for zero will fail and there will be a need to involve the kernel. The blocking thread can then use the futex() system call with the FUTEX_WAIT opcode to put itself to sleep on the futex, which is carried out by passing the address of the futex state variable in the uaddr argument. To release the lock, its owner changes the lock mode to zero and issues the FUTEX_WAKE opcode, which wakes the blocked thread up to return to the userspace and acquire the lock.

Now, based on these explanations, we consider implementing a mutex. Figure 5.23 demonstrates a simple library to implement the mutex synchronisation construct. The functions Parvicursor_mutex_init() and Parvicursor_mutex_destroy(), by simply setting the value of the mutex pointer to zero, initialise and destroy the mutex pointer, respectively. In this implementation, the built-in functions of the GCC compiler such as __sync_val_compare_and_swap and __sync_fetch_and_sub are employed. The implementation of such built-in functions as CAS for x86 and x64 processors will be discussed in detail in Section 5.3. The futex() system call is realised directly by calling the syscall() function and passing the SYS_futex system call number. Figure 5.24 shows a typical example of using the designed mutex object. This is a generalised example of Figure 5.18 in which threads are created based on the clone() system call. The pieces of code shown by the three-dot symbol are omitted sections in the example within Figure 5.18. The shared variable counter is incremented between the Parvicursor_mutex_lock() and Parvicursor_mutex_unlock() functions, which have been placed to establish a mutual exclusion, within an infinite loop.

```
1: int futex(int *uaddr, int op, int val, const struct timespec *timeout, int *uaddr2, int val3);
```

Figure 5.22 Prototype of futex() system call definition.

```
1: #include <unistd.h>
2: #include <limits.h>
3: #include <sys/syscall.h>
4: #include <linux/futex.h>
5: typedef unsigned int volatile Parvicrursor_mutex_t;
6.
7: void Parvicrursor_mutex_init(Parvicrursor_mutex_t *mutex) {
8:    *mutex = 0;
9: }
10:
11: void Parvicrursor_mutex_destroy(Parvicrursor_mutex_t *mutex) {
12:    *mutex = 0;
13: }
14:
15: static inline void Parvicrursor_mutex_lock(Parvicrursor_mutex_t *mutex) {
16:    unsigned int c;
17:    if((c = __sync_val_compare_and_swap(mutex, 0, 1)) != 0) {
18:       do {
19:          if((c == 2) || __sync_val_compare_and_swap(mutex, 1, 2) != 0)
20:             syscall(SYS_futex, mutex, FUTEX_WAIT_PRIVATE, 2, NULL, NULL, 0);
21:       } while((c = __sync_val_compare_and_swap(mutex, 0, 2)) != 0);
22:    }
23: }
24:
25: static inline void Parvicrursor_mutex_unlock(Parvicrursor_mutex_t *mutex) {
26:    if(__sync_fetch_and_sub(mutex, 1) != 1) {
27:       *mutex = 0;
28:       syscall(SYS_futex, mutex, FUTEX_WAKE_PRIVATE, 1, NULL, NULL, 0);
29:    }
30: }
```

Figure 5.23   Implementation of the mutex synchronisation using the `futex()` system call in the Linux operating system and atomic hardware primitives.

5.3 Non-Blocking Synchronisation and Transactional Memory

5.3.1 Introduction

As stated in the previous sections and chapters, in traditional multi-threaded programming, a variety of mutual exclusion constructs such as critical sections, mutexes, and semaphores are used to synchronise and ensure that regions of code do not run concurrently. If a thread attempts to acquire a lock that was previously held by another thread, that thread will be blocked until the lock is released. When one thread is blocked, it can do no other work. In addition, in most operating systems, including microkernels, to achieve such a function, a context switch must be made from userspace to kernel in order to acquire the desired lock; if a lock is attempted

```
 1: ...
 2: static int counter = 0;
 3: static Parvicrursor_mutex_t mutex;
 4: // The child thread will execute this function
 5: int thread_proc(void *arg) {
 6:    while(true) {
 7:        Parvicrursor_mutex_lock(&mutex);
 8:        counter++;
 9:        Parvicrursor_mutex_unlock(&mutex);
10:        printf("I'm child thread %d with pid %d counter %d\n", (int)arg, getpid(), counter);
11:    }
12:    return 0;
13: }
14:
15: int main(int argc, char *argv[]) {
16:    Parvicrursor_mutex_init(&mutex);
17:    ...
18:    Parvicrursor_mutex_destroy(&mutex);
19:    return 0;
20: }
```

Figure 5.24   An example using the designed mutex relied on futexes in a multi-threaded application.

to be acquired by multiple threads many times (namely, in a highly contended environment, as stated in Chapter 4), context switching overheads become very serious.

In addition, as noted in Chapter 4, the use of traditional blocking synchronisation methods poses several problems, such as deadlock, contention, and priority inversion, especially in highly concurrent environments. Using locks also creates a trade-off between coarse-grained synchronisation, which greatly reduces parallelism, and fine-grained synchronisation, which requires careful design and increases locking overhead and is prone to faults.

Two very popular methods that look at thread synchronisation from a totally different angle, which are much more efficient than mutual exclusion methods, include non-blocking synchronisation algorithms and transactional memory (TM). In the following, we will examine the first method thoroughly and then take a brief look at the second method.

5.3.2 Non-Blocking Synchronisation Algorithms

Non-blocking synchronisation is a multi-threaded programming model that avoids the nature of blocking and the problems stated for mutual exclusion. In turn, different synchronisation methods are used, which aim to provide certain progress guarantees even if some threads are arbitrarily delayed for a long time. This method is primarily employed to implement concurrent data structures such as stacks, queues, linked lists, and hash tables. Designing non-blocking concurrent data structures are much more difficult than their sequential counterparts, which are developed based on blocking synchronisation constructs but can be more efficient in the presence of high contention between threads.

As mentioned, non-blocking implementations are exploited to overcome the many problems associated with the use of locks. To formalise this idea, several non-blocking progress conditions are discussed in the literature, such as wait-freedom, lock-freedom, and obstruction-freedom.

- In a wait-free operation, each running thread is guaranteed to complete its operation, regardless of the speed of execution of other threads. Wait freedom ensures the absence of livelock and starvation.
- A lock-free operation ensures that a number of operations are completed after a finite number of steps. Lock freedom guarantees the absence of livelock, but not starvation.
- An obstruction-free operation is guaranteed to be completed within a finite number of its own steps after interfering with a collision from another operation.

Clearly, wait-freedom is a stronger condition than lock-freedom, and lock-freedom is instead stronger than obstruction-freedom. However, all of these conditions are strong enough to prevent the use of blocking structures such as locks. Whilst stronger progress conditions seem desirable, implementations that create weaker guarantees are generally simpler, more efficient in most cases, and easier to design and validate as well. It is difficult to argue about the correctness of concurrent programs because all possible interactions between running threads must be considered simultaneously. This is especially true for non-blocking algorithms in which threads interact in subtle ways through dynamically allocated data structures. Other advantages of non-blocking synchronisation algorithms are as follows:

- Non-blocking synchronisation minimises interference between process scheduling and synchronisation. For example, the highest-priority process can access a synchronised data structure without being delayed or blocked by a lower-priority process. Compared to blocking synchronisation, a low-priority process holding a lock can delay a higher-priority process, effectively neutralising the process schedule. Blocking synchronisation can also cause a process to be delayed by another process holding a lock that involves a page fault or a cache miss. This delay can be hundreds of thousands of cycles for a page fault. Non-blocking synchronisation also forms a lock convoy.
- Non-blocking synchronisation allows synchronised code to be executed anywhere, for example executable code at an interrupt or asynchronous signal handler without the risk of deadlock because synchronisation is handled by hardware.
- Non-blocking synchronisation aims at fault tolerance. They only allow a small inconsistency window (a window over which a data structure is in an inconsistent state). By contrast, in lock-based synchronisation methods, the inconsistency window may surround the entire locked critical section. These larger critical sections and lock protocols also increase the risk of deadlock or failure to release locks on certain code paths.

- Non-blocking synchronisation can reduce interrupt latencies. Systems that perform blocking synchronisation can avoid disabling interrupts for long periods of time. Instead, interrupts can make progress, and recently running operations will be re-attempted. Blocking algorithms dynamically give the system the ability to make decisions about a task with higher priority.
- Non-blocking algorithms support system maintainability. Independently designed modules can be combined without knowledge of their internal details (because synchronisation is universally handled by hardware based on the architectural specifications of a processor for all tasks).
- Non-blocking synchronisation increases the overall throughput of the system by allowing processes to proceed even if a single process modifying a shared data structure is delayed. It allows synchronisation even where mutual exclusion is prohibited due to the need to resolve confinement issue. (The confinement issue requires a system to suspend a program during its execution so that it cannot communicate with anyone other than its caller. Mutual exclusion on a shared resource provides a mechanism by which readers can modulate as a signal to establish a covert channel behind the writer, even if the information flow is unidirectional; in a non-blocking algorithm with the unidirectional flow of information, readers have no way of signalling the writer [1].

In the following, we will study in detail how non-blocking algorithms are implemented, and, as a result, the reader will have the ability to step into this attractive and promising avenue in terms of research and production. We first look at how a low-level non-blocking synchronisation routine is built on hardware synchronisation primitives for x86 and x64 processor architectures on Unix-like operating systems (such as Linux) and Windows. Then, based on this implemented single routine, we design and implement a counter, a stack (designed by the authors of this book), a dynamic memory allocator (designed by the authors of this book), and an array list (published using an existing algorithm). In this way, we will address many of the challenges that we faced during the implementation of these data structures.

The hardware primitive used here is the atomic compare-and-swap (CAS) operation shown in Figure 4.23. Let's first modify the definition prototype of the `compare_and_swap` function and then implement it in the assembly language. Figure 5.25 shows this prototype in line 9 for 32-bit and 64-bit x86 and x64 processors (such as Intel or AMD processors) for the Windows operating system (in the text of

```
1: // Define the long data type for x86 and x64 architectures targeting the Windows OS.
2: #if defined _M_IX86
3:    typedef signed long Long;
4: #else if (defined _M_X64)
5:    typedef signed long long Long;
6: #endif
7:
8: // The C's prototype of the function Parvicrursor_AtomicCompareAndSwap().
9: static inline bool Parvicrursor_AtomicCompareAndSwap(void volatile *accum, void volatile *dest, Long newval);
```

Figure 5.25 The definition prototype of the `compare_and_swap` function used in this book.

the book, we only describe the details of the implementation of this function for the Microsoft Visual C++ compiler). All the code for implementing this function on the Linux operating system, which is compiled using GCC, is also available in the "/Parvicursor/Parvicursor/atomic" path from the companion resources of this book (moreover, the implementation of a cross-platform CAS is available in this path and average readers can easily understand the assembly codes through its annotations). In this function, if the values pointed by the accum and dest pointers are equal, the value of newval is placed in the address of dest pointer and this function returns a value of true; otherwise, if these two values are inequal, or if another thread is updating the dest location, the value in the address of dest pointer is copied into the address of accum pointer and returns a value of false.

Since CAS function works on addresses in memory, this function must be used on 32-bit systems on values and pointers of four bytes, and 64-bit systems on values and pointers with eight-byte length, which in fact is indicative of the length of the address space that can be accessed by processes and threads. The Long data type for this purpose in x86 and x64 processors is defined as signed long and signed long long in Figure 5.25 using C pre-processors. Since the type of both accum and dest pointers is defined as void in the definition of CAS function, the compiler during the translation of C or C++ language codes based on the platform for which the code is compiled takes the length of the void data type as four or eight bytes into account. The inline keyword instructs the compiler to replace the contents of the CAS function directly where it is called, thus avoiding the overhead due to frequent function calls.

It is essential to explain the role of the volatile keyword in the CAS function prototype because in most textbooks of the C programming language, the role of this keyword is described by merely one or two lines. This keyword has special properties related to code optimisation by the compiler and threading. This keyword tells the compiler to avoid any optimisations to the guarded by it that assume the values of the variables cannot be changed on their own. In one sentence, this keyword prevents the compiler from optimising the code containing the volatile objects. A volatile variable should be to be declared volatile whenever its value could change unexpectedly. When using the CAS function, since the two addresses dest and accum are accessed randomly and indefinitely by multiple threads, they must be declared volatile.

With these principles in hand, we now implement the Parvicursor_ AtomicCompareAndSwap function in assembly code for 32-bit and 64-bit Windows operating systems. Figures 5.26 and 5.27 show this implementation. From lines 10 to 32 of Figure 5.26, the implementation of this function for 32-bit x86 processors is seen as an inline assembly code. Inline assembly is a C-compiler feature that allows very low-level code written in assembly language to be embedded in C or C++ codes. This embedding is commonly used for a variety of purposes, such as improving program performance, reducing memory requirements, and controlling hardware. This method likewise allows us to embed assembly language instructions directly into our program's codes without additional assembly and linking steps. An inline assembly is built into the compiler, so there is no need to use a separate assembler like MASM for Windows or NASM for Linux. In line 13, the address of the accum variable is loaded into the edx register. In line 14, the value of variable accum is loaded into the eax register. The cmpxchg instruction, which is made atomic using the atomic lock

```
 1: /*
 2:    The C's prototype of the Parvicrursor_AtomicCompareAndSwap function for x64 architectures.
 3:    In x64 architectures, use the assembly file atomic_x64.asm for the following CAS function in Windows OS.
 4:    We did this because Microsoft C++ Compiler for x64 architectures does not support assembly inlining.
 5: */
 6: extern "C" inline bool Parvicrursor_AtomicCompareAndSwap_x64(void volatile *accum, void volatile
*dest, Long newval);
 7:
 8: static inline bool Parvicrursor_AtomicCompareAndSwap(void volatile *accum, void volatile*dest, Long
newval)
 9: {
10:
11: #ifdef _M_IX86
12:    __asm {
13:        mov edx,accum       // Load the address of the accum variable into edx.
14:        mov eax,[edx]       // Load the value of the accum variable into eax.
15:        mov ebx,dest        // Load the address of the dest variable into ebx.
16:        mov ecx,newval      // Load the value of the newval variable into ecx.
17:        lock cmpxchg [ebx],ecx // Atomic compare and exchange between [ebx] and ecx.
18:        jne Unsuccessful    // If the values are not equal or the operation was failed
19:                            //   due to concurrent access of threads, then jump if ZF=0.
20:        mov eax,1           // Here, we must fill eax with the true values due to the successful
21:                            // operation of the cmpxchg instruction.
22:        jmp End
23:        // Don't call the ret instruction from the inline assembly, otherwise you'll skip the
24:        // epilog code that the compiler puts at the end of the function to clean the stack.
25:
26: Unsuccessful:
27:        mov [edx],eax       // Copy the eax content (the value of the location pointed by the dest)
28:                            // within the address of the pointer accum.
29:        mov eax,0           // Here, we must fill eax with the value false due to the unsuccessful
30:                            // operation of the cmpxchg instruction and return with result in eax.
31: End:
32:    }
33: #elif defined _M_X64
34:    return Parvicrursor_AtomicCompareAndSwap_x64(accum, dest, newval);
35: #else
36: #error Parvicrursor_AtomicCompareAndSwap function is only compiled for x86/x64 CPU architectures.
37: #endif
38: }
```

Figure 5.26 Implementation of the `Parvicursor_AtomicCompareAndSwap` function for x86 and x64 architectures used in this book based on the MASM assembly language.

prefix, performs an exchange-and-swap operation by comparing the value in the location of the address stored in the ebx register (which holds the address of dest pointer) and the ecx register value (which stores the value of the newval variable in itself). The result of this operation is stored by the processor in the ZF flag as a bit, in line 18; if this operation fails, a jump is made to line 26, which contains the label Unsuccessful. If the cmpxchg instruction succeeds in line 20, the value 1, which is true, returns as a value inside the eax register. If the cmpxchg operation in line 27 fails, we copy the contents of the eax register (which contains the current value of the dest pointer, which is atomically filled by the processor) into the location to where the edx register points (which is actually the address of the accum pointer)

```
 1: PUBLIC Parvicrursor_AtomicCompareAndSwap_x64
 2:
 3: .code
 4: Parvicrursor_AtomicCompareAndSwap_x64 PROC uses rdx
 5:    ;The Microsoft x64 calling convention (for long mode on x86-64) takes advantage of additional register
 6:    ; space in the AMD64/Intel 64 platform. The registers RCX, RDX, R8, R9 are used for integer and pointer
 7:    ; arguments (in that order left to right), and XMM0, XMM1, XMM2, XMM3 are used for floating point arguments.
 8:    ; Additional arguments are pushed onto the stack (right to left). Integer return values (similar to x86) are
 9:    ; returned in RAX if 64 bits or less. Floating point return values are returned in XMM0. Parameters less than 64
10:    ; bits long are not zero extended; the high bits contain garbage.
11:
12:    mov rax,[rcx] ; Load the value of the accum variable into rax. The rcx register contains the address of the
accum.
13:    lock cmpxchg [rdx],r8  ; The r8 register contains the value of newval and rdx contains the address of the
dest.
14:    jne Unsuccessful     ; Jump if ZF=0
15:    mov rax,1
16:    ret
17:
18: Unsuccessful:
19:    mov [rcx],rax  ;Copy the rax content into the location pointed by accum.
20:    mov rax,0
21:    ret
22:
23: Parvicrursor_AtomicCompareAndSwap_x64 ENDP
24:
25: End
```

Figure 5.27   Assembly implementation of the `Parvicursor_AtomicCompareAndSwap_x64` function for 64-bit x64 processors.

and the function returns by filling a zero value (which indicates `false` value) into the `eax` register. It is worth noting that the return value of a function in the MASM's inline assembly structure (whether a numeric value or the address of a variable) must be placed inside the `eax` register in the x86 architecture.

We now consider the implementation of the `Parvicursor_Atomic-CompareAndSwap_x64` function for 64-bit x64 architectures. This implementation is very different from what was stated for the 32-bit x86 architecture. In particular, on a 64-bit Windows operating system, it is not possible to use an inline assembly via the Microsoft Visual C++ compiler (such a problem does not exist for GCC compiler, and we implemented the CAS function for the Linux operating system based on inline assembly). Microsoft's abandonment of support for inline assembly coding for 64-bit platforms appears to further simplify the task of optimisation and development of newer versions of the C++ compiler.

Therefore, to implement a CAS function, you must either have intrinsic functions [2] (intrinsic functions are those whose implementation is handled by the compiler. They replace a sequence of automatically generated instructions to call the main function in the code, similar to an inline function), or link the external assembly files (by compiling the assembly file, an object file is generated that is linked to the output executable using a linker program). According to the prototype of the `Parvicursor_AtomicCompareAndSwap` function definition, we use the second method, which in addition to being fully compatible with the concepts stated for implementing the CAS function based on inline assembly and mentions interesting points about the 64-bit processor architecture for a better understanding of the reader.

Figure 5.27 shows the implementation of the CAS function in an external assembly code for x64 platforms. As can be seen, this code is very different from the inline assembly code of the CAS function for 32-bit x86 architectures. Since the number of CPU registers in x64 architectures is very large (the number of registers is 16, including, rax, rbx, rcx, rdx, rsi, rdi, rbp, rsp, and r8 to r15 registers), so the function calling convention is faster and more different than their x86 counterparts. In 32-bit x86 architectures, the calling convention describes the calling code interface. One of the most important parts of this agreement is how parameters are passed when calling a function, pushed on the stack, placed in registers, or a combination of both. Since the number of registers in x64 architectures is large, the stack space usage can be completely ignored, and when calling a function, a number of its arguments can be placed directly into registers. For example, in a 64-bit Windows operating system, up to four input arguments of a function for integer values or pointer addresses are inserted into the four registers rcx, rdx, r8, and r9 from left to the right side, and if there are more arguments, then more pushing on the stack is used. In Unix-style operating systems, calling convention benefits from six registers rdi, rsi, rdx, rcx, r8, and r9 for integer values or pointer addresses. Based on a simple experiment done on the GCC compiler for x64 platforms, we obtained a 1.4- to-1.5-fold performance increase on the same machine with the same C language code for a function call with two input arguments, indicating that the x64 platforms have taken an important step forward. In addition, the address space of 64-bit architectures is a maximum of 2^{64} as compared to 2^{32} for 32-bit processors.

After compiling the assembly code shown in Figure 5.27 (which is available in the "/Parvicursor/Parvicursor/atomic/atomic_x64.asm" path from the companion resources in this book), an object file is created, which must eventually be linked with the main executable program by a linker. For this purpose, when using the function written in assembly language in C codes, the definition prototype of this function should be declared as shown in line 6 of Figure 5.26. The extern "C" expression tells the compiler that the marked function must be compiled in a C style to combine with the implementation in the external assembly, and, in fact, this function has a C linkage. The value of the newval variable and the addresses of accum and dest pointers are set by C compiler to the three registers rcx, rdx, and r8, respectively. The implementation description of the Parvicursor_AtomicCompareAndSwap_x64 function written in the assembly language is the same as the implemented function in Figure 5.26; so, we will refrain from re-explanation. Now that the CAS function is fully implemented, we can develop several non-blocking algorithms for concurrent data structures. All code for these algorithms is available in the "/Parvicursor/Samples/LockFree" path.

Before giving examples of lock-free algorithms that leverage the developed CAS function, it is worthwhile to briefly address one of the key problems that you must bear in mind when designing such algorithms. Of course, all the examples described below do not suffer from this problem. When using the CAS function to design a lock-free algorithm, a problem called ABA may occur, so non-blocking algorithms must be designed to be ABA-free. This problem occurs when a thread reads an A

```
 1: // A simple, straightforward, lock-free counter.
 2: class LockFreeCounter : public Object
 3: {
 4:     /*--------------------fields---------------*/
 5:     private: Long volatile count;
 6:     /*--------------------methods---------------*/
 7:     // LockFreeCounter Class constructor.
 8:     public: LockFreeCounter();
 9:     // Gets the current value of the count variable.
10:     public: inline Long get_Count();
11:     // Incerements the count variable.
12:     public: inline void Increment();
13:     // Decrements the count variable.
14:     public: inline void Decrement();
15:     // Gets the current value of the count variable and increments it.
16:     public: inline Long get_Count_And_Increment();
17:     // Gets the current value of the count variable and decrements it.
18:     public: inline Long get_Count_And_Decrement();
19: };
```

Figure 5.28   Prototype definition of the lock-free counter class.

value from a shared location, and then other threads change that location to a different value, say B, and then change it to A.

The first, very simple lock-free (non-blocking) algorithm is to implement a counter based on the CAS function. Figure 5.28 shows the prototype of the counter class's definition. Since the variable count must be updated or accessed by the CAS function, we define it as volatile. The two main methods of this class are Increment() and Decrement(), which add or subtract a one to the count variable. In a blocking implementation, these two functions' bodies must be placed inside a critical section such as a mutex, which, as mentioned, has many disadvantages and overheads. Figure 5.29 illustrates the non-blocking implementation of these two methods. In the counter class's constructor, the count variable is filled by a value of zero for the first time. For an easier understanding of the implementation of the Increment() method, first, suppose that only a single thread has invoked it. It is important to note that since the first argument of the CAS function is defined as volatile, the volatile keyword is added to the temp1 variable in line 7 of Figure 5.29 as well. The value of temp1 is chosen to be -10 before coming at the loop in line 10 so that it is not equal to the value of the count variable when entering this method, and this makes the code execution flow to enter the while loop.

Since these two values are not equal, the CAS function sets the current value of the count variable to temp1, and in line 11 the temp2 value is added to this read value, and the loop continues; this time because the count and temp1 values are equal, the CAS function places the temp2 value into the address of count variable, and the code execution flow jumps out of the while loop. Now suppose that two or more threads invoke the Increment() method concurrently, since in this example only one location of memory is accessed and modified by the CAS function, so if

```
1: LockFreeCounter::LockFreeCounter() {
2:    count = 0;
3: }
4:
5: void LockFreeCounter::Increment() {
6:
7:    Long volatile temp1 = -10;
8:    Long temp2 = -10;
9:
10:    while(!Parvicrursor_AtomicCompareAndSwap(&temp1, &count, temp2)) {
11:        temp2 = temp1 + 1;
12:    }
13: }
14:
15: void LockFreeCounter::Decrement() {
16:
17:    Long volatile temp1 = -10;
18:    Long temp2 = -10;
19:
20:    while(!Parvicrursor_AtomicCompareAndSwap(&temp1, &count, temp2)) {
21:        temp2 = temp1 - 1;
22:    }
23: }
```

Figure 5.29 Lock-free implementation of the `Increment()` and `Decrement()` methods of the counter class.

the CAS function fails due to concurrent access to multiple threads, the `while` loop repeats until the value of `temp2` variable is successfully and indivisibly placed into the address of `count` variable. Implementing the rest of the lock-free counter class's methods is available in the "`/Parvicursor/Parvicursor/Samples/LockFree`" path.

Now let's consider implementing a lock-free stack. A stack is an abstract last-in first out (LIFO) data and a linear data structure. A stack can contain any abstract data type as an element and has two fundamental operations called `push` and `pop`. The `push` operation adds a new item to the top of the stack. If the stack is full and does not have enough space to accept a new item, in the simplest case the `push` operation can return a `false` value to indicate the stack is full. The `pop` operation removes an item from the top of the stack; if the stack is empty, a `false` value returns indicating that the stack is empty. The following is an implementation of a lock-free concurrent stack that relies on a doubly linked list. Figure 5.30 shows our designed data structure. In this implementation, to separate the logic of the proposed algorithm from memory operations, we now omit to describe dynamic memory allocation and assume that the stack elements have already been allocated, and, consequently, we discuss an implementation of a bounded stack (hereinafter, this problem is considered in full, and a lock-free dynamic memory allocator will be designed).

In this doubly linked list, the `next` and `prev` references point respectively to a successor node and a predecessor node of each element (or node) of the stack.

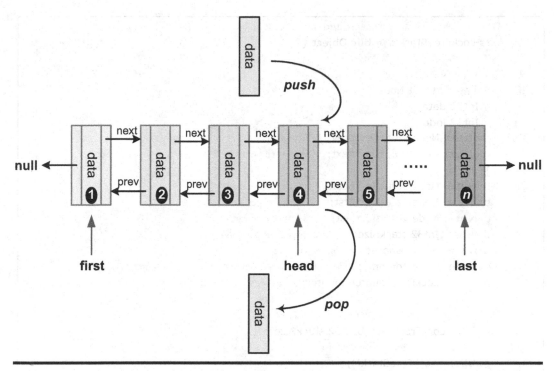

Figure 5.30   A specialised data structure designed as a doubly linked list to implement the lock-free stack.

For simplicity, we suppose that each node stores an integer data type. The first node points to the beginning and the last node to the end of the doubly linked list. n indicates the length of the bounded stack. The accompanying head reference points to the end of our main stack from where either a push or a pop operation is always performed. The stack is full when the head reference points to last, and the stack is empty when the prev field of the head reference points to null; otherwise, the stack is half full and the head pointer is located somewhere between the address of the first and last pointers. Figure 5.31 shows the prototype of the lock-free stack class definition. The PreAllocate() method is used in the constructor of this class to allocate the doubly linked list data structure. Figure 5.32 shows a lock-free implementation of the Push() and Pop() methods. The reader can refer to the "/Parvicursor/Parvicursor/Samples/LockFree" path to see the implementation of the rest of the methods for this class.

Since the head pointer's location only changes in this lock-free implementation, this pointer is used in the CAS function. The first time that line 4 executes, the current value of the head is read and placed into the current pointer; if the pointer is null, then the stack is empty, and the head address must be updated to the first node. Otherwise, if the next node of current is not null, the value of the temp variable is changed to the next node of current, and in the next iteration of the while loop, this value replaces the previous pointer of head. At this point, head points to a new location on the right-hand side of the stack. Because in this operation only one memory location is updated, in concurrent access of two or more

```
1: //The lock-free stack is implemented as a doubly linked list.
2: class LockFreeStack : public Object {
3:     /*---------------------fields----------------*/
4:     // The node definition.
5:     private: struct Node {
6:         Int32 data;
7:         Int32 index;
8:         struct Node volatile *prev; // The predecessor node with respect to this node.
9:         struct Node volatile *next; // The successor node with respect to this node.
10:    };
11:    private: Node volatile *head; // The head pointer.
12:    private: Node volatile *first; // The first pointer.
13:    private: Node volatile *last; // The last pointer.
14:    private: Int32 stackSize; // The stackSize is equivalent to the n.
15:    private: bool disposed; // For destructor use.
16:    private: Node *dummy; // A dummy node used in the stack implementation.
17:    private: LockFreeCounter counter; // Stores the number of elements in the stack.
18:    /*---------------------methods----------------*/
19:    // LockFreeStack Class constructor.
20:    public: LockFreeStack(UInt32 stackSize);
21:    // LockFreeStack Class destructor.
22:    public: ~LockFreeStack();
23:    // Preallocates the bounded doubly linked list.
24:    private: void PreAllocate();
25:    // Deallocates the bounded doubly linked list.
26:    private: void DeAllocate();
27:    // Inserts an element at the top of the stack.
28:    // This method is an O(1) operation.
29:    public: bool Push(Int32 data);
30:    // Removes and returns the element at the top of the stack.
31:    // This method is an O(1) operation.
32:    public: bool Pop(Out Int32 *data);
33:    // Gets the number of elements available in the stack.
34:    public: Long get_Count();
35: };
```

Figure 5.31   Prototype definition of the lock-free stack.

threads to the head pointer, this loop is executed atomically and there is no need to prove the functional correctness of the Push() method. In the Pop() method, some mechanisms are performed, but the difference is that this method uses the prev reference of the stack elements, using the CAS function shown between lines 18 and 29. In the Pop() method, the return value of the integer type is placed into the pointer of the data argument. The Out parameter in the Pop() method definition is just an empty predefined macro, which means that the argument is an output, not an input. The implementation of a test class (LockFreeStackTest class) to check the functionality of our lock-free stack can be found in the file "LockFreeStack/

```
 1: bool LockFreeStack::Push(Int32 data) {
 2:    Node volatile *temp = null;
 3:    Node volatile *current = dummy;
 4:    while(!Parvicrursor_AtomicCompareAndSwap(&current, &head, (Long)temp)) {
 5:       if(current == null) // The beginning of the stack was reached.
 6:          temp = first;
 7:       else {
 8:          if(current->next == null)
 9:             return true; // The stack is full.
10:          temp = current->next;
11:       }
12:       temp->data = data;
13:    }
14:    counter.Increment();
15:    return false; // The stack is not full.
16: }
17:
18: bool LockFreeStack::Pop(Out Int32 *data) {
19:    Node volatile *temp = null;
20:    Node volatile *current = dummy;
21:    while(!Parvicrursor_AtomicCompareAndSwap(&current, &head, (Long)temp)) {
22:       if(current == null)
23:          return false; // The stack is empty.
24:       *data = current->data;
25:       temp = current->prev;
26:    }
27:    counter.Decrement();
28:    return true; // The stack is not empty.
29: }
```

Figure 5.32 **Lock-free implementation of the** Push() **and** Pop() **methods of the stack class.**

LockFreeStack.h," where two threads named pusher and popper constantly invoke the Push() and Pop() methods for an object instance of the stack class simultaneously.

As stated in the lock-free stack design, we did not use dynamic memory allocation in the Push() and Pop() methods, and instead employed a pre-allocated data structure. In this section, we address the issue of concurrent dynamic memory allocation, and design and implement a memory allocator with fixed-size blocks for use in non-blocking concurrent systems such as lock-free data structures.

Dynamic memory management routines (malloc and free) are heavily used in C and C++ applications. This pair of routines are considered sufficiently fast and without performance bottlenecks for sequential programs. However, the dynamic memory allocator may severely degrade the performance of multi-threaded applications if it is not scalable [3]. To create a safe execution in multi-threaded environments, current allocators avail of mutual exclusion locks in a variety of ways, ranging from the use of a single lock wrapped around the malloc and free functions, to the distributed use of locks in order to let more concurrency and higher scalability. Using locks, in addition to the problems stated due to mutual exclusion, imposes limitations on efficiency, availability, robustness, and programmability. A desirably alternative method but challenging for achieving multi-threaded safety is lock-free synchronisation. First, let's look at why lock-free synchronisation makes dynamic memory management too difficult. The key problem is that a memory block (such as a node in a linked list) cannot be freed unless we can guarantee that no thread will subsequently modify that block. Otherwise, a thread might modify the memory block with potentially dangerous consequences after it has already been reallocated for another purpose. In those data structures that use locks, a common pattern is to ensure that a thread can obtain a pointer to a particular block only after it has been locked, and this warrants that there is only one active pointer to that block. Conversely, in lock-free data structures, it may be hard for a thread whilst releasing a block to ensure that no other thread has that pointer in a local variable. There are several benefits to using a non-blocking synchronisation in the design of a memory allocator, including below:

- To provide a general-purpose memory allocator for use in lock-free algorithms and data structures that employ dynamic memory.
- To improve scalability in highly contended concurrent systems, especially where the number of running threads exceeds the number of processors.
- To increase fault tolerance whilst the failure of one thread cannot block the progress of other threads.

In the following, we describe the design and implementation of a lock-free memory allocator. To reduce the complexity of a comprehensive allocator with arbitrarily variable size of data (because it is outside the scope of this book), we present a fixed-size allocator based on a memory pool model. A memory pool is a technique of pre-allocating a number of blocks of the same size that provides dynamic memory allocation comparable to the `malloc` function. A memory pool is a memory allocation with constant runtime and no memory fragmentation (memory fragmentation takes place when most of the memory is allocated to a large number of blocks or non-contiguous chunks, which leaves a high percentage of the whole memory unallocated, but this memory becomes unusable for most scenarios). Using a pair of `malloc` and `free` functions, when memory is severely fragmented, memory allocations are likely to take longer because the memory allocator has to do more to find suitable space for the new object. To design a dynamic memory allocator relied on a memory pool, there are at least four objectives that must be met:

- Requires a large contiguous memory block. This block can be allocated in different ways in an operating system such as heaps (e.g., calling the traditional `malloc` function) or by file mapping based on the `mmap` system function in Unix-style operating systems.
- Requires an algorithm to allocate the memory unit to the program code from the memory block. This is a non-trivial task and is discussed in great detail in operating system textbooks. For the implementation of a memory pool in this book, we divide the memory blocks into equally sized units.
- Furthermore, an algorithm must be considered to reclaim the memory unit from the program code. Exactly the same issue that is associated with the allocation of the memory unit.
- A more fundamental issue in designing a dynamic memory allocator is the synchronisation issue. Standard system memory allocators use a mutex to prevent

simultaneous access to the allocator's data structures and to maintain the consistency of these structures. Locking a mutex invokes only a handful of atomic instructions, and when there is no lock conflict, it is not accounted as a performance problem. But on multiple processors and multi-core platforms, multiple threads invoke the memory allocator simultaneously, which leads to spending a lot of processing time in performing context switches. Even if the threads work autonomously in an application (each thread is only accessing objects created by itself) and therefore do not require synchronisation, there is still only one memory allocator, and this results in a lot of conflict between threads. The result is that instead of increasing the expected linear performance, the addition of processors leads to an exponential decline in performance. Therefore, using a lock-free algorithm in designing a memory allocator on top of a memory pool is critical.

Figure 5.33 shows the data structure designed for the memory allocator based on our memory pool. A singly linked list is used to structure and organise memory slots. Each node in this list is called a `Header`, and its `next` reference points to the next node. After the pointer address of each node, a memory space with a fixed length equal to `slotSize` begins. Figure 5.34 shows the class prototype that implements this structure. Each time a memory slot is assigned to the program code (which may require one thread, or two or more threads simultaneously), each node must have a free flag indicating whether the slot is free for allocation or not. The simplest way to do this is to go through the beginning of the free linked list and check each node's flag, and if this value is `false`, we will assign it to the requesting thread's code. This practically forces us to traverse the entire free linked list from scratch, which will be corrected in later lines in our proposed algorithm for memory allocation and release. The `first` reference points to the beginning and the `last` reference to the `last` node of the linked list. The `head` reference is used to allocate and free the memory. After each memory allocation, the reference of the `head` pointer refers to the next location of its current value in the hope that the new location will have a free memory slot; moreover, the free flag of the memory slot relative to the `true` value must

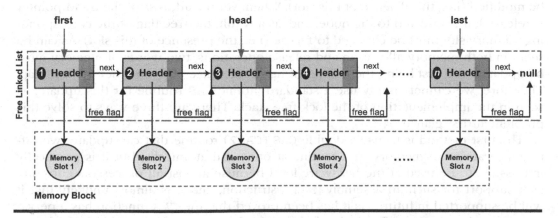

Figure 5.33 Dedicated data structure designed as a free singly linked list for our memory allocator based on memory pools.

```
1: // A lock-free memory pool based on a singly free linked list.
2: class LockFreeMemoryPool : public Object {
3:    /*--------------------fields----------------*/
4:    private: struct Header { // The header definition.
5:       struct Header volatile *next; // The successor node with respect to this node.
6:       // bool isFree;
7:       // Actually, this struct can locate in one word; we can use LSB of the next pointer as the free flag.
8:    };
9:    private: Header volatile *first; // The first pointer.
10:   private: Header volatile *last; // The last pointer.
11:   private: Header volatile *head; // The head pointer.
12:   private: Header volatile *dummy; // A dummy node used in the pool implementation.
13:   private: Header volatile *_dummy;
14:   private: bool disposed; // For destructor use.
15:   private: UInt64 poolSlots; // The number of slots within the memory block.
16:   private: UInt64 slotSize; // The fixed size of the allocated memory associated with every slot.
17:   private: void volatile *buffer; // The allocated memory for the memory block and free linked list.
18:   private: LockFreeCounter counter; // Indicates the number of non-free slots in the memory pool.
19:   /*--------------------methods----------------*/
20:   // LockFreeMemoryPool Class constructor.
21:   public: LockFreeMemoryPool(UInt64 slotSize, UInt64 poolSlots);
22:   // LockFreeMemoryPool Class destructor.
23:   public: ~LockFreeMemoryPool();
24:   // Pre-allocates the entire memory block and free linked list.
25:   private: void PreAllocate();
26:   // Deallocates the whole allocated memory regions.
27:   private: void DeAllocate();
28:   // Returns a void pointer to the allocated space or null if there is insufficient memory available.
29:   public: void *Malloc();
30:   // Deallocates or frees a memory slot.
31:   public: void Free(void *memslot);
32:   // Gets the number of non-free slots in the memory pool.
33:   public: Long get_Count();
34: };
```

Figure 5.34 Prototype definition of the lock-free memory pool class.

be modified (i.e., the absence of this slot). Whenever the address of the head pointer is released, it is updated to the node, and, as a result, the free flag of the corresponding memory slot must be changed to false (i.e., the presence of this slot). As can be seen, in both memory allocation and release operations, two words of memory must be updated, the first being the pointer of head reference and the other the free flag. Therefore, we cannot simply use a standard atomic CAS routine for this update, as seen in the implementation of the lock-free stack. There are three ways to solve this problem at first glance.

The first method is to use a double CAS (CAS2) routine that can update two different locations of memory in a routine at once and atomically, but it is practically impossible to be used at the hardware level because almost all processors currently lack support for such an assembly-level instruction, and it is almost unlikely that it will be supported in future, as it has been proved that the CAS function has a pervasive generality. At the software level, the CAS2 function can be implemented based on the CAS function, but in practice this method has an overhead and can severely affect the performance of the memory allocator. Since the free flag is a Boolean value and in practice just needs the space of a single bit, the third method can be to find a way in which the next reference of each node and the free flag can be updated simultaneously during a single invocation of the CAS function. The only practical method available for the third solution is to use the special and unique property of tagged pointers. This technique allows the value of the free flag of a node in the linked list to be smuggled (encoded) in the least significant bit (LSB) of the next reference of that node. Often a pointer to certain types of data is aligned as much as that data (such as four bytes, eight bytes, etc.), leaving a small number of bits unused. Therefore, the pointer can be tagged with additional information to the number of unused bits.

One of the advantages of tagged pointers, in addition to saving the occupied space (like our free linked list in this section), is to guarantee the atomicity of an operation that updates both the pointer and its tag within a single instruction. Besides its application in our memory pool example, this method can have a very efficient performance benefit, especially in operating systems. In 32-bit processor architectures, the number of these bits is equal to 2 and in 64-bit processors equal to 16. Figure 5.35 shows several functions to work with tagged pointers. The TaggedPointer_Smuggle

```
1: static inline void *TaggedPointer_Smuggle(void *ptr, Int32 value) {
2:     return (void *)( (Long)ptr | (value & 3) );
3: }
4:
5: static inline Int32 TaggedPointer_RecoverData(void *ptr) {
6:     return (Long)ptr & 3;
7: }
8:
9: static inline void *TaggedPointer_RecoverPointer(void *ptr) {
10:     return (void *)( (Long)ptr & (~3) );
11: }
12:
13: /* Gets the last bit of the LSB */
14: static inline bool Is_marked_reference(void *ptr) {
15:     return TaggedPointer_RecoverData(ptr) & 1;
16: }
17:
18: /* Sets the last bit of the LSB */
19: static inline void *get_marked_reference(void *ptr) {
20:     return TaggedPointer_Smuggle(ptr, 1);
21: }
22:
23: /* Clears the last bit of the LSB */
24: static inline void *get_unmarked_reference(void *ptr) {
25:     return TaggedPointer_RecoverPointer(ptr);
26: }
```

Figure 5.35   The implementation of typical functions to work with tagged pointers in C and C++ languages.

function smuggles a two-bit numeric value into two bits of the `ptr` pointer's LSB. The `TaggedPointer_RecoverData` function retrieves the value of two bits smuggled into the `ptr` pointer. The `TaggedPointer_RecoverPointer` function retrieves the original pointer whose LSB has already been manipulated. The three functions `is_marked_reference`, `get_marked_reference`, and `get_unmarked_reference` are written to make it easier to work with tagged pointers because in this book we only need one bit as a free flag for our free linked list.

We now discuss the implementation of the `LockFreeMemoryPool` class's methods as shown in Figure 5.36. In line 2, the traditional `malloc` system function is used to allocate the region needed to store the entire space of the free singly linked list data structure and memory slots in the `buffer` pointer. In every iteration of the `for` loop in line 8, we use the allocated memory in the `buffer` pointer to create the linked list and the memory slot associated with it. In the `Malloc()` method in line 23, we return the `null` value by checking the `counter` value if our memory pool does not have free space to allocate a slot. In line 33, the current location of `head`, which is required to prevent searching for free memory slots from the beginning of the linked list upon entering the `Malloc()` method, is placed in the `entrance` pointer via the CAS function. Inside the `while` loop and in line 40, if `current` is `null`, which indicates that we have reached the end of the linked list, we decide whether to search from the beginning of the list to find a free slot or return a value of `null` because no slot is free. In lines 47–55, we check to see if this slot is empty based on the LSB stored in the `next` reference of the `current` pointer. If it is empty, this free flag must be atomically modified to a `true` value so that no other thread can access it; this is done in line 50, and the loop iteration is used to update the free flag. If this operation fails due to simultaneous access of threads to the `current->next` address or the `current` slot is not free, in line 58 the location of the `current` pointer is changed to the next node of the link list. If a free slot is found for allocation, in lines 60–65, after changing the `head` reference to the `current` value in line 65, the free slot address is returned to the requesting thread's code.

The implementation of the `Malloc()` method is now complete, and, as can be seen, the proposed algorithm is very complex. Since in this method the free flag and the `next` reference are updated in one atomic operation and the `head` reference is updated in another atomic operation (namely, the `head` value is not read at all in line 63) and these two CAS operations have no data dependencies, the `Malloc()` method is ABA-free.

To complete the implementation of the `LockFreeMemoryPool` class, we consider developing the `Free()` method. In line 74, we first find the address of the `header` reference, which is actually the address of the node in our linked list based on the address of the `memslot` pointer, a simple subtraction is used to find the location of this node because we had used the sum operation on the pointers in line 9 of the `PreAllocate()` method. To release the `header` pointer after its calculation, we must atomically change the LSB of the `next` reference as its free flag in line 80 to a value of `false` (indicating that this slot is free). Finally, we require to change the address of the `head` reference to the `header` value so that we can allocate this free memory slot to another thread without probably looking a free slot up in the linked list when using the `Malloc()` method. In line 88, we decrement

```
 1: void LockFreeMemoryPool::PreAllocate() {
 2:     buffer = (void volatile *)::malloc(poolSlots * (slotSize + sizeof(struct Header)));
 3:     Header volatile *node = null;
 4:     Header volatile *temp = null;
 5:     head = null;
 6:     dummy = (struct Header volatile*)::malloc(sizeof(struct Header));
 7:     _dummy = dummy;
 8:     for(UInt64 i = 0 ; i < poolSlots ; i++) {
 9:         struct Header volatile *node = (struct Header volatile *)( (char *)buffer + i*(slotSize +
sizeof(struct Header)) );
10:         head = node;
11:         if(temp != null)
12:             temp->next = node;
13:         temp = node;
14:         if(i == 0)
15:             first = (Header *)head;
16:     }
17:     head->next = null;
18:     last = (Header *)head;
19:     head = first;
20: }
21:
22: void *LockFreeMemoryPool::Malloc() {
23:     if(counter.get_Count() == poolSlots)
24:         return null;
25:     Header volatile*temp1 = dummy;
26:     Header volatile *temp2 = null;
27:     Header volatile *current;
28:     Header *entrance;
29:     bool found = false;
30:     bool fullySearched = false;
31:     bool lsb = false;
32:
33:     Parvicrursor_AtomicCompareAndSwap(&temp1, &head, (Long)temp2);
34:     current = temp1;
35:     entrance = (Header *)temp1;
36:     while(true) {
37:         if(current == null) {
38:             if(fullySearched)
39:                 return null;
40:             if(entrance <= last && entrance > first) {
41:                 current = first;
42:                 fullySearched = true;
43:             }
44:             else
45:                 return null;
46:         }
47:         while(!Parvicrursor_AtomicCompareAndSwap(&temp1, &current->next, (Long)temp2)) {
48:             lsb = is_marked_reference((void *)temp1);
49:             if(!lsb) {
50:                 temp2 = (Header *)get_marked_reference((void *)temp1); // Set the LSB.
51:                 found = true;
52:             }
```

Figure 5.36 The implementation of the lock-free memory pool class's methods.

(Continued)

```
53:        else
54:          break;
55:      }
56:      if(found)
57:        break;
58:      current = (Header *)get_unmarked_reference((void *)temp1);
59:    }
60:    if(found) {
61:      temp1 = dummy;
62:      temp2 = current;
63:      while(!Parvicrursor_AtomicCompareAndSwap(&temp1, &head, (Long)temp2));
64:      counter.Increment();
65:      return (void *)( (char *)current + sizeof(struct Header) );
66:    }
67:    else
68:      return null;
69: }
70:
71: void LockFreeMemoryPool::Free(void *memslot) {
72:    if(memslot == null)
73:      return;
74:    Header *header = (struct Header *)( (char *)memslot - sizeof(struct Header) );
75:    if(header == null)
76:      return;
77:    Header volatile *temp1 = dummy;
78:    Header volatile *temp2 = null;
79:    /* Safely clear the head->next to indicate that this slot was freed. */
80:    while(!Parvicrursor_AtomicCompareAndSwap(&temp1, &header->next, (Long)temp2)) {
81:      temp2 = (Header volatile *)get_unmarked_reference((void *)temp1); // Clear the LSB.
82:    }
83:    /* Atomically update the head to the header (head = header;) */
84:    temp1 = dummy;
85:    while(!Parvicrursor_AtomicCompareAndSwap(&temp1, &head, (Long)temp2)) {
86:      temp2 = header;
87:    }
88:    counter.Decrement();
89: }
```

Figure 5.36 (Continued) The implementation of the lock-free memory pool class's methods.

the value of the `counter` field due to the release of this slot. An implementation of a test class (`LockFreeMemoryPoolTest` class), to check that the lock-free memory pool class is properly functioning, comes in the file "`LockFreeMemoryPool/LockFreeMemoryPool.h`", in which n threads of control are concurrently allocating and releasing memory by invoking the `Malloc()` and `Free()` methods successively.

At the end of our journey into the fascinating world of lock-free programming, we explore the implementation of a non-blocking algorithm for an array list that relies on a lock-free singly linked list [4]; we will make use of our developed lock-free memory allocator for this array list. Linked lists are one of the most basic data structures used in designing application programs, so building a lock-free linked list is of great interest. For example, a linked list can be used to construct more complex data structures, such as hash tables, graphs, and trees. Figure 5.37 demonstrates our implemented data structure for the lock-free array list. Following this section, we

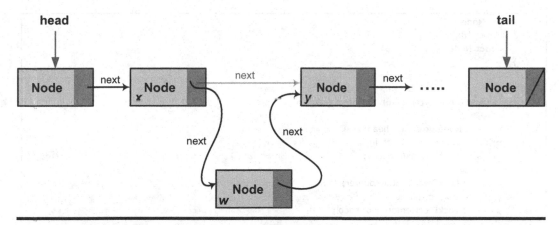

Figure 5.37 **The data structure designed for the singly-linked-link-based array list. Here node w is being added between nodes x and y of the linked list.**

will further explain the non-blocking linked list algorithm designed by Harris [4] and develop our own array list utilising it. In this figure, the two sentinel nodes, head and tail hold the beginning and ending references of the linked list without storing an element of the array list. A sentinel node is the one dedicated to be used in linked lists and trees as a traversal path terminator. Such a node does not hold actual data. Sentinels are used as an alternative method, instead of a null terminator, to speed up operations, and to reduce algorithmic complexity and code size.

Here node w is being added between nodes x and y of the linked list. The operation for adding an element is straightforward. After allocating a new node using our designed memory pool, this new node is added to the list using a single CAS operation on the next reference of the previous node. But removing a node from the link list is not so simple, because when physically deleting a node other threads may be deleting the predecessor nodes and before this node at the same time; hence, the deletion operation is inherently complicated.

The technique proposed by Harris for removing a node from the linked list is to use two separate CAS operations (similar to the one we employed in implementing the LockFreeMemoryPool class). The first is used to mark the next reference of the deleted node (logical removal), and the second is to delete the actual deletion (physical removal) of the node. Figures 5.38 and 5.39 show the prototype for defining and implementing the LockFreeArrayList class. Lines 29–33 of Figure 5.38 are the modified methods of Harris's original algorithm. For example, line 18 of Figure 5.39 shows Harris's CAS implementation based on the Parvicursor_AtomicCompareAndSwap function. The Malloc() and Free() methods of the memory pool object in lines 25, 33, and 67 of Figure 3.58 are used to allocate and release dynamic memory to create and delete nodes.

The Add() method uses Harris's modified insert function to add a unique object to an array list. In Harris's original algorithm, each node has a unique key; here we consider this key to be the address of objects. Therefore, our array list only allows the addition of unique objects that do not already exist in the linked list. If the address of the object requested to be added to the array list already exists, the Add() method returns the DuplicateData value. The insert method instead uses the

```
 1: struct Node {
 2:    Object *data;
 3:    struct Node volatile *next;
 4: };
 5:
 6: // A lock-free array list based on a lock-free singly linked list designed by Harris.
 7: class LockFreeArrayList : public Object {
 8:    /*---------------------fields---------------*/
 9:    private: Node volatile *head; // The head sentinel node.
10:    private: Node volatile *tail; // The tail sentinel node.
11:    private: UInt32 maxCapacity; // The maximum capacity of a LockFreeArrayList is the number of elements
that the LockFreeArrayList can hold.
12:    private: LockFreeCounter counter; // Indicates the number of non-free slots in the LockFreeArrayList.
13:    private: bool disposed; // For destructor use.
14:    private: LockFreeMemoryPool *pool; // The memory pool used to allocate and deallocate nodes.
15:    /*---------------------methods---------------*/
16:    // LockFreeArrayList Class constructor.
17:    public: LockFreeArrayList(UInt32 maxCapacity);
18:    // LockFreeArrayList Class destructor.
19:    public: ~LockFreeArrayList();
20:    // Adds an object to the end of the LockFreeArrayList.
21:    public: Status Add(Object *data);
22:    // Removes the occurrence of a specific object from the LockFreeArrayList.
23:    public: void Remove(Object *data);
24:    // Gets the number of elements actually contained in the LockFreeArrayList.
25:    public: Long get_Count();
26:    // Determines whether an element is in the LockFreeArrayList.
27:    public: bool Contains(Object *data);
28:    // Our methods based on Timotht L. Harris's modified methods.
29:    private: static inline bool CAS(void volatile *address, Long old, Long _new);
30:    private: Status insert(Object *data);
31:    private: bool find(Object *data);
32:    public: Status _delete(Object *data);
33:    private: Node volatile *search(Object *data, Node volatile **left_node);
34: };
```

Figure 5.38   Prototype definition of the lock-free array list class.

search function to locate pairs of nodes between new nodes that must be inserted. The update itself occurs in a single CAS function in line 37 from Figure 5.39, which changes the reference in left_node->next from right_node to a new node. The Contain() method uses Harris's modified find function to check whether the object is present as an input argument in the array list. The Remove() method uses Harris's technique to remove an object from the array list. The _delete method uses the search function to locate the node to be deleted and then a two-step process to perform the final deletion. For more details on Harris's algorithm and how the search method works, we refer interested readers to the main reference of the Harris algorithm [4]. An implementation of a test class (LockFreeArrayListTest class) to check the proper functioning of a lock-free array list class can be found in the "LockFreeArrayList/LockFreeArrayList.h" file, in which n threads repeatedly invoke the Add() and Remove() methods of the LockFreeArrayList class to dynamically add/remove objects.

```
 1: Status LockFreeArrayList::Add(Object *data) {
 2:    Status status = insert(data);
 3:    if(status == Success)
 4:       counter.Increment();
 5:    return status;
 6: }
 7:
 8: void LockFreeArrayList::Remove(Object *data) {
 9:    Status status = _delete(data);
10:    if(status == Success)
11:       counter.Decrement();
12: }
13:
14: bool LockFreeArrayList::Contains(Object *data) {
15:    return find(data);
16: }
17:
18: bool LockFreeArrayList::CAS(volatile void *address, Long old, Long _new) {
19:    if(Parvicrursor_AtomicCompareAndSwap(&old, address, _new))
20:       return true;
21:    return false;
22: }
23:
24: Status LockFreeArrayList::insert(Object *data) {
25:    Node *new_node = (Node *)pool->Malloc();
26:    if(new_node == null)
27:       return ArrayListIsFull;
28:    new_node->data = data;
29:    volatile Node *right_node, *left_node;
30:    do {
31:       right_node = search(data, &left_node);
32:       if ((right_node != tail) && (right_node->data == data)) { /*T1*/
33:          pool->Free(new_node);
34:          return DuplicateData;
35:       }
36:       new_node->next = right_node;
37:       if(CAS(&(left_node->next), (Long)right_node, (Long)new_node)) /*C2*/
38:          return Success;
39:    } while (true); /*B3*/
40: }
41:
42: bool LockFreeArrayList::find(Object *data) {
43:    Node volatile *right_node;
44:    Node volatile *left_node;
45:    right_node = search(data, &left_node);
46:    if((right_node == tail) || (right_node->data != data))
47:       return false;
48:    else
49:       return true;
50: }
51:
52: Status LockFreeArrayList::_delete(Object *data)
53: {
```

Figure 5.39 Implementation of the lock-free array list class methods.

(Continued)

```
54:    Node volatile *right_node;
55:    Node volatile *right_node_next;
56:    Node volatile *left_node;
57:    do {
58:        right_node = search(data, &left_node);
59:        if ((right_node == tail) || (right_node->data != data)) /*T1*/
60:            return NoSuchData;
61:        right_node_next = right_node->next;
62:        if(!is_marked_reference((void *)right_node_next)) {
63:            if(CAS(&(right_node->next), /*C3*/ (Long)right_node_next, (Long)get_marked_reference((void
*)right_node_next))) {
64:                if(!CAS(&(left_node->next), (Long)right_node, (Long)right_node_next)) /*C4*/
65:                    right_node = search(right_node->data, &left_node);
66:
67:                pool->Free((void *)right_node);
68:                return Success;
69:            }
70:        }
71:    } while (true); /*B4*/
72: }
73:
74: volatile Node *LockFreeArrayList::search(Object *data, volatile Node **left_node) {
75:    Node volatile *left_node_next;
76:    Node volatile *right_node;
77: ch_again:
78:    do {
79:        Node volatile *t = head;
80:        Node volatile *t_next = head->next;
81:        /* 1: Find left_node and right_node */
82:        do {
83:            if(!is_marked_reference((void *)t_next)) {
84:                (*left_node) = t;
85:                left_node_next = t_next;
86:            }
87:            t = (Node *)get_unmarked_reference((void *)t_next);
88:            if(t == tail)
89:                break;
90:            t_next = t->next;
91:        } while (is_marked_reference((void *)t_next) || (t->data != data)); /*B1*/
92:        //} while (is_marked_reference(t_next) || (t->data < data)); /*B1*/
93:        right_node = t;
94:        /* 2: Check nodes are adjacent */
95:        if (left_node_next == right_node) {
96:            if ((right_node != tail) && is_marked_reference((void *)right_node->next))
97:                goto search_again; /*G1*/
98:            else
99:                return right_node; /*R1*/
100:       }
101:       /* 3: Remove one or more marked nodes */
102:       if(CAS(&((*left_node)->next), (Long)left_node_next, (Long)right_node)) { /*C1*/
103:           if ((right_node != tail) && is_marked_reference((void *)right_node->next))
104:               goto search_again; /*G2*/
105:           else
106:               return right_node; /*R2*/
107:       }
108:   } while (true); /*B2*/
109: }
```

Figure 5.39   (Continued) Implementation of the lock-free array list class methods.

5.3.3 Transactional Memory

Transactional memory (TM) has been proposed as a mechanism for thread synchronisation. TM alleviates many lock-related problems and offers the benefits of transactions without posing its overhead found in relational databases. TM forces memory, which is shared by a thread, to behave like a database in a transactional manner. The key goal is to simplify the development of concurrent applications, which are increasingly growing due to the orientation of technology towards many-core processors and multi-processor systems.

Transactions provide an alternative way to coordinate concurrent threads. An application can wrap a computation inside a transaction. Failure atomicity ensures that the computation completes successfully and commits its result or aborts abnormally. Transactions replace critical sections in codes with atomic executable units. Suppose we have a BankAccout abstraction with a m_balance property that is updated by a ModifyBalance() method (see Figure 5.40). If BankAccout is accessible by threads at once, then we need to put the body of the ModifyBalance() method inside an indivisible block (rather than a lock). The atomic keyword is desirable from a programmer's point of view, but the compiler must convert the code inside this guarded region before compilation and using the TM system. The code on the right-hand side, which has a while loop, shows such a conversion. The StartTM() function begins a new transaction in the current thread. The ReadTM() function is used to read the value of the m_balance variable via its address and returns the data view of the transaction at the address. WriteTM() takes the m_balance variable's address and writes the newly calculated balance value to the address from the transaction's point of view. The set of places that a transaction can read and write is referred to as *readable-set* and *writable-set*, respectively. At the end of the while loop, the CommitTM() function attempts to commit the current transaction, which, if it succeeds, returns a value of true and, if it fails, returns a value of false.

A TM framework must perform three basic concurrency control operations for synchronisation. First, a conflict occurs when two transactions perform conflicting operations on the same data (e.g., a transaction writing to shared data and another reading from the data or writing twice simultaneously). Second, this conflict is detected when the TM framework determines that a conflict has occurred. Third, this conflict is resolved when the TM framework decides to prevent the conflict. A TM system uses two methods (or a combination of them) to implement this concurrency control. In a pessimistic concurrency control, when a transaction tries to reach a location in memory, the system detects a conflict and resolves it. In fact, this

```
1: class BankAccount {                          1: public: void ModifyBalance(Int32 amount) {
2:    private: Int32 m_balance;                  2:    do {
3:    public: void ModifyBalance(Int32 amount) { 3:       StartTM();
4:       atomic {                                4:       Int32 balance = ReadTM(&(m_balance));
5:          m_balance = m_balance + amount;      5:       balance = balance + amount;
6:       }                                       6:       WriteTM(&(m_balance), balance);
7:    }                                          7:    } while(!CommitTM());
8: }                                             8: }
```

Figure 5.40   A transactional method that runs inside the body of an indivisible block.

type of concurrency control requires dedicated ownership of the data before it can be executed, which in turn prevents other transactions from doing anything on the data. If conflicts are frequent, then pessimistic concurrency control is very useful, because when a transaction has its own lock, it can be executed for completion. In an optimistic concurrency control, conflict detection and resolution can occur after a conflict takes place. This type of concurrency allows multiple transactions to access data simultaneously and continue to execute even if they interfere, and as long as the TM framework detects and resolves these conflicts before it commits a transaction. If conflicts are rare in a concurrent environment, optimistic concurrency control is usually faster because it significantly avoids locking overhead and can increase concurrency between transactions.

A TM system must provide mechanisms for managing temporary writes that concurrent transactions are performing, which is called *version management*. The first method is eager version management, in which a transaction directly modifies data in memory. Each transaction maintains an undo-log record that holds the values overwritten. This log allows old values to be written to the previous value if that transaction subsequently ends abnormally. The second method is lazy version management, in which updates are delayed until a transaction is committed. The transaction keeps its temporary writes in a private-transaction redo-log record. Updates to a transaction are buffered in this log, and the reads of a write must use the log so that the older writes are seen. When a transaction commits, it updates the actual locations from these private copies.

Two methods of software and hardware transactional memory (STM and HTM) approaches have been developed to realise TM. STM is a software system that equips programmers with a transaction model through a library interface or compiler. STM has several advantages over HTM. Software is easier to modify and allows the implementation of a wider range of complex algorithms due to its flexibility. Nevertheless, in practice, STM systems suffer from complexity problems in implementation. Although STM can be fast, TM hardware support clearly promises significant performance improvements. Most HTM systems rely on direct modifications to cache coherency protocols. When a thread reads or writes a memory location on behalf of a transaction, the cache entry is flagged as a transaction. Transaction writes are stored in a cache or a write buffer but are not written to the memory whilst the transaction is active. If another thread invalidates a transaction entry, a data conflict occurs, thereby resulting in the transaction getting abnormally terminated and restarted.

If a transaction ends without any of its entries being invalidated, then the transaction is committed by marking its transaction entries as valid or dirty, allowing dirty entries to be written to the memory normally. One of the main limitations of HTM is that in-cache transactions are limited in size and scope. Most HTMs require the programmer to be aware of platform-specific resource constraints such as buffer and cache sizes, scheduling quanta, and the effects of context switching and process migration.

Finally, it should be noted that since TM is a general mechanism, a direct non-blocking implementation of specific data structures will likely be more efficient than a TM-based implementation, although their non-blocking implementation will be very difficult as seen in the previous section. For more information on TM, interested readers are encouraged to refer to [5].

References

[1] B.W. Lampson, A note on the confinement problem. *Communications of the ACM*, 16(5): 613–615, 1973.

[2] Compiler Intrinsics, Microsoft MSDN Library, Available from: http://msdn.microsoft.com/en-us/library/26td21ds.aspx

[3] U. Drepper, What every programmer should know about memory, 2022, 21 November 2007; Available from: http://www.akkadia.org/drepper/cpumemory.pdf.

[4] T. Harris, A pragmatic implementation of non-blocking linked-lists, In *Proceedings of Fifteenth International Symposium on Distributed Computing (DISC 2001)*, volume 2180 of Lecture Notes in Computer Science, Springer-Verlag, Lisbon, Portugal, pp. 300–314, 2001.

[5] T. Harris, A. Cristal, O. S. Unsal, E. Ayguad, F. Gagliardi, B. Smith, and M. Valero, Transactional memory: An overview. *IEEE Micro*, 27(3): 8–29, 2007.

Chapter 6

Storage Systems: A Parallel Programming Perspective

The human brain has a vast amount of memory storage. It made us curious and very creative. Those were the characteristics that gave us an advantage – curiosity, creativity and memory. And that brain did something very special. It invented an idea called "the future."

David Suzuki

6.1 Introduction

In this chapter, storage systems are introduced with a major emphasis on their parallel programming for distributed systems. We will discuss the structural underpinnings of storage system hardware and then delve into overlapping disc I/O with concurrency through the techniques presented in the earlier chapters.

6.2 Storage Systems and Disc Input/Output Mechanisms for Use in Distributed Systems

6.2.1 Introduction

Physical data storage and retrieval are one of the most important issues in operating systems and file systems, in terms of both hardware and software perspectives. In this section, we try to give the reader a first look at how their data is stored through the operating system on the hardware of a permanent storage system. Familiarity with these principles helps us design systems that are highly efficient with respect to input-output and meet our needs, especially in highly data-intensive and distributed environments. From an operating system's point of view, a general view of disc input/output mechanisms can be imagined. This view is shown in Figure 6.1.

DOI: 10.1201/9781003379041-6

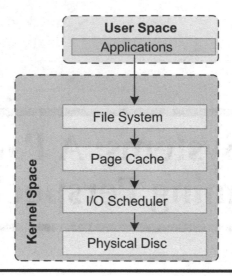

Figure 6.1   An overview of disc input/output layers in an operating system.

- Application programs are running in userspace. They initiate I/O transfers through the operating system's system calls by accessing memory pages mapped to files. These procedures will be fully explored in Section 6.3.
- File system translates requests from userspace into one or more block I/O requests. The file system also implements block allocation strategies, which specify physical placement on the disc and fragmentation. File systems will be discussed further in Section 6.3.
- Page cache is responsible for hiding a set of disc blocks that are likely being reused.
- Disc scheduler sorts, merges, and prioritises I/O requests, and then dispatches them to the disc.
- Physical disc services requests. Discs usually provide another caching layer to increase performance. With features like native command queuing (NCQ) and tagged command queuing (TCQ), discs can queue multiple requests, and rearrange them to minimise search time and increase efficiency.

6.2.2 Disc Drives from a Hardware Perspective

Ever since the introduction of personal computers, rotating hard discs have been the most common type of storage systems. One such disc is a unit containing a number of platters in a stack. They can be installed in a horizontal or vertical position. Figure 6.2 shows a view of a rotating disc. Electromagnetic read/write heads are located at the top and bottom of every platter. As the platters rotate, the drive heads move towards the inside of the central level and outside of the edge. In this method, the drive heads reach the entire surface of every platter. On each rotating hard disc, data is stored in thin, concentric bands called tracks. One end of the disc reads from or writes to a track. Tracks are made up of sectors, and sectors are the smallest physical storage units. A sector is always typically 512 bytes in size.

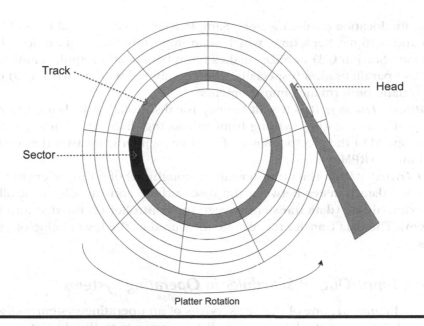

Figure 6.2   A view of the structure of a rotating disc.

In contrast to traditional rotating discs are solid state drives (SSDs). An SSD is a data storage device that uses integrated circuits as its underlying memory to store data permanently. The SSD technology employs electronic interfaces compatible with traditional block I/O hard drives. SSDs do not use any moving mechanical components and therefore differ from rotating discs in that they have read/write heads. Compared to mechanical rotating discs, SSDs are less vulnerable to physical shocks, are quieter, and have less access time and latency. SSDs are mostly based on volatile DRAMs or non-volatile NAND flash memories. The performance of an SSD can be increased by the number of parallel NAND flash chips.

In evaluating the performance of both types of these discs, there are a number of features that we should know:

- *Access Time*: Access time or response time of a rotating disc is the time it takes before the disc actually transfers data. Factors that control this time are largely dependent on the mechanical nature of discs and moving heads. For SSDs, this time does not rely on moving parts, but on electrical connections to solid state memory, so access time is very fast and stable.
- *Seek Time*: In rotating discs, seek time is a measure of the time that is taken by the drive to reach the platter where data will be read or written. When a disc needs to read or write data to a specific sector, it identifies which platter is located at the sector, and then moves the head to the particular platter. If the original location was at the top of the platter, then seek time would be zero. If the start platter was the farthest edge of the disc and the target platter was at the innermost edge, then seek time would be the longest for that disc. Seek times for rotating discs are non-linear. Since SSDs do not have removable parts, measuring seek time for them will only be possible by testing electronic circuits that are preparing

a specific location on the memory. Sample SSDs have a typical time of between 0.08 and 0.16 ms. Seek time, which is an important factor in random access to files (see Section 6.3) of SSDs, makes them beneficial to applications in which disc I/O parallelisation (especially when combined with network I/O) can lead to dramatic performance improvements.

- *Rotational Latency*: It is a wait latency for disc rotation to bring the required disc part under reading/writing from/to rotating discs. This latency is the rotational speed of the electric motor of the disc, which is measured in revolutions per minute (RPM).
- *Data Transfer Rate*: Data transfer rate (throughput) of a disc refers to the internal rate (data transfer between the disc surface and the disc controller) and the external rate (data transfer between the controller on the disc and the host system). The data transfer rate can be measured as the lower value of these two rates.

6.2.3 Disc Input/Output Scheduler in Operating Systems

As shown in Figure 6.1, one of the key services of an operating system is disc input/output scheduler. This scheduler passes all I/O requests to the disc. It implements policies that specify when I/O requests should be sent to the disc, and in which order. The I/O scheduler should make a balanced choice between general throughput, latency, and priority. On a rotating disc, for example, servicing a single random request may take 5 ms, whilst processor can execute millions of clock cycles per second. This means that there could be an opportunity to spend some CPU time scheduling I/O to improve overall system performance, and that is one of the chief tasks of an I/O scheduler. Another task of the scheduler is to implement a policy about how resources on a shared disc should be shared between multiple system processes.

One of the simplest I/O schedulers is the first-come, first-served (FCFS) scheduler, in which each request is sent to the disc in the same direction it arrives. FCFS efficiency is not suitable for random access on rotating discs because no attempt is made to reduce seeks. But this method is very suitable for SSD drives which are random devices. This simple example shows that the design of I/O schedulers and different scheduling algorithms is critical to different disc architectures and different for each architecture. For a more in-depth study of I/O disc schedulers, the interested reader can refer to operating system textbooks.

6.2.4 Benchmarking the Performance and Throughput of Disc I/O Based on the IOzone Tool

Now that we are familiar with the different concepts of disc input and output, we are going to test the performance of a general system based on a standard tool such as IOzone. IOzone allows us to monitor the performance of our file system based on how changing the size of records (block size) affects it. To download and install this tool, visit its website at [1]. With IOzone we can get detailed information for read, write, read/write randomly, and so forth. IOzone is very effective in finding areas where I/O files may not work well as expected. IOzone runs in a shell and can export its output to an Excel spreadsheet, and by using Excel software we can draw stylish and expressive 3D charts. In this example, we intend to make a 3D diagram with a report as a triplet (throughput, file size, record size) on the Linux operating system. To find the specifications of your disc drive, use the hdparm command in the shell as shown in Figure 6.3. As it is clear, the disc in question is a rotating HDD with 16 heads and a volume of 500 GB. Now we use the IOzone command to store the benchmark results in a file called output.xls. This command is illustrated in Figure 6.4. The -a parameter tells IOzone to perform all default tests. The -g parameter indicates that the maximum file size tested in this example is 2 GB. Figure 6.5 shows a 3D surface diagram for random writes generated by the IOzone tool and drawn in the Excel software. The throughput axis is measured in kilobits per second, and the other two axes are measured in kilobytes.

```
 1: [root@~]# hdparm -I /dev/sda
 2:
 3: /dev/sda:
 4:
 5: ATA device, with non-removable media
 6:        Model Number:       Hitachi HDS721050CLA362
 7:        Serial Number:      JPF570HK0D5XKR
 8:        Firmware Revision:  JP2OA3MA
 9: Standards:
10:        Supported: 8 7 6 5
11:        Likely used: 8
12: Configuration:
13:        Logical        max      current
14:        cylinders      16383    16383
15:        heads          16       16
16:        sectors/track  63       63
17:        --
18:        CHS current addressable sectors:   16514064
19:        LBA    user addressable sectors: 268435455
20:        LBA48  user addressable sectors: 976773168
21:        device size with M = 1024*1024:     476940 MBytes
22:        device size with M = 1000*1000:     500107 MBytes (500 GB)
```

Figure 6.3 Using hdparm shell command in Linux operating system to recover our disc drive data.

```
 1: ./iozone -a -b output.xls -g 2G
```

Figure 6.4 The use of iozone command to test a file system on the Linux operating system.

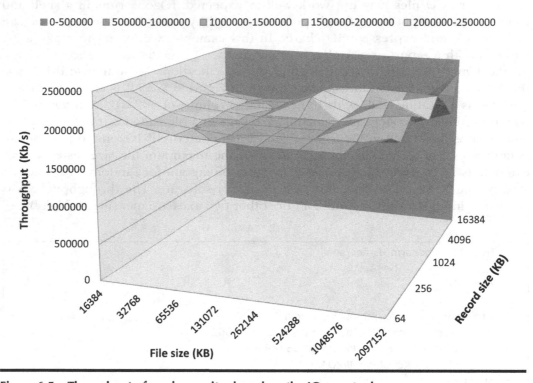

Figure 6.5   Throughput of random writes based on the IOzone tool.

As can be seen, throughput is maximised for record sizes between 1024 to 4096 KB and for files larger than 500 MB.

6.3 Cross-Platform Disc I/O Programming and Manipulation of Folders Based on the Parvicursor.NET Framework for Distributed Systems

File system is one of the most important components of an operating system for most users, especially programmers. File systems provide mechanisms for storing and accessing data and applications on the OS. This section describes programming files and folders based on the Parvicursor.NET Framework. The capabilities of the classes in the System::IO namespace are presented for this purpose, and then various examples, including the combination of concurrency with these classes, will be described. File system features are even more important in distributed systems.

6.3.1 *Storage and Retrieval of Data Files Based on the* `FileStream` *Class*

Files are an abstraction mechanism that provides a way to store information on a secondary storage (such as a disc) and read it at a necessary time. The operating system provides an interface through which information is stored and retrieved in such a way that the user does not need to know the details of how and where this information is stored. The most important and basic feature in working with files is the way they are named, which is different in each system. When a program needs to work with a file, it passes the file name to a system function, and after opening the file, it writes or reads it, and finally closes the file. The data of a file can be stored in any structure by the programmer and the operating system will have no knowledge of this structure. For example, the layout of a file can be structured by a programmer as a byte sequence, a record sequence, and a tree.

Locating an offset within a file can be complicated for an operating system. Disc storage systems typically have a well-defined block size determined by the size of a sector. All I/O activities are performed in units of one block (a physical record), and all blocks are of the same size. Logical records are user data records that are stored within these logical records. It is unlikely that the size of the physical record will match the size of a desired logical record. Logical records can even be variable in length. Packing a number of logical records into physical blocks is a common solution to this problem. In Unix-like operating systems, for example, a file is simply defined as a stream of bytes. Each byte can be addressed individually by offsetting from the beginning (or end) of the file. In this scenario, the logical record size is one byte. The file system automatically packs or unpacks bytes into the physical blocks of the disc (like blocks 512 bytes long). The easiest way to access files is through sequential access. The information in the file is processed sequentially, one after the other. This access mode is one of the mostly common techniques used by applications. An operation reads the next part of the file and automatically moves the file pointer forward, which tracks the I/O location. Similarly, a write operation appends to the end of the file and moves the file pointer to the end of the new written content. Another method is random access in that bytes or records of a file can be read and written out of order. This type of access is required in many applications, for example, databases. Figure 6.6 shows an example for sequential and random access to a file. In the random method, direct (random) jumps are sought from each byte of the file to another. Random access provides a special operation called seek to set the current position of the file pointer. After a seek, the file can be read or written sequentially from its current position. In implementing the xDFS protocol in Chapter 10, random-access property is used to achieve parallel transfers of a large file over multiple network channels.

Sequential access is much faster than random access because hardware works in the former way. Because random reads involve a higher number of seek operations than sequential ones, they deliver a lower throughput rate. This is also true for random writes. For workloads with high I/O rates, it is necessary to consider stripped sets because they add physical discs, thus increasing the system's ability to handle simultaneous disc requests.

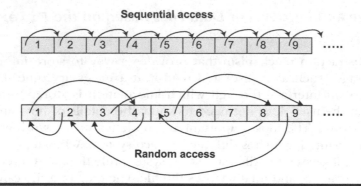

Figure 6.6   An example of sequential and random access to files.

In the Parvicursor.NET Framework, the FileStream class can be used to work with random and sequential files. Table 6.1 shows the methods and constructor of this class. If an error occurs whilst using any of the methods in this class, an exception with a type of Exception, ArgumentNullException, ArgumentException, ArgumentOutOfRangeException, IOException, or ObjectDisposedException is thrown by the Parvicursor.NET Framework. The constructor of this class has two features, FileMode and FileAccess. FileAccess has the following three values: Read—data can only be read from a file, write—data can only be written to a file, and ReadWrite—data can be written to or read from a file. FileMode values that specify how the file is opened by the operating system are listed in Table 6.2.

6.3.2 *Two Non-Concurrent and Concurrent Examples for Using the FileStream Class*

In this section, we describe two practical examples of the FileStream class, specifically oriented to use in file transfer systems such as xDFS. In the first example, we save a local file to another local file on a hard disc. Figure 6.7 portrays this example. Here, threads of control are not used and therefore it is a synchronous or sequential program. A file named readFilename is copied through the fsRead object to a file named writeFilename via the fsWrite object. Because the readFilename file must exist, we instantiate it in line 10 with Open mode and Read access to read it. The writeFilename file is modelled with OpenOrCreate mode (as this file may or may not exist) and with Write access to write to it. To perform a copy operation, lines 19–35 in a loop read the fsRead object repeatedly and the read contents are stored in the buffer, and the amount of data read in the buffer is written on line 24 to the fsWrite object with a read length. If the read value is zero, we are at the end of the fsRead file and jump out of the loop. In lines 36 and 37, the instance objects of open files are closed, and we free up the allocated memory. If in the execution of every step of the code an exception is thrown through the Parvicursor.NET Framework, we catch it with the C++ catch keyword, and after printing the corresponding error, we terminate the execution of the program by returning from

Table 6.1   Methods and Constructor of the `FileStream` Class in the Parvicursor.NET Framework

Name	Description
`FileStream(String path, FileMode mode, FileAccess access, Int32 bufferSize)`	A new instance of `FileStream` class initialises the specified path, creation mode, access method, and buffer length (used for internal data file buffering).
`Int32 Read(char array[], Int32 offset, Int32 count)`	Reads a block of bytes from the file stream and writes it to `array`. This operation is performed on `array` from its `offset` to the length of `count`. This method returns a value of zero if the end of the stream is reached. This method will block if there is no existing data from the stream.
`void Write(const char array[], Int32 offset, Int32 count)`	Writes a block of bytes stored inside `array` to this stream.
`void Close()`	Closes the stream and frees up consumed resources (such as file handles and allocated internal memory).
`void Flush()`	Clears all buffers associated with this instance and causes any buffered data to be written to the underlying file system.
`void Lock(Int64 position, Int64 length)`	Prevents other processes or threads from changing the open file from `position` to `length`. However, they are allowed to read in this range.
`void UnLock(Int64 position, Int64 length)`	Unlocks the range specified by a process or owner thread and allows other processes to modify this range.
`void Seek(Int64 offset, SeekOrigin origin)`	Performs a seek operation on the file and changes the current position of the file pointer to `offset` location based on `origin`. `origin` can be one of the following three values: `Begin`—indicates the beginning of the file, `Current`—states the current position of the file, `End`—states the end of the file.
`Int64 get_Length()`	Finds the length of bytes in the file instance.

the `main()` function. The code for this example is available in the "`/Parvicursor/Parvicursor/Samples/FileStream`" path.

The second example, as shown in Figure 6.8, is to perform the copy operation of the previous exercise using two threads simultaneously. This example is a combination of the codes in Figures 6.7, and 5.7. One thread reads the data of the `readFilename` file block by block and puts it inside our circular queue. In this example, each circular buffer cell shown in Figure 5.6 is a cell data structure defined in line 3. Each cell contains a buffer and the size of the actual contents read by the producer thread (which is responsible for reading the blocks of the file `readFilename`). In the `ConcurrentFileCopy` class constructor and lines 26 through 31, we allocate the memory of our circular buffer. Since in this and previous examples the `Read()` and

Table 6.2 Possible FileMode Values for Use in the `FileStream` Class Constructor

Name	Description
CreateNew	Specifies that the operating system should create a new file. If the file exists, an `IOException` will be thrown.
Create	Specifies that the operating system should create a new file. If the file already exists, it will be overwritten.
Open	Specifies that the operating system should open an existing file. The ability to open depends on the value specified by `FileAccess`.
OpenOrCreate	Specifies that the operating system should open a file if it exists; otherwise, a new file should be created.
Truncate	Specifies that the operating system should open an existing file. Once this file is opened, the file should be truncated so that its size becomes zero of bytes. Trying to read from a file opened in this mode throws an exception.
Append	Opens the specified file if it exists, then seeks to the end of it, or creates a new file. `FileMode.Append` can only be used in conjunction with `FileAccess.Write`. Attempting to seek for a position before the end of the file will throw an `IOException`, and any attempt to read will fail and a `NotSupportedException` is thrown.

`Write()` methods from the `FileStream` class block until their works are complete, the two intermediate buffers, `buffer_producer` and `buffer_consumer`, together as temporary storage that is between the `circular_buffer` circular queue and the two producer and consumer threads, are allocated to improve as much concurrency as possible (otherwise, the `buffer` variable takes up too much time by one thread). For example, in line 48, the `buffer_producer` buffer is used to read the file blocks, in line 48 to read a single block via the `fsRead->Read()` method, and in line 88 the contents of this buffer are used by the `memmove()` system function. The last circular buffer cell is copied (`circular_buffer[end].buff`). The same thing happens with `buffer_producer` in the consumer thread. Two Boolean flags `StopRequested` and `EndOfFileReached` are added to this example as shown in Figure 5.6. The producer thread may be done, but the loop buffer is still full and should be written by the consumer thread to the `fsWrite` file. In the execution of each thread, if an exception is caught, the Boolean `StopRequested` flag is used to terminate the execution of the other thread. This somewhat complex example makes the strength of the Parvicursor.NET Framework clearer to the reader for easier and uniform construction of distributed systems. The full code for this example is in the "/Parvicursor/Parvicursor/Samples/DiscIO/ConcurrentFileCopy" path.

6.3.3 *Management of Files and Folders Based on the Two Classes* `Directory` *and* `File`

Operating systems store files on discs. A system may have millions of files. To manage such a volume, we must be able to manage them. Folders are used for this purpose

```
1: int main(int argc, char *argv[]) {
2:     FileStream *fsRead, *fsWrite;
3:     String readFilename = "C:/test.dat";  //to change
4:     String writeFilename = "C:/test1.dat";  //to change
5:     printf("Copying %s to %s\n", readFilename.get_BaseStream(), writeFilename.get_BaseStream());
6:     Int32 bufferSize = 256*1024;
7:     char *buffer = new char[bufferSize];
8:     Int32 read = 0;
9:     try {
10:        fsRead = new FileStream(readFilename, System::IO::Open, System::IO::Read, 8*1024);
11:        fsWrite = new FileStream(writeFilename, System::IO::OpenOrCreate, System::IO::Write, 8*1024);
12:    }
13:    catch(Exception &e) {
14:        printf("1. Exception Message: %s\n", e.get_Message().get_BaseStream());
15:        char s[12];
16:        scanf("%s", s);
17:        return 0;
18:    }
19:    while(true) {
20:        try {
21:            read = fsRead->Read(buffer, 0, bufferSize);
22:            if(read <= 0)
23:                break;
24:            fsWrite->Write(buffer, 0, read);
25:            printf("\r...");
26:        }
27:        catch(IOException &e) {
28:            printf("2. Exception Message: %s\n", e.get_Message().get_BaseStream());
29:            return 0;
30:        }
31:        catch(Exception &e) {
32:            printf("3. Exception Message: %s\n", e.get_Message().get_BaseStream());
33:            return 0;
34:        }
35:    }
36:    fsWrite->Close(); fsRead->Close();
37:    delete fsRead; delete fsWrite; delete buffer;
38:    return 0;
39: }
```

Figure 6.7 Local, non-concurrent copy of one file to another using the FileStream class.

by an OS. A directory can be thought of a symbol table that translates file names into their directory entries. So, the directory itself can be organised in different ways. Such a system should allow to insert and delete entries, search for a named entry, and list all the entries within the directory. A complete reference for these operations is shown in Table 6.3, which is provided by the Parvicursor.NET Framework through the Directory class.

Directory systems are usually stored as a hierarchy (i.e., a tree of folders). In this method, there can be many folders whilst being used to group files in different ways. Figure 6.9 shows this technique. Folders are displayed by squares and files by circles. This directory system has a root node, which, for example, could be the name of a drive or file system partition. For example, the directory F is the parent of two

```
 1: class ConcurrentFileCopy : public Object {
 2:    /*---------------------fields----------------*/
 3:    private: struct Cell {
 4:       Int32 size;
 5:       char *buff;
 6:    };
 7:    private: ConditionVariable *bufferNotEmpty, *bufferNotFull;
 8:    private: Cell *circular_buffer;
 9:    //integers to index circular_buffer
10:    private: char *buffer_producer;
11:    private: char *buffer_consumer;
12:    private: FileStream *fsRead, fsWrite;
13:    private: Int32 bufferSize;
14:    private: Int32 cells;
15:    private: bool StopRequested;
16:    private: bool EndOfFileReached;
17:    ...
18:    /*---------------------methods---------------*/
19:    public: ConcurrentFileCopy(FileStream *fsRead, FileStream *fsWrite, Int32 bufferSize, Int32 cells,
Barrier *barrier)
20:    {
21:       ...
22:       start = 0;
23:       end = 0;
24:       buffer_producer = new char[bufferSize];
25:       buffer_consumer = new char[bufferSize];
26:       circular_buffer = new Cell[cells];
27:       for(Int32 i = 0 ; i < cells ; i++)
28:       {
29:          circular_buffer[i].buff = new char[bufferSize];
30:          circular_buffer[i].size = -1;
31:       }
32:       ...
33:    }
34:
35:    public: void Run() {
36:       producer_thread = new Thread(ConcurrentFileCopy::Wrapper_To_Call_producer, (void *)this);
37:       consumer_thread = new Thread(ConcurrentFileCopy::Wrapper_To_Call_consumer, (void *)this);
38:       producer_thread->Start();
39:       consumer_thread->Start();
40:       producer_thread->SetDetached();
41:       consumer_thread->SetDetached();
42:    }
43:
44:    private: void *producer(void *ptr) {
45:       Int32 read;
46:       while(true) {
47:          try {
48:             read = fsRead->Read(buffer_producer, 0, bufferSize);
49:             if(read <= 0) {
50:                mutex->Lock();
51:                {
52:                   EndOfFileReached = true;
```

Figure 6.8 Local, concurrent copy of a file to another using the `FileStream` class.

(*Continued*)

```
53:              // Wait until the consumer thread completes its execution.
54:                 while(end != start && !StopRequested)
55:                    bufferNotEmpty->Wait();
56:              }
57:           mutex->Unlock();
58:           break;
59:        }
60:     }
61:     catch(IOException &e) {
62:        printf("3. Exception Message: %s\n", e.get_Message().get_BaseStream());
63:        mutex->Lock();
64:        StopRequested = true;
65:        mutex->Unlock();
66:        break;
67:     }
68:     catch(Exception &e) {
69:        printf("4. Exception Message: %s\n", e.get_Message().get_BaseStream());
70:        mutex->Lock();
71:        StopRequested = true;
72:        mutex->Unlock();
73:        break;
74:     }
75:     mutex->Lock();
76:     {
77:        // Use modulo as a trick to wrap around the end of the buffer_producer back to the beginning
78:        // Wait until the buffer_producer is full
79:        while((end + 1) % cells == start && !StopRequested) {
80:           // Buffer is full - sleep so consumers can get items.
81:           bufferNotFull->Wait();
82:        }
83:        if(StopRequested) {
84:           mutex->Unlock();
85:           break;
86:        }
87:        circular_buffer[end].size = read;
88:        memmove(circular_buffer[end].buff, buffer_producer, read);
89:        end = (end + 1) % cells;
90:     }
91:     mutex->Unlock();
92:     // If a consumer is waiting, wake it.
93:     bufferNotEmpty->Signal(); //
94:  }
95:  // for (StopRequested==true)
96:  bufferNotFull->Signal();
97:  bufferNotEmpty->Signal();
98:
99:  barrier->SignalAndWait(); // Synchronizes with other threads before the completion of its execution.
100:   return ptr;
101: }
102:
103: private: void *consumer(void *ptr) {
104:    Int32 write_bytes;
105:    while(true) {
```

Figure 6.8 (Continued) Local, concurrent copy of a file to another using the FileStream class.

(Continued)

```
106:            mutex->Lock();
107:            {
108:              if(end == start && EndOfFileReached && !StopRequested) {
109:                mutex->Unlock();
110:                break;
111:              }
112:              // Wait until the buffer_producer is empty
113:              while(end == start && !StopRequested && !EndOfFileReached) {
114:                // Buffer is empty - sleep so producers can create items.
115:                bufferNotEmpty->Wait();
116:              }
117:              if(StopRequested) {
118:                mutex->Unlock();
119:                break;
120:              }
121:              write_bytes = circular_buffer[start].size;
122:              if(write_bytes != -1)
123:                memmove(buffer_consumer, circular_buffer[start].buff, write_bytes);
124:              circular_buffer[start].size = -1;
125:              start = (start + 1) % cells;
126:            }
127:            mutex->Unlock();
128:            bufferNotFull->Signal(); // If a producer is waiting, wake it.
129:            if(write_bytes <= 0)
130:              continue;
131:            try {
132:              fsWrite->Write(buffer_consumer, 0, write_bytes);
133:              printf("\r...");
134:            }
135:            catch(IOException &e) {
136:              printf("5. Exception Message: %s\n", e.get_Message().get_BaseStream());
137:              mutex->Lock();
138:              StopRequested = true;
139:              mutex->Unlock();
140:              break;
141:            }
142:            catch(Exception &e) {
143:              printf("6. Exception Message: %s\n", e.get_Message().get_BaseStream());
144:              mutex->Lock();
145:              StopRequested = true;
146:              mutex->Unlock();
147:              break;
148:            }
149:          }
150:          // for (StopRequested==true)
151:          bufferNotFull->Signal();
152:          bufferNotEmpty->Signal();
153:
154:          barrier->SignalAndWait(); // Synchronizes with other threads before the completion of its execution.
155:          printf("...\r");
156:          return ptr;
157:        }
158:
```

Figure 6.8 **(Continued) Local, concurrent copy of a file to another using the FileStream class.**

(Continued)

```
159:     public: static int Parvicursor_main(int argc, char *argv[]) {
160:         Int32 bufferSize = 256*1024, cells = 10;
161:         FileStream *fsRead = null, fsWrite = null;
162:         Barrier *barrier = new Barrier(3); // main thread + producer and consumer threads.
163:         String readFilename = "c:/test.exe"; //to change
164:         String writeFilename = "c:/test1.exe"; //to change
165:         printf("Copying %s to %s\n", readFilename.get_BaseStream(), writeFilename.get_BaseStream());
166:         try {
167:             fsRead = new FileStream(readFilename, System::IO::Open, System::IO::Read, 8*1024);
168:             fsWrite = new FileStream(writeFilename, System::IO::OpenOrCreate, System::IO::Write,
8*1024);
169:         }
170:         catch(Exception &e) {
171:             ...
172:         }
173:         catch(...) {
174:             ...
175:         }
176:         ConcurrentFileCopy cfc = ConcurrentFileCopy(fsRead, fsWrite, bufferSize, cells, barrier);
177:         cfc.Run();
178:         barrier->SignalAndWait(); // Waits until the completion of other threads' execution.
179:         delete barrier; delete fsRead;delete fsWrite;
180:         return 0;
181:     }
182: };
```

Figure 6.8   (Continued) Local, concurrent copy of a file to another using the FileStream class.

folders, G and H, whilst the directory D is the parent of this directory. The ability of programs to create any number of subdirectories provides a powerful tool for organising files. At the end of this section, to complete the capabilities of the FileStream and Directory classes, we bring Table 6.4. The File class has three main methods, all of which are described in this table. It is also worth noting that the Directory and File class methods, as stated in the FileStream class, throw an exception if an error occurs whilst being invoked.

6.3.4 Two Examples of Non-Concurrent and Concurrent Use of the Directory Class

The first example of using the Directory class deals with listing all files under folders of a particular directory. As mentioned, the structure of a directory system is a hierarchical tree. Therefore, to find all files in this example, we must meet all the nodes of the tree and find files in the subdirectory whenever we visit. As a result, we will use a recursive function to fully traverse this tree structure. The implementation of this example comes in Figure 6.10. Inside the main() function, the RecursiveDirectoryTreeTraversal() function is used to find all the files under the dir directory. In this example, the dir directory is, in fact, our root directory to which the traversal is performed. In implementing this function in line 2, we first find the subdirectories of the dir folder. Then in a for loop (line 5) with the number of subdirectories found, we first locate the files in it; this is done in line 7 using the

Table 6.3   Static Methods of the `Directory` Class

Name	*Description*
`static void CreateDirectory(const String &path)`	Creates the given directory. It will throw an exception if at least one of the parent folders of the `path` variable does not exist. If the specified directory exists, this method does nothing.
`static void Delete(const String &path, bool recursive)`	Deletes the specified directory. If the `recursive` value is true, folders, subdirectories, and files in the path will be deleted.
`static void Delete(const String &path)`	Removes an empty directory from the specified path. If the directory has at least one file or subdirectory, an exception is thrown.
`static bool Exists(const String &path)`	Specifies whether the given path refers to a directory on disc. If such a directory does not exist, this method returns a `false` value.
`static ArrayList *GetDirectories(const String &path)`	Finds the subdirectories in the `path` variable. If there is no subdirectory, a `null` value returns. Otherwise, the pointer is an array list containing subdirectories, each link list element stores the reference of an instance of the memory-allocated `String` object in itself. Note that after using this class, we must delete all the elements in this array list by calling the `delete` keyword. Since the return value of this method is of pointer type, so because the memory allocation for the returned instance is an array list, after finishing our work with the return array, we must delete it from the memory (using the `delete` operator) as well.
`static ArrayList *GetFiles(const String &path)`	Returns names of files in the `path` directory. If there is no file, a `null` value returns. The procedure for freeing up allocated memory in this function is exactly the same as the `GetDirectories()` method.
`static void Move(const String &sourceDirName, const String &destDirName)`	Moves a directory and its contents from the `sourceDirName` path to the new `destDirName` location.
`static String GetCurrentDirectory()`	Finds the current application directory.

`GetFiles()` method. In lines 7 through 13, if the current directory contains a file, we print its name. Since in each iteration of the first `for` loop each subdirectory may contain subdirectories, we invoke the `RecursiveDirectoryTreeTraversal()` method again each time we repeat the loop of line 5 in line 17 to return subdirectories. This can be found under the directory. According to those tips explained in Table 6.3, the allocated memory objects are freed in lines 12, 14, 15, 18, 20, and 21 by these two static methods.

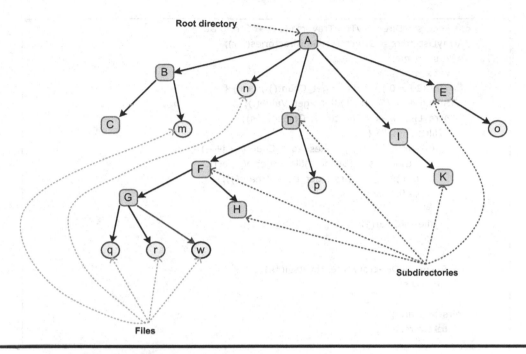

Figure 6.9   A hierarchical directory system.

Table 6.4   Static Methods of the `File` Class

Name	Description
`static void Delete(const String &path);`	Deletes the specified file. If the file does not exist, an exception is thrown.
`static bool Exists(const String &path);`	Specifies whether the given file exists or not. If such a file does not exist, this method returns a `false` value.
`static void Move(const String &sourceFileName, const String &destFileName);`	Moves a file from the existing `sourceFileName` path to the new `destFileName` location.

In the second and last example of this section, we describe a concurrent implementation of the cp shell command. Using this command on the command prompt of the Windows operating system or the shell of Unix systems such as Linux, one can completely copy a source directory (with all subdirectories and files in it) to a destination directory locally. Figure 6.11 shows the architecture of this example. Its implementation is shown in Figure 6.12. In the main() function, we want to copy the src directory to the dest directory. First, we create the src directory using the CreateDirectoryEx() method, then use the FindRootDirectoryFiles() method to find the files in the src directory; after finding each file in this directory on lines 96 and 97 using the data structure MethodInfo, we add the corresponding

```
 1: void RecursiveDirectoryTreeTraversal(const String &dir) {
 2:    ArrayList *dirs = Directory::GetDirectories(dir);
 3:    if(dirs == null)
 4:       return;
 5:    for(Int32 i = 0 ; i < dirs->get_Count() ; i++) {
 6:       String *s = (String *)dirs->get_Value(i);
 7:       ArrayList *files = Directory::GetFiles(*s);
 8:       if(files != null) {
 9:          for(Int32 j = 0 ; j < files->get_Count() ; j++) {
10:             String *ss = (String *)files->get_Value(j);
11:             printf("%s\n", ss->get_BaseStream());
12:             delete ss;
13:          }
14:          files->Clear();
15:          delete files;
16:       }
17:       RecursiveDirectoryTreeTraversal(*s);
18:       delete s;
19:    }
20:    dirs->Clear();
21:    delete dirs;
22: }
23:
24: int main(int argc, char *argv[]){
25:    String dir = "C:/"; // root director - to change
26:    RecursiveDirectoryTreeTraversal(dir);
27:    return 0;
28: }
```

Figure 6.10   Listing all files in the subdirectory of a directory by recursively traversing it.

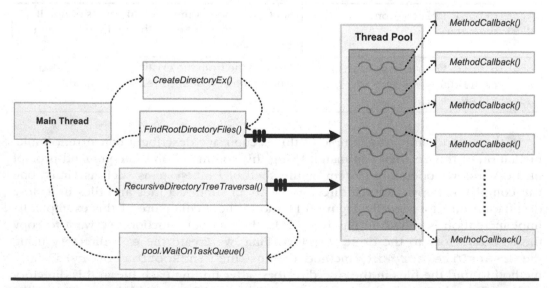

Figure 6.11   Architecture of the implemented code to concurrently copy one directory to another based on the `ThreadPool` class.

```
 1: class ConcurrentCP : public Object {
 2:    /*---------------------fields----------------*/
 3:    private: struct MethodInfo : public Object {
 4:       String *readFilename, *writeDir;
 5:       Int32 bufferSize;
 6:       public: MethodInfo(String *readFilename, String *writeDir, Int32 bufferSize) {
 7:          this->readFilename = readFilename;
 8:          this->writeDir = writeDir;
 9:          this->bufferSize = bufferSize;
10:       }
11:       public: ~MethodInfo() {
12:          if(readFilename != null) // allocated in FindRootDirectoryFiles or RecursiveDirectoryTreeTraversal
13:             delete readFilename;
14:          if(writeDir != null) // allocated in FindRootDirectoryFiles or RecursiveDirectoryTreeTraversal
15:             delete writeDir;
16:       }
17:    };
18:    /*--------------------methods---------------*/
19:    private: static void MethodCallback(Object *state) {
20:       MethodInfo *info = (MethodInfo *)state;
21:       String writeFilename = String(*info->writeDir) + "/" + info->readFilename->Substring(info-
       >readFilename->LastIndexOf("/") + 1);
22:       FileStream *fsRead = null, fsWrite = null;
23:       printf("Copying '%s' to '%s'\n", info->readFilename->get_BaseStream(),
       writeFilename.get_BaseStream());
24:       try {
25:          fsRead = new FileStream(*info->readFilename, System::IO::Open, System::IO::Read, 8*1024);
26:          fsWrite = new FileStream(writeFilename, System::IO::OpenOrCreate, System::IO::Write,
       8*1024);
27:       }
28:       catch(Exception &e) {
29:          ...
30:          return ;
31:       }
32:       catch(...) {
33:          ...
34:          return ;
35:       }
36:       Int32 read;
37:       if(info->bufferSize <= 0)
38:          info->bufferSize = 256*1024;
39:       char *buffer = new char[info->bufferSize];
40:       while(true) {
41:          try {
42:             read = fsRead->Read(buffer, 0, info->bufferSize);
43:             if(read <= 0)
44:                break;
45:             fsWrite->Write(buffer, 0, read);
46:          }
47:          catch(IOException &e) {
48:             ...
49:             break;
50:          }
```

Figure 6.12 Concurrent implementation of the directory copy operation reliant on the `Directory`, `FileStream`, and `ThreadPool` classes of the Parvicursor.NET Framework.

(Continued)

```
51:            catch(Exception &e) {
52:                ...
53:                break;
54:            }
55:            catch(...) {
56:                ...
57:                break;
58:            }
59:        }
60:        delete fsRead; delete fsWrite; delete buffer;
61:        delete info; // allocated in FindRootDirectoryFiles or RecursiveDirectoryTreeTraversal
62:        return;
63:    }
64:    /*----------------------------------------*/
65:    private: static void RecursiveDirectoryTreeTraversal(const String &dir, const String &newdir, const
String &root, ThreadPool *pool, Int32 bufferSize) {
66:        ArrayList *dirs = Directory::GetDirectories(dir);
67:        if(dirs == null)
68:            return;
69:        for(Int32 i = 0 ; i < dirs->get_Count() ; i++) {
70:            String *s = (String *)dirs->get_Value(i);
71:            String newstr = newdir + s->Substring(root.get_Length());
72:            if(!Directory::Exists(newstr))
73:                Directory::CreateDirectory(newstr);
74:            ArrayList *files = Directory::GetFiles(*s);
75:            if(files != null) {
76:                for(Int32 j = 0 ; j < files->get_Count() ; j++) {
77:                    String *ss = (String *)files->get_Value(j);
78:                    MethodInfo *info = new MethodInfo(ss, new String(newstr), bufferSize);
79:                    pool->QueueUserWorkItem(MethodCallback, info);
80:                }
81:                files->Clear();
82:                delete files;
83:            }
84:            RecursiveDirectoryTreeTraversal(*s, newdir, root, pool, bufferSize);
85:            delete s;
86:        }
87:        dirs->Clear();
88:        delete dirs;
89:    }
90:    /*----------------------------------------*/
91:    private: static void FindRootDirectoryFiles(const String &newdir, const String &root, ThreadPool
*pool, Int32 bufferSize) {
92:        ArrayList *files = Directory::GetFiles(root);
93:        if(files != null) {
94:            for(Int32 j = 0 ; j < files->get_Count() ; j++) {
95:                String *ss = (String *)files->get_Value(j);
96:                MethodInfo *info = new MethodInfo(ss, new String(newdir), bufferSize);
97:                pool->QueueUserWorkItem(MethodCallback, info);
98:            }
99:            files->Clear();
100:           delete files;
101:       }
```

Figure 6.12 (Continued) Concurrent implementation of the directory copy operation reliant on the Directory, FileStream, and ThreadPool classes of the Parvicursor.NET Framework.

(Continued)

```
102:   }
103:   /*-----------------------------------------*/
104:   // Creates a recursive directory pattern, e.g., /a/b/c/d/e.
105:   private: static void CreateDirectoryEx(const String &path) {
106:       String str = path;
107:       String temp;
108:       Int32 n = 0;
109:       while(true) {
110:           n = str.IndexOf("/", n + 1);
111:           if(n <= 0)
112:               break;
113:           temp = str.Substring(0, n);
114:           if(!Directory::Exists(temp))
115:               Directory::CreateDirectory(temp);
116:       }
117:       if(!Directory::Exists(path))
118:           Directory::CreateDirectory(path);
119:   }
120:   /*-----------------------------------------*/
121:   public: static int Parvicursor_main(int argc, char *argv[]) {
122:       Int32 bufferSize = 256*1024;
123:       Int32 threadNum = Environment::get_ProcessorCount()*4;
124:       String src = "C:/Users/Administrator/Desktop/Matrix Multiplication"; // to change
125:       String dest = "C:/test/c"; // to change
126:       if(!Directory::Exists(src)) {
127:           printf("src does not exist.\n");
128:           return 0;
129:       }
130:       ThreadPool pool = ThreadPool(threadNum, 10000); // Initialises the thread pool instance.
131:       try {
132:           if(!Directory::Exists(dest))
133:               CreateDirectoryEx(dest);
134:           FindRootDirectoryFiles(dest, src, &pool, bufferSize);
135:           RecursiveDirectoryTreeTraversal(src, dest, src, &pool, bufferSize);
136:       }
137:       catch(Exception &e) {
138:           ...
139:       }
140:       catch(...) {
141:           ...
142:       }
143:       pool.WaitOnTaskQueue(); // Waits until all methods (or threads within the ThreadPool) complete.
144:       return 0;
145:   }
146:   /*-----------------------------------------*/
147: };
```

Figure 6.12 (Continued) Concurrent implementation of the directory copy operation reliant on the Directory, FileStream, and ThreadPool classes of the Parvicursor.NET Framework.

file to the instance of our thread pool using the `QueueUserWorkItem()` method. In this example, the number of threads in our pool is chosen four times the count of the machine processor cores on line 123. The `CreateDirectoryEx()` method creates the desired path (like `/a/b/c/d/e`) in a loop by identifying the characters in path. After completing these steps, the `RecursiveDirectoryTreeTraversal()` method is called, and as in the example in Figure 6.10, in addition to finding the file, and like the `FindRootDirectoryFiles()` method (lines 78 and 79), it puts them in the thread pool's work queue and also creates subdirectories. Our thread pool implements the `MethodCallback()` callback method for copying files.

What follows in the implementation of this method in lines 19–23 is exactly the example code in Figure 6.7 of the `FileStream` class used to copy one file locally to another. In the end, we invoke the `WaitOnTaskQueue()` method of our thread pool class. This leads to waiting in the `main()` function for the completion of all operations until the thread pool's work queue still is not empty (namely, all files have not been copied by the thread pool yet). The complete source code examples of this section can be found in the "`/Parvicursor/Parvicursor/Samples/DiscIO/DiscIO`" path.

Reference

[1] IOzone Filesystem Benchmark, 2022; Available from: https://www.iozone.org

Chapter 7

Computer Networks: A Parallel Programming Approach

Major power and telephone grids have long been controlled by computer networks, but now similar systems are embedded in such mundane objects as electric meters, alarm clocks, home refrigerators and thermostats, video cameras, bathroom scales, and Christmas tree lights – all of which are, or soon will be, accessible remotely.

Charles C. Mann

7.1 Substantial Concepts of Computer Networks for Distributed Systems Design

7.1.1 Introduction

In the definition of a distributed system, it comes that a distributed system is composed of distributed processes in a computer network that communicate with one another through a computer network. Therefore, taking communication issues into account is fundamental to constructing a distributed system. Of course, it should be noted that the emergence and advancement of computer networks, as an indispensable part of distributed systems, has conducted distributed systems to their current form. In this chapter, we first examine necessary concepts in computer networks and then instruct the reader with different software techniques to implement communications in software and middleware layers. We also attempt, unlike traditional books in distributed systems that mostly discuss communications from high-level and algorithmic aspects, to arrive at two different approaches. First, we teach you to directly take your hands into coding and design communication protocols by yourself (we will not at all use ready methods such as RPC; rather, we build such a feature). Second,

DOI: 10.1201/9781003379041-7

unlike network programming books available on the market which rarely investigate the design of highly complex concurrent client-server systems (and it is not usually examined), in this chapter we only deal with this type of complex systems to leverage the processing power of modern multi/many-core processors throughout Sections 7.4–7.6. Although this complexity may lead to a steep learning curve for the reader, but the performance achieved from such systems can be a motivational factor for you to follow up on the hard materials within this chapter. In this respect, we will design a highly asynchronous and concurrent framework from the ground up. In Section 7.6, we teach our experience gained from constructing this framework to the interested readers. The section can become a standard candidate to build higher-level communication systems, because this framework has been designed based on optimum exploitation of the computing power available in multi/many-core systems to properly and performantly handle highly scalable communication mechanisms. In this chapter, we assume the reader has enough skills with the concepts of computer networks and even network programming, and we teach him/her with more advanced topics. However, since this book is intended for a broad audience of readers with various interests and experiences, we will discuss those topics in a nutshell that are needed from computer networks and network programming (i.e., socket programming).

7.2 An Introduction to Modern Computer Networks

A computer network consists of a collection of computers (or any computing entity such as portable mobile devices) and other hardware components that are connected by communication channels and allow sharing of resources and information. In the topology created within this computer network, threads (or processes) can send and receive messages and information. Communication protocols in computer networks provide the rules and structures of data to exchange information and create a basis for network programming which are discussed in detail herein.

There are two transport technologies: broadcast links and point-to-point links. Point-to-point links connect individual pairs of machines. This type of transport is usually referred to as unicast. In a broadcast network, the communication channel is shared between all the machines on the network, and packets sent by any machine are received by all other machines. Some broadcast systems support transmission to a subset of machines, which is known as multicast. In this chapter, we explain unicast transports entirely grounding upon TCP/IP protocol, because the book's skeleton exclusively utilises this type of transport. Multicast or broadcast transports based on such protocols as UDP are commonly used for transferring messages and collective communications of dozens of network nodes. Because the concepts covered in this book do not require multicast transports, which are outside the scope of the book, we omit to describe them and refer the interested reader to references like [1].

Computer networks are classified into four major categories based on distance and speed parameters: local-area networks[1], metropolitan-area networks[2], wide-area networks[3], and high-speed networks such as InfiniBand interconnects.

LANs are computer networks that are formed from joining a set of machines in a restricted local region like a university. Amongst the most significant cabling

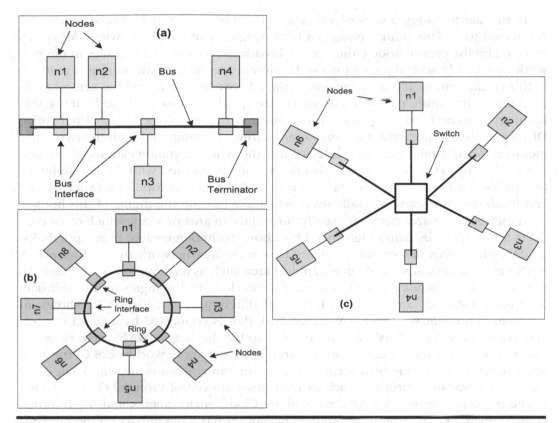

Figure 7.1   Three typical types of topologies used in the wiring of a LAN network: (a) bus topology, (b) ring topology, and (c) star topology.

approaches used to construct LAN networks is Ethernet. The wiring of LAN networks is done in different varieties, including, bus, ring, star, tree, mesh, and so on. Some of these topologies appear in Figure 7.1.

In the bus topology, a single cable is used for all devices on the network. This cable is often referred to as the term *network backbone*. When a connection happens between nodes, the sender device broadcasts its message to all nodes, but only the intended recipient picks that message up (this action is done by a unique hardware address called MAC[4] address for each device on the network). This topology makes the installation of cables very easy but limits overall network performance in a large number of nodes.

In the ring topology, every node is connected to other nodes on the network, whilst the first and last nodes are connected to each other. Messages from one node to others travel from the originator towards the destination through a set of intermediary nodes. The intermediary nodes function as active repeaters for messages intended for other nodes. In this topology, messages can move both clockwise and counterclockwise. The ring topology usually creates relatively long transmission times in comparison with the bus topology, and has a much more compact effect on network communication in the event of a cable failure between any two nodes.

In the star topology, a upper-level central node is used in that all other nodes are connected to it. This central node can be a computer or simply a switch. Messages received by the central node either can be broadcast to all available nodes in the network or are only sent to a target node. The internode delay of messaging is reduced in this configuration. If one of the connections between a node and the central node goes down, the entire network will not be disrupted. Because of these benefits, this topology is more used in contrast to the bus and ring topologies in LAN networks. Of course, this configuration requires more wirings as compared with the two other methods. Also, should the central device fail, the whole communications of the network will stop. This topology has also restrictions concerned with the scalability of the number of network nodes. Due to these problems, other topologies such as tree and mesh structures are generally used, which are beyond the theme of this book.

A metropolitan-area network usually surrounds an area or a city, which often connects a few LANs by using high-speed backbone technologies like fibre-optic links. A MAN often provides communications to a wide-area network or the Internet. A WAN network encloses a wide geographical area such as a country or a continent. In practice, WANs operate more as computer networking technologies to transmit data over long distances, and between LANs and different WANs. Figure 7.2 shows an example of a client/server on a WAN network that is connected by a cloud of routers. Routers are the WNAs' building blocks. Today the largest WAN network is the Internet, which connects a network of large WAN networks worldwide. In the next section, we will examine how a client and server can communicate with each other on top of a transport protocol such as Transmission Control Protocol (TCP/IP). One of the important issues in WANs, particularly Cloud environments and the Internet, is the transmission optimisation problem because it has a big impact on the network throughput in addition to a large number of users and long distances. Most of them that are mainly caused by TCP protocol include throughput, bandwidth requirements, latency, protocol optimisation, congestion (in lost packets), and the scalability

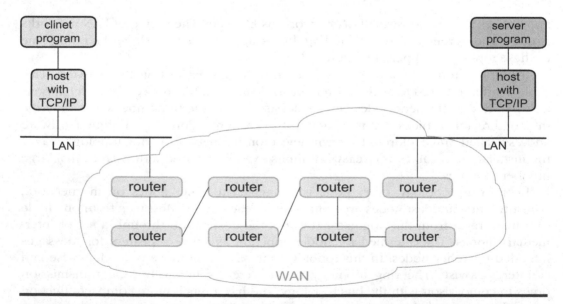

Figure 7.2   A client and server on different LANs are connected via a WAN link.

issue. WAN optimisation has been one of the subjects of extensive academic research almost since the emergence of WANs. In this chapter and in Chapter 10, we will discuss this issue in detail, especially at the application layer, protocol design, and operating system.

In the last classification of computer networks, we briefly refer to high-speed networks that are built reliant on InfiniBand communication links. InfiniBand is a switched fabric communication link in High-Performance Computing, enterprise data centres, and Cloud Computing. The dramatic increase in the performance of modern processors requires I/O subsystems to satisfy the ability in data delivery with a rate that is needed by the processor subsystem. In order to achieve higher performance and scalability with lower costs, system architects have encountered concepts like clustering, grid and cloud computing. To achieve the benefits of these new technologies, the protocol used for communications between physical machines must supply high bandwidth and low latency. Unfortunately, fully-fledged network protocols such as TCP (as we extensively examine it within this book), to achieve a good performance on LANs and WANs, have become so complicated that they cause significant latencies. InfiniBand is the answer to this key issue in data transmission.

In transmitting a piece of data from one machine to another, the latency due to the overhead and the latencies that are added to the time needed for actual data transfer exhibit themselves. The most important contributors to this latency can be studied from three aspects: (a) the execution overhead of network transport protocol inside the operating system kernel, (b) several context switchings to move inside and outside of the kernel for sending and receiving data, and (c) extra data copies between userspace buffers and NIC memory.

A typical topology of an InfiniBand network looks like the star topology shown in Figure 7.1. Communications between nodes, switches, and routers are point-to-point and serial connections. InfiniBand specification defines the raw bandwidth of base connection 1x to 2.5 Gb per second, and also other bases such as 4x, 12x, and so on are specified. In this specification, channel adapters are divided into Host Channel Adapters[5] and Target Channel Adapters[6]. Figure 7.3 illustrates the InfiniBand communication stack. If an application wants to communicate with another application over InfiniBand, it must first create a work queue that is comprised of Queue Pair[7].

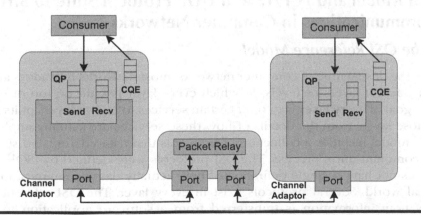

Figure 7.3 InfiniBand communication stack.

The application to be able to perform an operation must put a Work Queue Element[8] into the work queue. From there, that operation is selected by the channel adapter. Thus, the work queue establishes a communication medium between applications and channel adaptors and relieves the operating system from having to deal with this responsibility. Each process may create one or more QP(s) for communication purposes with another application. Instead of having to use a single queue of an NIC card in a typical operating system, each queue pair has a context associated. Because both the protocol and the structures are all very clearly defined, queue pairs can be implemented in hardware, and in this way, most of the work is offloaded from the CPU. As soon as a WQE is properly processed, a Completion Queue Element[9] is created and the WQE is placed into the CQE. The advantage of using a completion queue for notifying the caller of the completed WQEs is to reduce interrupts that may otherwise be generated. For the receive queue, only a type of operation is defined: Post Receive Buffer. The list of the operations supported by InfiniBand architecture at the transport level for send queue comes as follows:

1. Send/Receive: supports the typical send/receive operations where one node submits one message and another node receives the message. A difference between the implementation of the send/receive operations in InfiniBand architecture and conventional networking protocols is that InfiniBand defines the send/receive operations as operating along the queue pairs.
2. RDMA[10]-Send/Receive: these operations allow a node to write/read directly to/from the memory buffer on a remote node. The remote node must already have some registered memory buffers for remote access.
3. RDMA Atomics: perform atomic CAS operations, which were discussed in Chapter 5, with RDMA type on a remote node.

Other transports are also supported in InfiniBand, including multicast and transactional operations. On the whole, InfiniBand provides high throughput, low latency, quality of service[11], high scalability, and failover.

7.3 OSI Model and TCP/IP and UDP Protocol Suite to Structure Communications in Computer Networks

7.3.1 The OSI Reference Model

To reduce the design time of computer networks, most networks nowadays are organised as a stack of layers or levels, in which every layer is built on top of the lower layer. The goal of every layer is to offer certain services to higher layers of itself whilst hiding those layers from the details of how these services are actually implemented. The OSI[12] model includes a collection of protocols that try to define and standardise the data communication process. The OSI protocols were defined by ISO[13]. The OSI model does not have a single definition of how actually data communications occur in the real world. Several protocols exist in every layer. The OSI reference model describes how information is transferred from a software application to another machine via a network environment. Figure 7.4 shows the OSI reference model.

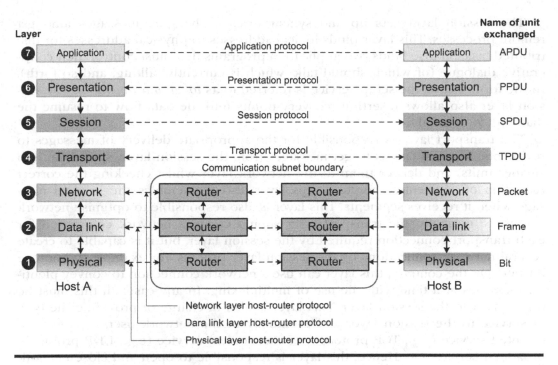

Figure 7.4   The OSI reference model.

OSI splits communications into seven layers. Layers are organised into two groups. The upper four layers are used when a message passes from/to a user. The lower three layers are used when a message passes through the host machine. Messages intended for another host are not passed to the upper layers and, in turn, are forwarded to another host. The application layer of the OSI model lays closest to the end user, which means that the application layer and the user interact directly with the software application. This layer interacts with software programs that implement a communication component. For instance, programs such as a web server, a mail server, and a file server are implemented on this layer. The role of this layer is to identify communication partners, determine resource availability, and synchronise communications. When identifying communication partners, the application layer determines the identification and availability of the communication partners for an application along with the data to be transferred. When determining the resource availability, this layer must decide whether sufficient network resources for the requested communication exist or not. In synchronising the communication, all communications amongst applications require cooperation that is managed by the application layer. This layer is one of the widely used layers throughout this book. All existing protocols in this book, in particular this chapter and Chapter 10, will be implemented on this layer.

The presentation layer takes care of the syntax and semantics of transferred data: this layer processes the data to be accommodated between communication tasks. This layer guarantees independence between user and data transmission. This layer can usually convert, format, encrypt, and compress the data. For example, the secure data transfer protocol (xSec) for the Parvicursor platform is implemented within this layer in Chapter 10.

The session layer sets up and synchronises exchanging messages amongst remote processes. This layer binds logical addresses to physical addresses for distributed tasks. It also binds two application programs that must control their cooperative dialogue (of which should talk, which is currently talking, and so forth). In the former case, the setup service is referred to as *token management*. The session layer also allows inserting recovery points into the data flow to resume the dialogue after a failure.

The transport layer is responsible for the appropriate delivery of messages to recipients. Its main task is to get messages from the session layer, split them into smaller units, and deliver them to the network layer whilst checking the correct reception of segments. Therefore, this layer also reassembles the original message when it receives segments. This layer is also responsible to optimise network resources: normally, the transport layer should create a network connection for each transport connection required by the session layer, but it is capable to create several network connections by the session layer process, for example to improve bit rate. On the contrary, this layer can use a network connection to convey plentiful messages at a time with the use of multiplexing. In any case, all this must be transparent to the session layer. This layer is also in charge of providing the type of service to the session layer and eventually to the network users: connection-oriented service (e.g., TCP protocol), connectionless service (e.g., UDP protocol), broadcast service, etc. Hence, this layer is responsible to open and close network connections. This also has the duty of flow control. This layer is one of the most important layers because it provides fundamental services to the user and controls the entire connection process with all corresponding constraints. The information unit for this layer is a *message*. We will further discuss this layer in the rest of this section.

The network layer is responsible for the subnet, which means the routing packets over subnets and the interconnection of various subnets. When designing this layer, determining a routing mechanism and calculating routing tables (static or dynamic tables) are very important. This layer controls the subnet congestion as well. The information unit for this layer is a packet. IP protocol is one of the most essential protocols of this layer, which will be discussed in the remainder of this section as well.

The data link layer provides practical and procedural tools for data transmission between network entities, and to find and probably correct the errors that may happen in the physical layer. This layer divides the sender input data into frames, sends these frames sequentially, and manages acknowledgement frames sent by the recipient. This layer must be able to signal a transmission problem by sending a proper frame. This layer also integrates a control flow operation to avoid blocking a receiver. The information unit of this layer is a *frame* that is composed of a few hundred up to a few thousand bytes.

The physical layer has the task to transfer raw bits over the transmission channel. This layer must ensure the complete transfer of data. In fact, this layer must standardise electrical characteristics (e.g., a bit set to 1 is expressed with a potential voltage of 5 volts), mechanical and functional characteristics of data circuits, establishment procedures, and maintenance and release of data circuits. The typical information unit of this layer is a *bit* that is expressed by a given voltage.

7.3.2 The TCP/IP Protocol Suite

TCP[14]/IP protocol suite is a layered network protocol, which includes Internet Protocol[15] and a variety of other protocols layered on top of it. The code that implements its various layers is usually known as the *Protocol Stack*. Encapsulation is one of the significant principles of layered network protocols. Figure 7.5 depicts a sample of this mechanism in the layers of TCP/IP protocol. The key idea behind encapsulation is that the information (e.g., application data, a TCP segment, and an IP datagram) passed from an upper layer to a lower layer is dealt as opaque data by the lower layer. In other words, the lower layer does not perform any effort to interpret the information sent from an upper layer, but it merely puts the information into any type of packet that is used in the lower layer and adds its own layer's special header before passing the packet downwards to the next lower layer. When data is passed from a lower layer to an upper layer, a reverse-unpacking process occurs.

In the TCP/IP protocol suite, the IP protocol functions in the OSI model's network layer. This protocol has two versions, 4 and 6, in which addresses respectively are 32 and 128 bits in length. The IP protocol is described as a connectionless protocol because it does not provide the image of a virtual circuit connecting two hosts. IP is also an unreliable protocol: it performs the best effort to move datagrams from the sender to the recipient but does not guarantee that the packets will reach their destination from where they had been sent, or that they will not duplicate, or even that they will never arrive. IP also does not provide error recovery; the packets with overhead errors are silently discarded. Reliability must be obtained either by a reliable transport-layer protocol (such as TCP and SCTP[16]) or within the application itself.

The IPv4 datagrams can be up to 65,535 bytes. By default, IPV6 datagrams allow the maximum length of 65,575 bytes and provide an option for larger datagrams (which are called *jumbograms*). An IP address consists of two parts: a network

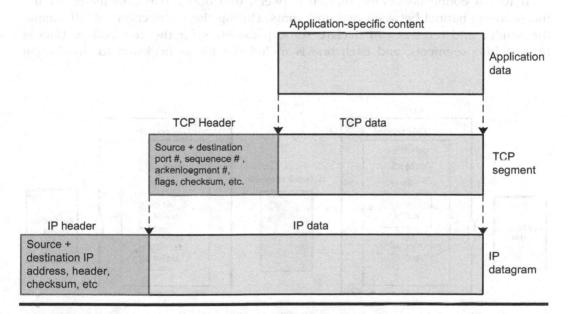

Figure 7.5   Encapsulation within the layers of TCP/IP protocol.

ID, which specifies the network in which a host is located, and a host ID. An IPv4 address is made up of 32 bits and displayed as a dotted decimal representation when it comes to human readable form, for example, the address `192.168.1.2` is one of the addressees in a LAN network's range. IPv6 addresses are typically written as a series of 16-bit hexadecimal numbers that are separated by colons (their general representation is in the form of `F000:0:0:0:0:0:A:1`).

There are two types of transport-layer protocols in the TCP/IP protocol suite. UDP[17] protocol is used for connectionless transmission of datagrams. UDP uses a simple model with a minimal protocol mechanism. This is not a reliable protocol and is commonly used for multicast and VoIP[18] applications. In this book, according to this issue and that the UDP protocol is not used in this context, we will not examine it. The TCP protocol is the most widely used transport protocol on the Internet, Cloud environments, and particularly WAN networks and distributed systems.

The task of a transport protocol is to provide end-to-end communication for applications residing on different hosts. To perform such a function, the transport layer requires a way to distinguish between applications on a host. In TCP and UDP, this distinction is made by a 16-bit port number. For instance, a web server and a file server serve their clients on ports 80 and 21, respectively.

TCP provides a reliable, connection-oriented, bidirectional, and byte-stream communication channel between two endpoints (i.e., applications). Figure 7.6 illustrates a scenario in which two applications A and B interact with each other via TCP sockets. Connection-oriented TCP socket programming is comprehensively discussed in the next sections. In this figure, the term *TCP endpoint* has been used to denote the information maintained by the kernel for an end of a TCP connection. This information includes the `send()` and `receive()` buffers for this end of the connection along with state information which is maintained to synchronise the operation of two connected endpoints.

Before a connection is established between two hosts, TCP establishes a communication channel between two endpoints. During the connection establishment, the sender and receiver can declare some parameters for the connection. Data is broken into segments, and each one is included with a checksum to provide an

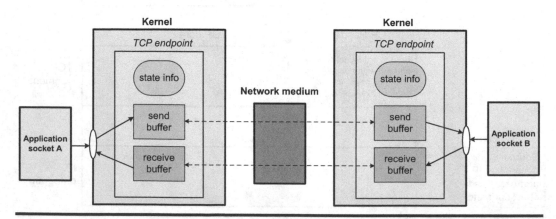

Figure 7.6   The transition between two applications' sockets based on the TCP protocol.

end-to-end transmission error detection. Every segment is transferred within a single datagram. When a TCP segment arrives at its destination without any error, the receiving TCP entity sends a positive acknowledgement to the sender and informs it of the successful delivery of the data. If a segment comes with errors, TCP ignores it, and no acknowledgement is sent. To handle segments that will never arrive or are ignored, the sender of every segment starts a timer when every segment is being transferred. If an acknowledgement is not received before the timer expires, the segment is retransmitted.

A logical sequence number is assigned to each byte that is transferred over a TCP connection. This number indicates the byte position within the data stream for the connection. When a TCP segment is transmitted, it has a field containing the sequence number of the first byte in the segment. Flow control in TCP protocol prevents a fast sender from overwhelming a slow receiver. To implement the flow control, the TCP receiver maintains a buffer for incoming data. Each TCP entity advertises the size of this buffer upon connection establishment. Data accumulates in this buffer whilst it is received from the sending TCP entity and is removed when the application reads it. With every acknowledgement, the receiver notifies the sender of the amount of space that is available in its input data buffer (i.e., how many bytes can be transferred by the sender). TCP has also several congestion control algorithms to prevent a fast sender from overwhelming a network. Provided that a sending TCP entity transmits the packets faster than they can be relayed by a router, the router drops the packets. If the sender TCP retransmitted these dropped packets, it could lead to high rates of packet loss and finally a dramatic performance degradation. Thus, as seen, TCP congestion control algorithms are very important. A comprehensive evaluation of the TCP protocol suite is beyond the space of this chapter. We refer the interested reader to reference [2] for further study. In the remainder of this chapter, we follow the implementation of the communication subject relied on socket programming and the Parvicursor platform.

7.4 Network Programming Based on TCP Sockets and Thread-Level Parallesim to Develop Distributed Client-Server Programs Atop the Parvicursor.NET Framework

7.4.1 An Introduction to the Socket Programming Model

The standard model used for the development of networked applications is socket programming. A socket is an endpoint that can be named and addressed. Socket programming in this chapter shows how we can use the Socket class's methods in the namespace System::Net::Sockets from Parvicursor platform to establish communication links between local and remote processes. Sockets are generally used for client/server interactions and have an essential role in the construction of a broad taxonomy of applications in distributed systems, the Internet and WANs. The typical system configuration places the server on one machine with clients on other machines. Clients connect to the server, exchange information, and then disconnect the connection.

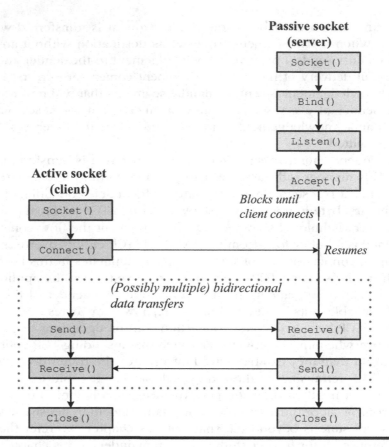

Figure 7.7 A typical flow of events for a connection-oriented socket.

A socket has a typical flow of events. In a client-server model, a socket on the server process waits for requests of a client. To do this, the server first establishes (binds) an address that the clients can use to locate the server. The server waits for clients' requests when the address is established. The client-to-server data exchange occurs when a client connects to the server through a socket. The server performs the client request and sends a reply to the client. Figure 7.7 illustrates a typical flow of the events and the order of use of the socket methods for a connection-oriented socket session. The figure's methods are located between the application layer and the transport layer in the communication model. On the other hand, the socket methods allow programs to interact with the network or transport layer. We explain these methods in short as follows.

1. The method Socket() opens a communication endpoint and returns a reference that represents the endpoint.
2. When a program has a socket reference, it can bind a unique name to the socket. Servers must bind an address immediately accessible from the network.
3. The method Listen() indicates an interest to accept client connection requests. When the Listen() method is issued on a socket, the socket cannot actively initiate the connection request. The Bind() method binds a name to the socket. The Listen() method must be issued before the Accept() method can be called.

4. The client program uses the method `Connect()` on a connection-oriented (stream) socket to establish a connection to the server.

5. The server program makes use of the `Accept()` method to accept a client connection request. The server must call the methods `Listen()` and `Bind()` before invoking the method `Accept()`.

6. When a connection is established between the client and server stream sockets, you can use the methods `Send()` and `Receive()` for actual data transmission.

7. When the server or the client is going to stop the operation, it calls the `Close()` method to release any resources acquired by the socket.

7.4.2 A General Description of Network Programming Classes in the Parvicursor.NET Framework

Now that we are familiar with socket concepts, in this section, we describe classes from the Parvicursor.NET Framework that can be used in most cases to develop communication systems for distributed applications. In Sections 7.5 and 7.6, advanced concepts to develop highly scalable, high-performance, complex programs are presented in addition to this section's classes. This is important from two aspects: first, a client must be able to convert a server address (e.g., which is in the form of a domain) into a numerical IP address, and second, the server must be able to listen on a specific IP address and port to incoming network connections. The four classes `IPEndPoint`, `IPAddress`, `Dns`, and `IPHostEntry` of the `System::Net` namespace carry out these functionalities for us.

Domain Name System[19] is an Internet standard protocol that locates machines on an IP-based network. IP networks, such as the Internet, are concerned with numerical addresses for data processing. Users can usually remember name addresses easier than numerical ones, so it is required to translate user-friendly domain names (e.g., www.example.com) into addresses that can be recognised by the network (such as `198.23.57.53`). Table 7.1 shows the `Resolve()` method of the `Dns` class. To understand how to use the classes in the `System::Net` namespace, follow Example 1 at the end of this section.

The most key class for network programming in the Parvicursor.NET Framework is the `Socket` class in the `System::Net::Sockets` namespace. Because we discussed existing methods for a connection-oriented socket at the beginning of this section, here we just explain a number of the `Socket` class's important methods just for emphasis (see Table 7.2). Note that an exception such as `SocketException`, `Exception`, and so on is thrown in the case of any error after using these methods.

Table 7.1 The DNS Class's Static Method in the Parvicursor.NET Framework

Name	Description
`IPHostEntry Resolve(const String &hostName)`	Queries a DNS server for IP addresses associated with a hostname or an IP address and returns an instance of the class `IPHostEntry`. If this method fails to find at least one IP address (e.g., due to connectivity problems), an exception of the `SocketException` class is thrown.

Table 7.2   The `Socket` Class's Constructor and Methods in the Parvicursor.NET Framework

Name	Description
`Socket(Address-Family addressFamily, SocketType socketType, ProtocolType protocolType)`	Initialises a new instance of a socket class along with address family, and socket and protocol type. The values of `InterNetwork` and `InterNetworkV6` can be specified as the argument `addressFamily` for IPv4 and IPv6 protocols. To use connection-oriented and connectionless sockets, you can specify the `socketType` parameter to be `Stream` and `Dgram`, respectively. To specify the type of the working protocol of TCP or UDP, you can use `tcp` and `udp`. In this book, we always employ the following class constructor for instantiation (i.e., for connection-oriented sockets depending on the TCP protocol): `Socket(InterNetwork, Stream, tcp)`
`void Connect(IPEndPoint &remoteEP)`	Establishes a blocking connection to a server specified by the variable `remoteEP`. `remoteEP` can be initialised by the information returned from the `System::Net::Dns::Resolve()` method and a port number (see the Example 1 of this section).
`void Bind(IPEndPoint &localEP)`	Binds a socket instance on an IP address (or a series of IP addresses) and a port. To use the `Listen()` method, this method must be invoked in advance.
`void Listen(Int32 backlog)`	Makes a connection-oriented socket instance be set to a listening state for incoming connection attempts.
`Socket *Accept() const`	Dequeues simultaneously the first pending connection from the connection request queue of the listening socket, and then creates and returns a new socket. Since a pointer address to the `Socket` class returns, it means that a memory allocation has been made. Therefore, we must use the `delete` keyword to release the memory allocated to this new instance after getting our work completed with it (in this situation, we should first call the `Close()` method of the socket instance). The `Accept()` method blocks until an incoming connection attempt is queued. Once a connection is accepted, the original socket continues to enqueue incoming connection requests as long as the socket is closed by the `Close()` method.
`Int32 Send(const char buffer[], Int32 offset, Int32 size, SocketFlags socketFlags)`	Sends the specified number of bytes from an offset to a connected socket by using the parameter `SocketFlags`. In this book, we just deal with the `None` value of this flag. This method returns the number of bytes sent. To use this method, you must make sure that the send buffer size does not exceed the maximum size provided by the underlying service provider. In connection-oriented sockets, this method blocks until the requested bytes are sent.
`Int32 Receive(char buffer[], Int32 offset, Int32 size, SocketFlags socketFlags)`	Receives the number of bytes specified into the buffer from the location `from` and fills it. If the connection is closed by the endpoint, then this method returns a value of zero, otherwise it returns the number of bytes received on the socket. The behaviour of this method is akin to the `Send()` method.

(Continued)

Table 7.2 (Continued) The Socket Class's Constructor and Methods in the Parvicursor.NET Framework

Name	Description
void Shutdown(Socket-Shutdown how)	Disables the send or receive operation on a socket. When using connection-oriented sockets, call this method before closing the socket. This ensures that all data on the connected socket are sent and received before it is closed. The parameter how can have one of these three values: Send, Receive, and Both. For example, the value of Both simultaneously disables the send and receive operations on the socket.
void Close()	Closes the remote host connection and releases all system resources consumed by the socket instance.
Int32 get_Handle() const	Gets the operating system handle for the respective socket. Because the current implementation of the Socket class in the Parvicursor.NET Framework supports for what is needed in this book, for calling the operating system APIs that provide more operations than to this class, you can use this method and get the desired socket handle. This handle can be passed to some socket system routines such as sendto(), getsockopt(), setsockopt(), select(), etc.

7.4.3 A Short Overview of the HTTP[20] Protocol

In this section, we briefly take a look at the HTTP protocol, because we will extensively take benefit of this protocol in the examples of this chapter as well as this protocol has great importance especially on the Internet and Cloud Computing to form distributed systems.

The HTTP/1.1 protocol in RFC 2616 is defined as an application-level standard protocol for distributed, collaborative, and hypermedia systems. HTTP is a stateless protocol that has been used for many tasks beyond hypertext applications. HTTP is based on a request/response model. In simple terms, a client sends a request consisting of a request method, URI[21] (a page or object address) and the protocol version to a web server followed by a MIME[22]-style message containing client information, request modifiers, and possibly body contents (for POST requests). The server then replies to the client with a status code including the protocol version, and a success or error code followed by a MIME-like message containing server information, metadata, and probably entity-body contents.

In this request/response chain, there may be one or more intermediate systems that are referred to as gateways, tunnels, or proxies. A proxy simply is a sender agent that receives the requests for a URI, rewrites some or the entire message, and sends the formatted request to a remote server. In the second example of Section 7.6, a complete proxy server is designed and implemented.

HTTP is usually implemented over TCP/IP sessions and on the default port 80. Also, always keep in mind that the connections of request/response protocols like HTTP (unlike file transfer protocols such as xDFS and FTP; refer to Chapter 10) rarely exist for extended periods of time. Instead, these connections tend to be short-lived and are generated for the duration of request/response chains which are being carried. HTTP has seven request operations, including DELETE, CONNECT, POST, GET, PUT, HEAD, and TRACE. they are sent by a client to a server, which we will explain only the first three. The GET method retrieves any information that is in the URI request. The POST method tells the server it must accept the message body sent; this method is used generally to send the contents of an HTML form, upload a file, and in web services based on SOAP[23] protocol. The CONNECT method is employed for tunnelling protocols such as SSL/TLS[24] and other protocols through a proxy server.

Earlier HTTP versions established a separate TCP connection to fetch each URL[25]. This meant that we were greatly increasing the load processing on HTTP servers, and, finally, this resulted in unnecessary congestion in both the Intranet and Internet. For instance, inline images and other data could mean that one client made multiple requests to a web server over a short amount of time. To overcome this issue, HTTP/1.1 introduced persistent connections. Such a concept also exists in file transfer protocols like xDFS, of course, in terms of reusable channels. In general, an HTTP/1.1 server assumes that all requests are persistent connections unless the Connection header issued by the client is in the type of close. The clients that are usually connected to a web server via a proxy use the Proxy-Connection header with the value of keep-alive in their requests, indicating the client is going to establish a persistent connection to the proxy and consequently to the web server. The proxy should remove the Proxy- part of the header when it sends the Proxy-Connection header. This makes the server not detect that a client is connecting through a proxy server. Persistent connections have several advantages including:

- Opening and closing fewer TCP connections mean that CPU time can be saved in routers and hosts (clients and servers), and also less memory is needed to store TCP control blocks on host machines.
- Requests and responses can be made pipeline, which allows multiple requests to be embedded into a message body without waiting to be returned separately for each response. Also, with a persistent connection, a single connection can be used more efficiently resulting in less latency and the avoidance of re-establishing connections.
- The overall network congestion reduces because we do not need to constantly open connections anymore, and thus the overhead of packets caused by establishing TCP connections decreases. Similarly, the latency associated with these excessive connections reduces because the connection remains open.

Now, we examine three examples to use the methods POST, GET, and CONNECT (in direct and indirect connection mode of a client to a web server or through a proxy) so that you see how the HTTP messages are formatted and exchanged between clients and servers. These examples are shown in Figure 7.8 through Figure 7.10. In the direct GET example, the client requests the page /index.html from a server with the Host header containing the value of www.example.com. The server returns the page contents with a 200 OK success status code which includes an HTML page with a length of 20 bytes in line 8 of Figure 7.8(c). In all these examples, persistent connections have been made with the header of Connection: keep-alive. In the request of a client through a proxy for GET/POST methods, the client in line 1 of Figure 7.8(b) must send the absolute address of a page or web object to the proxy

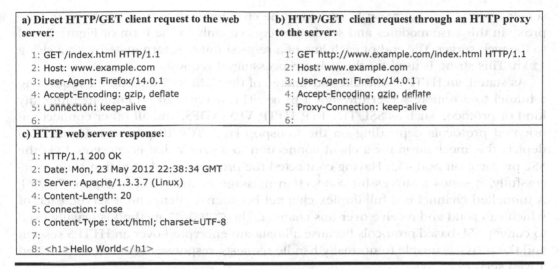

a) Direct HTTP/GET client request to the web server:	b) HTTP/GET client request through an HTTP proxy to the server:
1: GET /index.html HTTP/1.1	1: GET http://www.example.com/index.html HTTP/1.1
2: Host: www.example.com	2: Host: www.example.com
3: User-Agent: Firefox/14.0.1	3: User-Agent: Firefox/14.0.1
4: Accept-Encoding: gzip, deflate	4: Accept-Encoding: gzip, deflate
5: Connection: keep-alive	5: Proxy-Connection: keep-alive
6:	6:

c) HTTP web server response:

1: HTTP/1.1 200 OK
2: Date: Mon, 23 May 2012 22:38:34 GMT
3: Server: Apache/1.3.3.7 (Linux)
4: Content-Length: 20
5: Connection: close
6: Content-Type: text/html; charset=UTF-8
7:
8: \<h1>Hello World\</h1>

Figure 7.8 An example of a GET method in the request/response of a client from an HTTP web server to retrieve a web page (c), directly (b) and through a proxy server (c).

a) Direct HTTP/POST client request to the web server:	b) HTTP/POST client request through an HTTP proxy to the server:
1: POST /login.php HTTP/1.1	1: POST http://www.example.com/login.php HTTP/1.1
2: Host: www.example.com	2: Host: www.example.com
3: User-Agent: Firefox/14.0.1	3: User-Agent: Firefox/14.0.1
4: Content-Length: 28	4: Content-Length: 28
5: Content-Type: application/x-www-form-urlencoded	5: Content-Type: application/x-www-form-urlencoded
6:	6:
7: username=test&password=test*	7: username=test&password=test*

c) HTTP web server response:

1: HTTP/1.1 200 OK
2: Date: Mon, 23 May 2012 22:38:34 GMT
3: Server: Apache/1.3.3.7 (Linux)
4: Content-Length: 20
5: Connection: close
6: Content-Type: text/html; charset=UTF-8
8:
9: \<h1>Hello World\</h1>

Figure 7.9 An example of the POST method in the directly (a) and through (b) a proxy server of a client from an HTTP web server to upload a login form's filled forms, directly (a) and through (b) a proxy server

a) HTTP/CONNECT client request to the proxy server:	b) HTTP/CONNECT proxy response:
1: CONNECT www.example.com:443 HTTP/1.1	1: HTTP/1.1 200 Connection established
2: User-Agent: Firefox/14.0.1	2: Proxy-Agent: Parvicursor.NET-AsynchProxy-v1
3: Proxy-Connection: Keep-Alive	3:
4:	

Figure 7.10 An example of the CONNECT method in the request (a) and response (b) of a client from an HTTP proxy server to tunnel a channel to a remote server on port 443 for secure transmission relied upon the HTTPS/SSL protocol.

server and the `Connection` header must be changed to `Proxy-Connection`. The proxy in this case modifies and sends the requests only in the form of Figure 7.8(a) to the web server. The end of each line of a request must be terminated with a string `\r\n`. This string is used for the string processing of requests.

As stated, an HTTP client takes advantage of the `CONNECT` method for requesting a tunnel to a remote server through a proxy. This server can be implementing any kind of protocol, such as SSL/TLS, FTP, HTTP, VPN, xDFS, and all other connection-oriented protocols depending on the transport-layer TCP/IP protocol. Figure 7.10 depicts this mechanism for a client connection to a server that is encrypted via the SSL protocol on port 443. Having connected the proxy to the destination server successfully, it sends a successful connection message to the client in Figure 7.10(b). A tunnelled channel is a full-duplex channel between a client and a server, each of which can send and receive over this channel. The `CONNECT` method is usually used to convey SSL-based protocols because all data are encrypted over an HTTPS session and the proxy is unable to normally handle requests/responses between a client and a web server.

7.4.4 Example 1: A Simple Client Program of the HTTP Protocol to Retrieve a Web Page

In the first example for this section, we examine a simple code in which a client directly (without traversing through an HTTP proxy) connects to a web server and requests the first page of a domain name through the HTTP protocol. See Figure 7.11. In line 10, we find IP addresses associated with the domain `www.example.com` using the `Dns::Resolve()` method. Because the number of these IP addresses returned by the DNS server may be more than one, we carry them onto the console inside a loop for display in lines 11 to 15. We have already found the web server's IP address; in line 18, we instantiate a connection-oriented TCP/IP socket. In lines 20–22, we use an `IPEndPoint` instance to put the IP address and port number (port 80 in this example) into it.

In line 24, the client socket is connected to the created endpoint by using the `Connect()` method. We prepare the buffer for `GET` requests to retrieve the main page of our domain in lines 26–30 based on the HTTP/1.1 protocol. Then, we send the request to the web server in line 32. Note that we choose the fourth parameter of the `Send()` and `Receive()` methods representing the `SocketFlag` Enum to be the `None` type here and in our future examples. We have already sent the request to the web server; thus, we read the server response into the buffer. The receive operation has been placed inside a loop because the server may send fewer bytes than the buffer length at any receive time. In line 36, we fill the buffer from the offset to the size of `bufferSize - read`.

Be aware that in this example, we have assumed that the sent response's length is less than or equal to our buffer's size. Otherwise, since a web server usually sends the response length in the `Content-Length` header, we can somehow handle the read from the client socket ourselves. For example, if the returned object's length is not very large, we can dynamically allocate the buffer. Or if the client has requested a large file to download, we must open a file, fill the buffer piece by piece equal to the size of `bufferSize` by calling the `Receive()` method, and write the buffer

```
 1: using namespace System;
 2: using namespace System::Net;
 3: using namespace System::Net::Sockets;
 4:
 5: int main(int argc, char* argv[]) {
 6:     Socket *client = null;
 7:     IPAddress ip;
 8:     try {
 9:         // Finds the IP address associated with the domain.
10:         IPHostEntry hostEntry = Dns::Resolve("www.example.com");
11:         // Prints all of the found IP addresses into the console.
12:         for(Int32 i = 0 ; i < hostEntry.get_AddressListLength() ; i++) {
13:             ip = hostEntry.get_AddressList(i);
14:             printf("IP Address %d: %s\n", i , inet_ntoa(*(struct in_addr *)ip.GetAddressBytes())));
15:         }
16:
17:         // Instantiates the Socket object for a TCP-based connection-oriented transport.
18:         client = new Socket(System::Net::Sockets::InterNetwork, System::Net::Sockets::Stream,
System::Net::Sockets::tcp);
19:
20:         // Sets up the remote endpoint to connect on port 80.
21:         ip = hostEntry.get_AddressList(0);
22:         IPEndPoint inp = IPEndPoint(ip, 80);
23:         // Connects to the remote web server.
24:         client->Connect(inp);
25:
26:         const Int32 bufferSize = 256*1024;
27:         char buffer[bufferSize + 1];
28:
29:         String request = "GET / HTTP/1.1\r\nHost: www.example.com\r\nConnection: close\r\n\r\n";
30:         printf("Client said to server:\n\n%s\n", request.get_BaseStream());
31:         // Sends the request to get the HTTP page from the web server.
32:         client->Send(request.get_BaseStream(), 0, request.get_Length(), System::Net::Sockets::None);
33:
34:         // Read the entire response from the web server until the end of the connection is reached.
35:         Int32 n, read = 0;
36:         while((n = client->Receive(buffer, read, bufferSize - read, System::Net::Sockets::None)) > 0)
37:             read += n;
38:
39:         // Prints the buffer into console if any data was received.
40:         if(read > 0) {
41:             // Formats the buffer to indicate the received response as an ASCII string.
42:             buffer[read] = '\0';
43:             printf("Server said to client:\n\n%s\n", buffer);
44:         }
45:     }
46:     catch(SocketException &e) {...}
47:     catch(ObjectDisposedException &e) {...}
48:     catch(Exception &e){...}
49:
50:     // Closes and releases the Socket instance.
51:     if(client != null) {
52:         try {
53:             client->Shutdown(Both);
54:             client->Close();
55:         } catch(...){}
56:         delete client;
57:     }
58:     return 0;
59: }
```

Figure 7.11 **A simple client-side code that connects to a web server on port 80 and requests its first page.**

into our file. The second example of this section will implement such a scenario to upload a file from a client to a server depending on a simple protocol. In lines 50 through 57, we close and release the client socket. Take notice of the invocation for the Shutdown() method with the Both input parameter has been made prior to calling the Close() method in line 53, which disables the send and receive operations on the client socket. Because there may be thrown an exception within the program execution by the Parvicursor.NET Framework at runtime, we handle these likely exceptions in lines 46 to 48, the complete codes of this section have been omitted due to space limitation. To view the full code of this sample, refer to the path "/Parvicursor/Parvicursor/Samples/ClientSocket" of the companion resources of the book.

7.4.5 *Example 2: A Concurrent Client/Server Program Based on Threads to Upload a File from a Client to a Server*

In the previous example, no concurrency, through the computing power of multi/many-core systems, was exploited. As discussed in the previous chapters, concurrency and multi-threaded programming have great importance in building the next generation of distributed applications. Concurrency has drawn significant attention in the design of network services and distributed systems. All the remainder of this chapter and the next chapters take this issue seriously. As a starting point, let's assume a server does not use threads (i.e., there is no concurrency at all); it is evident that this server can only serve one client at each moment of time until a client needs the service. Therefore, no other client(s) can use the service as long as the first client has not finished its work with the server. One of the important techniques of concurrency is to create one thread for each incoming request, and this thread takes responsibility to handle the client connection. This model owing to its simplicity in programming benefits from the processing power of multi/many-core processors. However, it has an important problem with respect to scalability and high overheads, which cannot be extended to a large number of connections. The reason for this issue was discussed in the previous chapters. This issue will be comprehensively discussed and analysed in the rest of this chapter and in Chapter 10. In the stated sections and chapters, we employ hybrid techniques to integrate thread-based concurrency with event-driven concurrency. But so far, it is enough to know that the traditional model of *one thread per connection* is adequate for ordinary applications with a few clients (e.g., a typical number of 200). Of course, the more system cores, the lower limitation we will face with.

As the second example of socket programming, let's suppose that we intend to design and implement a simple protocol for uploading a file with a variable size from a client to a file server. This very simple sample plays an essential foundation for the architecture and implementation of the xDFS file transfer protocol in Chapter 10. At a glance, we propose and examine such a protocol. The client connects to the file server at first and sends a filename as a string request which will be uploaded to the server. The server upon receiving the filename opens a file and sends a byte containing a value of zero to the client; this value notices the client that no error has occurred when opening the file on the server side. If an error takes place at this stage, the server sends one byte with the value of one to the client and closes the connection. The client, after receiving the error byte and if there is no error on the server, sends the file contents to the server. When the client reaches the end of the file, it closes the connection to the server. At this point, the server supposes that the end of the file was reached; it closes the file handle and terminates the transfer session.

At first, we consider the server-side implementation of this simple file transfer protocol in upload mode. Figure 7.12 illustrates the main skeleton of a concurrent file server based on threads atop the Parvicursor.NET Framework. The server socket is created in line 49 and inside the main() function. We assume that the server is listening to incoming connections on port 3128 and all network interfaces (the get_Any() method satisfies this for us in line 51); see lines 50 through 56. Inside the while loop in lines 59–72, a new connection is accepted and then we create a thread; the state of this thread is set to detached so that the flow of the loop can move to line 61 after initiating the thread in order to accept another client connection. As mentioned at the beginning of this section, the server object's Accept() method in line 64 blocks until there is at least one connection inside the incoming connection queue. The class ClientContext stores the file transfer session's state. This class has members such as a buffer (for file and network I/O operations), the object fsWrite (the file that we are going to write to), the client socket, and the file name to be written. Notice the descriptions of the ClientContext class's constructor (line 15) and destructor (line 26). In line 68, after the Accept() method gets a new connection, an object of the ClientContext class is instantiated and passed as an argument into the worker thread (lines 66 to 69). The ProcessClient() function pointer, which is run by the worker thread, implements the main part of our simple file transfer protocol and services the clients. The implementation of the function ProcessClient() appears in Figure 7.13.

In line 4 of the ProcessClient() function, we first cast the client state from the pointer arg to the type of the ClientContext class. In line 8, the filename sent by the client is read. Since file systems support filenames with a maximum of 256 characters, we read 256 bytes from the client socket in the Receive() method. If Receive() returns a value of zero, it means that the connection has been suddenly closed and we must jump to the Cleanup label in line 10. Below the Cleanup label in line 46, the cx pointer that had been allocated is released in line 68 of Figure 7.12. In lines 12 through 14, we construct the filename requested by the client from the buffer into the string writeFilename. In line 17, a FileStream instance is created to write the uploading file contents to the client socket (the fsWrite object). On line 20, by sending one byte to the client that contains the false value (i.e., no error occurred when opening the file to write), we notify the client to begin to send the file blocks. Now, we receive file blocks inside a while loop in lines 26 and 27 from the client socket and write them into fsWrite from the buffer to the size of the read. The loop execution continues until the Receive() method returns a value of zero, which means that the client has closed the connection and the end of the file is reached. At this stage, we are in lines 46 and 47 and the ProcessClient() function returns. As shown in the ClientContext class's destructor in Figure 7.12, both fsWrite and sock objects

```
1: // Represents a client context created by acceptor thread and passed to ProcessClient().
2: class ClientContext : public Object {
3:     // The buffer to transfer data between the client connection, file system, etc.
4:     public: char *buffer;
5:     // Indicates the size of the buffer in bytes.
6:     public: Int32 bufferSize;
7:     // The client Socket instance.
8:     public: Socket *sock;
9:     // The local FileStream instance to write the received data from the client.
10:     public: FileStream *fsWrite;
11:     // The local server-side file name requested by the client.
12:     public: String writeFilename;
13:     private: bool disposed;
14:     // The ClientContext constructor.
15:     public: ClientContext(Socket *acceptedSocket) {
16:         sock = acceptedSocket;
17:         // Default buffer size.
18:         bufferSize = 256 * 1024;
19:         // We must allocate the buffer from the heap, because a concurrent server servicing a large
20:         // number of clients cannot allocate the buffer from the stack due to the stack limit size.
21:         buffer = (char *)::malloc(bufferSize * sizeof(char));
22:         fsWrite = null;
23:         disposed = false;
24:     }
25:     // The ClientContext destructor.
26:     public: ~ClientContext(){
27:         if(disposed)
28:             return ;
29:         // Closes and releases the FileStream instance.
30:         if(fsWrite != null) {
31:             try { fsWrite->Close(); } catch (...){}
32:             delete fsWrite;
33:         }
34:         // Closes and releases client connection.
35:         if(sock != null) {
36:             try { sock->Shutdown(Both); sock->Close(); } catch (...){}
37:             delete sock;
38:         }
39:         // Deallocates the buffer.
40:         ::free(buffer);
41:     }
42: };
43:
44: // The worker's function pointer to handle a new accepted connection.
45: void *ProcessClient(void *arg);
46:
47: int main(int argc, char* argv[]) {
48:     // Creates the server socket (connection-oriented and TCP/IP-enabled).
49:     Socket *server = new Socket(System::Net::Sockets::InterNetwork, System::Net::Sockets::Stream,
System::Net::Sockets::tcp);
50:     // We will listen on port 3128 and all network interfaces.
51:     IPEndPoint hostEndPoint = IPEndPoint(IPAddress::get_Any(), 3128);
52:     // Binds the server socket to the hostEndPoint.
```

Figure 7.12 Concurrent implementation of our simple file server's main body to upload a file from the client to the server.

(Continued)

```
53:    server->Bind(hostEndPoint);
54:    // Listens on the server socket with the 'backlog; set to 100 concurrent connections.
55:    server->Listen(100);
56:    printf("The file server is listening on port 3128.\n");
57:
58:    // The main acceptor thread's loop.
59:    while(true) {
60:        // Blocks on the server socket until an incoming connection arrives.
61:        Socket *s = server->Accept();
62:        if(s == null)
63:            continue;
64:        printf("New client connection was accepted.\n");
65:
66:        // Allocates the client context, creates a worker thread, passes the cx to that worker, and
67:        // starts the worker to serve the client request. The ProcessClient() function will serve the client.
68:        ClientContext *cx = new ClientContext(s);
69:        Thread thread = Thread(ProcessClient, (void *)cx);
70:        thread.Start();
71:        thread.SetDetached();
72:    }
73:    return 0;
74: }
```

Figure 7.12 **(Continued) Concurrent implementation of our simple file server's main body to upload a file from the client to the server.**

are first closed and then released. At this point, a server-side file transfer session has ended. To see the complete file server code, refer to the path "/Parvicursor/ Parvicursor/Samples/FileTransferServer" from the companion resources of the book.

Finally, we in short examine the client-side implementation of our simple file transfer protocol. Figure 7.14 shows the code program of the client. The local file that is intended to upload is opened in line 20. The client socket is created in lines 21 through 29 and connected to the remote file server on port 3128. In line 33, we send the remote file name, which must be created by the server in its local file system, to the server. The function CheckServerResponseForError() in line 33 checks to see whether an error has occurred on the server side to open the remote file or not, we jump to the Cleanup label if there is any error. In lines 36 to 45, the file contents are read block by block and sent to the server. The first loop is used to read the entire file contents. If we are at the end of the file, the Read() method returns a zero or negative value and the execution of the first loop finishes, so the second loop will never run. The second loop is used to send the whole bytes in the buffer to the server. The rationale behind using both loops is the same descriptions as given for the code of the file server part. All allocated system resources (file and client socket) are released in lines 51 to 64. To have a full look at the full client code, refer to the path "/Parvicursor/Parvicursor/Samples/FileTransferClient" from the companion resources of the book.

```
 1: // The worker's function pointer to handle a newly accepted connection.
 2: void *ProcessClient(void *arg) {
 3:    // A type-casting to caste the arg variable into a ClientContext object.
 4:    ClientContext *cx = (ClientContext *)arg;
 5:    char errorOccured = false;
 6:    try {
 7:       // Reads the writeFilename from the client.
 8:       Int32 read = cx->sock->Receive(cx->buffer, 0, 256, System::Net::Sockets::None);
 9:       if(read <= 0)
10:          goto Cleanup;
11:
12:       // Builds the writeFilename string from the buffer.
13:       cx->buffer[read] = '\0';
14:       cx->writeFilename = String((const char *)cx->buffer);
15:
16:       // Instantiates a FileStream instance to which the write operation will be performed.
17:       cx->fsWrite = new FileStream(cx->writeFilename, System::IO::OpenOrCreate, System::IO::Write,
8*1024);
18:
19:       // Notifies the client that it can now begin the transfer flow.
20:       try { cx->sock->Send(&errorOccured, 0, sizeof(char), System::Net::Sockets::None); } catch(...) {}
21:
22:       // Receives the file blocks sent by the client and writes them into the fsWrite object.
23:       // The while() loop executes until the end of the file represented by the client by closing the
24:       // connection. In this stage, Receive() returns 0.
25:       read = 0;
26:       while( (read = cx->sock->Receive(cx->buffer, 0, cx->bufferSize, System::Net::Sockets::None)) > 0 )
27:          cx->fsWrite->Write(cx->buffer, 0, read);
28:    }
29:    catch(SocketException &e) {
30:       // This kind of exception indicates that the socket could not be used anymore, and then
31:       // we must jump to the 'Cleanup' label.
32:       printf("Error occurred. SocketException message: %s\n", e.get_Message().get_BaseStream());
33:       goto Cleanup;
34:    }
35:    catch(IOException &e) {
36:       printf("Error occurred. IOException message: %s\n", e.get_Message().get_BaseStream());
37:       errorOccured = true;
38:    }
39:    catch(Exception &e) {
40:       printf("Error occurred. Exception message: %s\n", e.get_Message().get_BaseStream());
41:       errorOccured = true;
42:    }
43:
44: Cleanup:
45:    // Frees the cx instance created by acceptor thread.
46:    delete cx;
47:    return arg;
48: }
```

Figure 7.13 The implementation of the `ProcessClient()` function. This function is the thread worker function pointer which handles every accepted connection on the server. The implementation of our simple protocol is done in this function.

```
 1:  // Checks whether there was a server-side error during the file transfer session.
 2:  bool CheckServerResponseForError(Socket *client) {
 3:     char errorOccured = false;
 4:     if(client->Receive(&errorOccured, 0, sizeof(char), System::Net::Sockets::None) > 0)
 5:        if(errorOccured)
 6:           printf("There was a server-side error during the file transfer session.\n");
 7:     else {
 8:        printf("The server has been closed the connection, and thus we could not determine if there is a server-
side error during the file transfer session.\n");
 9:        return true;
10:     }
11:     return (bool)errorOccured;
12: }
13:
14: int main(int argc, char* argv[]) {
15:     Socket *client = null; FileStream *fsRead = null;
16:     String localFilename = "c:/test.pdf"; String remoteFilename = "c:/test1.pdf";
17:     const Int32 bufferSize = 256 * 1024; char buffer[bufferSize];
18:     try {
19:        // Opens the local file to read.
20:        fsRead = new FileStream(localFilename, System::IO::Open, System::IO::Read, 8*1024);
21:        // Finds the IP address associated with the domain.
22:        IPHostEntry hostEntry = Dns::Resolve("localhost");
23:        // Instantiates the Socket object for a TCP-based connection-oriented transport.
24:        client = new Socket(System::Net::Sockets::InterNetwork, System::Net::Sockets::Stream,
System::Net::Sockets::tcp);
25:        // Sets up the remote endpoint to connect on port 3128.
26:        IPAddress ip = hostEntry.get_AddressList(0);
27:        IPEndPoint inp = IPEndPoint(ip, 3128);
28:        // Connects to the remote file server.
29:        client->Connect(inp);
30:        // Sends the remote file name to be created by server.
31:        client->Send(remoteFilename.get_BaseStream(), 0, remoteFilename.get_Length(),
System::Net::Sockets::None);
32:        // Checks whether there was a server-side error during the file transfer initiation.
33:        if(CheckServerResponseForError(client))
34:           goto Cleanup;
35:        printf("The file transfer session was started.\n");
36:        // Reads a file block from fsRead.
37:        Int32 read, sent, total;
38:        while( (read = fsRead->Read(buffer, 0, bufferSize)) > 0 ) {
39:           total = 0;
40:           // Tries to send all read content within the buffer until all bytes are sent.
41:           while( (read - total) > 0 ) {
42:              sent = client->Send(buffer, total, read - total, System::Net::Sockets::None);
43:              total += sent;
44:           }
45:        }
46:        printf("The file transfer session was successfully completed.\n");
47:     }
48:     catch(Exception &e) {
```

Figure 7.14   The client program of our simple file transfer protocol to upload a local file to a remote file server.

(Continued)

```
49:        printf("Error occurred. Exception message: %s\n", e.get_Message().get_BaseStream());
50:    }
51: Cleanup:
52:    // Closes and releases the Socket instance.
53:    if(client != null) {
54:        try {
55:            client->Shutdown(Both);
56:            client->Close();
57:        } catch(...){}
58:        delete client;
59:    }
60:    // Closes and releases the FileStream instance.
61:    if(fsRead != null) {
62:        try {fsRead->Close();} catch(...){}
63:        delete fsRead;
64:    }
65:    return 0;
66: }
```

Figure 7.14 (Continued) The client program of our simple file transfer protocol to upload a local file to a remote file server.

7.5 Asynchronous Methods in Parvicursor Platform: An Optimum Computing Paradigm to Exploit the Processing Power of Multi/Many-Core Systems for Increasing the Performance of Distributed Systems

7.5.1 Introduction

In the entire book materials discussed so far, all the method invocations have been routed as a stream of execution from one method to another. It is often desirable to fork the stream of execution into two branches and allow one branch to run a given method whilst the remaining branch continues its usual execution. Figure 7.15 depicts this concept. In a multiprocessor machine, two branches are actually executed concurrently. The chief reason for forking the execution is to allow the processing to

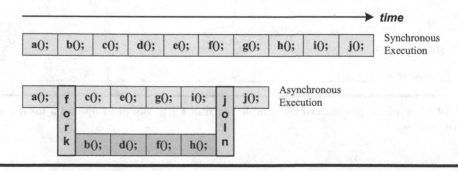

Figure 7.15 Synchronous execution in comparison with asynchronous execution.

continue whilst part of the program is blocked and waits for I/O completion or other events. Forking the execution also can significantly increase throughput on multi/ many-core machines due to parallelism; however, as stated in the previous chapters, this kind of design leads to a thorough attention for synchronisation amongst shared resources. The main advantage of forking the instruction stream is to implement asynchronous method invocations. An asynchronous method call forks the execution into two streams. The new stream runs the source method's body. The main stream continues its processing.

As a practical example, suppose we want to write a web server which processes thousands of concurrent client requests. If we were using the model of *one thread per request* (as discussed in the former section), we had to consume gigabytes of the physical memory along with severe overhead caused by frequent context switches. Asynchronous methods directly address this problem by using a pattern in that concurrent activities are handled by thread pools. In the following, we examine a complete example for the concept of asynchronous methods. Primarily, we describe how to use the designed asynchronous interface as a sample, and then how this interface can be designed and implemented on top of the Parvicursor platform. This example provides an easier understanding of asynchronous methods for the reader, and the strategy established in the next section helps us design and implement a sophisticated framework library for asynchronous sockets.

7.5.2 Example: Asynchronous Translation of Domain Names to IP Addresses Based on an Asynchronous DNS Resolver

Assume we are going to translate thousands of domains into their corresponding IP addresses concurrently. The only tool that we have introduced to you in this chapter is the `Resolve()` method of the `Dns` class. We first explain the extended functionality of this class with two new asynchronous methods and then solve the problem to find concurrent IP addresses. Table 7.3 shows the `AsyncDns` class's asynchronous methods. As seen, the `Dns::Resolve()` method is turned into two equivalent asynchronous methods of `BeginResolve()` and `EndResolve()`. The difference between the signature of a synchronous method and an asynchronous `BeginXXX()` method is that `BeginXXX()` always returns a reference to a calling object from the `IAsyncResult` class. This class has a member called `AsyncState` that stores a reference to the state object passed into the `BeginXXX()` method. All `BeginXXX()` methods take a callback function corresponding to the definition of the `AsyncCallback` function pointer to execute after the completion of the asynchronous operation. The execution sequence of each `BeginXXX()` method inside the `AsyncCallback` callback function must terminate with an `EndXXX()` method.

Figure 7.16 shows the code example in which the `AsyncDns` class's methods are used. The class `ResolveState` stores the state of asynchronous calls during the methods of `BeginResolve()` and `EndResolve()` to resolve every domain name. In lines 38 to 55 and inside the `main()` function, we initialise the program objects. In this example, ten domain names are asynchronously and concurrently resolved. Within the `for` loop in line 50, the resolution operation's state is instantiated for every domain, and in line 54 we pass them to the `BeginResolve()`

Table 7.3 The `AsyncDns` Class's Static Methods in the Parvicursor.NET Framework

Name	Description
`IAsyncResult *BeginResolve(const String &hostName, AsyncCallback requestCallback, Object *stateObject)`	Begins an asynchronous request to resolve a DNS hostname or an IP address to an `IPHostEntry` instance. `requestCallback` specifies the reference to the function that is invoked when the resolution operation is completed. `stateObject` is an object defined by the user, which contains information about the operation. In fact, we use this state to store the main state object during asynchronous calls. `stateObject` plays a key role throughout the programming abstraction of asynchronous methods. When `requestCallback` is called, this object is passed into it.
`IPHostEntry EndResolve(IAsyncResult *asyncResult)`	Ends the asynchronous request for DNS information. This method returns an `IPHostEntry` object that contains DNS information about a host. This method must be invoked inside the `requestCallback` callback function passed to the `BeginResolve()` method.

method. The `OnResolve()` callback function is invoked when the resolution operation completes. Because ten asynchronous resolution operations must be first completed in this example, a mutex object, a condition variable and a global variable `completedNum`, which stores the number of completed asynchronous methods, have been used for this program. Therefore, we wait in lines 57 through 61 inside the `main()` thread until all asynchronous method operations complete. In lines 63–67, the whole allocated objects are released. The most important function of this example is the `OnResolve()` function. First, we cast the object state (`ar->AsyncState`), which was passed to the `BeginResolve()` static method by the programmer, to the `ResolveState` type in line 12. In line 15, the `EndResolve()` is called so that we can retrieve and store the resolved value of the current domain as a `hostEntry` object. The description of lines 17–20 is precisely the same as the example in Figure 7.11. At the end of this method (because the `OnResolve()` callback function is executed by a different thread other than the main program thread), we must inform the main thread of the completion of the resolution operation in lines 30 through 34.

7.5.3 Implementation of an Asynchronous DNS Resolver Based on the Parvicursor.NET Framework

Now, you are familiar with the concept of asynchronous methods and have seen a practical example about it; we examine how you can generally implement asynchronous methods. In this section, we consider an implementation of the `AsyncDns` class's asynchronous static methods. One straightforward technique to implement asynchronous methods is to make use of a work queue with a thread pool.

```
 1: // State object for resolving the domain asynchronously
 2: class ResolveState : public Object {
 3:    public: String domain;
 4: };
 5: // The following parameters are used to synchronise between the main thread and the execution of asynchronous
requests.
 6: static Mutex mutex = Mutex();
 7: static ConditionVariable cv = ConditionVariable(&mutex);
 8: static Int32 completedNum = 0;
 9:
10: static void OnResolve(IAsyncResult *ar) {
11:    // Converts the ResolveState object to a ResolveState object.
12:    ResolveState *state = (ResolveState *)ar->AsyncState;
13:    try {
14:       // Ends the asynchronous request.
15:       IPHostEntry hostEntry = AsyncDns::EndResolve(ar);
16:
17:       // Prints all of the found IP addresses into console.
18:       for(Int32 i = 0 ; i < hostEntry.get_AddressListLength() ; i++) {
19:          IPAddress ip = hostEntry.get_AddressList(i);
20:          printf("Domain: %s IP Address %d: %s\n", state->domain.get_BaseStream(), i , inet_ntoa(*(struct
in_addr *)ip.GetAddressBytes())));
21:       }
22:    }
23:    catch(Exception &e) {
24:       printf("Error occurred in OnResolve)() for %s. Exception message: %s\n", state-
>domain.get_BaseStream(), e.get_Message().get_BaseStream());
25:    }
26:    catch(...) {
27:       printf("Error occurred in OnResolve() for %s. Unknown exception.\n", state-
>domain.get_BaseStream());
28:    }
29:
30:    // Signals the main thread that the current asynchronous method was finished.
31:    mutex.Lock();
32:    completedNum++;
33:    cv.Signal();
34:    mutex.Unlock();
35: }
36:
37: int main(int argc, char *argv[]) {
38:    // Allocates the domain set to be resolved.
39:    const Int32 DomainNum = 10;
40:    String *domains = new String[DomainNum];
41:    domains[0] = "www.example.com"; domains[1] = "www.microsoft.com"; domains[2] = "www.kernel.org";
42:    domains[3] = "www.yahoo.com"; domains[4] = "www.google.com"; domains[5] = "www.msn.com";
43:    domains[6] = "mail.google.com"; domains[7] = "mail.yahoo.com"; domains[8] = "www.facebook.com";
44:    domains[9] = "www.nytimes.com";
45:
46:    // Allocates the asynchronous states and issues the BeginResolve() method for each resolve request.
47:    ResolveState **states = new ResolveState*[DomainNum];
48:    for(register Int32 i = 0 ; i < DomainNum ; i++) {
49:       // Creates an instance of the ResolveState class.
```

Figure 7.16   The example of the asynchronous resolution of domain names into their equivalent IP addresses.

(Continued)

```
50:        states[i] = new ResolveState();
51:        states[i]->domain = domains[i];
52:        // Begins an asynchronous request for information like host name, IP addresses, or
53:        // aliases for specified the specified URI.
54:        IAsyncResult *asyncResult = AsyncDns::BeginResolve(domains[i], OnResolve, states[i]);
55:    }
56:
57:    // Waits until all asynchronous request complete.
58:    mutex.Lock();
59:    while(completedNum != DomainNum)
60:        cv.Wait();
61:    mutex.Unlock();
62:
63:    // Releases the allocated objects.
64:    for(register Int32 i  = 0 ; i < DomainNum ; i++)
65:        delete states[i];
66:    delete []states;  delete []domains;
67:    return 0;
68: }
```

Figure 7.16 (Continued) The example of the asynchronous resolution of domain names into their equivalent IP addresses.

When a method is called asynchronously, we must encapsulate the method parameters along with its callback function into an instance of the IAsyncResult class. Then, we can put this request into the work queue of our thread pool. At this stage, the thread pool designed in Chapter 5 takes over the remaining job. Figure 7.17 depicts the objects and the necessary class prototype to implement the AsyncDns class. In line 5, the thread pool is instantiated. The AsyncDnsInfo class, which inherits from the base (interface or abstract) IAsyncResult class, stores the parameter information of every asynchronous BeginResolve() method call. Lines 10 to 13 show the variables used for storing the BeginResolve() method parameters. The code in lines 14 through 19 indicates the internal variables that are required at the time of asynchronous execution by the designed class.

Because of inheritance, all these fields remain hidden from the programmer who is using the AsyncDns class and only the base IAsyncResult class's members are visible. hostEntry stores the return data of the synchronous Dns::Resolve() function in the implementation of the AsyncDns class's methods. The members HasException and exceptionMessage store an exception that possibly has occurred at an asynchronous execution, and if there is any exception, then we must re-throw it into the calling thread when invoking the EndResolve() method. Examine carefully the descriptions given within the codes. Now that we have a working knowledge of asynchronous methods, we can discuss the implementation of two methods of BeginResolve() and EndResolve() as shown in Figure 7.18.

In the BeginResolve() method within lines 26–33, we must first encapsulate the required parameters for asynchronous execution into an instance of the AsyncDnsInfo class. The asynchronous request is added to the thread pool's work queue in line 35. The thread pool will run the ResolveCallback() callback, which is considered as an internal function and is not visible to the user. The implementation of the ResolveCallback() function, in lines 1 through 19, simply uses the synchronous Dns::Resolve() function to resolve the domain name, and if any error occurred,

```
1: // A thread pool instance is used to simulate an asynchronous DNS resolver by calling
2: // the synchronous Dns::Resovle() method. This sample project is just a simple learning
3: // example. In general, we should consider a system-wide thread pool for all asynchronous
4: // method invocations across Parvicursor.NET framework instead of a thread pool per class.
5: static ThreadPool dnsThreadPool = ThreadPool(System::Environment::get_ProcessorCount()*2, INT_MAX);
6:
7: // An internal class that provides to encapsulate the necessary information allocated by
8: // the BeginResolve() method and used by the EndResolve() method.
9: class AsyncDnsInfo : public IAsyncResult {
10:    // Stores the hostName passed to the BeginResolve() method.
11:    public: String hostName;
12:    // Stores the callback passed to the BeginResolve() method.
13:    public: AsyncCallback requestCallback;
14:    // Stores the return of the synchronous Dns::Resovle() method
15:    public: IPHostEntry hostEntry;
16:    // Indicates whether there is an error during the calling synchronous Dns::Resovle() method.
17:    public: bool HasException;
18:    // Stores the message of the thrown exception by synchronous Dns::Resovle() method.
19:    public: String exceptionMessage;
20: };
21:
22: // Provides simple asynchronous domain name resolution functionality.
23: class AsyncDns : public Object {
24:    // Begins an asynchronous request to resolve a DNS hostname or IP address to an IPAddress instance.
25:    public: static IAsyncResult *BeginResolve(const String &hostName, AsyncCallback requestCallback,
Object *stateObject);
26:    // Ends an asynchronous request for DNS information.
27:    public: static IPHostEntry EndResolve(IAsyncResult *asyncResult);
28: };
```

Figure 7.17 **Objects and the necessary class prototype to implement the `AsyncDns` class.**

then it stores its information into the info object. At the end of this function, which is indicating the asynchronous operation execution in the thread pool, we must invoke the requestCallback callback specified by the user within the BeginResolve() method in line 18 and pass the info object to it. In the implementation of the EndResolve() method, we check if there is an error registered by the ResolveCallback() method; an exception must be thrown into the calling code, otherwise we return the result of the resolution operation in line 54. Note that in line 53 we must release the info object that has been already allocated inside the BeginResolve() method. To see the full client code, refer to the path "/Parvicursor/Parvicursor/Samples/AsyncResolver" from the companion resources of the book.

7.6 Addressing the Scalability Issue of Communication Systems in the Parvicursor Platform

7.6.1 Introduction

In this section, we try to address this important challenge: How can we design and implement highly scalable, standardised applications for next-generation distributed systems such as HPC, Cloud, and the Internet? The development of complex network applications is somewhat difficult to learn. To write applications that can service

```
 1: // This internal callback is executed by the ThreadPool instance.
 2: static void ResolveCallback(Object *asyncDnsInfo) {
 3:     // Casts asyncDnsInfo into the AsyncDnsInfo class.
 4:     AsyncDnsInfo *info = (AsyncDnsInfo *)asyncDnsInfo;
 5:     try{
 6:         // The Resolve() method is a synchronous method.
 7:         info->hostEntry = System::Net::Dns::Resolve(info->hostName);
 8:     }
 9:     catch(Exception &e) {
10:         info->HasException = true;
11:         info->exceptionMessage = e.get_Message();
12:     }
13:     catch(...) {
14:         info->HasException = true;
15:         info->exceptionMessage = "Unknown exception";
16:     }
17:     // Invokes the callback passed to the BeginResolve() method.
18:     info->requestCallback(info);
19: }
20:
21: IAsyncResult *AsyncDns::BeginResolve(const String &hostName, AsyncCallback requestCallback, Object
*stateObject) {
22:     if(hostName.get_BaseStream() == null)
23:         throw ArgumentNullException("hostName");
24:     if(requestCallback == null)
25:         throw ArgumentNullException("requestCallback");
26:     // Allocates a placeholder to keep the asynchronous request.
27:     AsyncDnsInfo *info = new AsyncDnsInfo();
28:     info->hostName = hostName;
29:     info->requestCallback = requestCallback;
30:     info->AsyncState = stateObject;
31:     info->IsCompleted = false;
32:     info->CompletedSynchronously = false;
33:     info->HasException = false;
34:     // Enqueues the request into the ThreadPool instance.
35:     dnsThreadPool.QueueUserWorkItem(ResolveCallback, info);
36:     return info;
37: }
38:
39: IPHostEntry AsyncDns::EndResolve(IAsyncResult *asyncResult) {
40:     if(asyncResult == null)
41:         throw ArgumentNullException("asyncResult");
42:     // Casts asyncResult into the AsyncDnsInfo class.
43:     AsyncDnsInfo *info = (AsyncDnsInfo *)asyncResult;
44:     // Was there an error while the asynchronous execution?
45:     if(info->HasException) {
46:         String exceptionMessage = info->exceptionMessage;
47:         delete info;
48:         // Re-throws the caught exception within the ResolveCallback() function.
49:         throw Exception(exceptionMessage);
50:     }
51:     IPHostEntry hostEntry = info->hostEntry;
52:     // Releases the allocated memory for AsyncDnsInfo instance within the BeginResolve() method.
53:     delete info;
54:     return hostEntry;
55: }
```

Figure 7.18   The implementation of the `AsyncDns` class's asynchronous methods.

thousands of clients and implement concurrency on multi/many-core systems are much more difficult and complicated. In this section, we try to deal with the very important issue of scalability in client/server programs and propose the implementation of a standard-based framework in order to reduce this complexity. The main reason for such a strategy was discussed in the previous sections: to increase performance. The I/O subsystem is one of the main bottlenecks in distributed systems, which makes the development of such applications complex. Here, we first examine different strategies for network-based application development, and after describing the classification of networked I/O systems, we will discuss the solution proposed by the Parvicursor platform in detail. Numerous practical examples will be also presented. The reader will get a much deeper attitude to concurrency; because we put your hands directly into programming and teach you how we can integrate concurrency with I/O (i.e., the communication issue) for constructing scalable distributed systems. Note that, unlike any other book or web resource, we examine the scalability issue simultaneously for both clients and servers in this section.

7.6.2 Design Strategies of Client-Server Applications

The architecture of a client or server program can be classified into two taxonomies: high throughput and a large number of connections. However, what this book will teach you is to combine them and introduce hybrid architectures. We consider the hybrid architectures in the rest of this chapter and in Chapter 10. A high-throughput architecture mainly deals with pushing as much data as on a few numbers of connections. Of course, the meaning of the term *a few numbers of connections* relatively refers to the number of existing resources on a machine. The architecture with a large number of connections mostly copes with handling too many network connections whilst it does not push much data to the connections. The integration of these two architectures is the issue that is examined particularly for the xDFS protocol to provide a high-throughput and high-performance framework for the next generation of distributed systems in this chapter and Chapter 10.

A traditional file server (such as NFS and FTP) is an example of a high-throughput architecture in which we deal with the issue of bulk delivery. In this case, the server copes with the processing of every connection to minimise the amount of time required for data transmission. To achieve this goal, the server must limit the number of concurrent connections because too many concurrent connections deliver lower throughput on every individual connection. The purpose of this architecture is I/O. The server should keep enough send/receive operations posted to maximise throughput. The server may also accept a large number of connections continuously, but I/O operations must be restricted to a small set of connections.

Maximising the number of concurrent connections is more difficult between these two strategies expressed above. Handling I/O on every connection becomes difficult. A server cannot easily post one or more send/receive operations on every connection. In this scenario, the server is interested in handling connections at the expense of throughput. An instance of this scenario could be a DNS server that must handle many thousands of connections to send a large number of a few bytes. Providing a procedure in which both strategies can be supported is challenging.

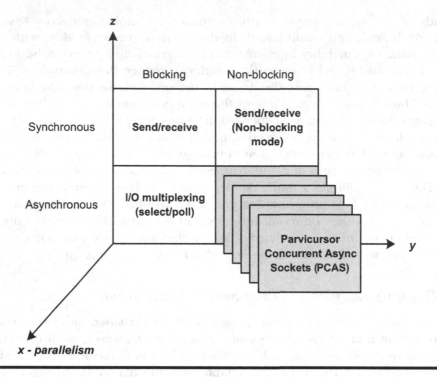

Figure 7.19 The different possible models of socket I/O in the Parvicursor platform.

To address these strategies and the hybrid strategy, we can divide I/O models into four general categories. We limit our attention only to the network I/O subsystem in this book. Figure 7.19 shows the three-dimensional models: synchronous and asynchronous, and blocking and non-blocking with the hybrid and concurrent Parvicursor Concurrent Asynchronous Sockets (PCAS) model. Every one of these models has use patterns that make them beneficial to specific applications; however, PCAS architecture makes it a general-purpose paradigm for a broad family of network applications (for instance, Cloud environments, HPC and the Internet).

One of the popular models is the synchronous blocking model which was described in the socket programming section at the beginning of this chapter. In this model, a userland thread executes a system call that results in blocking the program thread. This means that the thread is blocked as long as the system call completes (completion of data transfer or any error occurred). The calling thread is in a state that does not consume any CPU cycles and simply waits for a response, so this model is efficient in terms of processing. Figure 7.20 illustrates this traditional blocking model. This model is well understood, and its use for ordinary applications is optimum. When the recv() system call is invoked, the thread is blocked and its state is mode switched into the kernel. The send operation is started, and when the response returns, the data is moved to the userspace buffer. Finally, the thread is unblocked. From the thread's perspective, the recv() call spends a lot of time. But, in fact, the thread gets actually blocked whilst the receive operation is multiplexed with another work inside the kernel.

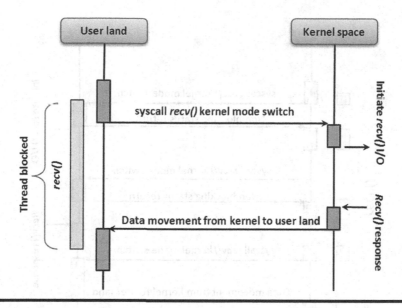

Figure 7.20   A typical flow of the synchronous blocking I/O model.

Another variant with less performance than the former is the synchronous non-blocking model. In this model, a socket is created as non-blocking. This means that instead of immediately getting an I/O completion, a recv() request may return an error code indicating that this request could not be immediately satisfied. This model appears in Figure 7.21. The outcome of the non-blocking feature is that an I/O request may not be immediately satisfied and requires the respective thread to issue several calls for waiting on the operation completion. This technique can be extremely inefficient because the thread must perform busy waiting (spinning) until the data becomes available. As seen in Figure 7.21, this technique creates latency in I/O because the gap between the data being available in the kernel and the user calling the recv() function to return it can reduce the total data throughput.

Another model in the classification of I/Os is the non-blocking I/O pattern with blocking notification. See Figure 7.22. In this model, first, a socket is set as non-blocking, and then the blocking select() system call is used to determine the status of the socket. The select() system function provides the status notification of multiple sockets. The properties of this system function will be fully described in Chapter 10. One chief problem with this system function is that it is not performant for a large collection of sockets.

Finally, the latest model is the asynchronous, concurrent, and non-blocking PCAS provided by the Parvicursor platform. Figure 7.23 shows this model. In this model, a request like BeginReceive() immediately returns and represents that the receive operation has got successfully begun. The desired thread can perform other processing whilst the receive operation is being completed in the background on another dedicated thread. When the response of a request like BeginReceive() arrives, a callback function that has already been passed to the BeginXXX() method is invoked by PCAS to complete the I/O transaction. The ability to overlap computations with I/O processing in a single thread potentially makes multiple I/O requests

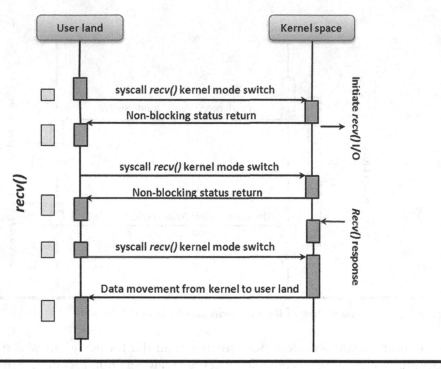

Figure 7.21 A typical flow of the synchronous non-blocking model.

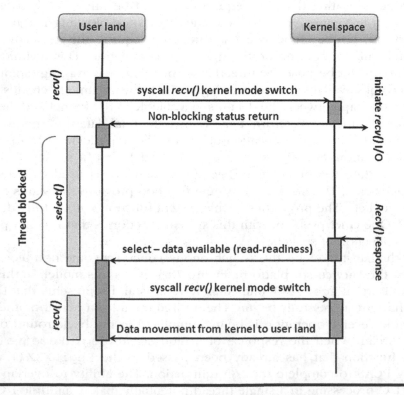

Figure 7.22 A typical flow of the asynchronous blocking I/O model.

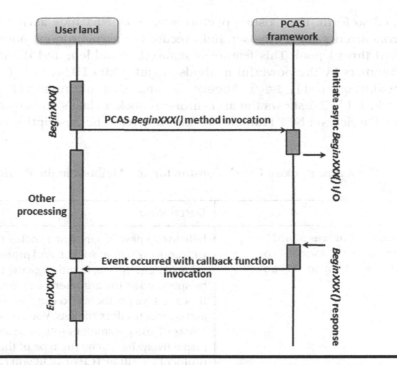

Figure 7.23 A typical flow of I/O based on the PCAS model in the Parvicursor platform.

exploit multi/many-core processors and the gap between processing speed and I/O speed. Whilst one or more slow I/O requests are pending, processor can execute other works, or generally, on previously completed I/O requests whilst other I/O requests have begun, in parallel. In the blocking model, it is impossible to overlap the processing and I/O at the same time. The concurrent non-blocking model allows the processing and I/O to be overlapped but requires the desired thread to check the status of I/O relied upon a recurring primitive. This issue indicates the high importance of the PCAS model. In the remainder of this section, we examine PCAS with miscellaneous examples.

7.6.3 Asynchronous Sockets in Parvicursor Platform as a Proposed Standard to Develop Highly Scalable Optimum Communication Systems for Distributed Systems

In this section, we describe the PCAS framework's methods to develop highly scalable network applications. Since the interface has been designed to comply with the .NET ECMA standard, the PCAS framework can be widely used as a standard interface for communications in distributed systems. In addition to the full PCAS compatibility with .NET Framework's asynchronous socket methods, our framework brings extra methods and their implementation to the developer, so that they can have direct access to the underlying concurrency of threads, which execute on processor cores, and take control over them. It is worthwhile to note that this feature is unique amid all existing asynchronous socket frameworks, including Java, C#, the Boost library, and so forth. The existing platforms such as .NET hide asynchronous input/ output concurrency from the user and execute the asynchronous operations within an internal thread pool. This feature is realised, unhidden, and directly accessible to programmers by the powerful methods of get_CoreID(), get_CoreCount(), TryMigrateToCore(), BeginAccept(), and BeginConnect() in the PCAS Framework. Table 7.4 shows the asynchronous socket class's constructor and methods in the Parvicursor.NET Framework. Carefully read the description of every of the

Table 7.4 The `AsyncSocket` Class's Constructor and Methods in the Parvicursor.NET Framework

Name	Description
AsyncSocket(AddressFamily addressFamily, SocketType socketType, ProtocolType protocolType)	Initialises a new instance of a socket class along with address family, socket, and protocol type. The values InterNetwork and InterNetworkV6 can be specified as the argument addressFamily for IPv4 and IPv6 protocols. To use connection-oriented and connectionless sockets, you can specify the socketType parameter as Stream and Dgram, respectively. To specify the type of the working protocol for either TCP or UDP, you can use tcp and udp. In this book, we always employ the following class to instantiate (i.e., for connection-oriented sockets depending on the TCP protocol): AsyncSocket(InterNetwork, Stream, tcp)
void Bind(IPEndPoint &localEP)	The description of this method comes in Table 7.2, and thus we omit it here.
void Listen(Int32 backlog)	The description of this method comes in Table 7.2, and thus we omit it here.
IAsyncResult *BeginAccept(AsyncCallback callback, Object *state)	Begins an asynchronous operation to accept an incoming connection attempt. The description of the parameters callback and state are the same as what was discussed for the BeginXXX() and EndXXX() methods of the AsyncDns class in Table 7.3.
IAsyncResult *BeginAccept(AsyncCallback callback, Object *state, bool GuaranteeMulticoreExecution)	This method is similar to the former method except that the Boolean GuaranteeMulticoreExecution parameter guarantees the execution of the accepted connection on the next processor core. For example, if the previous connection is running on core 0, a new connection is executed on the next core assigned, which is core 1 in this scenario.
AsyncSocket *EndAccept(IAsyncResult *asyncResult)	Asynchronously accepts an incoming connection attempt and creates a new AsyncSocket instance to handle the remote host communication.

(Continued)

Table 7.4   (Continued) The `AsyncSocket` Class's Constructor and Methods in the Parvicursor.NET Framework

Name	Description
IAsyncResult *BeginConnect(IPEndPoint &remoteEP, AsyncCallback callback, Object *state)	Begins an asynchronous request for a remote host connection.
IAsyncResult *BeginConnect(IPEndPoint &remoteEP, AsyncCallback callback, Object *state, bool GuaranteeMulticoreExecution)	This method is similar to the former method except that the Boolean `GuaranteeMulticoreExecution` parameter guarantees the execution of the accepted connection on the next processor core. For example, if the previous connection is running on core 0, a new connection is executed on the next core assigned, which is core 1 in this scenario.
void EndConnect(IAsyncResult *state)	Ends a pending asynchronous remote connection request.
IAsyncResult *BeginSend(char buffer[], Int32 offset, Int32 size, SocketFlags socketFlags, AsyncCallback callback, Object *state)	Asynchronously sends the data buffer to a connected socket. The description of the first four parameters of this method is exactly the same as the `Socket` class's `Send()` method mentioned in Table 7.2.
Int32 EndSend(IAsyncResult *asyncResult)	Ends a pending asynchronous send request, and if the send operation is successful, it returns the number of sent bytes to the `AsyncSocket` object.
IAsyncResult *BeginReceive(char buffer[], Int32 offset, Int32 size, SocketFlags socketFlags, AsyncCallback callback, Object *state)	Asynchronously begins to receive data from a connected or accepted socket. The description of the first four parameters of this method is exactly like the `Socket` class's `Receive()` method mentioned in Table 7.2.
Int32 EndReceive(IAsyncResult *asyncResult)	Ends a pending asynchronous receive request and returns the number of bytes received. If the return value is zero, it means that the remote host has closed the connection.
Socket *get_BaseSocket() const	Gets the base object instance of the `Socket` class.
void Close()	The description of this method comes in Table 7.2, and thus we omit it here.
void Shutdown(SocketShutdown how)	The description of this method comes in Table 7.2, and thus we omit it here.
Long get_CoreID() const	Gets the logical, physical processor core ID of the current socket instance that is running on it.
Int32 get_CoreCount() const	Gets the number of logical, physical processor cores on the current machine.

(Continued)

Table 7.4 (Continued) The `AsyncSocket` Class's Constructor and Methods in the Parvicursor.NET Framework

Name	Description
`bool TryMigrateToCore(Int32 DestCoreID)`	Atomically tries to make the `AsyncSocket` instance migrate from the current core to the destination core specified by `DestCoreID`. If the return value is false, this indicates that the destination core has not enough empty slots to enqueue the `AsyncSocket` instance, and therefore the migration operation fails. Also, this method may throw an exception indicating the error occurred during the socket migration process, and we must catch this exception and ensure that only the migration process has failed, and the program can continue with its normal execution. Of course, we can try again later. If we want to be able for invoking this method, we must have already called at least once one of the `BeginSend()` or `BeginReceive()` methods (this implicitly states that one background thread must be first assigned to the `AsyncSocket` instance internally through one of these two methods). This method can be only issued on a socket with a connected or accepted state.
`static void InitClientModeRuntime(void)`	If the `BeginConnect()` method is executed at least once in a program, the developer should invoke the static `InitClientModeRuntime()` method at the beginning of the `main()` function. In other words, this function initialises the client-side runtime, which contains the internal thread pool and dynamic object allocation for the asynchronous operations implemented. In the PCAS Framework, two separate thread pools are maintained for both client and server modes. The server thread pool is automatically initialised after the first call to the `BeginAccept()` method on the server socket, and it is destroyed after invoking the `Close()` method on a listening stateful socket instance. If this method has not already been invoked, the implementation of the `BeginConnect()` method internally calls the `InitClientModeRuntime()` method by default.
`static void DestroyClientModeRuntime(void)`	Destroys the client-side runtime initiated by the `InitClientModeRuntime()` method and releases all the resources in this state.

methods within the table. The implementation of the current PCAS version is presently only supported in the Linux operating system. The source code of the PCAS Framework is located at the path "`/Parvicursor/Parvicursor/AsyncSocketLib`" from the companion resources of the book. Due to the high complexity in the implementation of the AsyncSocket class, we avoid describing it and refer interested readers to the source code that was written to be easy to understand. For further study, interested readers can consult with the reference [3] and Chapter 10 to get more familiar with asynchronous methods and event-driven patterns.

7.6.4 Example 1: An Asynchronous Echo Client-Server

Now that you know enough about the AsyncSocket class, we describe an asynchronous echo client/server as the first example. Here, a server echoes the whole received data back to the client. Figure 7.24 shows the asynchronous echo server program.

In the main() function, having prepared the server socket to initiate accepting the incoming connections, we invoke the BeginAccept() method inside the while loop. Because this method is non-blocking, we must wait in lines 41 through 44 to synchronise between the main() thread and the thread executing the OnAccept() callback until no new connection is accepted by the EndAccept() method. After a new connection is accepted, the PCAS Framework invokes the OnAccept() callback. Within OnAccept(), we inform the main thread of getting accepted a new connection; then after preparing the StateObject for the accepted connection in line 70, we issue the BeginReceive() method to commence the receive operation on the client socket. After the receive operation completes, the PCAS Framework invokes the OnReceive() callback.

In line 80, the data receive request ends. If there is no error occurred and the client has not yet closed its connection to the server, in line 102 we call the BeginSend() method to start sending the data received from the client back to the client. After the send operation completes, the OnSent() function is invoked by the PCAS Framework. We consider two modes inside the implementation of the OnSent() callback function. If all the data received from the client still has yet been sent to it, again we must issue the BeginSend() method to send the remaining number of bytes. Otherwise, we wait to receive other data from the client by calling the BeginReceive() method. This sequence continues as long as the client closes the connection, and we in lines 81 to 86 free the client socket and the state object associated with it after detection of this occurrence.

In this example, note that choosing the value of true for the Guarantee-MulticoreExecution parameter when calling the BeginAccept() method ensures the concurrent execution of all accepted connections on different cores. Here, when the key combination CTRL+C is pressed on the console, we immediately terminate the program execution through the caught signal inside the StopRequested_signal_handler() interrupt handler by calling the exit() system function. The SIGINT signal event has been registered for this purpose in line 29 using the signal() system call.

Finally, we glimpse the implementation of an asynchronous echo client, as shown in Figure 7.25. Since we are at client-side runtime within this code, we invoke the InitClientModeRuntime() method in line 5. In line 81, the DestroyClientModeRuntime() method corresponding to this method is called. In this example, two parallel, asynchronous clients have been instantiated and connected to the remote server by calling the asynchronous BeginConnect() method. The implementation of the OnReceive() and OnSent() has been removed from

```
1: // State object for reading/writing client data asynchronously
2: class StateObject : public Object {
3:    // Client socket.
4:    public: AsyncSocket *workSocket;
5:    // Size of receive buffer.
6:    public: const static Int32 BufferSize = 1024;
7:    // Receive buffer.
8:    public: char buffer[BufferSize];
9:    // Size of received buffer.
10:    public: Int32 n_read;
11:    public: Int32 n_written;
12: };
13: // Asynchronous callbacks.
14: static void OnAccept(IAsyncResult *ar);
15: static void OnReceive(IAsyncResult *ar);
16: static void OnSent(IAsyncResult *ar);
17: // The following parameters are used to synchronise between the main thread and the execution of asynchronous
requests.
18: static Mutex mutex = Mutex();
19: static ConditionVariable cv = ConditionVariable(&allDone_mutex);
20: static bool conditionMet = false;
21:
22: static void StopRequested_signal_handler(int sig) {
23:    printf("\nCTRL+C was pressed.\n");
24:    printf("The server is terminating.\nPlease wait ...\n");
25:    exit(0);
26: }
27:
28: int main(int argc, char* argv[]) {
29:    my_signal(SIGINT, StopRequested_signal_handler);
30:    printf("Service was started.\n");
31:    AsyncSocket *listener = new AsyncSocket(InterNetwork, Stream, tcp);
32:    IPEndPoint hostEndPoint = IPEndPoint(IPAddress::get_Any(), 9000);
33:    listener->Bind(hostEndPoint);
34:    listener->Listen(1000);
35:    while(true) {
36:        conditionMet = false;
37:        // Start an asynchronous socket to listen for connections.
38:        printf("Waiting for a connection...\n");
39:        listener->BeginAccept(OnAccept, listener, true);
40:        // Wait until a connection is made before continuing.
41:        mutex.Lock();
42:        while(!conditionMet)
43:            cv.Wait();
44:        mutex.Unlock();
45:    }
46:    printf("The server is terminating.\nPlease wait ...\n");
47:    listener->Close();
48:    delete listener;
49:    // Here, we should also close all accepted connections. For example, you could
50:    // store a reference to every client connection into an array list
51:    // and close them altogether in a loop.
52:    return 0;
```

Figure 7.24   The echo server program depending upon asynchronous sockets in the Parvicursor platform.

(Continued)

```
53: }
54:
55: void OnAccept(IAsyncResult *ar) {
56:    // Signals the main thread to continue.
57:    mutex.Lock();
58:    conditionMet = true;
59:    cv.Signal();
60:    mutex.Unlock();
61:    // Gets the socket that handles the client request.
62:    AsyncSocket *listener = (AsyncSocket *)ar->AsyncState;
63:    AsyncSocket *handler = listener->EndAccept(ar);
64:    printf("new connection accepted.\n");
65:    // Creates the state object.
66:    StateObject *state = new StateObject();
67:    state->workSocket = handler;
68:    state->n_read = 0;
69:    state->n_written = 0;
70:    handler->BeginReceive(state->buffer, 0, state->BufferSize, System::Net::Sockets::None, OnReceive,
state);
71: }
72:
73: void OnReceive(IAsyncResult *ar) {
74:    // Retrieves the state object and the handler socket from the asynchronous state object.
75:    StateObject *state = (StateObject *) ar->AsyncState;
76:    AsyncSocket *handler = state->workSocket;
77:    // Reads data from the client socket.
78:    Int32 bytesRead;
79:    try {
80:       bytesRead = handler->EndReceive(ar);
81:       if(bytesRead <= 0) {
82:          printf("Error occurred in OnReceive. The AsyncSocket has been closed\n");
83:          handler->Close();
84:          delete handler; // This has been already allocated via invoking EndAccept();
85:          delete state;
86:          return ;
87:       }
88:    }
89:    catch(Exception &e) {
90:       printf("Error occured in OnReceive. Exception message: %s\n", e.get_Message().get_BaseStream());
91:       handler->Close();
92:       delete handler; // This has been already allocated via invoking EndAccept();
93:       delete state;
94:       return ;
95:    }
96:    catch(...){ ... }
97:    if(bytesRead > 0) {
98:
99:       printf("CoreID: %d bytesRead: %d\n", handler->get_CoreID(), bytesRead);
100:      state->n_read = bytesRead;
101:      // Echoes the data back to the client.
102:      handler->BeginSend(state->buffer, 0, bytesRead, System::Net::Sockets::None, OnSent, state);
103:   }
104:   else
```

Figure 7.24 (Continued) The echo server program depending upon asynchronous sockets in the Parvicursor platform.

(Continued)

```
105:        handler->BeginReceive(state->buffer, 0, state->BufferSize, System::Net::Sockets::None, OnReceive,
state);
106:    return;
107: }
108:
109: void OnSent(IAsyncResult *ar) {
110:    // Retrieves the state object and the handler socket from the asynchronous state object.
111:    StateObject *state = (StateObject *) ar->AsyncState;
112:    AsyncSocket *handler = state->workSocket;
113:    // Completes sending the data to the remote device.
114:    Int32 bytesSent;
115:    try {
116:        bytesSent = handler->EndSend(ar);
117:    }
118:    catch(Exception &e) {
119:        printf("Error occured in OnSent. Exception message: %s\n", e.get_Message().get_BaseStream());
120:        handler->Close();
121:        delete handler; // This has been already allocated via invoking EndAccept();
122:        delete state;
123:        return ;
124:    }
125:    catch(...) {...}
126:    if(bytesSent > 0) {
127:        printf("CoreID: %d bytesSent: %d\n", handler->get_CoreID(), bytesSent);
128:        state->n_written += bytesSent;
129:        Int32 remaining = state->n_read - state->n_written;
130:        if(remaining > 0)
131:            handler->BeginSend(state->buffer, state->n_written, remaining, System::Net::Sockets::None,
OnSent, state);
132:        else {
133:            state->n_read = 0;
134:            state->n_written = 0;
135:            handler->BeginReceive(state->buffer, 0, state->BufferSize, System::Net::Sockets::None,
OnReceive, state);
136:        }
137:    }
138:    else
139:        handler->BeginSend(state->buffer, 0, state->n_read, System::Net::Sockets::None, OnSent, state);
140: }
```

Figure 7.24   (Continued) The echo server program depending upon asynchronous sockets in the Parvicursor platform.

Figure 7.25 due to similarity with the server code. In lines 57 to 71 upon the completion of every send/receive operation on the client sockets, we migrate them to the opposite socket CPU core by calling the `TryMigrateToCore()`. One of the most important practical applications of the `TryMigrateToCore()` method can be used for uniformly load balancing amongst all the processor cores for network communications. For instance, this method allows moving a connection that requires a lot of processing into an idle or low-load core. The codes of the client and server are located at the path "`/Parvicursor/Parvicursor/Samples/AsyncEchoClient`" and "`/Parvicursor/Parvicursor/Samples/AsyncEchoServer`" from the companion resources of the book.

```
 1: ...
 2: int main(int argc, char* argv[]) {
 3:    printf("The client program was started.\n");
 4:    // Sets up the asynchronous client mode runtime.
 5:    AsyncSocket::InitClientModeRuntime();
 6:    // Establish the remote endpoint for sockets.
 7:    // The name of the remote device is "localhost".
 8:    IPHostEntry ipHostInfo = Dns::Resolve("localhost");
 9:    IPAddress ipAddress = ipHostInfo.get_AddressList(0);
10:    IPEndPoint remoteEP = IPEndPoint(ipAddress, 9000);
11:    AsyncSocket *client1 = new AsyncSocket(InterNetwork, Stream, tcp);
12:    AsyncSocket *client2 = new AsyncSocket(InterNetwork, Stream, tcp);
13:    // Create the state object.
14:    StateObject *state1 = new StateObject();
15:    state1->workSocket = client1;
16:    StateObject *state2 = new StateObject();
17:    state2->workSocket = client2;
18:    conditionNum = 0;
19:    // Connect to the remote endpoints.
20:    try {
21:       client1->BeginConnect(remoteEP, OnConnected, state1, true);
22:       client2->BeginConnect(remoteEP, OnConnected, state2, true);
23:    }
24:    catch(SocketException &e) {
25:       printf("Error occurred in OnConnected. Exception message: %s\n",
e.get_Message().get_BaseStream());
26:       return -2;
27:    }
28:    catch(...){ ... }
29:    // Waits until the two client connect.
30:    mutex.Lock();
31:    while(conditionNum != 2)
32:       cv.Wait();
33:    mutex.Unlock();
34:    const char *str = "Alireza Poshtkohi";
35:    Int32 len = strlen(str) + 1; // 1 for '\0' (the end of string)
36:    memmove(state1->sendBuffer, str, len);
37:    state1->len = len;
38:    memmove(state2->sendBuffer, str, len);
39:    state2->len = len;
40:    if(state1->hasException || state2->hasException)
41:       goto Cleanup;
42:    for(register Int32 i = 1 ; i <= 10 ; i++) {
43:       conditionNum = 0;
44:       printf("I: %d\n", i);
45:       client1->BeginSend(state1->sendBuffer, 0, state1->len, System::Net::Sockets::None, OnSent, state1);
46:       client2->BeginSend(state2->sendBuffer, 0, state2->len, System::Net::Sockets::None, OnSent, state2);
47:       // Waits until the two send operations complete.
48:       mutex.Lock();
49:       while(conditionNum != 2)
50:          cv.Wait();
51:       mutex.Unlock();
52:       if(state1->hasException || state2->hasException)
```

Figure 7.25 The echo client program relied upon asynchronous sockets in the Parvicursor platform.

(Continued)

```
53:          break;
54:          printf("Client1 Cores: %d CoreID: %d sendBuffer: %s receiveBuffer: %s\n", client1->get_CoreCount(),
client1->get_CoreID(), state1->sendBuffer, state1->receiveBuffer);
55:          printf("Client2 Cores: %d CoreID: %d sendBuffer: %s receiveBuffer: %s\n", client2->get_CoreCount(),
client2->get_CoreID(), state2->sendBuffer, state2->receiveBuffer);
56:          // Swaps cores.
57:          Int32 client1_CurrentCore = client1->get_CoreID();
58:          Int32 client2_CurrentCore = client2->get_CoreID();
59:          if(client1_CurrentCore != client2_CurrentCore) {
60:              printf("Tries to swap client cores ...\n");
61:              bool success = client1->TryMigrateToCore(client2_CurrentCore);
62:              if(success)
63:                  printf("client1 was swapped.\n");
64:              else
65:                  printf("client1 was not swapped.\n");
66:              success = client2->TryMigrateToCore(client1_CurrentCore);
67:              if(success)
68:                  printf("client2 was swapped.\n");
69:              else
70:                  printf("client2 was not swapped.\n");
71:          }
72:      }
73: Cleanup:
74:      printf("The client program is terminating.\nPlease wait ...\n");
75:      // Here, we should also close all accepted connections. For example, you could
76:      // store a reference to every client connection into an array list
77:      // and close them altogether in a loop. The client program was started.
78:      client1->Close(); delete client1; delete state1;
79:      client2->Close(); delete client2; delete state2;
80:      // Disposes the asynchronous client mode runtime.
81:      AsyncSocket::DestroyClientModeRuntime();
82:      return 0;
83: }
84:
85: void OnConnected(IAsyncResult *ar) {
86:      // Retrieve the state object and the handler socket
87:      // from the asynchronous state object.
88:      StateObject *state = (StateObject *) ar->AsyncState;
89:      AsyncSocket *handler = state->workSocket;
90:      try {
91:          // Completes the connection.
92:          handler->EndConnect(ar);
93:          printf("Socket connected.\n");
94:      }
95:      catch(Exception &e) {
96:          state->hasException = true;
97:          printf("Error occurred in OnConnected. Exception message: %s\n",
e.get_Message().get_BaseStream());
98:      }
99:      catch(...){ ... }
100:     // Signals the main thread to continue.
101:     mutex.Lock();
102:     conditionNum++;
103:     cv.Signal();
104:     mutex.Unlock();
105:     return;
106: }
107: ...
```

Figure 7.25 (Continued) The echo client program relied upon asynchronous sockets in the Parvicursor platform.

7.6.5 Example 2: The Design and Implementation of a Highly Concurrent and Scalable HTTP Proxy Server Supporting Tens of Thousands of Client Connections

As the last example of asynchronous sockets, we concentrate on the implementation of a highly scalable, concurrent, and complex HTTP proxy server atop the PCAS Framework. In Section 7.4, the HTTP protocol was elaborated for both direct and proxy (indirect) modes. Based upon the material presented therein, we shortly report a typical implementation of an HTTP proxy server supporting the GET/POST/CONNECT methods. Because the code of this example is very well understood, the reader should follow and read the entire codes line by line; this helps the reader get a better understanding of asynchronous sockets as well as enjoy the power of C and C++ languages in the construction of complex software systems (such as middleware frameworks), particularly for distributed systems on top of the Parvicursor platform.

Figure 7.26 illustrates the finite-state machine[26] of the implemented source code. The C++ code snippets of this FSM appear in Figure 7.27. An HTTP proxy server, first of all, must process and parse the client request inside the ProcessQuery() function after receiving a connection. After retrieving the request method, the proxy server connects to the remote server and relays between the client and the

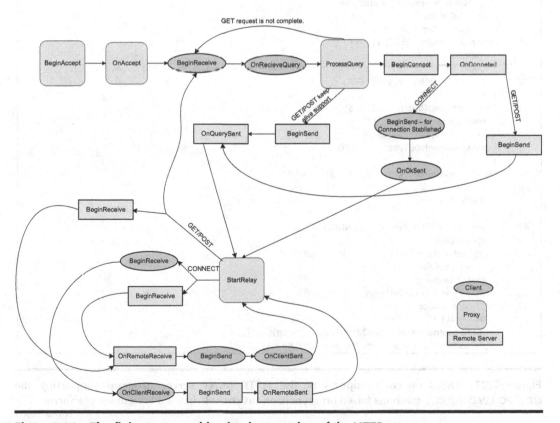

Figure 7.26 The finite-state machine implementation of the HTTP proxy server.

```
 1: // Called when there's an incoming client connection waiting to be accepted.
 2: private: static void OnAccept(IAsyncResult *ar) {
 3:    HttpProxyServer *proxy = (HttpProxyServer *)ar->AsyncState;
 4:    // Signal the Start() thread to continue.
 5:    proxy->accepted_mutex->Lock();
 6:    proxy->accepted = true;
 7:    proxy->accepted_cv->Signal();
 8:    proxy->accepted_mutex->Unlock();
 9:    // Gets the socket that handles the client request.
10:    AsyncSocket *clientSocket = proxy->listener->EndAccept(ar);
11:    printf("new connection accepted.\n");
12:    Session *session = new Session(__BUFFER_SIZE__);
13:    session->clientSocket = clientSocket;
14:    session->clientClosed = false;
15:    session->serverClosed = true;
16:    try {
17:        session->clientSocket->BeginReceive(session->clientBuffer, 0, session->bufferSize,
System::Net::Sockets::None, OnReceiveQuery, session);
18:    }
19:    ...
20: }
21: // Parses a specified query and modifies to the HTTP request.
22: private: static bool ParseRequest(InOut Session *session) {
23:    if(session->clientBuffer == null)
24:        return false;
25:    // Parses the HTTP METHOD request.
26:    char *begin = session->clientBuffer;
27:    char *end = null;
28:    Int32 methodLen = 0;
29:    if(strncmp(begin, "GET ", 4) == 0) {
30:        methodLen = 4;
31:        begin += 4;
32:        session->methodType = __GET;
33:    }
34:    else if(strncmp(begin, "POST ", 5) == 0) {
35:        methodLen = 5;
36:        begin += 5;
37:        session->methodType = __POST;
38:    }
39:    else if(strncmp(begin, "CONNECT ", 8) == 0) {
40:        // Finds hostname, e.g., CONNECT www.example.com:443 HTTP/1.1
41:        methodLen = 8;
42:        begin += 8;
43:        session->methodType = __CONNECT;
44:        char *end;
45:        if((end = strstr(begin, " HTTP/")) == null)
46:            return false;
47:        char *delimiter;
48:        if((delimiter = strchr(begin, ':')) == null)
49:            return false;
50:        delimiter++; // for ':'
51:        Int32 hostnameSize = (Int32)(delimiter - begin);
52:        if(hostnameSize > Session::MaxHostnameLen - 1)
```

Figure 7.27 **The C++ code snippets of the HTTP proxy server program supporting the GET/POST/CONNECT methods based on asynchronous sockets in the Parvicursor platform.**

(Continued)

```
53:          return false;
54:        memmove(session->hostname, begin, hostnameSize);
55:        session->hostname[hostnameSize - 1] = '\0';
56:        Int32 portSize = (Int32)(end - delimiter);
57:        if(portSize > 5)
58:          return false;
59:        char port_str[6]; // maximum port number is 65536 + 1 for '\0'
60:        port_str[portSize - 1] = '\0';
61:        memmove(port_str, delimiter, portSize);
62:        session->port = atoi(port_str);
63:        return true;
64:      }
65:      else
66:        return false;
67:    if(session->methodType == __GET || session->methodType == __POST) {
68:      // Finds pathname and protocol version.
69:      begin += 7;
70:      if((end = strchr(begin, '/')) != null) {
71:        char *pathnameBegin = begin - 7;
72:        char *pathnameEnd = end;
73:        Int32 transferLen = end - begin + 7;
74:        begin = end;
75:        if((end = strstr(begin, " HTTP/")) != null) {
76:          // Modifies line 1.
77:          memmove(pathnameBegin, pathnameEnd, session->clientRecv - transferLen);
78:          pathnameBegin -= methodLen;
79:          session->clientBuffer = pathnameBegin;
80:          session->clientRecv -= transferLen;
81:        }
82:      }
83:      // Removes Proxy-xxx
84:      if((begin = strstr(session->clientBuffer, "Proxy-")) != null) {
85:        // Proxy-Connection: Keep-Alive
86:        // Proxy-Connection: Close
87:        if(strncasecmp(begin, "Proxy-Connection: keep-alive", 28) == 0)
88:          session->KeepAlive = true;
89:        else if(strncasecmp(begin, "Proxy-Connection: Keep-Alive", 28) == 0)
90:            session->KeepAlive = true;
91:        else
92:          session->KeepAlive = false;
93:
94:        end = begin;
95:        end += 6; // strlen("Proxy-");
96:        //printf("clientRecv: %d begin: %d end: %d len: %d\n", session->clientRecv , (Int32)begin, (Int32)end, len);
97:        memmove(begin, end, ((Int32)session->clientBuffer + session->clientRecv) - (Int32)end);
98:        session->clientRecv -= 6;
99:      }
100:   }
101:   begin = session->clientBuffer;
102:   // Finds hostname, e.g., Host: www.example.com:8000
103:   if((begin = strstr(begin, "Host: ")) == null)
104:       return false;
105:   begin += 6;
```

Figure 7.27 (Continued) The C++ code snippets of the HTTP proxy server program supporting the GET/POST/CONNECT methods based on asynchronous sockets in the Parvicursor platform.

(Continued)

```
106:    end = null;
107:    if((end = strstr(begin, "\r\n")) == null) // Finds the end of the current line.
108:        if((end = strstr(begin, "\n")) == null)
109:            return false;
110:    char *delimiter = null;
111:    delimiter = strchr(begin, ':');
112:    if(delimiter == null || delimiter > end) {
113:        end++;
114:        delimiter = end;
115:        session->port = 80;
116:    }
117:    else {
118:        delimiter++; // for ':'
119:        Int32 portSize = (Int32)(end - delimiter);
120:        if(portSize > 5)
121:            return false;
122:        char port_str[6]; // maximum port number is 65536 + 1 for '\0'
123:        port_str[portSize - 1] = '\0';
124:        memmove(port_str, delimiter, portSize);
125:        session->port = atoi(port_str);
126:        if(session->port > 65536)
127:            return false;
128:    }
129:    Int32 hostnameSize = (Int32)(delimiter - begin);
130:    if(hostnameSize > Session::MaxHostnameLen - 1)
131:        return false;
132:    memmove(session->hostname, begin, hostnameSize);
133:    session->hostname[hostnameSize - 1] = '\0';
134:    return true;
135: }
136: // Disposes of the resources (other than memory) used by the Client.
137: // Closes the connections with the local client and the remote host. Once Dispose() has been called, this object should
not be used anymore.
138: private: static void Dispose(Session *session, bool clientMode) {
139:
140:    session->mutex->Lock();
141:    if(clientMode) {
142:      if(!session->clientClosed) {
143:        session->clientSocket->Close();
144:        session->clientClosed = true;
145:        if(session->serverClosed || session->serverSocket == null) {
146:          if(session->serverSocket != null)
147:            delete session->serverSocket;
148:          delete session->clientSocket;
149:          session->clientSocket = null;
150:          session->mutex->Unlock();
151:          delete session;
152:          session = null;
153:          return;
154:        }
155:        session->mutex->Unlock();
156:        return ;
157:      }
```

Figure 7.27 (Continued) The C++ code snippets of the HTTP proxy server program supporting the GET/POST/CONNECT methods based on asynchronous sockets in the Parvicursor platform.

(Continued)

```
158:    }
159:    else {
160:       if(!session->serverClosed) {
161:          session->serverSocket->Close();
162:          session->serverClosed = true;
163:          if(session->clientClosed) {
164:             if(session->clientSocket != null)
165:                delete session->clientSocket;
166:             delete session->serverSocket;
167:             session->clientSocket = null;
168:             session->serverSocket = null;
169:             session->mutex->Unlock();
170:             delete session;
171:             session = null;
172:             return;
173:          }
174:          session->mutex->Unlock();
175:          return ;
176:       }
177:    }
178:    session->mutex->Unlock();
179: }
180: // Called when we received some data from the client connection.
181: private: static void OnReceiveQuery(IAsyncResult *ar) {
182:    Session *session = (Session *)ar->AsyncState;
183:    try {
184:       Int32 Ret = session->clientSocket->EndReceive(ar);
185:       if(Ret <= 0) {
186:          Dispose(session, true);
187:          return;
188:       }
189:       if(session->methodType == __GET && !session->hasGetMethodCompleted) { // for large GET requests
190:          session->clientRecv += Ret;
191:          session->clientBuffer[session->clientRecv] = '\0';
192:          goto UncompletedGetMethod;
193:       }
194:       else
195:          session->clientRecv = Ret;
196:    }
197:    ...
198:    session->clientBuffer[session->clientRecv] = '\0';
199:    if(!ParseRequest(session)) {
200:       SendErrorToClientAndDispose(session, &errorCodes[__BadRequest__]);
201:       return;
202:    }
203:    session->clientBuffer[session->clientRecv] = '\0';
204: UncompletedGetMethod:
205:    if(session->methodType == __GET) {
206:       bool found = false;
207:       if(strstr(session->clientBuffer, "\r\n\r\n") != null)
208:          found = true;
209:       else if(strstr(session->clientBuffer, "\n\n") != null)
210:          found = true;
```

Figure 7.27 (Continued) The C++ code snippets of the HTTP proxy server program supporting the GET/POST/CONNECT methods based on asynchronous sockets in the Parvicursor platform.

(Continued)

```
211:     if(found) {
212:         session->hasGetMethodCompleted = true;
213:         goto Continue;
214:     }
215:     else {
216:         session->hasGetMethodCompleted = false;
217:         // Here, we must read the remaining content of the GET request from client.
218:         try {
219:             session->clientSocket->BeginReceive(session->clientBuffer, session->clientRecv, session->bufferSize - session->clientRecv, System::Net::Sockets::None, OnReceiveQuery, session);
220:             return;
221:         }
222:         ...
223:     }
224: }
225: Continue:
226:     if(session->methodType != __CONNECT && !session->isFirstTimeHttpRequest && session->KeepAlive)
227:     {
228:         if(strcmp(session->lastHostname, session->hostname) == 0) { // HTTP/1.1 Keep-Alive Support
229:             try {
230:                 session->serverSocket->BeginSend(session->clientBuffer, 0, session->clientRecv,
System::Net::Sockets::None, OnQuerySent, session);
231:             }
232:             ...
233:             return;
234:         }
235:     }
236:     session->mutex->Lock();
237:     if(session->serverSocket != null) {
238:         session->serverSocket->Close();
239:         delete session->serverSocket;
240:         session->serverSocket = null;
241:         session->serverClosed = true;
242:     }
243:     session->isFirstTimeHttpRequest = false;
244:     session->mutex->Unlock();
245:     // Establish the remote endpoint for sockets.
246:     // The name of the remote device is "session->hostname".
247:     IPHostEntry ipHostInfo;
248:     try {
249:         ipHostInfo = Dns::Resolve((const char*)session->hostname);
250:     }
251:     catch(...) {
252:         SendErrorToClientAndDispose(session, &errorCodes[__GatewayTimeout__]);
253:         return ;
254:     }
255:     IPEndPoint remoteEP;
256:     try {
257:         IPAddress ipAddress = ipHostInfo.get_AddressList(0);
258:         remoteEP = IPEndPoint(ipAddress, session->port);
259:         session->serverSocket = new AsyncSocket(InterNetwork, Stream, tcp);
260:         session->serverClosed = false;
261:         /* Sets the option active */
```

Figure 7.27 **(Continued) The C++ code snippets of the HTTP proxy server program supporting the GET/POST/CONNECT methods based on asynchronous sockets in the Parvicursor platform.**

(Continued)

```
262:        if(session->KeepAlive) {
263:            int one = 1;
264:            ::setsockopt(session->serverSocket->get_BaseSocket()->get_Handle(), SOL_SOCKET,
SO_KEEPALIVE, &one, sizeof(one));
265:        }
266:    }
267:    ...
268:    try {
269:        session->serverSocket->BeginConnect(remoteEP, OnConnected, session, true);
270:        printf("server socket: %d\n", session->serverSocket->get_BaseSocket()->get_Handle());//
271:    }
272:    catch(Exception &e) {
273:        printf("Error occured in OnReceiveQuery() 7. Exception message: %s\n",
e.get_Message().get_BaseStream());
274:        SendErrorToClientAndDispose(session, &errorCodes[__GatewayTimeout__]);
275:        return ;
276:    }
277:    ...
278: }
279: // Called when we're connected to the requested remote host.
280: private: static void OnConnected(IAsyncResult *ar {
281:    Session *session = (Session *)ar->AsyncState;
282:    try {
283:        session->serverSocket->EndConnect(ar);
284:        if(session->KeepAlive)
285:            memmove(session->lastHostname, session->hostname, strlen(session->hostname) + 1); // Copies
hostname into lastHostname.
286:    }
287:    catch(Exception &e) {
288:        printf("Error occured in OnConnected() 1. Exception message: %s\n",
e.get_Message().get_BaseStream());
289:        SendErrorToClientAndDispose(session, &errorCodes[__GatewayTimeout__]);
290:        return ;
291:    }
292:    ...
293:
294:    if(session->methodType == __CONNECT) { //HTTPS
295:        ::sprintf(session->clientBuffer, "HTTP/1.%d  200 Connection established\r\nProxy-Agent:
Parvicursor.NET-AsynchProxy-v1\r\n\r\n", 1);
296:        printf("Successfully connected to %s on port %d.\n", session->hostname, session->port);
297:        try {
298:            session->clientSocket->BeginSend(session->clientBuffer, 0, strlen(session->clientBuffer),
System::Net::Sockets::None, OnOkSent, session);
299:        }
300:        ...
301:    }
302:    else { //Normal HTTP
303:        printf("Successfully connected to %s on port %d.\n", session->hostname,session->port);
304:        try {
305:            session->serverSocket->BeginSend(session->clientBuffer, 0, session->clientRecv,
System::Net::Sockets::None, OnQuerySent, session);
306:        }
307:        ...
```

Figure 7.27 **(Continued) The C++ code snippets of the HTTP proxy server program supporting the GET/POST/CONNECT methods based on asynchronous sockets in the Parvicursor platform.**

(Continued)

```
308:    }
309: }
310: // Called when an OK reply has been sent to the client.
311: private: static void OnOkSent(IAsyncResult *ar) {
312:    Session *session = (Session *)ar->AsyncState;
313:    try {
314:       Int32 Ret = session->clientSocket->EndSend(ar);
315:       if(Ret == -1) {
316:          Dispose(session, true);
317:          return;
318:       }
319:    }
320:    ...
321:    StartRelay(session);
322: }
323: // Called when the HTTP query has been sent to the remote host.
324: private: static void OnQuerySent(IAsyncResult *ar)
325: {
326:    Session *session = (Session *)ar->AsyncState;
327:    try {
328:       if(session->serverSocket->EndSend(ar) == -1)
329:       {
330:          Dispose(session, false);
331:          return;
332:       }
333:    }
334:    ...
335:    StartRelay(session);
336: }
337: // Starts relaying data between the remote host and the local client.
338: // This method should only be called after all protocol specific communication has been finished.
339: private: static void StartRelay(Session *session)
340: {
341:    if(session->methodType == __CONNECT) {
342:       try {
343:          session->clientSocket->BeginReceive(session->clientBuffer, 0, session->bufferSize,
System::Net::Sockets::None, OnClientReceive, session);
344:       }
345:       ...
346:       try {
347:          session->serverSocket->BeginReceive(session->serverBuffer, 0, session->bufferSize,
System::Net::Sockets::None, OnRemoteReceive, session);
348:       }
349:       ...
350:    }
351:    else if(session->methodType == __GET || session->methodType == __POST) {
352:       try {
353:          session->clientSocket->BeginReceive(session->clientBuffer, 0, session->bufferSize,
System::Net::Sockets::None, OnReceiveQuery, session);
354:       }
355:       ...
356:       try {
357:          session->serverSocket->BeginReceive(session->serverBuffer, 0, session->bufferSize,
```

Figure 7.27   (Continued) The C++ code snippets of the HTTP proxy server program supporting the GET/POST/CONNECT methods based on asynchronous sockets in the Parvicursor platform.

(Continued)

```
System::Net::Sockets::None, OnRemoteReceive, session);
358:      }
359:      ...
360:    }
361: }
362: // Called when we have received data from the local client. Incoming data will immediately be forwarded to the remote host
363: private: static void OnClientReceive(IAsyncResult *ar) {
364:    Session *session = (Session *)ar->AsyncState;
365:    try {
366:       Int32 Ret = session->clientSocket->EndReceive(ar);
367:       if(Ret <= 0) {
368:          Dispose(session, true);
369:          return;
370:       }
371:       session->clientRecv = Ret;
372:    }
373:    ...
374:    try {
375:       session->serverSocket->BeginSend(session->clientBuffer, 0, session->clientRecv,
System::Net::Sockets::None, OnRemoteSent, session);
376:    }
377:    ...
378: }
379: // Called when we have received data from the remote host. Incoming data will immediately be forwarded to the local client.
380: private: static void OnRemoteReceive(IAsyncResult *ar) {
381:    Session *session = (Session *)ar->AsyncState;
382:    try {
383:       Int32 Ret = session->serverSocket->EndReceive(ar);
384:       if(Ret <= 0) {
385:          Dispose(session, false);
386:          return;
387:       }
388:       session->serverRecv = Ret;
389:    }
390:    ...
391:    try{
392:       session->clientSocket->BeginSend(session->serverBuffer, 0, session->serverRecv,
System::Net::Sockets::None, OnClientSent, session);
393:    }
394:    ...
395: }
396: // Called when we have sent data to the remote host. When all the data has been sent, we will start receiving again from the local client.
397: private: static void OnRemoteSent(IAsyncResult *ar) {
398:    Session *session = (Session *)ar->AsyncState;
399:    try {
400:       Int32 Ret = session->serverSocket->EndSend(ar);
401:       if(Ret <= 0) {
402:          printf("Error occurred in OnRemoteSent() 1.\n");
403:          Dispose(session, false);
404:          return;
```

Figure 7.27 **(Continued) The C++ code snippets of the HTTP proxy server program supporting the GET/POST/CONNECT methods based on asynchronous sockets in the Parvicursor platform.**

(Continued)

```
405:      }
406:    }
407:    ...
408:    StartRelay(session);
409: }
410: // Called when we have sent data to the local client. When all the data has been sent, we will start receiving again
from the remote host.
411: private: static void OnClientSent(IAsyncResult *ar) {
412:    Session *session = (Session *)ar->AsyncState;
413:    try {
414:       Int32 Ret = session->clientSocket->EndSend(ar);
415:       if(Ret <= 0) {
416:          Dispose(session, true);
417:          return;
418:       }
419:    }
420:    ...
421:    StartRelay(session);
422: }
423: // Sends an error to the client.
424: private: static void SendErrorToClientAndDispose(Session *session, ErrorStruct *error) {
425:       ::sprintf(session->clientBuffer, "HTTP/1.1 %d %s\r\nConnection: close\r\nContent-Type:
text/html\r\n\r\n\r\n<html><head><title>Parvicursor.NET-AsynchProxy-v1: %d %s</title></head><body><div
align=\"centre\"><table border=\"0\" cellspacing=\"3\" cellpadding=\"3\" bgcolor=\"#C0C0C0\"><tr><td><table
border=\"0\" width=\"500\" cellspacing=\"3\" cellpadding=\"3\"><tr><td bgcolor=\"#B2B2B2\"><p
align=\"centre\"><strong><font size=\"2\" face=\"Verdana\">Parvicursor.NET-AsynchProxy-v1: %d
%s</font></strong></p></td></tr><tr><td bgcolor=\"#D1D1D1\"><font size=\"2\"
face=\"Verdana\">%s</font></td></tr></table></centre></td></tr></table></div></body></html>",
426:                error->number, error->message,
427:                error->number, error->message,
428:                error->number, error->message,
429:                error->description);
430:    try {
431:       session->clientSocket->BeginSend(session->clientBuffer, 0, strlen(session->clientBuffer),
System::Net::Sockets::None, OnErrorSent, session);
432:    }
433:    ...
434: }
435: // Called when the Bad Request error has been sent to the client.
436: private: static void OnErrorSent(IAsyncResult *ar) {
437:    Session *session = (Session *)ar->AsyncState;
438:    try {
439:       session->clientSocket->EndSend(ar);
440:    }
441:    ...
442:    Dispose(session, true);
443: }
```

Figure 7.27   (Continued) The C++ code snippets of the HTTP proxy server program supporting the GET/POST/CONNECT methods based on asynchronous sockets in the Parvicursor platform.

server to communicate and transmit the data (the StartRelay function). The ProcessQuery() function has been implemented grounding on the ANSI C string functions for high-performance purposes; herein, we avoided for any additional memory allocation to manipulate strings (this makes the implementation complicated in favour of a performance increase). Whereas the length of the send buffer may be less than the length of the proxy buffer in the GET method, at the proxy side we must read from the server socket until the end of the request is reached as advertised by the string \r\n\r\n.

This issue is also valid for POST method, especially when a client is uploading an object or a file that has specified its length in the Content-Length header; the current implementation does not support this feature and we leave it as an exercise to the reader. Because connections in the HTTP protocol version 1.1 are persistent, we must support it when the client sends frequent requests to a single proxy (line 228). Due to the lengthy code, we invite the reader to look at the entire code carefully with the inline comments.

In the end, we talk a little about the Dispose() method. Since the client and remote server sockets are running on individual threads, terminating a session between the client and server is a bit more challenging. For this reason, when a connection is closed, we have to make use of a mutex in this function and close the socket at the side that has been closed and also release its object; however, we cannot release the other side socket because its thread is running. To solve this problem, we just close the opposite side socket in this case; this makes an exception to be thrown inside the thread, and, at this moment, because the thread can catch this exception, it itself can call the Dispose() function safely and close its socket; finally, we also free the current session reference (i.e., the variable session). The codes of this sample are available at the path "/Parvicursor/Parvicursor/Samples/HttpProxyServer" from the companion resources of the book.

We hope that the contents within this chapter could convey the author's experience to the respected readers in the area of parallel network programming. Furthermore, we will be so pleased to hear that this chapter has motivated you about the very interesting and key topic of integrating communication with concurrency for distributed systems.

Notes

1 LANs
2 MANs
3 WANs
4 Media Access Control
5 HCA
6 TCA
7 QP
8 WQE
9 CQE
10 Remote Direct Memory Access
11 QoS
12 Open Protocol Architecture
13 International Organization for Standardization
14 Transmission Control Protocol
15 IP
16 Stream Control Transmission Protocol
17 User Datagram Protocol
18 Voice over Internet Protocol

19 DNS
20 Hypertext Transfer Protocol
21 Uniform Resource Identifier
22 Multipurpose Internet Mail Extensions
23 Simple Object Access Protocol
24 Secure Socket Layer/Transport Layer Security
25 Uniform Resource Locator
26 FSM

References

[1] B. Forouzan, and D.A. College, *TCP/IP Protocol Suite*, 4th Edition, McGraw-Hill, New York, 2010, ISBN 978-0070166783.

[2] Asynchronous Programming Patterns, MSDN, 2022; http://msdn.microsoft.com/en-us/library/ms228969.aspx

[3] D. Makofske, and K. Almeroth, *Multicast Sockets: Practical Guide for Programmers*, Morgan Kaufmann, London, New York, 2002, ISBN 978-1558608467.

Chapter 8

Parvicursor.NET Framework: A Partial, Native, and Cross-Platform C++ Implementation of the .NET Framework

Computer programming is an art because it applies accumulated knowledge to the world, requires skill and ingenuity, and especially because it produces objects of beauty.

Donald Knuth

8.1 Introduction

DotGrid project was introduced to create a Grid infrastructure atop .NET Framework [1–5]. The current DotGrid structure does not offer a Grid middleware, but rather it provides an infrastructure for creating and implementing middleware in distributed, Cluster, Grid, and Cloud environments. DotGrid anatomy utilises a peer-to-peer abstraction which can form a distributed environment between network nodes. Using and extending DotGrid APIs and developing the P2P concept, one can easily arrive at different low-level networked topologies, including the master-slave, hierarchical master-slave, and perfect graph. In the year 2005, DotGrid Grid Computing Framework was implemented on top of MONO.NET and Microsoft.NET Frameworks using the ECMA standards 334 and 335 [6, 7]. DotGrid was the first project employing.NET technologies that were implemented in a cross-platform fashion to create heterogeneous Grid environments with the notion of a homogenised system on the most recent operating systems like Windows, Linux, and Unix.

During the design period, whilst the DotGrid project was being developed, we faced substantial problems in the efficiency of the .NET Framework; hence, in the year 2006 the conception of a new project, currently referred to as the term *Parvicursor*, emerged. DotGrid platform had been designed accurately by using very

DOI: 10.1201/9781003379041-8

low-level design methods of software systems. We did not make use of special features provided by the .NET Framework, which could not be ported to other runtimes (platforms) like Java and native code. Parvicursor project, using the open standard-based benefits from the DotGrid platform, provides a new cross-platform framework to easily port C#-based DotGrid source codes directly to the native code which relied heavily on the .NET ECMA standards [6–8].

Parvicursor project is an essential effort to establish an OS-based framework to fast develop new high-performance distributed paradigms. The basic infrastructure is inspired by concepts mostly available in Cluster, Grid, and Cloud environments. From the viewpoint of the developer users, the Parvicursor.NET Framework provides a set of rich, cross-platform, object-oriented, high-performance, and low-level C++ class libraries which enable quick and solid development of the next-generation networked/distributed applications and paradigms. From the viewpoint of the Parvicursor core, it supplies some critical services developed with parts in kernel mode and some other parts in userspace.

In this chapter, we briefly introduce the .NET Framework and existing technologies within the platform. The presented material herein will make the understanding of the Parvicursor.NET Framework more tangible to the reader.

The rest of the chapter is organised as follows. In Section 8.2, we present Common Language Infrastructure (CLI). Section 8.3 describes Parvicursor.NET Framework. Sections 8.4 and 8.5 concentrate on the compilation and loading process of .NET-CLI and Parvicursor.NET application programs. The Parvicursor.NET Socket Interface (PSI), Parvicursor Object Passing Interface (POPI), and Parvicursor.NET Remoting Architecture (PR) will be discussed in Sections 8.6–8.8. Section 8.9 focuses on native programming with the Parvicursor.NET Framework. In Section 8.10, we provide some example programs developed atop Parvicursor.NET Framework.

8.2 Common Language Infrastructure (CLI)

CLI is an international open standard (defined in ECMA-335 and ISO/IEC 23271 standards) developed by Microsoft Corporation that provides the basics to create development and execution environments in which languages and libraries work together seamlessly. The most important major and integral parts of CLI fall into four cores: Common Type System (CTS), Metadata, Common Language Specification (CLS), and (VES) Virtual Execution System.

VES isolates CLI-compliant programs from the underlying operating system. The VES has been implemented for a broad spectrum of operating systems (such as Microsoft.NET in Windows and MONO.NET in Unix-style operating systems like FreeBSD, Linux, and Solaris) so that the programs written in CLI-compliant languages (like C#, F#, C++/CLI, and J#) can be executed on different systems without recompilation or rewriting. The programming to the CLI-compliant languages eventually offers a simple model but is rich in where the use of this platform can cause developing programs in different languages, taking advantage of code reuse techniques and removing the most structural problems involved in traditional programming models. CLI provides many facilities for modules, including to be self-registered, to be able to execute remote processes, to be possible to deal with errors through exception handling mechanisms, and so on.

The CTS builds an infrastructure of data types in the CLI. The data types are something beyond the concept of bits that data reside in them. The original idea behind the CTS is to provide compatible types, which give interoperability to various languages. The CTS has been designed for a wide class of objected-oriented, procedural, and functional languages.

CLS is a subset of CTS. CLS is a set of bytes that may be used in external calls within codes for portability purposes. This entire standardised framework (including the Base Class Library, XML Library, Network Library, Reflection Library, and Extended Numeric Library) is expected to be used on any system that runs compliant VES or in any CLS-compliant language.

Standard .NET Framework conforms to the CLS and mainly aims to be cross-language. In the definition of CLI, a profile is a collection of libraries grouped into a structure that makes up a strong general entity, and in turn this procedure provides a functional firm level. A basic CLI profile is the kernel profile which contains C# class libraries.

.NET Class Framework is a huge set of classes. This structure is an interface encapsulating the operating system that is implemented above the operating system APIs. .NET Framework only uses the basic functionalities of the operating system, thus eventually leading to a limitation in terms of feature set.

The term *Common Language Runtime (CLR)* is one core component of Microsoft's .NET initiative which is the implementation of CLI standard. CLR allows developers and programmers to forget the detail of dozens of processor architectures, which execute their programs. Moreover, the CLR arranges several services, including Memory Management, Garbage Collector, Thread Management, Exception Handling, and Security.

Despite the strength and the emerging innovations of CLI, this abstraction significantly degrades performance in executing programs because of its multiple layers in the conversion of codes into native code by the CLR. Of course, this issue is not accounted for in usual enterprise and desktop applications but rather the CLI weakness is meaningful in server systems and HPC environments. In other words, one of the main goals of the Parvicursor.NET Framework is to eliminate this performance issue whilst preserving the unique features of the .NET Framework and C# language in such platforms depending upon the native C/C++ runtime.

8.3 Parvicursor.NET Framework

To realise the goal to eliminate the overheads concerned with the multi-layer architecture of the .NET Framework, the perception of the Parvicursor project in following up the DotGrid project emerged. The Parvicursor.NET Framework is a native and cross-platform implementation of the standard CLI profiles and libraries based on the standard ISO C++. The main aim of the Parvicursor project is actually to provide an infrastructural software framework to easily port the source codes of the .NET-based DotGrid Grid Computing Framework into native code with the minimum time and cost spent and to increase the efficiency of the protocols that had been implemented in DotGrid platform. Therefore, in addition to porting the DotGrid structure to native code, a high-performance implementation of the CLI standard leaves to enterprise and scientific communities. Figure 8.1 shows the current layered architecture of the Microsoft .NET Framework.

Each of the layers according to the inherent nature of CLI poses extra overheads upon application programs developed atop Microsoft .NET Framework. The Just-In-Time (JIT) compiler emits the CIL code into native executable code within the operating system through two methods at runtime, bytecode compilation and dynamic compilation. One important overhead of this compilation process is that the .NET assembly modules must be dynamically compiled and loaded into memory.

When a method is called for the first time, the CLR passes control to the JIT compiler, which converts the MSIL for that method into native code and modifies the code state to point directly to the generated native code. Subsequent calls to the JIT-compiled method, therefore, proceed directly to the native code.

Section 8.4 mentions a number of these overheads in comparing the performance of executed codes by Microsoft .NET and MONO .NET Frameworks with Parvicursor. NET Framework.

Figure 8.2 portrays the four-layer architecture of the Parvicursor.NET Framework. As implicitly shown in this framework, only native C/C++ codes are compiled and after linking with the Parvicursor.NET Framework, which implements CLI classes and

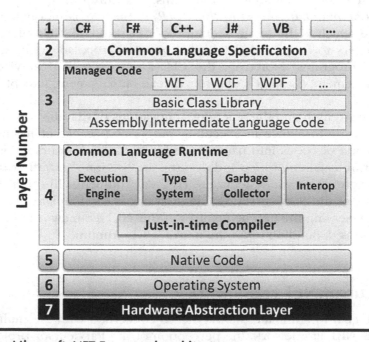

Figure 8.1   The Microsoft .NET Framework architecture.

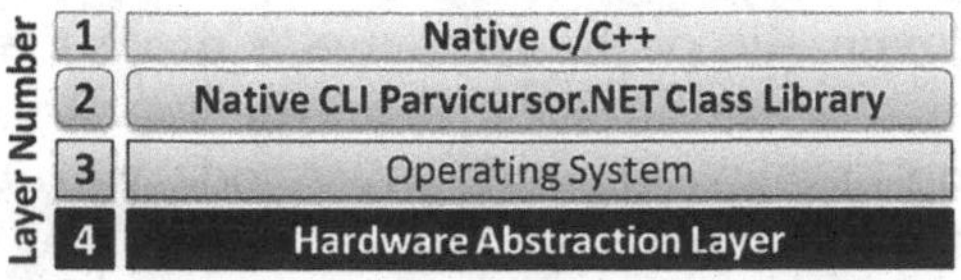

Figure 8.2   The Parvicursor.NET Framework architecture.

profiles, an executable image file is executed by the operating system. Also, there is no additional layer and no overhead on applications that make use of the framework.

The number of layers with respect to the .NET Framework is seven and it is four for the Parvicursor.NET Framework. Layer 1 of the Parvicursor.NET Framework has replaced layers 1–4 of the .NET Framework. The comparison of Figures 8.1 and 8.2 together show that the native runtime within the Parvicursor.NET Framework supersedes the .NET Framework's CLR.

Architecturally, the primary differences between the Parvicursor.NET Framework layout system and the Microsoft .NET Platform are the lack of distinction between core and framework and the execution runtime (native runtime for Parvicursor.NET versus virtual machine nature for Microsoft .NET); the three-layer architecture including the CLS, Managed Code, and CLR, as shown in Figure 8.1, has high-performance costs which are deemed excessive for server-based applications and HPC environments.

Furthermore, since the application of Parvicursor.NET Framework is part of low-level operating system services, the interoperability and product lifecycle scenarios are generally simplified compared to those of desktop applications, so the benefits of the layer separation are minimal.

In this section, we examine a practical example as an attempt to describe how porting the Microsoft .NET Framework classes written in C# language into native code through the standard C++ for Parvicursor.NET Framework is achieved. At the end, we point out a lot of technical points for developers targeting the Parvicursor platform in porting their applications from C# to native C++.

Figure 8.3 illustrates the `Socket` class prototype in `System.Net.Sockets` namespace from profiles and libraries of the CLI standard written in C# language.

.NET Platform Invoke Technology [9] has been used to implement the main methods of this class in the existing implementations such as Microsoft .NET [10], Shared Source Common Language Infrastructure (SSCLI) [11], MONO .NET [12], DotGNU [13], and the Portable .NET [14]. As seen in this sample, the `DllImport` attribute has taken benefit of the .NET P/Invoke.

.NET Platform Invoke technology is built right into the CLR runtime to enable managed programs (i.e., the CLI runtime) to invoke ordinary dynamically linked unmanaged code (.dll files in Windows and .so files in Unix-class style operating systems such as Linux and Solaris). It is logically equivalent to a DLL or SO in native C++ for routines exported and annotated by `delclsspec(dllexport)`. The result of linking against an ordinary DLL or SO in the Microsoft C++ compiler or GNU GCC C++ compiler is an executable that inserts small proxy stubs which, when invoked, redirect to the actual code at native runtime. P/Invoke is very similar, except that the CLR is responsible for loading, binding, and making necessary transformations between data types whilst a function is called. As is the case with pure unmanaged code (i.e., the native runtime), the operating system will share code with multiple processes accessing that DLL or SO simultaneously.

When working with unmanaged code, whether it is a native system function or native libraries in C++, there is a type system gap that must be bridged. For instance, a string to the .NET Framework is not the same as a string in C++. Marshalling performs transformations to bits such that data instances can be used on both sides of the runtimes (managed runtime against unmanaged runtime). This operation may be a simple bit-for-bit copy from the managed to unmanaged runtime and vice versa,

```
using  System;
using  System.Collections;
using  System.Net;
using  System.Runtime.InteropServices;

namespace  System.Net.Sockets
{
    /* .NET Platform Invoke */
    [DllImport("Ws2_32.dll", SetLastError=       true )]
    static    extern   int socket( int af,   int type,   int protocol);

    public  class  Socket : Object
    {
        private  int sock;
        public   Socket(AddressFamily addressFamily, SocketType socketType,
                              ProtocolType protocolType)
        {
            /* through .NET Paltform Invoke*/
            this .sock = socket(addressFamily, socketType, protocolType);
            //...
        }
        public   Socket Accept();
        public   void  Bind(EndPoint localEP);
        public   void  Close();
        public   void  Connect(EndPoint remoteEP);
        public   void  Listen( int backlog);
        public   int Receive( byte [] buffer,   int offset,   int size, SocketFlags socketFlags);
        public   static   void  Select(IList checkRead, IList checkWrite, IList checkError,
                                       int microSeconds);
        public   int Send( byte [] buffer,   int offset,   int size, SocketFlags socketFlags);
        public   void  Shutdown(SocketShutdown how);
        public   AddressFamily AddressFamily {       get ; }
        public   bool Connected {    get ; }
        public   IntPtr Handle {    get ; }
        public   ProtocolType ProtocolType {      get ; }
        public   SocketType SocketType {    get ; }
    }
}
```

Figure 8.3   .NET C# CLI class implementation sample.

but just as well might involve a complete reorganisation of the contents of a data structure as the copy occurs. This translation adds extra overheads. Hence, the marshalling mechanism can be very expensive; it can add tens of native instructions per argument for even simple native function calls.

Along with these overheads imposed by P/Invoke as mentioned at the beginning of this section, the various .NET layers, especially the VES, pose another heavy overhead on the programs developed atop CLI. As seen in Figure 8.4, the socket() native function is called through P/Invoke from a DLL named Ws2_32.dll, which implements the native WinSock system routines.

Figure 8.4 shows an implementation example of the CLI profiles and libraries in native C++ for the Parvicursor.NET platform. The fundamental differences between Microsoft .NET Framework and Parvicursor.NET Framework can be understood by the structural comparison of Figures 8.3 and 8.4. As derived from Figure 8.4, the architectural structure of the Parvicursor.NET Framework makes use of the standard C++ for the sake of implementing available classes in CLI. The main idea behind this approach is inspired by the structural similarities between two C++ and C# languages, and this process can provide an integrated flow easily to port the .NET-based DotGrid Platform into native code in addition to creating a new and native object-oriented framework to develop high-performance applications relying on the concept of .NET technologies.

```
using   namespace   System;
using   namespace   System::Collections;
using   namespace   System::Net;

#if defined  WIN32 || WIN64
#include   <winsock2.h>
#pragma   comment (lib , "ws2_32.lib")
#pragma   comment (lib , "Mswsock.lib")
#else
#include   <sys/socket.h>
#endif

namespace   System
{
namespace   Net
{
namespace   Sockets
{
        // native CLI C++ Socket Class Implementation
        class  Socket :    public  Object
        {
                private:    int sock;
                public : Socket(AddressFamily addressFamily, SocketType socketType,
                                ProtocolType protocolType)
                {
                        /* through native WinSock (for Windows)
                                or Berkeley Socket (for Linux) call */
                        this ->sock = socket(addressFamily, socketType, protocolType);
                        //...
                }
                public : ~Socket();
                public : Socket *Accept()        const ;
                public : void Bind(IPEndPoint &localEP);
                public : void Connect(IPEndPoint &remoteEP);
                public : void Close();
                public : void Listen( int backlog);
                public : int Receive( char buffer[],   int offset,   int size, SocketFlags socketFlags);
                public : static  void  Select(ArrayList &checkRead, ArrayList &checkWrite,
                                        ArrayList &checkError,       int microSeconds);
                public : int Send( const  char buffer[],   int offset,   int size, SocketFlags socketFlags);
                public : void Shutdown(SocketShutdown how);
                public : AddressFamily get_AddressFamily()        const ;
                public : bool get_Connected()    const ;
                public : int get_Handle()   const ;
                public : ProtocolType get_ProtocolType()        const ;
                public : SocketType get_SocketType()        const ;
        };
}
}
}
```

Figure 8.4   Native and cross-platform CLI C++ Parvicursor.NET class implementation sample.

As the comparison of the two figures tells us, we have tried to use the syntax similarities between C# and C++ languages as much as possible so that the implemented C++ codes become close to the C# codes and the defining features of the classes, methods, and the functional state of the CLI libraries are preserved.

The prototypes defined in the Parvicursor.NET Framework and their implementation architecture can present a new and novel solution to standardise the CLI and .NET Framework in the standard C++ level as a cross-platform and portable software framework, of course with the unique feature of being native, for heterogeneous platforms. To further clarify features in the context of Parvicursor.NET Framework, we explore the efforts of Microsoft Corporation to standardise CLI in C++ since 2000.

On 13 February 2002, Microsoft released the first version of the .NET Framework. In this regard, Managed Extensions for C++, or in a more accurate phrase Managed C++, was born. Managed C++, by introducing a series of new keywords, syntaxes, pragmas, preprocessor directives, and attributes, announced the C++ language as an infrastructural development environment with performance somewhat more improved than the C# language to develop .NET Framework and to achieve the execution of managed codes alongside the native machine target codes within the CLR.

But in general, Managed C++ code (MSIL) is faster or more efficient than code (MSIL) compiled by using the C# compiler.

Because the Managed C++ used a few keywords to preserve the simplicity and the main syntax of standard C++, it produced problems for programmers who wanted to develop their programs based upon C++ demanding .NET Framework. The following major issues can be pointed out:

1. Code development dependent on the C++ imposed more time spend than other .NET Framework languages for developers, a problem that could have been caused by new keywords, and syntax changes of the Managed C++ language than the standard C++.
2. Although one of the unique features of Managed C++ is the ability to use unmanaged system APIs within managed codes, once again data marshalling is performed automatically by the CLR, and the overheads originating from the multi-layered abstraction of the .NET Framework and P/Invoke remain intact.
3. Multiple inheritances were not supported in Managed C++. The problem was chiefly because a class managed by Garbage Collector (GC) related to CLR could not inherit from more than one class.
4. One other disadvantage of using Managed C++ was that the assembly written in Managed C++ could not utilize the verification mechanisms of .NET security, so it was required to run in a trusted environment.
5. Managed C++ was the first attempt by Microsoft and did not allow a standard implementation on other platforms. So, it did not support generic programming via templates.

To fix up some problems mentioned above, Microsoft introduced the ECMA-372 standard referred to as the term C++/CLI in the year 2005 [8]. C++/CLI can be thought of as a language within a language.

In fact, C++/CLI is a set of extensions to the standard ISO C++ that provides a complete "binding" of the C++ language to the CLI. Although C++/CLI demonstrates all the CLI features in C++ and even though C++/CLI is coherent and easier to understand than its predecessor Managed C++, but C++/CLI with the introduction of many new structures (the CLI features like interfaces, properties, generics, pointers, inheritance, enumeration, etc.) makes itself to become very far from the standard C++. Table 8.1 shows the most important keywords introduced in C++/CLI (the notation ⫶ is equivalent to space over there). A full description of these keywords is beyond the scope of this context (more information can be found in [8]).

Because C++/CLI akin to Managed C++ executes on the VES, it exposes the same overheads stated in this subsection on developed applications. Standard C++ over the past decades has been famous as a sophisticated language for learning and using properly. Although Microsoft is attempting to register the C++/CLI as an ISO/

Table 8.1 Some New C++/CLI Keywords

abstract delegate event finally generic in initonly internal literal override property sealed where enum⫶class enum⫶struct for⫶each gcnew interface⫶class interface⫶struct nullptr ref⫶class ref⫶struct value⫶class value⫶struct #using __cplusplus_cli interior_ptr pin_ptr array ...

IEC standard, but it is necessary nothing that the complexity of the C++ language is increased by more than 60% if this standardisation happens (however, the newer versions of CLI like Microsoft .NET Framework 4 could increase greatly this percentage due to creating new structural complications).

In addition, the C++/CLI is merely supported as platform-specific presently by Microsoft VC++ on Windows operating system and no version has been provided for other platforms since 2005 yet. The fact absolutely fails the application of C++/CLI as a standard platform to develop portable programs and makes most programmers develop their applications based on native C++ language and standard cross-platform libraries (such as C++ STL and Boost) to maintain code portability.

Figures 8.5–8.7 represent an example of evolution from managed C++ and C++/CLI to Parvicursor.NET CLI C++. By conceptual comparison of these three figures, the reader familiar with C++ language can deduce the essential differences between Parvicursor.NET Framework and Managed C++ and C++/CLI. As seen in these three figures, all of them promote a single operation unit from the operating system's point of view. Figure 8.5 to medium and Figure 8.7 to a large extent are closer to the existing structures in the C# language. Whilst Figure 8.6 is expressing the fact that C++/CLI language has created a new language in the heart of standard C++. In Figures 8.5 and 8.6, the .NET CLR execution environment has been used by importing the managed `mscorlib.dll` library, as in Figure 8.7 the same functionality is achieved by importing the native `ParvicursorLib.lib` library within the Parvicursor.NET Framework but the compiled and linked codes by the `ParvicursorLib.lib` take advantage of pure native runtime to execute.

As Figure 8.7 recounts, we can construct a framework by employing standard C++ language in which a simple, flexible, highly extensible, high-performance, and cross-platform environment, in addition to preserving the features of C++ language, is provided for CLI standard.

```
// Managed extensions for C++
#using <mscorlib.dll>
using namespace System::Collections;
__gc class referencetype
{
protected:
    String* stringVar;
    int intArr __gc[];
    ArrayList* doubleList;
public:
    referencetype(String* str, int* pointer, int number)
    {
        doubleList = new ArrayList();
        System::Console::WriteLine(str->Trim() + number.ToString());
    }
    ~referencetype();
};
```

Figure 8.5 Managed extensions for C++ sample.

```cpp
// C++/CLI
#using <mscorlib.dll>
using namespace System::Collections::Generic;
ref class referencetype // : IDisposable (this is added by the compiler)
{
protected:
    String^ stringVar;
    array<int>^ intArr;
    List<double>^ doubleList;
public:
    referencetype(String^ str, int* pointer, int number)
    {
        doubleList = gcnew List<double>();
        System::Console::WriteLine(str->Trim() + number);
    }
    ~referencetype();
                /* (deterministic) destructor
                   (turned into IDisposable.Dispose() by the compiler) */
protected:
    !referencetype();
                /* finalizer (non-deterministic destructor)
                   (former destructor syntax => virtual void Finalize()) */
};
```

Figure 8.6   C++/CLI sample.

```cpp
// Native Parvicursor.NET CLI C++
#include <Parvicursor.h>
#pragma comment(lib, "ParvicursorLib.lib")
using namespace System;
using namespace System::Collections;
class referencetype : public Object
{
protected:
    String* stringVar;
    int intArr [];
    ArrayList* doubleList;
public:
    referencetype(String* str, int* pointer, Int32 number)
    {
        doubleList = new ArrayList();
        Console::WriteLine(str->Trim() + number.ToString());
        // or
        cout << str->Trim() << number << endl;
    }
    ~referencetype()
    {
        if(doubleList != null)
            delete doubleList;
        doubleList = null;
    }
};
```

Figure 8.7   Native Parvicursor.NET CLI C++ sample.

One of our challenges in the design and implementation of the Parvicursor.NET Framework was the adaptation between the linguistic structures of standard C++ and the architecture of CLI standard. Thus, a standardised framework could be built from the aspects of prototyping, declaration and how to use it, in which their users could implement their programs with spending minimal time and cost and prevent learning new concepts and confusion.

Furthermore, it is worth noting that, after the implementation of the Parvicursor. NET Framework whilst porting the DotGrid Platform into native code, we found out that the Parvicursor.NET Framework's architecture can become a suitable infrastructure for developers who want to create their object-oriented application programs on top of the native framework, and even for people who have not had familiarity or worked with .NET technologies. This is due to the unique features of CLI and this reason that CLI is the result of extensive research by several companies including Microsoft, Intel, Hewlett-Parked, and many groups in the industry and academia sectors.

Table 8.2 distinguishes between the C# language (versions 1 and 2), the standard C++ and Parvicursor.NET CLI C++ Framework. The mapping forms a preliminary

Table 8.2 Mapping Between C# and Standard C++/Parvicursor.NET CLI C++ Framework

C# 1 & 2	*Standard C++/Parvicursor. NET CLI C++ Framework*
No included file is needed.	Reference to a class in another file of a project requires an included file.
No .LIB file needed.Add a reference to the DLL in the build(example: csc /r:external.dll helloworld.cs)	Reference to a class in an external DLL requires an include file and the DLL's ParvicursorLib.LIB and other .LIB file passed to the linker.
No declspec or .DEF file.Public symbols are exported, private/protected are not."internal" symbols are only available within the module.	Exported symbols must use declspec or .DEF file.
Forward declaration not needed. Declaration order is insignificant.	Referencing a class/structure before it is declared requires forward declaration.
Unicode is the native string format.	ASCII and Unicode are the native string format provided by Parvicursor.NET Framework.
null is a keyword. It is not equivalent to 0.	null is a concept, not part of the language. It is typically defined as 0 and thus is the equivalent of 0.
All C# types can accept null as a value • For type T with null support, use type T? • For example, int with null support is int?	Basic data types (int, float, char, etc.) cannot accept a "null" value. Only pointers can have a "null" value.
foreach keyword for iterating over a collection.	No direct support for "foreach".
try-catch-finally support.finally is always called, regardless of exception or not.	Support for try and catch. Support fully for "finally" is emulated with catch(...) structure with help of Parvicursor.NET exception handling classes.

(Continued)

Table 8.2 (Continued) Mapping Between C# and Standard C++/Parvicursor.NET CLI C++ Framework

C# 1 & 2	Standard C++/Parvicursor. NET CLI C++ Framework
Using checked/unchecked you can get overflow or exception thrown behaviour.	Overflow or thrown exception behaviour is handled by underlying Parvicursor.NET exception class handling like Exception, OverFlowException, etc classes.
lock keyword for critical sections	Native support for critical sections provided by mutex libraries.
a break is required (to prevent bugs from accidentally forgetting to add a break)	For switch statements, a break is optional.
XML documentation via "///"- prefixed comment. Used by IntelliSense in Visual Studio	Fully documented by Parvicursor.NET Framework.
Partial classes allow breaking up a source file (useful when multiple people are working on a class or when part of a class is auto-generated)	Cannot split the definition of a class across multiple files.
Can mix library versions without breaking existing code.	No support for mixing versions of libraries.
Garbage collection: • No memory leaks • Cannot read uninitialised variables • Cannot index past array boundaries	The developer must manage the deletion of memory and potential issues from reading/writing to invalid memory. The garbage collector was not initially designed for Parvicursor.NET Framework to keep optimum code execution performance and no extra runtime overhead. We will plan to provide a native and high-performance GC library to future Parvicursor.NET releases that will not be enabled by default.
All types are derived from the base "object."	All types are derived from the base "object."
C# has a ref keyword to support reference types.	C++ natively supports reference types by & and * operators.
C# natively provides basic data types like int, string, float, long, Array, etc.	Parvicursor.NET Framework in more conformance with CLI standards in native C++ only provides a solid basic data type system like Int32, String, Float, Int64, ArrayList, etc.
Cross-platform and interoperability features are supported by various C# CLI implementations like Microsoft.NET and MONO.NET for different operating systems.	Cross-platform and interoperability features are supported natively based on a unified standard C++ library implementing the CLI standard and compiled for most of the current operating systems by Parvicursor.NET Framework.
Strong support for .NET Framework Standard Class Library.	Strong support for CLI Parvicursor.NET Framework Standard Class Library.

attitude for C# and C++ developers on how the new Parvicursor.NET Framework, with the enormous similarities of C# and standard C++ languages, gives them the necessary tools to program high-performance applications in native code.

Cross-platform (multi-platform) and performance issues are the two important topics to design software components and create underlying libraries and frameworks, by which different applications are developed. This is also true and even possesses more importance about Parvicursor.NET Framework, since this platform has primarily been designed for HPC/distributed environments and server programs that have critical requirements. Of course, these two factors can give rise to a trade-off between choosing the proper implementation anatomy in different structures to maintain both of them. For instance, the development of an application founded on C# language and the CLI virtual machine may choose the portability trade-off in favour of preserving the cross-platform property as distinct from the performance issue.

The present-day implementation of Parvicursor.NET Framework enjoys simultaneously balancing these two principles in context, not as a trade-off from the CLI standard. Figure 8.8 illustrates an overall view of a small subset of the Parvicursor. NET Base Class Library (PBCL) hierarchy.

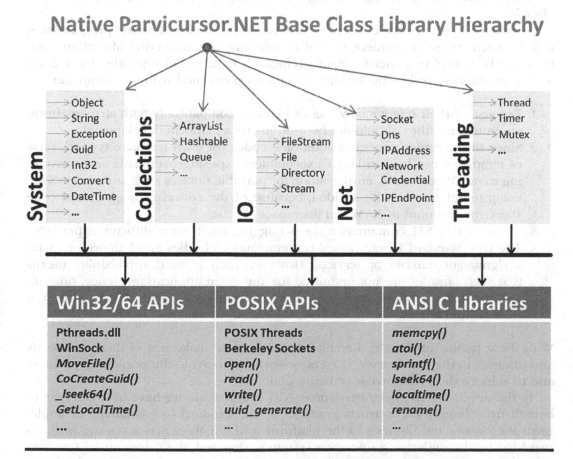

Figure 8.8   A small subset of the Parvicursor.NET base class library hierarchy.

To satisfy the feature of being a cross-platform framework, Parvicursor.NET should have allowed the developed applications to execute on most computer architectures and operating systems. To achieve this key goal in the design of the Parvicursor.NET platform at the lowest level to implement the native C++ base class library hierarchy shown in Figure 8.8, three sets of standards were used: Win32/Win64 APIs, POSIX APIs and ANSI C Libraries (with ISO/IEC 9899 Libraries). These standards provide necessary APIs that enable the Parvicursor.NET Framework to execute on existing heterogeneous platforms. Because of using these three standard sets, which have been developed for a dozen operating systems, in the Parvicursor.NET implementation, so much of the time devoted to programming the Parvicursor platform was to build a cross-platform infrastructure incredibly in compliance with the standard CLI profiles and libraries.

Using these three standards at the lowest-level layer of Parvicursor.NET Framework implicitly reveals that we have not employed standard or cross-platform C++ libraries to keep the execution runtime performance at the level of native code. There are such libraries, including Boost and C++ Standard Library.

These libraries developed based on the C++ language can have negative effects on performance from two aspects. First, they are implemented by different developers for a wide variety of operating systems; second, they are available as template-based libraries.

Templates introduce the concept of generic programming. Generic programming is a data structure-independent way of developing and delivering algorithms that need not be bound to a specific object. Templates have negative pitfalls that are not widely researched. Following are the chief issues concerned with C++ templates:

1. Because of their relative newness and lack of compatibility with cross-platform environments, they should not be used in cross-platform development.
2. Since the compiler generates additional codes for each template type, the use of templates can lead to larger executables, exposing overheads and consuming more OS resources. Furthermore, for portable devices such as smartphones, using templates must be avoided, because of the concern for generated code size (small amount of RAM and disc space).
3. Complex C++ STL containers make debugging much more difficult in practice.
4. The C++ Standard Library based on templates embodies good algorithms with a significant number of services. However, their general applicability means that such libraries are not optimised for any given application. Hence, one can achieve better runtime, and often better compile-time, performance, with their own custom library.

With these points, obviously, the chief reasons not to make use of these standards and libraries in the Parvicursor.NET Framework are to avoid the portability problem and to achieve the performance of native code.

In the development of the Parvicursor.NET Framework, we have tried our best to benefit from linguistic constructs available in the standard C++ language to implement the classes and libraries of the platform; and, finally, when accessing facilities provided by the underlying operating system is required, the three sets of standard APIs shown in Figure 8.8 are used. This leads to more cross-platform and performance features. For example, in implementing all the methods of String class and all the classes within the System::Collections namespace from the CLI standard, the keywords, the concept of link lists, and structures of C++ language have been used.

From the most significant classes in Figure 8.8, which have key roles in the Parvicursor platform and for building server and distributed programs, we can note Socket, FileStream, and Thread. To keep the performance parameter in mind during the implementation of the Parvicursor.NET Framework's classes, we have always tried to make use of low-level system functions at the time when accessing hardware functionality through OS APIs. Let's say that Figure 8.9 depicts the layered model of FileStream class implementation within the Parvicursor.NET Framework.

In this figure, processes A and B can easily access low-level file I/O operations through the FileStream class from a high-level perspective. To use maximal efficiency, the Parvicursor employs three major components: C Runtime Library, Parvicursor Disc Buffers, and Parvicursor Zero-Copy Functions. The main interface used in the FileStream class is the C runtime unbuffered family of APIs [open(), and so forth] that are supported on all platforms.

These functions invoke the operating system directly for lower-level operations than those provided by ANCI C stream I/O, other native libraries, or OS-specific APIs. Low-level input and output calls do not buffer or format data.

The buffering operation is directly handled by Parvicursor.NET Framework at a higher level if the application requests it from the FileStream class. In the design of this class to eliminate the two layers of C Runtime Library and OS Caches, which diminish drastically the performance and disc I/O throughput (because of excessive system calls and the buffering of Disc Controller Hardware Cache in OS Caches), the Parvicursor.NET Framework transparently in a platform-specific fashion serves zero-copy functions directly to move the content of Parvicursor Disc Buffers into Disc Controller Hardware Cache for xDFS protocol. This technique significantly improves the throughput and performance as a whole.

Another example of the Parvicursor classes' low-level and cross-platform implementation is the Thread class located at the System::Threading namespace. As shown in Figure 8.8, the POSIX Threads in Unix-like operating systems and its equivalent in Windows platform through a dynamic link library called pthread.dll are used to implement the Thread class. Open-source POSIX Threads for Windows provide a high-quality solution to currently implementing a large subset of the POSIX standard threads-related API.

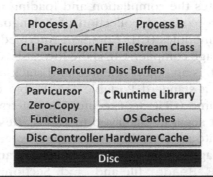

Figure 8.9 The layered model of Parvicursor.NET's FileStream class implementation.

The head advantages of the Parvicursor.NET Framework can be summarised as follows:

1. To create a standard, cross-platform, portable infrastructure grounded upon the CLI standard and to develop the next-generation paradigms of distributed systems for scientific and enterprise communities (indeed, porting the DotGrid project into native code is the proof-of-concept of this aim as a typical prototype through the state-of-the-art platform).
2. To build a native, object-oriented platform in C++ and to ignore the complexities of the multi-layer abstractions in the .NET Framework for developing critical applications in the area of high-performance computing and distributed systems on behalf of performance improvements at the native code level or even the kernel. Moreover, to reduce the total system resource usage such as CPU and RAM by contrast to the Microsoft .NET Framework's virtual machine.
3. The most superior advantage over Parvicursor.NET Framework is to supply an integrated process to port the C# codes of the DotGrid platform into native code that relied on C++. In this way, with the direct porting DotGrid platform to native code, the performance of native machine code will considerably contribute to the execution speed of algorithms that had been implemented in DotGrid. Also, having fully ported the DotGrid platform and due to being Parvicursor as native and cross-platform, this new platform can be executed as part of the operating system services and provide manifold services to its upper layers.
4. To resolve the problems in Managed C++ and C++/CLI, and to create an integrated platform seamlessly close to the C# language and CLI standard for programmers interested in .NET technology and language to develop their applications as portable identical to conventional C++ programming. To help those who are familiar with C# and .NET Framework, one can make use of the Parvicursor.NET Framework and common benefits between C# and C++ to increase their programs' efficiency.

8.4 The Compilation and Loading Process of .NET-CLI-Based Application Programs

In this section, we study the compilation and loading process of .NET-based applications and accurately examine overheads due to using the .NET Framework within them. Figure 8.10 illustrates the compilation and loading process stages of a .NET-based collection of source codes. A collection of X language source codes can be converted into managed modules (CIL: Common Intermediate Language and metadata) through the X language compiler. CIL is the lowest-level programming language that is defined by CLI. CIL is an object-oriented and stack-based assembly language. The managed module is a standard Portable Executable (PE) file, which requires Common Language Runtime (CLR) to execute. Having translated the source code files and created different separate managed modules, these modules at stage 4 are synthesised and turned into an assembly. A managed executable file consists of five parts that are shown in stage 5. At the time when linking an assembly, specific information is added to the PE Header file and .txt Section. When an executable file is invoked, this information causes the CLR to load and initialise. When creating an

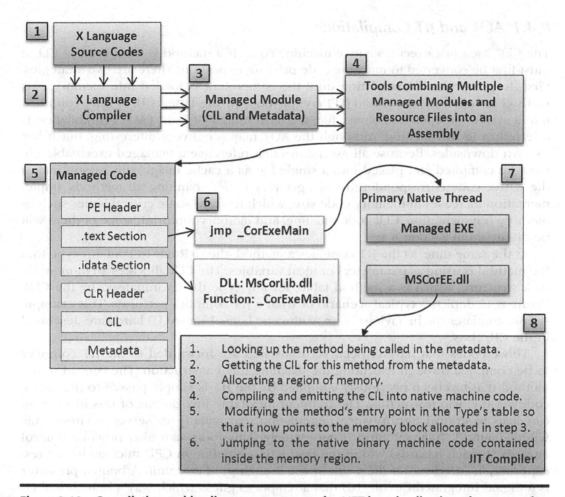

1 X Language Source Codes

2 X Language Compiler

3 Managed Module (CIL and Metadata)

4 Tools Combining Multiple Managed Modules and Resource Files into an Assembly

5 Managed Code
- PE Header
- .text Section
- .idata Section
- CLR Header
- CIL
- Metadata

6 jmp _CorExeMain

DLL: MsCorLib.dll
Function: _CorExeMain

7 Primary Native Thread
- Managed EXE
- MSCorEE.dll

8
1. Looking up the method being called in the metadata.
2. Getting the CIL for this method from the metadata.
3. Allocating a region of memory.
4. Compiling and emitting the CIL into native machine code.
5. Modifying the method's entry point in the Type's table so that it now points to the memory block allocated in step 3.
6. Jumping to the native binary machine code contained inside the memory region.   JIT Compiler

Figure 8.10   Compilation and loading process stages of a .NET-based collection of source codes.

executable assembly, the linker adds the jmp _CorExeMain routine stub imported from MsCorEE.dll dynamic-link library.

The primary thread for the created process executes this routine stub and quickly jumps to the _CorExeMain function. _CorExeMain initialises the CLR and searches the CLR Header so that it determines what entry point method must be executed. The CIL code for that method is compiled into native CPU instructions, and, finally, the CLR jumps to the native code. This compilation process is carried out by the JIT compiler as detailed in stage 8 of Figure 8.10. The _CorDllMain function is loaded onto memory through the system function calls of LoadLibrary() in Windows and dlopen() in Unix-class operating systems. As seen, several complex stages must be passed for transforming a CLI-based set of source codes into native code. These additional heavyweight layers can expose extra overheads upon application programs to convert a .NET-based source code into native machine code. However, we can divide the major overheads concerned with the use of CLR and the CLI standard into four classifications, including, Ahead Of Time (AOT) and JIT compilations, cross-mode execution switches (C++/CLI managed/unmanaged interop transitions), platform invocation services, and .NET memory footprint.

8.4.1 AOT and JIT Compilations

The CLR itself just executes native machine code. If a method is composed of CLI, it must first be converted to machine code prior to invocation. There are two strategies. First, to postpone the translation until the component is loaded into memory; this method is called Just-In-Time (JIT) compilation. In the latter, CIL is fully compiled into a system-independent binary file; the term Ahead-Of-Time (AOT) compilation is referred to in this method. Although the AOT may seem very interesting, but it has its own downsides. Because all assemblies that reference a managed executable file must be compiled and placed into a single file as a cache image, this reason makes the native code corresponding to CIL get very large. Spanning all methods' implementation increases in-memory code size, which leads to some critical issues such as memory fragmentation, CLR code pitching, and memory footprint; some of them will be discussed in Section 8.4.

At the same time, as the JIT compiles a method, the CLR has to load any type that the method is using as parameters or local variables. The CLR allocates an in-memory data structure, which is a method table, for any type that is initialised by the CLR. Figure 8.11 depicts a typical scenario of what a JIT compiler performs. This example simply emulates the behaviour of an Arithmetic Logic Unit (ALU) hardware described in the CIL class.

Those codes that haven't been yet translated are forwarded to the JIT compiler to be compiled through executing the machine `call` instruction. The control of the method that has been previously compiled by the JIT is simply passed to the native code via the `jmp` instruction. The frequent inevitable invocations of this instruction can lead to critical performance degradation, particularly in server environments where memory fragmentation occurs widely. This jump can also provoke control hazards (branch hazards) within the instruction pipeline in CPU microarchitectures; especially it can disorder the work of the branch predictor unit. A branch predictor is a digital Integrated Circuit (IC) that attempts to guess which way a branch will go

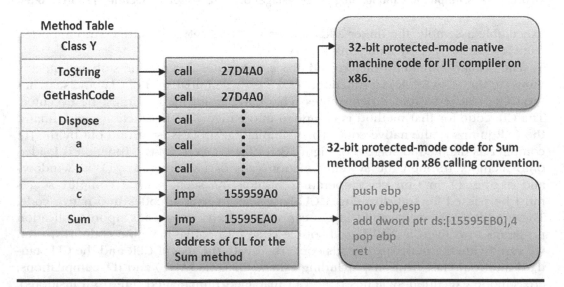

Figure 8.11   A typical ×86 JIT-compilation scenario for a CIL class.

before this is known for sure. The purpose of the branch predictor is to improve the flow in the instruction pipeline. Branch predictors are crucial in today's pipelined microprocessor architectures for achieving high performance.

These conditions, particularly for long jumps by the `jmp` instruction, get more obvious meanings through virtual memory. For example, in the implementation of the DotDFS protocol [1] on top of the .NET Framework, the native instructions like `recv()` and `read()` must pass periodically this extra `jmp`. This critical phenomenon indicates that .NET virtual machine is not a good candidate platform for developing server applications and distributed systems. A more comprehensive review of overheads posed by JIT is outside the theme of this chapter (e.g., overheads due to CLI interfaces, delegates, and virtual methods).

8.4.2 Cross-Mode Execution Switches (C++/CLI Managed/Unmanaged Interop Transitions)

Almost all runtimes, particularly virtual execution environments, provide interfaces to be integrated with libraries based on system routines written/emitted in assembly/machine language or C language through an additional layer such as P/Invoke and Java Native Interface. However, these extra layers contain costs. Without exception, the transition from managed to native C runtime causes nontrivial performance costs. Due to this classification, the CLR supports two modes of execution: managed mode and unmanaged mode. In managed mode, the CLR can inspect the stack frame (activation record) of every thread of control (such as parameters and local variables). In unmanaged mode, the CLR has no control over the code that is executed in the native C runtime. The mode of execution can be changed relying on a method's invocation.

C++/CLI language is an enabling technology that is accounted as a connecting interface of the standard C++ language with CLI to provide direct access to the underlying operating system APIs in managed code [8]. In C++/CLI, every method can be marked as managed or unmanaged via the metadata. Because CLR controls method prologs and epilogs for managed methods, it can easily traverse managed regions of the call stack, which is often achieved by the CPU's ebp (extended base pointer) register. The ebp register is used to point to the beginning of the activation record and sometimes is also called a stack pointer. A stack frame is a contiguous area of the process stack that is used to store local variables, parameters, return addresses, and temporary variables in the callee. The design of a frame layout usually requires specific features of an Instruction Set Architecture (ISA) and the high-level programming language compiled to it. However, a standard layout is usually used to take benefit of the maximum interoperability with cross-calls amongst different languages implementing the runtime functions (e.g., see Figure 8.12(b)). Stack pointers, according to this discussion, are employed to generate the backtrace stack in debuggers. The use of frame pointers in natively compiled code can have crucial performance costs at runtime, particularly for CPU-bound and server applications. That is why native language compilers remove the debugging information and emit the code without them in release or optimisation mode. One of the clear reasons for this optimisation is that the ebp register as a general-purpose register remains ready to be accessed for the rest of the code's execution flow. Therefore, using the ebp register for tracing

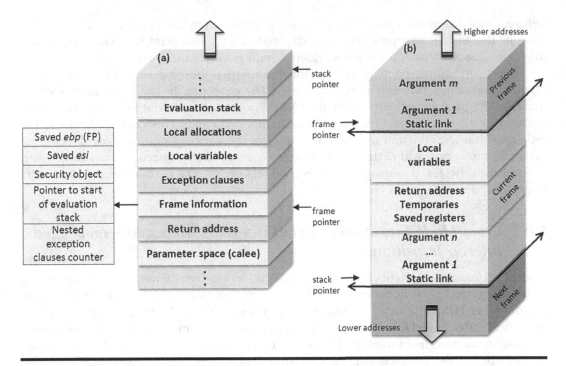

Figure 8.12 Different layouts of ×86 stack frames: (a) The CLR activation record layout and (b) the native C activation record layout.

can lead to critical performance pressures. Figure 8.12 portrays different layouts of x86 stack frames for CLR (managed methods) and native C runtime.

Cross-mode and heterogeneous invocations are not very simple mechanisms. Cross-mode invocation occurs when a managed method calls an unmanaged method (and vice versa). The emitted code for cross-mode invocations is significantly different in comparison with the same-mode calls. The cross-mode invocations are important to achieve low-level operating system functionalities. The cross-mode calls require additional work to distinguish between the changes in execution structure. In this state, the caller has to push some information onto the stack to specify the start of a new chain of stack frames. CLR divides the stack frame into several chains. Every chain indicates a series of same-mode calls. When the JIT compiler translates a cross-mode call, it emits additional code that pushes a transition frame onto the stack. After the transition frame is pushed onto the stack, the caller subsequently constitutes a normal stack frame that is expected by the target method. This gives rise to creating the stack frames for a cross-mode invocation, one for each mode.

The CLR's actual layout is the synthesis of Figures 8.12(a) and (b) for cross-mode execution switches. After the stack is prepared for the target cross-mode method, the execution state of the current thread is adjusted to reflect the change in the mode of execution. Besides, a flag bit must be changed in thread-local storage that indicates which execution mode the thread is currently executing in. After the thread state is prepared, the jump to the target method's body is done. When the target method returns, it returns the main transition code that resets the thread state and pops the transition frame from the stack. For invocations with simple method signatures, the overall cost of making these transitions are at least 32 processor instructions. Since the cross-mode calls require setting up a second stack frame after the transition frame, the cost of cross-mode calls depends on the number and types of parameters passed to the method. The more the number of parameters makes, the more transition costs.

As a final result, we can easily conclude that the overheads due to cross-mode execution switches in accessing to operating system's APIs, which are inevitable, can get server systems underutilised and overloaded in highly concurrent environments. In the Windows family of operating systems that C++/CLI is supported, Microsoft has implemented most of the .NET Base Class Libraries (BCL) in this way. The C++/CLI does not exist for Linux and Unix with the MONO .NET target. Although using C++/CLI in Windows can decrease needless context switches and memory requirements so as to improve the performance, but this way may result in unavoidable phenomena including double thunking and OS loader lock.

8.4.3 Platform Invocation Services (P/Invoke)

P/Invoke is an integral part of the CLI implementation that allows the managed code to call unmanaged code and vice versa. The .NET Platform Invoke technology is built right into the CLR runtime to enable managed programs to invoke ordinary dynamically linked unmanaged code (.dll files in Windows and .so files in Unix-like operating systems such as Linux and Solaris). It is the logical equivalent to a DLL or SO in native C++ for routines exported annotated by `delclsspec(dllexport)`. The result of linking against an ordinary DLL or SO in the Microsoft C++ compiler or GNU GCC C++ compiler is an executable that inserts small proxy stubs which, when invoked, redirect to the actual code at native runtime. P/Invoke is very similar, except that the CLR is responsible for loading, binding, and making necessary transformations between data types as a function is called. As is the case with pure unmanaged code, the operating system will share code with multiple processes accessing that DLL or so simultaneously. The indirection to the native code is performed by the CIL `calli` instruction with a P/Invoke target.

P/Invoke is indeed a superset of the managed and unmanaged transitions discussed in Section 8.4.2. P/Invoke accommodates a collection of type conversion facilities to deal with the inherent differences between the legacy C dynamic (shared) linked libraries and CLR. In addition to implementing the change in the execution mode explored in Section 8.4.2, P/Invoke provides transformations called marshalling to match between managed and unmanaged modes. Each transition from managed to unmanaged code remains overhead. The CLR interop layer enjoys the interop invocation optimisation levels that are grounded on the type of transition and types of parameters: JIT inlining compiled assembly stubs and interpreted marshalling stubs. The approximate overhead for a platform invokes call begins at least from ten machine instructions up. Figure 8.13 presents a P/Invoke scenario in which a transition from managed code is made to the native `libc` runtime for native POSIX `sendto()` socket function call in Unix-class operating systems. Let's examine the steps shown for this example in detail.

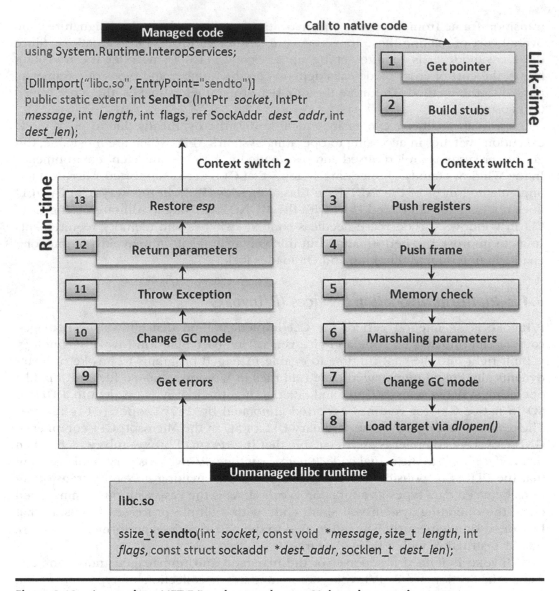

Figure 8.13 A complete .NET P/Invoke sample atop Unix-style operating systems.

1) The CLR loads the POSIX system functions dlopen() and dlsym().
2) The CLR constructs a DllImport method stub from the signature enfolding the target address.
3) Pushing the callee's saved registers.
4) Setting up a DllImport activation record and pushing it onto the stack frames.
5) Should a temporary chunk of memory has already been allocated, the CLR initialises a clean-up list for quick freeing at the time when the invocation completes.
6) Marshalling parameters. When working with unmanaged code, whether it is a native system function or native libraries in C++, there is a type system gap that must be bridged. For instance, a string to .NET Framework is not the same

thing as a string in C++. Marshalling performs the conversions to the bits so that data instances can be used on both runtime sides. Interop marshalling governs how data is passed in method arguments and the return values between managed and unmanaged memory during calls. Marshalling is a runtime activity performed by the CLR's marshalling service. Marshalling may be a simple bit-for-bit copy from one runtime to another, but just as well might involve a full reorganisation of the contents of a data structure whilst the copy occurs. For simple types, such as integers and floating-point numbers, marshalling is a bitwise-copy ("blitting"), just as would be the case for unmanaged code. This mechanism can add tens of machine instructions per argument even for simple unmanaged function invocations and contributes dramatically to the exposed overheads. Marshalling is not a panacea, as marshalling implies frequent data copies. Marshalling may be problematic because data translation is a complex, time-consuming process. Alternatively, it may be problematic because it is not possible to copy the data, as the data is not known or is likely to change.

7) Changing the .NET Garbage Collection (GC) mode from cooperative to pre-emptive so that a GC can happen at any time. It is worth here noting some issues concerned with the .NET GC system. When the garbage is actually collected can be unpredictable, resulting in stalls scattered throughout an application domain or the entire VES. Unpredictable CPU stalls, particularly in the instruction pipeline, can be unacceptable in real-time environments such as long-running servers and distributed systems. For a garbage collection to happen, it is important that the threads are in a known state and do not modify the heap in a way that cannot be tracked by the GC. So typically, all running threads are suspended, the collection is done, and then the threads are resumed. This operation can cause a big performance cost (far more than the overheads of thread-related context switches) and high-latency behaviour in server systems, for instance the hybrid DotDFS concurrency pattern (HCP) [1]! In addition, a thread executing unmanaged code can have a reference to a managed object. But in that case, the object would be alive and pinned. Thus, it would not be collected anyway. To prevent an unmanaged thread from entering into managed code, a barrier is used. Fundamentally, the JIT detects the stack frame where the thread went from managed code to unmanaged. The return address of this stack frame is pirated and made to point to a stub which suspends the thread.

8) The CLR loads the target address and invokes it via native function pointers.

9) If any error occurs, the CLR makes use of the `errno` global variable, a macro or an identifier declared with external linkage that contains the last error code generated in any function using the `errno` facility, and `_sys_errlist` array string to fill the information in a thread abstraction stored in thread-local storage (TLS).

10) Coming back to cooperative GC mode.

11) If the native exported function causes any runtime error, CLR throws an appropriately managed exception.

12) If there are not any thrown exceptions, CLR back-propagates `out` and by-`ref` parameters.

13) In the last step, CLR restores the extended stack pointer (`esp`) register to its original value for caller-popped arguments.

Under these elaborations, the reader can infer the overheads associated with P/Invoke. In non-Windows environments, due to the lack of a feasible C++/CLI implementation, all CLI classes are developed depending upon the P/Invoke standard from scratch. This fact implies that more critical overheads emerge in executing managed CLI-based frameworks such as MONO .NET in Unix/POSIX-compliant systems in contrast to Microsoft's .NET Framework implementation in Windows.

8.4.4 .NET Memory Footprint

Performance optimisation in one clause can be making the computer programs run faster. The execution of machine instructions is cheap for modern hardware, whereas fetching the instruction operands is expensive. Therefore, memory usage can influence how a program could execute fast, and it is indeed a significant metric to be optimised. Modern processors have a hierarchy of caches to improve the hardware cost. The Level-1 (L1) cache is the fastest one, but it is small. The next memory hierarchies are L2 cache, Random Access Memory (RAM), and hard disc. Managed CLI-based applications are pretty bloated in terms of memory usage. The main reason .NET applications have such a huge memory footprint is that the JIT compiler loads when the application starts, and all that bootstrap code and a ton of the execution engine and its components are loaded and compiled at start-up and get loaded into the process. Besides the fact that this takes up processor cycles, it also consumes a lot of memory. Also, the .NET Framework itself pulls a lot of code as well as that gets compiled.

Ideally, caches ought to have both short access times and low miss rates to minimise average memory access latency. Power optimisation is also one of the most critical problems in how designing and using caches. Lower power dissipation means a longer battery life for mobile devices. Higher power consumption leaves evidence of heating and reliability issues, which have evolved into a limiting factor in achieving higher performance. Increasing faults and hot spots are other concerns in the area of deep submicron and nanometric CMOS transistors. Because of shrinkage in feature sizes, variation in the fabrication process increases the faulty devices along with additional latency and leakage power.

This shows how managed .NET platform can result in critical overheads for increasing the dissipated power at the hardware level, particularly processors and realistic systems. If hot data paths access more memory, operators need to be fetched from slower memory. Because slower memory is slow by an order of magnitude, even low L2 cache misses can cause huge negative performance. In addition to these on-chip memory footprints, the items discussed in Sections 8.4.1 through 8.4.3 and .NET code bloat are other factors to increase memory usage. These overheads can easily disrupt the hardware units of instruction cache, data cache, and Translation Lookaside Buffer (TLB) cache in server systems. Increasing the number of TLB entries degrades TLB hit ratio and increases Cycles Per Instruction (CPI).

Furthermore, huge memory usage is another reason to emerge as memory fragmentations due to using the managed CLI. For example, because the method locations cannot be changed in the AOT-generated image after the code is generated, each of the methods may occupy a different virtual memory page. These memory fragmentations have a substantial downside on the working set of the application program.

Another critical issue in .NET-based applications is that programs that rely on the garbage collector often exhibit poor locality (interacting badly with cache and virtual memory systems), occupy more address space than the program uses at any one time, and touch otherwise idle pages. These may combine in a phenomenon referred to as thrashing, in which a program spends more time copying data between various grades of storage than performing worthwhile work. Moreover, the garbage collection consumes computing resources in determining which memory ought to be freed. A memory leak may take place despite the presence of the garbage collector if references to unused objects are not themselves manually finalised.

Also, the .NET memory footprint that results in extra page faults (hard faults) degrades the performance of a program and in the degenerate case can cause thrashing. Optimisations to programs that reduce the number of page faults that occur enhance the performance of the application program or even the entire system. The two primary aspects of the optimisation effort can be concentrating on reducing overall memory usage and improving memory locality.

8.5 The Compilation and Loading Process of Native Parvicursor. NET-Based Application Programs

In this section, we examine the compilation and loading process of Parvicursor.NET-based application programs, so that the reader can understand more the importance of the Parvicursor.NET Framework compared to the .NET Framework for server and HPC environments. To realise the aim to eliminate the overheads concerned with the multi-layer architecture of the .NET Framework, the perception of the Parvicursor project in following up the DotGrid project emerged. In fact, the Parvicursor.NET Framework is a native and cross-platform implementation of the standard CLI profiles and libraries which relied upon standard ISO C++. The main goal of the Parvicursor project actually is to provide an infrastructural software framework to easily port the source codes of the .NET-based DotGrid Grid Computing Framework [3–5] into native code with the minimum time and cost spent and to increase the more efficiency of the protocols that had been implemented in DotGrid platform. Therefore, in addition to porting the DotGrid structure to native code, a high-performance implementation of the CLI standard leaves to enterprise and scientific communities.

Figure 8.2 portrays the four-layer architecture of the Parvicursor.NET Framework. As implicitly shown in this framework, only native C/C++ codes are compiled, and after linking with the Parvicursor.NET Framework, which implements CLI classes and profiles, the executable image file is executed by the operating system. Also, there is no additional layer and no overhead on applications that make use of the framework.

As stated earlier in this chapter, the Parvicursor.NET platform complies itself with the CLI standard by providing a concrete native C++ wrapper library. In fact, this wrapper that constitutes the main Parvicursor.NET core implements a hierarchy of the .NET Base Class Library (BCL), which makes Parvicursor.NET capable of being used in distributed systems. The BCL indeed is a standard library that is available to all languages targeting the .NET Framework. The BCL in order to encapsulate a large number of common functions like disc and network I/O, threading and data structures, which make the programming easier, has been created. Figure 8.8 illustrates an overall view of a small subset of the Parvicursor.NET Base Class Library (PBCL) hierarchy.

Now given a brief description of PBCL, we explore the conversion process of the C++ Parvicursor.NET source codes into native machine code. Normally, the construction process of programs demanding the Parvicursor platform includes five stages in which each stage applies specific tools: preprocessor, compiler, assembler, linker, and loader. These stages appear in Figure 8.14. File objects are generated after assembling source codes, and then the executable image is produced after linking these object files. Several formats exist to store the image such as Executable and Linking Format (ELF) and Common Object-File Format (COFF). Parvicursor platform offers two methods to execute application programs: one being statically linked with a static library extension and the other being dynamically linked using a dynamic shared library. The loading process of an application executable image generated

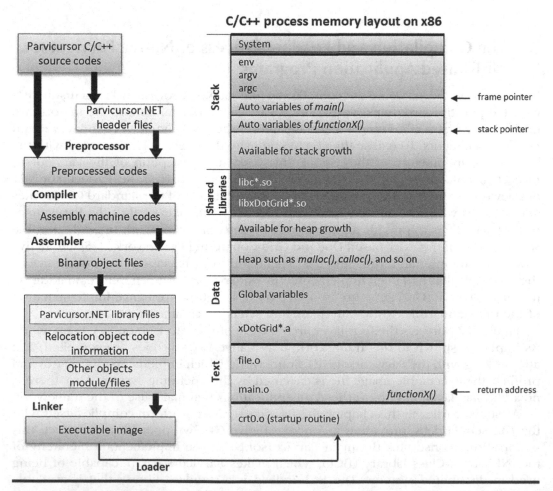

Figure 8.14 Compilation and loading process stages of a Parvicursor.NET-based collection of source codes.

targeting the Parvicursor runtime is performed under direct intervention of the native OS loader, and native compiled machine codes are loaded onto memory.

In the C/C++ process memory layout on the x86 architecture, the process's load segments are located at the base address of the process. The main stack is located at the bottom and grows downwards. Each extra thread or routine call that is created has its own stack, which locates at the bottom of the main stack. Each of the stack frames is separated by a protective page to detect stack overflow amongst stack frames. Heap memory is located above the process code and grows upwards. In the middle of a process's address space, there is a region that is reserved for shared objects.

Also, the slow native C++ backend compiler wins heavily over the JIT compiler at runtime. If one wraps an int inside a class for abstraction purposes, and he/she accesses it strictly as an int, the native C++ compiler can decrease the overhead of the wrapper to practically nothing. We can add many levels of abstraction to the wrapper without increasing the overhead cost. The JIT compiler is unable to take the time needed to eliminate this cost.

The C/C++ languages have been designed to ensure space overhead and minimal runtime. These two languages have been heavily used for decades in systems programming including implementing operating systems and embedded systems, due to optimum integration of features such as portability and performance, the ability of direct access to hardware addresses, and the demand for low execution time. The Parvicursor framework thus is lacking all of the overheads that are exposed by the .NET Framework discussed in Section 8.4.

8.6 Parvicursor.NET Socket Interface (PSI)

PSI is an encapsulating abstraction layer for transport protocols. From the developer's standpoint, this interface is an API that unifies network protocols and relied on the concept of well-known socket programming as a set of APIs. PSI helps reduce the necessary development time and effort to create and prototype network protocols. The layered model of PSI appears in Figure 8.15. This interface provides a fundamental abstraction for the entire Parvicursor infrastructure. All major services and APIs developed in the Parvicursor platform utilise this interface or it can be extended for new protocols. For example, an important application of PSI is to implement protocols such as SSL3, xSec, and TLS1 to secure network communications. It also brings the benefits of underlying network I/O mechanisms to the developers who want to work with low-level transport protocols.

As shown in Figure 8.15, a layer is a set of conceptually similar functionality that furnishes services to the layer above it and receives service from the lower below it.

The structure of Figure 8.15 is made up of five layers. From the most important services of this interface, we can point to POPI, Direct Memory Transfer, and Exception Handling. The Direct Memory Transfer service in conformance with traditional socket programming offers a flexible interface for transferring memory buffers directly to lower layers. The POPI service establishes a mechanism to exchange the Parvicursor.NET Framework's objects through low-level serialisation/deserialisation approaches with high performance (for details see Section 8.7). The Exception Handling service allows exchanging occurred exceptions between endpoints.

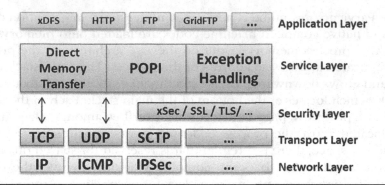

Figure 8.15   The layered model of Parvicursor.NET Socket Interface (PSI).

This can make feasible the use of PSI as a remote method invocation mechanism. Security and transport layers provide transparent transfer of data between users, and also secure and make reliable data transfer services to upper layers.

8.7 Parvicursor Object Passing Interface (POPI) over PSI

POPI is a collection of APIs that allows processes (or threads) to exchange objects over PSI sessions within the Parvicursor.NET Framework. In POPI architecture, serialisation/deserialisation mechanisms play the main role. POPI introduces services to applications so that they can transfer their desired objects through pointer-based buffering methods across remote endpoints. In Parvicursor.NET Framework, serialisation is the low-level process of converting the state of an object into a form that can be persisted or transported. Serialisation is also used when an object is passed across a remoting boundary in Parvicursor nodes.

Although serialisation libraries like .NET Remoting and Boost C++ Serialisation take advantage of general-purpose serialisation protocols and provide equipment to make binary a hierarchy of inherited classes, they impose critical performance overheads upon programs. In the design of POPI bearing this issue in mind, the direct serialisation of basic data types, such as Int32, Int64, String, Float and so on, are supported. Application developers can implement their own favourite serialisation protocols by designing a suitable and optimal algorithm, which supports object versioning, with minimal effort through extending POPI APIs. This flexible method can be used to develop customised serialisers/deserialisers in achieving high performance. POPI provides the ability to access low-level internal buffers through reference types so that extra copy operations are prevented to increase performance (these mechanisms are partly similar to zero-copy concepts).

8.8 Cross-Process, Cross-Language and Cross-Platform Parvicursor.NET Remoting Architecture (PR)

This section introduces Parvicursor.NET Remoting architecture. PR allows a vast array of programs and processes, regardless of the programming language, runtime, operating system, and hardware platform used (desktop, mobile, server, and embedded platforms), to perform low-level remoting operations for various purposes over cross-process boundaries. PR actually proposes and implements a basic infrastructure to make the key concepts of cross-language, cross-process, and cross-platform practical. Therefore, we can think of the design of the Parvicursor project and PR based on C/C++ languages as a move towards a cross-process, cross-language, and cross-platform framework.

Parvicursor project, by combining the features of PSI and POPI (described respectively in Sections 8.6 and 8.7), proposes and implements the PR architecture shown in Figure 8.16. There, it is assumed that process 1 intends to transmit some objects to process 2 located at a remote boundary towards process 1 via PR. Processes 1 and 2 may be written in any programming language, and executed on heterogeneous operating systems or hardware in terms of CPU architecture (x86 or x64). Language Binding Interface (LBI) provides a language-natural interface to applications and processes in cross-process boundaries.

LBI states specifications in which different programming languages can use PR. Native C/C++, CLI-compliant languages, and Java are the major types of these languages. Because PR has been implemented in the native C/C++ stack, it is directly accessible without any specification in any of the C and C++ languages. PR has been implemented as native C++ classes. Therefore, in order to straightforward use PR

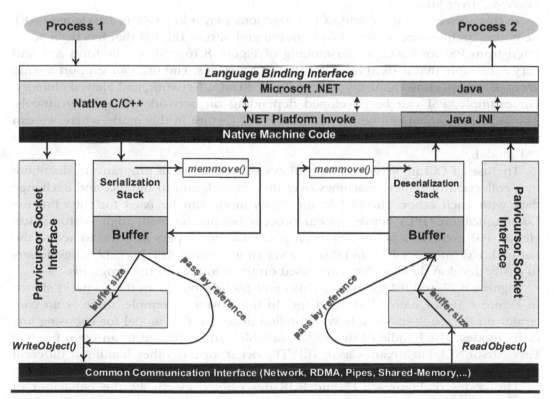

Figure 8.16 Cross-process, cross-language, and cross-platform Parvicursor.NET Remoting architecture (PR).

stack in other languages, LBI must explain specifications, so that they can conveniently be accessed, and be bound to the PR classes. By implementing an interface through .NET Platform Invoke and Java Native Interface (JNI), C# and Java programmers can access LBI through PR APIs.

As seen, therefore, LBI makes the cross-language concept for a broad family of programming languages practical. In Figure 8.16, the requests of processes are driven towards Serialisation/Deserialisation Stack and PSI. In the Processes 1 side, the serialisation is performed by copying objects into a pre-allocated buffer by calling the `memmove()` system function. The `WriteObject()` method, which is one of the main methods of PSI APIs, puts the content of the buffer onto Common Communication Interface (CCI) with the associated size of the dirty data buffer (on the other hand, from the POSIX standard's point of view, the write operation is performed at this stage). To avoid unnecessary copies of the content of the buffer within Serialisation Stack in the input arguments of the `WriteObject()` method, the buffer pointer is passed as pass-by-reference to this method, which this approach indeed is a type of zero-copy mechanism to significantly increase the PR performance. In the Process 2 side, the `ReadObject()` method, after receiving the content of objects sent by Process 1 over CCI, passes the received buffer pointer and data buffer size to the Deserialisation Stack. Deserialisation is done by calling the `memmove()` system function. The received objects stored in the buffer as binary can be retrieved as the main variables of rebuilt objects, and they are delivered to Process 2 over LBI.

In this scenario, the PSI and CCI abstractions play a key role in Parvicursor.NET Remoting architecture. In fact, CCI is an integral part of the PSI that has been separated from PSI for easier understanding of Figure 8.16. PSI is a uniform API and very extensible that is used to exploit the CCI services. The CCI can support a wide array of transport mechanisms such as Pipes, RDMA, Network, and Shared Memory. For example, PSI can be developed depending on network transport protocols. The TCP/IP protocol can be the most basic PSI feature in this mode where we can benefit from other protocols like HTTP to run on the TCP/IP stack by extending the PSI model.

The use of CCI in Network mode allows the processes of programs to distribute in a collection of remote machines over the network and to interact and exchange data with each other. The CCI in the Pipes mode can be used for Inter-Process Communication (IPC) between local process boundaries with high performance. Hence, PSI presents a set of I/O mechanisms for developers in order to access the network I/O, memory I/O, and disc I/O via an integrated API. It enables developers to easily develop their applications based on the demands of the programs.

Figures 8.17 and 8.18 illustrate a piece of pseudocode from the scenario shown in Figure 8.16 for native C++ language. In this abstract example, there is no constraint on the `socket` variable which relied upon the CCI model for choosing any of its modes. The handle of the socket variable can be related to an open file (via Parvicursor.NET FileStream class), TCP/TP socket, or any other handle of different I/O models.

The codes of Figures 8.17 and 8.18 describe, respectively, the behaviour of Process 1 and Process 2 in accessing PR functions shown in Figure 8.16. The `Serializer` class constructor takes its primary internal buffer size for serialisation

```
// All declared types here are defined by Parvicursor.NET Framework
// such as System, Parvicursor::Serialization and Parvicursor::Net
namespaces.
ParvicursorSocket *socket ... ;
Int32 a = 10;
String str = "Hello World";
Serializer se(512);
se.Write(str);
se.Write<Int32>(a);
socket->WriteObject(se.get_BaseBuffer(), se.get_BaseBufferSize());
```

Figure 8.17   A client-side example of Parvicursor.NET Remoting for native C++ (local objects serialisation and send to remote process boundary).

```
// All declared types here are defined by Parvicursor.NET Framework
// such as System, Parvicursor::Serialization and Parvicursor::Net
namespaces.
ParvicursorSocket *socket ... ;
Int32 objSize = 0;
Byte *buffer = socket->ReadObject(objSize);
Int32 a;
String str;
DeSerializer de(buffer, objSize);
str = de.Read();
a = de.Read<Int32>();
```

Figure 8.18   A server-side example of Parvicursor.NET Remoting for native C++ (receive buffer of objects from remote process boundary and local deserialisation of objects).

operation; of course, the length of this buffer may be automatically increased by the class during the life cycle of processes. The `get_BaseBuffer()` method actually passes the internal buffer pointer of the `Serialiser` class to the `WriteObject()` method for zero-copy purposes.

PR is a flexible and highly extensible framework to transfer objects in a variety of networks. One of the primary aims of PR is to provide the basic facilities for developing Remote Procedure Calls RPCs), as expected, in the Parvicursor's xThread model. The flexibility of PR makes it suitable to be applied to the set of the Web services' protocols over HTTP channels in CCI so that a single framework can be developed atop PR for a wide spread of software platforms and programming languages.

8.9 Parvicursor.NET Framework Programming Reference Guide

The Parvicursor.NET Framework provides the fundamental framework libraries and classes to easy and quick develop and port the .NET-based DotGrid platform to native C++ for all operating systems in Windows by Win32 and Win 64 APIs and in Linux and Unix-style operating systems by POSIX-compliant APIs.

The Parvicursor.NET Framework really implements a native and cross-platform implementation of the ECMA-334 and ECMA-335 in C++ stack with the following ECMA references:

1. ECMA-334: C# Language Specification, `http://www.ecma-international.org/publications/standards/Ecma-334.htm`. 2022.
2. ECMA-335: Common Language Infrastructure (CLI), `http://www.ecma-international.org/publications/techreports/E-TR-084.htm`. 2022.

The Parvicursor.NET Framework includes classes, interfaces, and value types that expedite and optimise the development process and provide access to system functionality.

The Parvicursor.NET Framework types are the foundation on which Parvicursor.NET applications and components are built. The Parvicursor.NET Framework includes types that perform the following functions:

- Represent base data types and exceptions.
- Encapsulate data structures.
- Perform I/O.
- Access information about loaded types.
- Invoke Parvicursor.NET Framework security checks.

The Parvicursor.NET Framework provides a rich set of interfaces shown in Figure 8.19, as well as abstract and concrete (non-abstract) classes. You can use the concrete classes as is or, in many cases, derive your own classes from them. To use the functionality of an interface, you can either create a class that implements the interface or derive a class from one of the Parvicursor.NET Framework classes that implement the interface.

For more help, you can see the Microsoft MSDN for .NET Framework Class Library. `http://msdn.microsoft.com/en-us/library/ms229335.aspx`

Additionally, it is necessary to note that a comprehensive package for easing the development of Parvicursor-based applications has been provided by the authors that is accessible via `https://github.com/poshtkohi/pads`.

8.9.1 Using Namespace System

```
#include "System/Object/Object.h"
#include "System/BasicTypes/BasicTypes.h"
#include "System/Convert/Convert.h"
#include "System/String/String.h"
#include "System/DateTime/DateTime.h"
#include "System/Guid/Guid.h"
#include "System/Type/Type.h"
#include "System/Exception/Exception.h"
#include "System/ArgumentException/ArgumentException.h"
#include "System/ArgumentException/ArgumentNullException.h"
#include "System/ArgumentException/ArgumentOutOfRangeException.h"
#include "System/NotSupportedException/NotSupportedException.h"
#include "System/InvalidOperationException/InvalidOperationException.h"
```

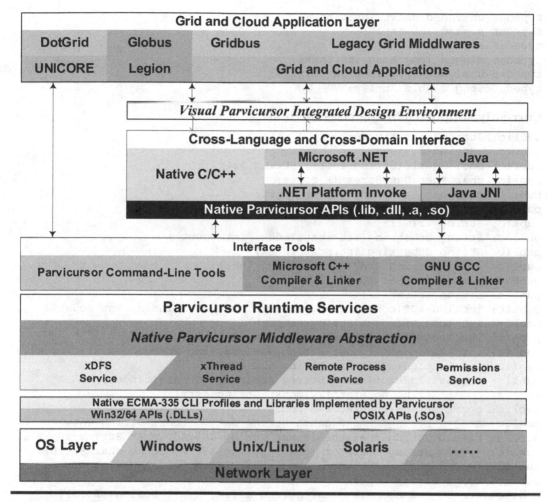

Figure 8.19 **The native layered Parvicursor infrastructure architecture.**

```
#include "System/ObjectDisposedException/ObjectDisposedException.h"
#include "System/FormatException/FormatException.h"
#include "System/OverflowException/OverflowException.h"
```

The System namespace is the root namespace for fundamental types in the .NET Framework Parvicursor. This namespace includes classes that represent the base data types used by all applications: Object (the root of the inheritance hierarchy), Byte, Char, Array, Int32, String, and so on. Many of these types correspond to the primitive data types that your programming language uses. When you write code using Parvicursor.NET Framework types, you can use your language's corresponding keyword when a Parvicursor.NET Framework base data type is expected.

Currently supported BasicTypes:

```
#define null 0
typedef signed char Int8;
typedef unsigned char UInt8;
typedef signed short int Int16;
```

```
typedef unsigned short int UInt16;
typedef signed int Int32;
typedef unsigned int UInt32;
typedef signed long long int Int64;
typedef unsigned long long int UInt64;
typedef long double Int128;
```

Currently supported String class methods:

```
public: String(char *buffer);
public: ~String();
public: bool Equals(String &str1, String &str2);
public: char *get_BaseStream() const;
public: char get_Value(int index) const;
public: int get_Length() const;
public: String Trim();
public: String Substring(int startIndex, int count);
public: String Substring(int startIndex);
public: static String Copy(const String &str);
public: String ToUpper();
public: String ToLower();
public: int IndexOf(const String &search, int startIndex, int count);
public: int IndexOf(const String &search);
public: int IndexOf(const String &search, int startIndex);
public: int LastIndexOf(const String &search, int startIndex, int count);
public: int LastIndexOf(const String &search);
public: int LastIndexOf(const String &search, int startIndex);
public: const String &operator+=(const String &str);
public: const String &operator+=(const char *str);
public: static String Concat(const String &str0, const String &str1);
public: friend String operator+(const String &StrA, const String &StrB);
public: friend String operator+(const String &StrA, const char *StrB);
public: friend String operator+(const char *StrA, const String &StrB);
public: const String &operator =(const String & str);
public: static int Compare(const String &StrA, const String &StrB);
public: friend bool operator ==(const String &StrA, const String &StrB);
public: friend bool operator !=(const String &StrA, const String &StrB);
public: String Replace(const String &oldValue, const String &newValue);
```

Currently supported Convert class methods:

```
public: static Int16 ToInt16(const String &value);
public: static UInt16 ToUInt16(const String &value);
public: static Int32 ToInt32(const String &value);
public: static UInt32 ToUInt32(const String &value);
public: static Int64 ToInt64(const String &value);
public: static double ToDouble(const String &value);
public: static UInt64 ToUInt64(const String &value);
public: static String ToString(Int16 value);
public: static String ToString(Int32 value);
public: static String ToString(Int64 value);
```

Current supported Guid class methods:

```
public: static String NewGuid();
```

Currently supported DateTime class methods:

```
public: static DateTime get_Now();
```

```
public: int get_Year();
public: int get_Month();
public: int get_DayOfWeek();
public: int get_Day();
public: int get_Hour();
public: int get_Minute();
public: int get_Second();
public: int get_Milliseconds();
```

8.9.2 Using Namespace System::IO

```
#include "System.IO/FileStream/FileStream.h"
#include "System.IO/Directory/Directory.h"
#include "System.IO/File/File.h"
#include "System.IO/IOException/IOException.h"
```

The System::IO namespace contains types that allow synchronous and asynchronous reading and writing on data streams and files.

The following distinctions help clarify the differences between a file and a stream. A file is an ordered and named collection of a particular sequence of bytes having persistent storage. Therefore, with files, one thinks in terms of directory paths, disc storage, and file and directory names. In contrast, streams provide a way to write and read bytes to and from a backing store that can be one of several storage mediums. Just as there are several backing stores other than discs, there are several kinds of streams other than file streams. For example, there are network, memory, and tape streams.

Currently supported FileStream class methods:

Use the **FileStream** class to read from, write to, open, and close files on a file system, as well as to manipulate other file-related operating system handles including pipes, standard input, and standard output. You can specify read and write operations to be either synchronous or asynchronous. **FileStream** buffers input and output for better performance.

FileStream objects support random access to files using the Seek method. Seek allows the read/write position to be moved to any position within the file. This is done with byte offset reference point parameters. The byte offset is relative to the seek reference point, which can be the beginning, the current position, or the end of the underlying file, as represented by the three properties of the SeekOrigin class.

```
public: FileStream();
public: ~FileStream();
public: FileStream(String path, FileMode mode, FileAccess access, int
bufferSize);
public: FileStream(String path, FileMode mode, FileAccess access);
public: int Read(char array[], int offset, int count);
public: void Write(const char array[], int offset, int count);
public: void Close();
public: void SetLength(Int64 value);
public: void Flush();
public: void Lock(Int64 position, Int64 length);
public: void UnLock(Int64 position, Int64 length);
public: void Seek(Int64 offset, SeekOrigin origin);
```

```
public: long get_Position();
public: void set_Position(Int64 position);
public: String get_Name();
public: Int64 get_Length();
public: bool get_CanRead();
public: bool get_CanWrite();
```

Currently supported File class methods:

File class provides static methods for the creation, copying, deletion, moving, and opening of files, and aids in the creation of FileStream objects.

```
public: static void Delete(const String &path);
public: static bool Exists(const String &path);
public: static void Move(const String &sourceFileName, const String &destFileName);
```

Currently supported Directory class methods:

Exposes static methods for creating, moving, and enumerating through directories and subdirectories. This class cannot be inherited.

```
public: static void CreateDirectory(const String &path);
public: static void Delete(const String &path);
public: static void Delete(const String &path, bool recursive);
public: static bool Exists(const String &path);
public: static ArrayList *GetDirectories(const String &path);
public: static ArrayList *GetFiles(const String &path);
public: static void Move(const String &sourceDirName, const String &destDirName);
```

8.9.3 Using Namespace System::Threading

```
#include "System.Threading/Thread/Thread.h"
#include "System.Threading/Timer/Timer.h"
```

The **System::Threading** namespace provides classes and interfaces that enable multi-threaded programming.

Currently supported Thread class methods:
Creates and controls a thread, sets its priority, and gets its status.

```
public: Thread(void *(*start)(void *), void *arg);
public: void Start();
public: bool IsAlive();
public: void Abort();
public: void SetDetached();
public: void Join();
public: static void SleepThread(int millisecondsTimeout);
```

Currently supported Timer class methods:
Provides a mechanism for executing a method at specified intervals.

```
typedef Object *(*Callback)(Object *);
class TimerCallback : public Object
{
        public: TimerCallback(Callback &callback);
```

```
        public: TimerCallback();
        public: Callback &get_BaseCallback();
};
class Timeout : public Object
{
public: const static Int32 Infinite = -1;
};
class Timer : public Object
{
        public: Timer(const TimerCallback &callback, Object *state, Int32
dueTime, Int32 period);
        public: Timer();
        public: ~Timer();
        public: void Finalize();
        public: void Dispose();
        public: bool Change(int dueTime, int period);
};
```

8.9.4 Using Namespace System::Collections

```
#include "System.Collections/ArrayList/ArrayList.h"
#include "System.Collections/Hashtable/Hashtable.h"
#include "System.Collections/Queue/Queue.h"
```

The **System::Collections** namespace contains interfaces and classes that define various collections of objects, such as lists, queues, bit arrays, and hash tables.

Currently supported ArrayList class methods:
Implements the IList interface using an array whose size is dynamically increased as required.

```
public: ArrayList();
public: ~ArrayList();
public: void Clear();
public: void Add(Object *data);
public: void Insert(int index, Object *value);
public: int get_Count();
public: bool Contains(Object *item);
public: void Remove(Object *data);
public: void RemoveAt(int index);
public: Object *get_Value(int index);
public: void set_Value(int index, Object *obj);
public: Object *operator[](int index);
```

Currently supported Hashtable class methods:
Represents a collection of key/value pairs that are organised based on the hash code of the key.

```
public: Hashtable();
public: ~Hashtable();
public: virtual int get_Count();
public: virtual Object *get_Item(const String &key);
public: virtual Object *get_Value(int index);
public: virtual void Add(const String &key, Object *value);
public: virtual void Clear();
```

```
public: virtual bool Contains(const String &key);
public: virtual bool ContainsKey(const String &key);
public: virtual void Remove(const String &key);
public: virtual int GetHashKey(const String &key);
```

Currently supported Queue class methods:
Represents a first-in, first-out collection of objects.

```
public: Queue();
public: ~Queue();
public: void Enqueue(Object *obj);
public: Object *Dequeue();
public: int get_Count();
public: void Clear();
public: bool Contains(Object *obj);
public: Object *Peek();
```

8.9.5 Using Namespace System::Net

```
#include "System.Net/Dns/Dns.h"
#include "System.Net/IPHostEntry/IPHostEntry.h"
#include "System.Net/IPAddress/IPAddress.h"
#include "System.Net/IPEndPoint/IPEndPoint.h"
```

The **System::Net** namespace provides a simple programming interface for many of the protocols used on networks today.

Currently supported Dns class methods:
Provides simple domain name resolution functionality.
public: static IPHostEntry Resolve(const String &hostName);

Current supported IPHostEntry class methods:
Provides a container class for Internet host address information.

```
public: IPHostEntry();
public: IPHostEntry(hostent *host);
public: ~IPHostEntry();
public: IPAddress get_AddressList(int index);
public: int get_AddressListLength();
```

Currently supported IPAddress class methods:
An Internet Protocol (IP) address.

```
public: IPAddress();
public: IPAddress(char address[], int len);
public: AddressFamily get_AddressFamily();
public: static long get_Any();
public: static long get_Broadcast();
public: static long get_Loopback();
public: static long get_None();
public: char *GetAddressBytes();
public: int GetAddressBytesLength();
```

Currently supported IPEndPoint class methods:
Represents a network endpoint as an IP address and a port number.

```
public: IPEndPoint(long address, int port);
public: IPEndPoint(const IPAddress &address, int port);
public: IPEndPoint();
public: int get_Port();
public: void set_Port(int port);
public: IPAddress get_Address();
public: long get_LongAddress();
public: void set_Address(IPAddress address);
public: AddressFamily get_AddressFamily();
```

8.9.6 Using Namespace System::Net::Sockets

```
#include "System.Net.Sockets/Socket/Socket.h"
#include "System.Net.Sockets/SocketException/SocketException.h"
#include "System.Net.Sockets/AddressFamily/AddressFamily.h"
#include "System.Net.Sockets/ProtocolType/ProtocolType.h"
#include "System.Net.Sockets/SocketType/SocketType.h"
#include "System.Net.Sockets/SocketFlags/SocketFlags.h"
#include "System.Net.Sockets/SocketShutdown/SocketShutdown.h"
```

The **System::Net::Sockets** namespace provides a managed implementation of the Windows Sockets (Winsock) and Beckley Sockets interface for developers who need to tightly control access to the network.

Currently supported Socket class methods:
The **Socket** class provides a rich set of methods and properties for network communications. The **Socket** class allows you to perform both synchronous and asynchronous data transfer using any of the communication protocols listed in the ProtocolType enumeration.

```
public: Socket(AddressFamily addressFamily, SocketType socketType,
ProtocolType protocolType);
public: ~Socket();
public: AddressFamily get_AddressFamily() const;
public: SocketType get_SocketType() const;
public: ProtocolType get_ProtocolType() const;
public: int get_Handle() const;
public: bool get_Connected() const;
public: void Connect(IPEndPoint &remoteEP);
public: void Bind(IPEndPoint &localEP);
public: void Listen(int backlog);
public: static void Select(ArrayList &checkRead, ArrayList &checkWrite,
ArrayList &checkError, int microSeconds);
public: int Send(const char buffer[], int offset, int size, SocketFlags
socketFlags);
public: int Receive(char buffer[], int offset, int size, SocketFlags
socketFlags);
public: void Close();
public: void Shutdown(SocketShutdown how);
public: Socket *Accept() const;
public: void SetReceiveTcpWindowSize(int size);
public: void SetSendTcpWindowSize(int size);
```

8.9.7 Using Namespace Parvicursor::Net

```
#include "Parvicursor/Parvicursor.Net/ParvicursorSocket/
ParvicursorSocket.h"
```

The **Parvicursor::Net** namespace provides a new high-performance object-oriented Message Passing Interface paradigm proposed by Parvicursor.

Currently supported ParvicursorSocket class methods:

```
public: ~ParvicursorSocket();
public: ParvicursorSocket(Socket *socket);
public: bool get_IsSecure();
public: Socket *get_BaseSocket();
public: void WriteException(Exception &e);
public: void WriteNoException();
public: void CheckExceptionResponse();
public: void Close();
public: char *ReadObject(int &objSize);
public: String ReadString();
public: void WriteObject(const char obj[], int size);
public: void WriteString(const String &str);
public: int Read(char array[], int offset, int count);
public: char *Read(int size);
public: char ReadByte();
public: int Write(const char array[], int offset, int count);
public: int Write(const char array[], int count);
public: void WriteByte(char buffer);
public: CheckedExceptionResponseState get_IsCheckedExceptionResponse();
public: void set_IsCheckedExceptionResponse(CheckedExceptionResponseState
value);
```

8.9.8 Using Namespace Parvicursor::Serialisation

```
#include "Parvicursor/Serialisation/Serialiser.h"
#include "Parvicursor/Serialisation/DeSerialiser.h"
```

The Parvicursor.NET Framework features the following high-performance native serialising technology:

- Binary serialisation preserves type fidelity, which is useful for preserving the state of an object between different invocations of an application. For example, you can share an object between different applications by serialising it to the Clipboard. You can serialise an object to a stream, to a disc, to memory, over the network, and so forth. **ParvicursorSocket** uses serialisation to pass objects "by value" from one computer or application domain to another.

Currently supported Serialiser and DeSerialiser class methods:

```
class Serialiser : public Object
{
public: Serialiser(int maxBufferCapcity);
       public: ~Serialiser();
       public: void Write(const String &str);
       public: template <class Object> void Write(const Object &obj)
```

```
        {
                this->Write(&obj, sizeof(obj));
        }
        public: char *get_BaseBuffer() const;
        public: int get_BaseBufferSize() const;
        public: void Reset();
};
class DeSerialiser : public Object
{
        public: DeSerialiser(char *buffer, int BufferSize);
        public: template <class _Object> const _Object Read()
        {
                _Object obj;
                this->Read(&obj, sizeof(obj));
                return obj;
        }
        public: const String Read();
        public: void Reset();
};
```

8.10 Presented Parvicursor.NET Sample Usages

In Windows, run all source codes by using Microsoft Visual Studio .NET 2003 or later versions and in Linux by using g++-enabled-compiler Code::Blocks.

1. ClientSocket sample shows a simple scenario in which a client connects to an HTTP server and requests the first page on a typical domain.
2. FileStream sample shows a file copy scenario from target to destination file system via using the well-known and good-featured System.IO.FileStream class.
3. RecursiveDirectoryTreeTraversal sample presents the full implemented features of .NET System.IO.File and System.IO.Directory class methods. This example traverses all directories under a specified path and lists all files on the storage system recursively.
4. The threading sample shows the use of a similar declaration of .NET Framework threads by utilising the POSIX Threads on Linux and its port to Windows by pthreads.dll dynamic link library.
5. The timer sample shows a System.Threading.Timer class usage.
6. The serialisation sample shows Parvicursor.NET serialisation/deserialisation tools.

References

[1] A. Poshtkohi and M.B. Ghaznavi-Ghoushchi, DotDFS: A Grid-based High-Throughput File Transfer System. *Parallel Comput.*, 37: 114–138, 2011. doi: 10.1016/j.parco.2010.12.003
[2] A. Poshtkohi and M.B. Ghaznavi-Ghoushchi, A Concurrent Framework for High Performance File Transfers in Grid Environments, In *Proceedings of the 3th International Conference on Computer and Electrical Engineering (ICCEE 2010)*, 16–18 November 2010, Chengdu, China. Available from: http://citeseerx.ist.psu.edu/viewdoc/summary?doi=10.1.1.174.6969, 2022.

[3] A. Poshtkohi, A.H. Abutalebi, and S. Hessabi, Parvicursor: A .NET-based Cross-Platform Software for Desktop Grids. *Int. J. Web Grid Serv.*, 3(3): 313–332, 2007. Available from: http://citeseerx.ist.psu.edu/viewdoc/summary?doi=10.1.1.112.1042, 2022.

[4] A. Poshtkuhi, A. Abutalebi, L. Ayough, and S. Hessabi, Parvicursor: A .NET-based Infrastructure for Global Grid Computing, in: *Proceedings of the 6th IEEE International Symposium on Cluster Computing and the Grid*, 16–19 May 2006, (CCGrid'2006), Singapore. Available from: http://citeseerx.ist.psu.edu/viewdoc/summary?doi=10.1.1.118.3976, 2022

[5] A. Poshtkuhi, A. Abutalebi, L. Ayough, and S. Hessabi, Parvicursor: A .NET-based Cross-Platform Grid Computing Infrastructure, In *Proceedings of the IEEE International Conference On Computing and Informatics 2006 (ICOCI'06)*, 6–8 June 2008, Malaysia. Available from: http://citeseerx.ist.psu.edu/viewdoc/summary?doi=10.1.1.113.2481, 2022

[6] ECMA-334: C# Language Specification, 2022; Available from: http://www.ecma-international.org/publications/standards/Ecma-334.htm.

[7] ECMA-335: Common Language Infrastructure (CLI), 2022; Available from: http://www.ecma-international.org/publications/techreports/E-TR-084.htm

[8] ECMA-372: C++/CLI Language Specification, 2022; Available from: http://www.ecma-international.org/publications/standards/Ecma-372.htm

[9] J. Clark, Calling Win32 DLLs in C# with P/Invoke, MSDN Magazine, The Microsoft Journal for Developers, July 2003; Available from: http://msdn.microsoft.com/en-us/magazine/cc164123.aspx, 2022.

[10] Microsoft Corporation, .NET Framework Home, 2022; Available from: http://msdn.microsoft.com/netframework/

[11] Microsoft Corporation, Shared Source Common Language Infrastructure 2.0 Release, 2022; Available from: http://www.microsoft.com/download/en/details.aspx?displaylang=en&id=4917

[12] MONO .NET Project Home Page, 2022; Available from: http://www.mono-project.com/

[13] DotGNU Project Home Page, 2022; Available from: http://www.gnu.org/software/dotgnu/

[14] DotGNU Portable.NET Home Page, 2022; Available from: http://www.gnu.org/software/dotgnu/pnet.html

Chapter 9

Parvicursor Infrastructure to Facilitate the Design of Grid/Cloud Computing and HPC Systems

The future is here. It's just not widely distributed yet.

William Gibson

9.1 Parvicursor: A Native and Cross-Platform Peer-to-Peer Framework to Design the Next-Generation Distributed System Paradigms

9.1.1 Introduction

In this chapter, we examine the main philosophy behind the Parvicursor platform and will complete some parts of it that have not been discussed in the previous chapters. The Parvicursor platform will be at first investigated as a fundamental infrastructure to implement the next-generation peer-to-peer (P2P) distributed middleware systems, and then we will consider the architecture of the xThread framework, which provides the ability to distributed execution of threads over a network of computers, in detail. Having solved several parallel and distributed problems, we will try to perform the practical proof-of-concept of the Parvicursor platform in order to develop the next-generation distributed systems. At the end of this chapter, we teach the reader how a distributed complex P2P middleware can be designed, implemented, and deployed.

DOI: 10.1201/9781003379041-9

9.2 Cross-Platform and High-Performance Parvicursor Platform to Develop the Next-Generation Distributed Middleware Systems

As seen so far, the design of distributed components of a system (or in general, the design of a complete distributed system) somewhat comes with very high complexity. In the past decades, to reduce this complexity, a software pattern has emerged referred to as the term *middleware*, which makes it easier to construct distributed applications. Middleware is a collection of technologies and software infrastructures that are used to facilitate the management and development of application programs in complex environments and heterogeneous distributed systems. The common definition of a middleware over the past two decades introduces the middleware as a software layer on top of operating systems (OSs) and beneath the application programs; with this definition, the middleware provides a common programming abstraction in a distributed system, as shown in Figure 9.1 (to this point, we assume that Parvicursor layer has been removed).

In practice, a middleware supplies a set of higher-level Application Programming Interfaces (APIs) than OS APIs. Middleware frameworks are designed to hide some kinds of heterogeneity that the programmers of distributed systems often face with them. These middleware frameworks also often hide the heterogeneity of OSs, programming languages, or either of them, transparently.

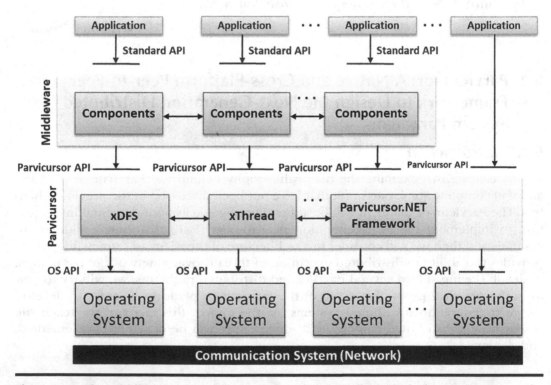

Figure 9.1 **The middleware abstraction and the role of Parvicursor platform to construct the next-generation distributed middleware systems.**

The use of a middleware has many benefits, including, hiding the low-level details, providing language and platform independence, exploiting code reuse, and facilitating the evolution of application programs. As it can be deduced, the use of middleware systems could result in reducing the cost and time of developing applications, portability and interoperability, and ultimately better quality. One of the potential disadvantages of making use of middleware in the development of complex and stand-alone systems can be attributed to the significant reduction of performance degree because of multiple software layers used to build the middleware.

The most important requirements of a distributed system, which have been taken into consideration in the design of the Parvicursor platform, are network communication, heterogeneity, scalability, standardisation, performance, resource sharing, support of multicore multiprocessor concurrency and distributed threading, and security. These requirements are more important in dynamic Grid and Cloud environments. The satisfaction of these requirements is accomplished by adding a light Parvicursor layer in Figure 9.1, on which one can build powerful next-generation middleware frameworks based upon it. In the following, we discuss these features.

9.2.1 Network Communication

As shown in Figure 9.1, different components of a distributed middleware may reside on various hosts. So, they must connect. This communication is done through network protocols and socket programming, which was discussed in Chapter 7, at the lowest possible level. Most distributed systems have been implemented atop transport layers such as TCP and User Datagram Protocol (UDP). These layers are provided by the OS at the lowest level. In the Parvicursor platform, in addition to supporting traditional sockets, which supply primitive communication, Parvicursor.NET Socket Interface (PSI), as described in Chapter 8, allows software components to use extra communication protocols such as Stream Control Transmission Protocol (SCTP) and UDP-based Data Transfer (UDT) Protocol. Advances in network hardware and new network protocols reveal the importance of the PSI interface. Therefore, the middleware that is designed based upon Parvicursor.NET Framework ensures the developers that if network transport protocols are evolved, then his/her implementations stay unchanged, and their system always works. A middleware also requires that complex data structures are converted into a format to transmit over a network. Such a facility in the Parvicursor platform, as described in Chapter 8, is provided through Parvicursor.NET Remoting Architecture (PR) and Parvicursor Object Passing Interface (POPI) interfaces. POPI makes it possible to send objects as serialised to another endpoint in native code and to reconstruct that object into the original one.

9.2.2 Heterogeneity

Heterogeneity means that the system has to run on a wide range of software and hardware platforms, including, networks, computer hardware, OSs, and programming languages. As mentioned in Chapter 8, the Parvicursor.NET Framework provides a native cross-platform implementation of the ECMA.NET standard for distributed systems.

In recent years, in addition to the heterogeneity issue of OSs and hardware, heterogeneous computing has been proposed due to a greater efficiency of multi/ many-core processors. A heterogeneous processing unit can be composed of a general-purpose processor, a special-purpose processor (such as a DSP[1] or GPU[2]), a co-processor, or a customised accelerator logic (such as an ASIC[3] or FPGA[4]). In general, a heterogeneous computing platform consisting of processors with different ISAs[5] is usually used to satisfy higher performance (e.g., networking applications). The heterogeneity level in modern computing systems gradually rises whilst the chip area is increasing, and scaling in the fabrication technologies allows the integration of more discrete components as parts on a system-on-chip (SoC). Therefore, the next-generation middleware systems in distributed systems must be able to interact with heterogeneous units. Since the Parvicursor platform has been implemented and runs in native code, so it can be easily connected with legacy libraries (such as OpenCL) and ISAs (through the machine assembly language) of such systems.

9.2.3 Scalability

A distributed system can exist on many computers. Scalability signifies the system is simply scalable. Scalability can be studied from different aspects. The system should remain stable when the number of its nodes changes. The design of scalable distributed systems requires a completely different collection of principles and patterns when compared with usually integrated systems. In the computer science literature, scalability is divided into two general categories: vertical and horizontal. Horizontal scalability points to adding more nodes in a system. One of the highly horizontal scalable architectures is P2P systems, to which extensive research has been devoted to them in the past decade. In Section 9.3, we will discuss this issue within the Parvicursor platform in detail. Vertical scalability means adding the resources to a single node in a system or the use of software architectures that improve the scalability. In the design and implementation of the Parvicursor platform, we have widely paid attention to vertical scalability. For instance, asynchronous sockets in Chapter 7 propose a kind of vertical scalability that can scale up to thousands of network connections. The xDFS and DotDFS protocols in Chapter 10, with a hybrid architecture (integrating the thread-based and event-driven concurrency models), realise scalability at the protocol level. Removed overheads from frameworks like .NET and the native execution of applications on top of the ECMA standard in the Parvicursor platform manifest vertical scalability at the software system level.

9.2.4 Standardisation

A standardised software platform is a set of standard interfaces that are accepted by a broad spectrum of software developers. These standards establish interoperability between various applications created by different developers as possible. The use of these standards has greater importance in designing distributed systems due to their high complexity. The use of open standards can make the system more flexible and adaptable. Taking advantage of software standards enhances the management of the software development lifecycle. Encapsulating the best practices avoids unnecessary repetition of past mistakes. New programmers can easier understand the structure of project codes by the standards used. Multiple projects can also easily and quickly be implemented by a common code base. To provide such an interface in the Parvicursor platform, we have made use of the ECMA-334 and ECMA-335 standards to create an open standard-based infrastructure for distributed systems as explained in Chapter 8. When the existing interfaces are not adequate in these two standards, we attempt to implement Parvicursor services and libraries as much as possible close to the structure of their equivalents in the .NET Framework.

9.2.5 Performance

Writing programs that have higher performance is a lot more art than science. For this purpose, a developer must simultaneously look at different aspects during code development, such as OS, hardware, concurrency, memory hierarchy, and network transport protocols. This issue becomes more difficult in distributed systems where they have relatively higher complexity. As a result, it is necessary to design an optimised interface and provide high-performance standard APIs on top of the OS. We have considered the performance metric from various aspects in the Parvicursor platform and refer to a number of them as follows. As discussed in Chapter 5, to increase the performance of multi-threaded applications, lock-free algorithms can be taken benefit. Parvicursor platform, against .NET Framework, gives the full advantage of native code performance to programmers. The native-execution feature allows us to benefit from available high-performance third-party libraries for various computing purposes in the Parvicursor platform. Asynchronous sockets (by reducing the number of running threads equal to the number of system cores) and the use of event-driven techniques (to overlap computation and communication) leverage the maximum efficiency of multicore multiprocessor machines in a distributed environment.

9.2.6 Resource Sharing

Resource sharing refers to the ability to use hardware, software, or data anywhere in the system. Distributed objects provide a comprehensive model of resource sharing. Processor sharing between two nodes is provided by the xThread service in the Parvicursor platform. The most basic type of resource sharing is data and file sharing. xDFS protocol fulfils such a necessity between two nodes as a P2P structure. For example, we can provide a complete distributed file system by extending the basic services presented by the xDFS framework for file sharing.

9.2.7 Concurrency Support of Multicore Processors and Distributed Threading

Nowadays, all computers have multiple processor cores. As was pointed out in Chapter 4, these processors have several advantages, such as improved performance through parallelism and reducing power consumption. Parvicursor platform supports a wide family of low-level classes and functions to implement any complex high-level concurrency for programmers, including thread abstraction, mutexes, condition variables, fibres, thread pools, and lock-free algorithms. Because one of the fundamental requirements of a distributed system is remote code execution in distant nodes and parallel programmers are already familiar with conventional thread program-ming styles, a distributed threading model, called xThread with unique features, is designed in this chapter which has close similarities to the class `Thread`. Therefore, we suggest an integrated environment for parallel and distributed programming based on distributed threads, which turns out to be very powerful.

9.3 Peer-to-Peer Paradigms and the Use of the Parvicursor Platform to Construct Large-Scale P2P Distributed Middleware Platforms such as Supercomputers and Traditional Distributed Systems

As discussed in the previous section, the scalability issue is one of the main chal-lenges in the design of next-generation distributed systems. The latest conventional supercomputers have at least one million processor cores. The emergence of new computing paradigms, such as Grid and Cloud Computing, has even eliminated the restriction on the number of processors used. The increase in the number of proces-sors and the communication issue do highlight the key importance of scalability. In the computer science literature, one of the highly scalable architectures to build supercomputers and large-scale grid environments is P2P systems. In this section, we briefly survey such systems and explain the role of the Parvicursor platform to construct distributed P2P middleware systems.

P2P computing has been noticed as a promising technology that rebuilds the architecture of distributed computing (or even the whole Internet). This is because it can exploit different resources (including computation, storage, and bandwidth), of course with high scalability. P2P is a computer network in which each computer on the network acts as either a client or a server for other computers. P2P is a dis-tributed application architecture that segregates tasks or workloads amongst peers. The owner of each computer on a P2P network exposes some of its resources to be directly available to other participants without requiring central coordination by stable servers or hosts. Within this model, peers are both providers and resource con-sumers, in contrast to the client/server model where servers only provide resources and clients consume them.

P2P systems are classified into centralised and decentralised (however, a com-bination of these two models is also possible to build a hybrid P2P system). In centralised P2P systems, like a client/server system, there are one or more central servers, which help peers locate their desired resources or act as task schedulers to coordinate actions amongst them. To locate resources, a peer sends messages to a central server to determine the peers' addresses that contain the desired resources, or to directly fetch job units from a central server. However, like a decentralised sys-tem, once a peer has its data or information, it can directly communicate with other peers without the intervention of a central server. In all centralised systems, a single-failure point exists. Furthermore, when there are a large number of peers, the central server will become a bottleneck, and it will significantly result in performance and scalability degradation. In a decentralised P2P system, each peer has the same rights and responsibilities. Each peer only has a partial view of the overall P2P network and offers the data/services that may be just related to some of the peers/queries. Locating peers, who offer data/services, can quickly turn into a challenging and critical issue. Benefits of these systems are: immunity against single-point failures, high efficiency, scalability, robustness, and other favourite properties.

P2P systems are divided into flat or hierarchical from a network structure's perspective. In a flat structure, functions and loads are distributed uniformly amongst the participating nodes. In a hierarchical structure, there are principally multiple routing structures. Hierarchical structures have several advantages such as fault and security isolation, effective caching and exploiting bandwidth, hierarchical storage, and so forth. Following this section, we conceptually prove how we can benefit from essential Parvicursor services to design and implement distributed P2P middleware systems for next-generation distributed systems. Since the current aim of the Parvicursor project is not to build such systems, in Section 9.6 we will examine a limited middleware for third-party data transfers atop the xDFS framework to practically show this philosophy.

Suppose we want to consider two nodes of a distributed P2P network built upon the Parvicursor platform. Figure 9.2 shows this notion. To build such an abstraction,

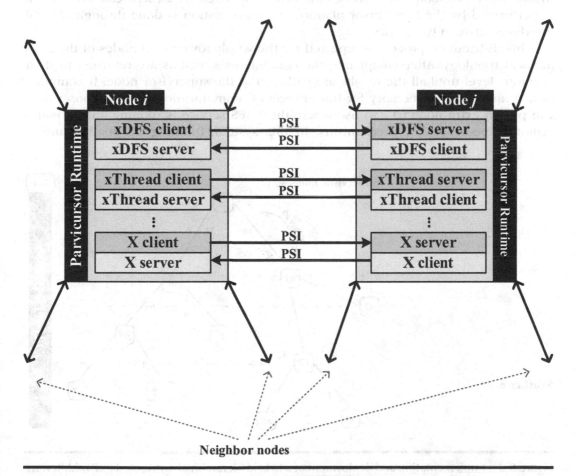

Figure 9.2 Two i and j nodes of a P2P system built upon the Parvicursor platform.

we need at least three services: xDFS service to transfer and share files between two nodes, xThread service to execute arbitrary codes on a remote node dynamically, and PSI service for communication between two nodes. In a node of a P2P network, Parvicursor runtime provides a set of servers and APIs equivalent to each service. As seen at node i, service X can act as a server for node j and vice versa. Acting as both client and server are one of the main principles in the definition of P2P networks. In this figure, each node can connect to neighbouring nodes by the PSI interface.

Now, we examine a real example to implement a distributed hierarchical hybrid P2P middleware based on the Parvicursor platform. In Figure 9.3 let's assume that we have a hierarchical P2P network composed of ten worker nodes, one supervisor node and an xDFS node. Also, suppose that 21 tasks have been submitted by a client to the supervisor. The designed middleware has to distribute tasks evenly, maintain the load-balancing issues amongst network nodes as P2P, and execute them on remote nodes. The node s just knows that there are two worker nodes on its underneath, each of which has several sub-nodes; therefore, it distributes 10 and 11 of these 21 jobs respectively between nodes n1 and n6 (to calculate how many sub-nodes of a node there are, we might make use of queries as multicast communications). Distribution of a work unit that is declared as an xThread abstraction is performed by the Parvicursor platform. Communication is done through the PSI interface between two nodes.

This distribution process is repeated for the whole lower-level nodes of the hierarchical topology. After completing the computations, results are returned to their previous level until all the results are gathered at the supervisor node. If computations require shared memory for Inter-Process Communication (IPC) purposes, one can put an extra node n11 to use where the xDFS service is running and provides remote pipe-based IPC mechanisms. In this system, fulfilling the load-balancing

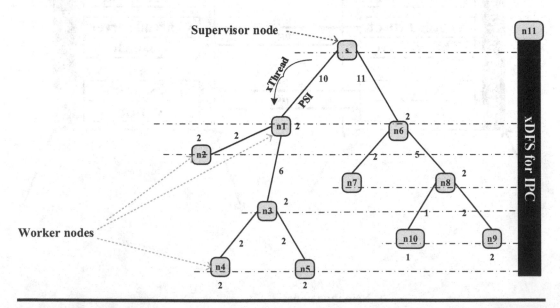

Figure 9.3 **Implementation and deployment of a hybrid hierarchical distributed P2P middleware constructed by the Parvicursor platform.**

problem must be performed through a special middleware that is implemented atop the Parvicursor platform. The Parvicursor platform supports fault tolerance directly in the xThread service between two nodes. Management of this facility should be done by designed middleware, which we will address in Section 9.4. As seen in this middleware, nodes n11 and s together function as a central controller whilst the worker nodes have been arranged as decentralised components, so we can conclude that this architecture realises a hierarchical hybrid P2P network.

9.4 xThread Abstraction: The Distributed Multi-threaded Programming Model Proposed by Parvicursor Platform for Distributed Systems

In this section, we introduce distributed multi-threading which relies on the xThread abstraction in the Parvicursor platform. Assume, in Figure 9.2, we are going to send a collection of threads from node i to the remote node j to execute and to wait on the completion of the remote code execution. xThread abstraction gives a rich set of operations, features, and controls over the established session to the developers. The conceptual functionality of xThread is similar to DotThreading from the DotGrid platform in [1] but with major differences. Since DotThreading had been implemented on a virtual machine platform (.NET CLR) with internal .NET Framework features employed, we could not port this abstraction directly into native code with the help of the Parvicursor.NET Framework. Hence, xThread abstraction emerged and developed based on native code from scratch. First, let's review how a client-side user can compile and run a program to harness the power of distributed multi-threading.

Figure 9.4 illustrates the client-side compilation process for distributed multi-thread programs depending on the xThread abstraction in the Parvicursor platform. The threads intended to be executed on remote nodes must inherit from the base class xThreadBase (interface) and implement its methods. The class MyThreadClass's implementation has to be compiled into a dynamic link library (DLL) file in the Windows OS or a shared object (SO) file in Unix-like OSs such as Linux. This generated shared file is passed to an instance of the class xThreadCollection within the function main() in the main program, and we use the class xThreadClient, for which Table 9.1 lists the description of the class's methods and constructor, to execute the threads on a remote xThread server. Finally, all compiled files converted into object files are linked to an executable by a linker program. The OS loader loads and executes this file, and the xThread runtime sends the thread instances for execution to a remote node. If an error occures in the entire xThread execution or its methods, an exception is thrown, and the program is notified of the error; upon receiving this error, the code should decide how to deal with the situation based on the type of the raised exception for the correct behaviour of the system.

The base class xThreadBase is a key object to work with xThread abstraction based on polymorphism concepts in object-oriented languages like C++ and C#. The class xThreadBase is usually referred to as an abstract class (or its equivalent in C# language, the interface class) because all of its methods are declared as virtual member functions. A pure virtual method is a virtual function that shall be implemented

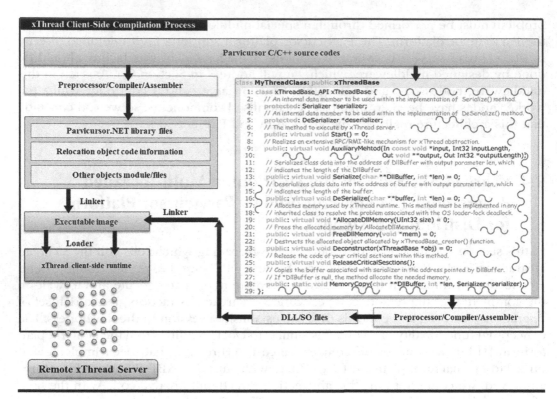

Figure 9.4 The client-side compilation process for distributed multi-threading relies on the xThread abstraction in the Parvicursor platform.

Table 9.1 The Constructor and Methods of the `xThreadClient` Class in Parvicursor. NET Framework

Name	Description
`xThreadClient(xThreadColl ection *collection, const String &xThreadServerAddress, NetworkCredential *nc, bool secure, ArrayList *errors)`	Instantiates a new object from the `xThreadClient` class. The argument `collection` specifies a set of xThread-based threads that must be run in a remote node with the associated `xThreadServerAddress` address and `nc` authentication information. The parameter `errors` stores the exception instances that occurred in the xThread server. After using the array list `errors`, we must free the allocated memory within every element of the list.
`void Run()`	Asynchronously executes the `xThreadClient` instance by creating a local thread as a detached state.
`void WaitForSessionInitiation()`	Waits until the remote xThread session on the server begins.

(Continued)

Table 9.1 (Continued) The Constructor and Methods of the `xThreadClient` Class in Parvicursor.NET Framework

Name	Description
`bool get_IsAlive()`	Gets a value indicating the execution status of the current xThread session.
`void SuspendAllThreads()`	Either suspends all the remote threads or has no effect if all the remote threads have already been suspended.
`void ResumeAllThreads()`	Resumes all remote threads that have already been suspended.
`void SuspendOneThread(Int32 index)`	Either suspends the remote thread specified by index or has no effect if the remote thread has already been suspended.
`void ResumeOneThread(Int32 index`	Resumes the remote thread specified by index that has already been suspended.
`void SyncReceiveOneThread(Int32 index)`	Executes a checkpoint operation on a remote thread specified by index and synchronises the data of the local class instance derived from the xThreadBase class in the client with its remote instance on the server.
`void SyncSendOneThread(Int32 index)`	Performs a restore operation on a remote thread specified by index and synchronises the data of the remote class instance derived from the xThreadBase class on the server with its local instance in the client.
`void AbortOneThread(Int32 index)`	Causes a remote thread specified by index to begin the process of termination. Calling this method usually terminates the remote thread immediately.
`void TerminateSession()`	Terminates the current xThread session and releases the whole consumed resources.
`void AuxiliaryMehtodOneThread(Int32 index, In const void *input, Int32 inputLength, Out void *output, Out Int32 *outputLength)`	Invokes the `AuxiliaryMehtod()` method of the interface xThreadBase class on the remote node, specified by index, in the xThread server. The parameter input is sent to the server based upon its length inputLength in order to invoke the `AuxiliaryMehtod()` method. The programmer is responsible for properly adjusting the address in that the `AuxiliaryMehtod()` method's output is stored, along with its length outputLength. The Parvicursor platform conveys the parameter output to the client-side xThread code and makes it accessible to the developer through the `AuxiliaryMehtodOneThread()` method. This method realises xRMI concept, which will be described in Section 9.6, in xThread abstraction.

by an inherited class (i.e., the classes derived from the abstract class `xThreadBase` in the Parvicursor platform), if and only if the derived class is not abstract itself. Classes containing pure virtual methods are referred to as the term `abstract`, which cannot be directly instantiated. A subclass of an abstract class can only be instantiated directly if all inherited pure virtual methods have been implemented by the class or a parent class. In fact, such a feature in the `xThreadBase` class makes the programmer implement all methods of this class that will be invoked at runtime by the xThread platform. In C++ language, pure virtual functions are declared using the specifier =0, as shown in the prototype of the xThread class's methods. In Section 9.5, we will explain several practical examples to work with the xThread abstraction, and how to derive from the interface `xThreadBase` class and implement its pure virtual methods.

Carefully see the descriptions of the pure virtual functions related to the abstract `xThreadBase` class in Figure 9.4. The code or algorithm implementation that will be executed as a distributed thread in a remote server must be placed into the method `Start()`'s body. The remote xThread server invokes this method for the first time to run a thread remotely. Memory allocation is done inside the DLL or SO file, which contains the implementation of the derived class, through a library by an OS; therefore, the server, which loads this DLL/SO file and does not know the type of the memory allocator used, must use two methods of `AllocateDllMemory()` and `FreeDllMemory()` necessarily implemented in the derived class from the base class xThreadBase. Parvicursor platform takes advantage of these two methods for allocating and releasing the memory that is needed during loading the objects from DLL/SO files at runtime to avoid OS loader-lock deadlock (LLD) concerning DLL files. To describe the problem incurred by LLD, we shortly express the basics of DLL/SO files; of course, since xThread loads the implementation of threads from DLL/SO files, it is worth discussing these basics as well.

A DLL/SO file is shared codes and data that an application can load and call at runtime. A DLL/SO file typically exports a collection of routines to be employed in programs and contains other routines for internal use. This technique allows code reuse (and particularly its use for distributed threads over a network of computers based upon the Parvicursor platform) by multiple programs to share a common feature in a library and to load them on demand. Advantages of using DLLs/SOs include reduced code footprint, using less memory due to single-copy-sharing, flexible development and testing, modularity, and functional isolation. Creating DLL/SO files leads to several challenges for developers. DLLs/SOs have no system-enforced versioning. When multiple versions of a DLL/SO exist on the system, the ease of being overwritten coupled with the lack of a versioning schema creates dependency and API conflicts. Complexity in the development environment, the OS loader implementation, and the DLL/SO dependencies have created fragility in load order and application behaviour.

The loader lock is a process-wide synchronisation primitive that the loader program depends on to guarantee the serialised loading of DLLs/SOs. Each function that has to read or modify the loader-library data structures for each process must acquire this lock before performing such an operation. Loader lock is recursive, which means that it can be re-acquired by the same thread. Inconvenient synchronisation within a DLL/SO can cause deadlocks for an application or access to data or code in an uninitialised DLL/SO. Calling certain functions from inside or outside a DLL/SO creates such problems.

The methods `Serialize()` and `DeSerialize()` function as a bridge between xThread runtime and the class implementation derived from the interface `xThread-Base`. xThread runtime to receive the serialised data of the `MyThreadClass` instance first allocates a `DLLBuffer` by calling the `AllocateDllMemory()` method, and then passes it to the `Serialize()` method, and this method implemented by the programmer performs a copy operation of the serialised data into `DLLBuffer`. The length of the filled buffer is stored in the pointer `len`'s address. Similar mechanisms are performed for the `DeSerialize()` method. The protected members `serializer` and `deserializer` have been considered as two internal objects to be used inside the `Serialize()` and `DeSerialize()` methods. Programs that have to use critical sections inside the `Start()` method should release them within the method `ReleaseCriticalSections()`, which is called before invoking the `Deconstructor()` method in the xThread server at runtime. The method `MethodAuxiliaryMehtod()` that utilises a powerful remote procedure call(RPC)/ remote method invocation (RMI) style for xThread abstraction will be described in Section 9.6.

Now that we have been sufficiently acquainted with the compilation process of client-side xThread programs from a developer's point of view, we focus on the implementation details of the xThread abstraction on both client and server sides. Figure 9.5 shows the Communicating Finite-State Machine (CFSM) of the `xThreadClient` class

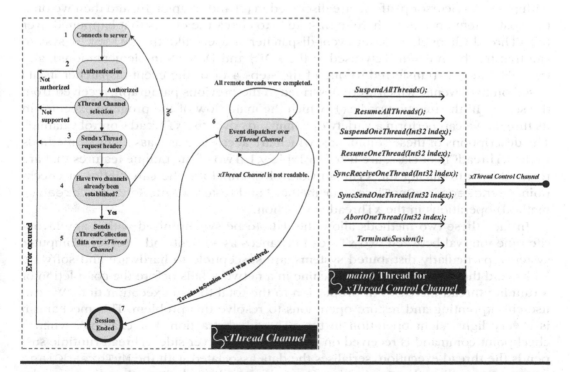

Figure 9.5 **The client-side CFSM implementation of the `xThreadClient` class in the Parvicursor platform.**

implementation in the Parvicursor platform. The red dotted rectangular boundaries execute concurrently in two separate threads of control. In the proposed xThread abstraction during each xThread session, in which n remote threads are running, two channels are created between the client and server: xThread Channel and xThread Control Channel. Events that take place in the server are reported to the client over the xThread Channel. Clients can issue frequent event-driven commands at the server side over the xThread Control Channel to accomplish and execute the functionalities offered by the xThread abstraction. In the current Parvicursor version, only two events have been defined over an xThread Channel, AllThreadsCompleted and TerminateSession; the former indicates that the execution of the whole remote threads has already been completed, and the latter notifies the client that the server is interested in terminating the xThread session abnormally (and therefore the client must inform the thread main(), which is controlling the current xThread session, of this occurrence).

In step 2, upon establishing the connection to the server the client performs the authentication process. If the client is allowed, it requests a new xThread session from the server in stage 3 (as noted in [2] and Chapter 10, the client can ask for various modes from the server such as xDFS, xThread, etc.). These stages are carried out for both channels (steps 1–4); in state 5, threads' data are packed into a class called xThreadCollection (every element within this collection contains some information such as the serialised data of the instance derived from the class xThreadBase and the main binary DLL/SO file) and sent to the server, and an xThread session actually begins. The full details of establishing a session between a client and a server within the Parvicursor platform are discussed in [2] and Chapter 10, and then we omit to debate them once more herein. In state 6, to check the events that happened over the xThread Channel, a socket event-dispatcher is used (like the select() system call that has been extensively used in the xDFS and DotDFS implementations), and the CFSM flow is transferred to one of the steps 4 or 6 (the event-dispatcher itself) based on two events, which were described in the previous paragraph, received from the server. In the function main(), which the main flow of the program executes in its thread, we can perform a variety of commands over the xThread Control Channel. The descriptions of these commands, which are accessible as class member methods in the xThreadClient class, are listed in Table 9.1. Two of the unique features that are realised by introducing the xThread Control Channel are the capabilities of checkpoint (SyncReceiveOneThread() method) and restore (SyncSendOneThread() method) operations in the xThread abstraction.

In fact, these two methods allow the data to be synchronised within any favourite time interval between two xThread instances as a client and a server. Computer systems, particularly distributed systems, are susceptible to hardware and software faults, and the probability that a machine in a network fails before the completion of a running thread increases in proportion to the total thread execution time. We can use checkpointing and restore operations to resolve this problem. This mechanism is a very lightweight operation in the xThread abstraction. For example, when a checkpoint command is received on the server, the server-side xThread runtime suspends the thread execution, serialises the data associated with the MyThreadClass instance by calling the Serialize() method and sends it to the client (on the other hand, the client data is synchronised with the server at this time), and restores the execution of the suspended thread. Since the user in the `Serialize()` and `DeSerialize()` methods can directly serialise or deserialise what is needed (of course, the programmer to use the checkpoint and restore functionalities must consider this case for storing the context of his/her code inside the `Start()` method's body), only the required data are transferred between the client and server, and thus the overall system performance improves dramatically due to saving the bandwidth and the increase in communication throughput. By combining features of two `SyncReceiveOneThread()` and `SyncSendOneThread()` methods, using critical sections and condition variables available in the Parvicursor platform inside the `Start()` method, and adding other events over the xThread Channel, one can build a very complicated system with functionalities similar to an asynchronous two-way RPC (the two-way feature means that every node during an xThread session can functions as a client or a server at any moment in time) and a Message Passing Interface (MPI)-like scenario with just two nodes. We don't discuss this subject, because it is beyond the scope of this book and the high complexity of such a system. Instead, we will examine somewhat a simpler variant called xRMI atop xThread in Section 9.6.

In a nutshell, we describe the xThread server, which encompasses the most complex part of the xThread architecture inside itself, as shown in Figure 9.6. The hybrid Parvicursor server upon establishing an xThread session transfers the CFSM state from 7 to 9 (steps 1 through 8 have already been discussed in [2] and Chapter 10 comprehensively). In stage 9, the `xThreadCollection` pack sent from the client over the xThread Channel is read through the PSI interface, we assume that the number of members of the collection is equal to n. Stages 10–13 executes for i=1 to i=n. In step 10, the DLL/SO file that is stored within a file with a GUID specified by the client for every element of the `xThreadCollection` object (these files are stored in a directory named to the GUID of the current xThread session) is loaded by the `LoadLibrary()` system call in Windows OS or the `dlopen()` system call in Unix-class OSs at runtime. Inside the DLL/SO file, the programmer must implement a function with the prototype `void *xThreadBase_creator()`. The return value of this function has to be the address of an instance of the `MyThreadClass` class. In stage 11, the server finds the function address within the DLL/SO file through the `GetProcAddress()`/ `dlsym()` system call. Now that we have the main `MyThreadClass` instance prepared, in state 12 the server deserialises the serialised data received from the client by calling the `DeSerialize()` method. In step 13, a thread is created and takes the `Start()` method's execution of the `MyThreadClass` instance. Stages 15, 17, and 18 respectively implement the xThread Channel and the xThread Control Channel. As seen, stages 14 through 18 have been placed into an infinite loop, and also these two channels are controlled through two separate event dispatchers associated with timeouts. For instance, if the command `TerminateSession` is received from a client over the xThread Control Channel, then the CFSM state moves to the final state (i.e., state 20) and the xThread session terminates.

At the end of this section, we point out a few remarks about the xThread abstraction. xThread facilitates a client (e.g., running on a Windows operating system) to be able to easily run a thread on any type of remote OS besides the target OS (e.g., on a remote Linux OS), which this can be done by compiling the instance `MyThreadClass` into two different DLL and SO files, and vice versa. Therefore, to

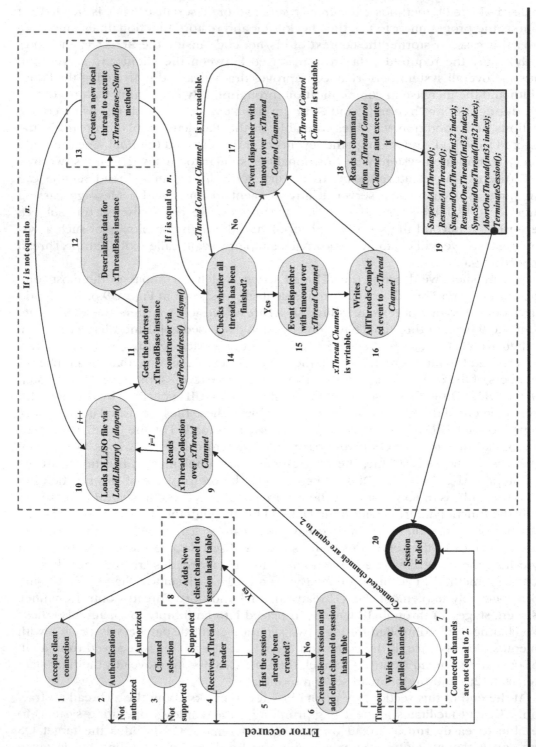

Figure 9.6 CFSM implementation of the xThread server in the Parvicursor platform.

perform computations, the network can be thought of by xThread heterogeneously, but the user notices the distributed network as a homogenous entity. We can develop distributed and parallel programs with MPMD and SPMD architectures through the xThread interface. In xThread abstraction, the framework code is separated from the algorithm code, but in some systems like MPI, the framework code must be embedded into the algorithm source code. As a result, xThread can extremely reduce the code complexity chiefly due to its high compatibility with the conventional, local multi-thread programming styles.

9.5 Practical Examples Using the xThread Abstraction

9.5.1 Example 1: A Simple Sum of Two Numbers Based on a Distributed P2P Architecture with Two Nodes

In our first example, we implement the sum of two numbers on two distributed nodes. The first node (as the client) sends the sum code request to the second node (as the server) as a DLL/SO file through the xThread abstraction and prints the result back into the console after completing the remote code execution. As illustrated in Figure 9.4, to develop a distributed program that relies on xThread, we must create a DLL/SO file implementing the distributed algorithm code and an executable program which controls the flow of the remote thread execution. The DLL/SO code of this example appears in Figure 9.7. The class `Sample` has inherited from the class `xThreadBase`, and then we must implement all of the pure virtual methods from the abstract class `xThreadBase`. Carefully pay attention to the descriptions within the codes. Whereas the Parvicursor platform, at first, has to load the sent object from a client on the server node at runtime, each DLL/SO implementation must contain an exported function named `xThreadBase_creator()`. As seen in lines 128 through 140, a reference to the object instantiated from the class `Sample` is returned. This function uses the class `Sample`'s constructor implemented in line 37 because the Parvicursor platform has no information about the constructor in line 5 or the internal implementation of the class `Sample` when it is calling the function `xThreadBase_creator()`. In the method `Start()`, in which we must place the implementation of our code, we simply add two numbers x and y and put the result into the variable z. The constructor in line 22 in the client is used to initialise the class `Sample` by the local native-code runtime. Within the method `Serialize()` in line 95, first, we compute the maximum length of bytes of the class `Sample` that must be transferred between two nodes based upon POPI over PSI. The allocation and de-allocation of two objects `serializer` and `deserializer` should always be performed respectively inside the methods `Serialize()` and `DeSerialize()`. In lines 105–107, we serialise our needed data members; as mentioned in the previous section, we must benefit from the static method `MemoryCopy()` of the class `xThreadBase` for mapping the C++ runtime memory with the used memory inside the DLL/SO file. The pointer `DllBuffer` stores the serialised contents of our class data members that must be transferred by the Parvicursor platform between two nodes. The function `MemoryCopy()` itself allocates the `DllBuffer` and the programmer does not need to allocate it. To deserialise our class data members, we must

```
 1: class Sample_API Sample : public xThreadBase, public Object {
 2:    public:
 3:        Int32 x, y, z;
 4:    public:
 5:        Sample(Int32 x, Int32 y);
 6:        Sample();
 7:        ~Sample();
 8:        void Start();
 9:        void Serialize(char **DllBuffer, Int32 *len);
10:        void DeSerialize(char **buffer, Int32 *len);
11:        void FreeDllMemory(void *mem);
12:        void *AllocateDllMemory(UInt32 size);
13: };
14:
15: // Important notice:
16: // To run your code correctly, please carefully read the template-like code comments.
17: // You MUST not use global variables in this shared library (DLL or SO),
18: // because it causes loader-lock deadlock at the OS kernel.
19: // You MUST not create threads in this class and MUST not use any
20: // synchronisation mechanism such as mutexes, semaphores and critical sections
21: // (if used, provide releasing the locks within the deconstructor).
22: Sample::Sample(Int32 _x, Int32 _y) {
23:    this->x = _x;
24:    this->y = _y;
25:    this->z = 0;
26:    // Here, you MUST set the values of serializer and deserializer pointers to null,
27:    // otherwise your program will have to crash.
28:    // SURE you have allocated all memories here and provided the de-allocation of them
29:    // in the ~Sample() deconstructor. This means YOU must not allocate memory in Start() method
30:    // with new operator or malloc() function call.
31:    // For example, if you need an opened file handle in Start() method,
32:    // you MUST provide closing the file handle in ~Sample() deconstructor.
33:    this->serializer = null;
34:    this->deserializer = null;
35: }
36:
37: Sample::Sample() {
38:    this->x = 0;
39:    this->y = 0;
40:    this->z = 0;
41:    // Here, you MUST set the values of serializer and deserializer pointers to null,
42:    // otherwise your program will have to crash.
43:    this->serializer = null;
44:    this->deserializer = null;
45: }
46:
47: Sample::~Sample() {
48:    // Here, you MUST release the allocated C++ stack memory for
49:    // Serializer and DeSerializer objects to avoid memory leaks for your entire multi-threaded application.
50:    if(this->serializer != null) {
51:        delete this->serializer;
52:        this->serializer = null;
53:    }
```

Figure 9.7 The DLL/SO code for the sum of two numbers is distributed on two nodes.

(Continued)

```
54:     if(this->deserializer != null) {
55:         delete this->deserializer;
56:         this->deserializer = null;
57:     }
58: }
59:
60: void Sample::Start() {
61:     // NOTE: You MUST never use the Thread::Sleep() or other thread sleep APIs in this method.
62:     // Because it may cause loader-lock deadlock in the OS kernel.
63:     // Don't define any variable that allocates memory from the heap in this method. Use instead
64:     // the class variable members to allocate memory from the heap. Don't declare local System::String
65:     // primitive data type in this method since it allocates memory from the heap.
66:     // This method is very useful in a pure compute-bound loop without Sleep() for execution
67:     // of scientific algorithms.
68:     this->z = this->x + this->y;
69:     printf("Start\n");
70:     printf("x: %d, y: %d, z: %d\n", this->x, this->y, this->z);
71: }
72:
73: void Sample::FreeDllMemory(void *mem) {
74:     // You MUST implement this method since Parvicursor.NET Framework uses it extensively.
75:     // If the memory has been allocated by the malloc() function, you MUST call here free() function.
76:     // If the memory has been allocated by C++ new operator, you MUST call here C++ delete operator.
77:     if(mem != null) {
78:         delete mem;
79:         mem = null;
80:     }
81: }
82:
83: void *Sample::AllocateDllMemory(UInt32 size){
84:     // You MUST implement this method since Parvicursor.NET Framework uses it extensively.
85:     // If the memory has been allocated by the malloc() function, you MUST call here the free() function.
86:     // If the memory has been allocated by C++ new operator, you MUST call here C++ delete operator.
87:     return (void *)new char[size];
88: }
89:
90: void Sample::Serialize(char **DllBuffer, Int32 *len) {
91:     // Don't change the values of len and DllBuffer variable pointers, since your program will have to crash.
92:     // These variables are to be used by Parvicursor.NET Framework for high-performance buffer transfers to
93:     // remote (or local) cross-process boundaries by Parvicursor Object-Passing Interface (POPI).
94:
95:     Int32 bufferSize = sizeof(this->x) + sizeof(this->y) + sizeof(this->z); // To avoid successive memory
allocation overhead, use the pre-allocated memory and
96:                                                     // increase POPI performance;
97:                                                     // you MUST consider keeping constant the bufferSize
length in mind.
98:                                                     // Also, you can select a default size that you guess is always
99:                                                     // greater than or equal to your real objects size. (e.g., a
large 1MB buffer size)
100:    if(this->serializer == null)
101:        this->serializer = new Serializer(bufferSize);
102:    else
103:        this->serializer->Reset(bufferSize);
```

Figure 9.7 (Continued) The DLL/SO code for the sum of two numbers is distributed on two nodes.

(Continued)

```
104:
105:    this->serializer->Write<Int32>(this->x);
106:    this->serializer->Write<Int32>(this->y);
107:    this->serializer->Write<Int32>(this->z);
108:
109:    xThreadBase::MemoryCopy(DllBuffer, len, this->serializer);    // Mapping between C++ memory and DLL C
Runtime memory.
110:                                    // If this line of code is removed at the end of this method
implementation,
111:                                    // your program will have to crash.
112: }
113:
114: void Sample::DeSerialize(char **buffer, Int32 *len) {
115:    // Don't change the values of len and buffer variable pointers, since your program will have to crash.
116:    // These variables are to be used by Parvicursor.NET Framework for high-performance buffer transfers to
117:    // remote (or local) cross-process boundaries by Parvicursor Object-Passing Interface (POPI).
118:    if(this->deserializer == null)
119:        this->deserializer = new DeSerializer(*buffer, *len);
120:    else
121:        this->deserializer->Reset(*buffer, *len);
122:
123:    this->x = deserializer->Read<Int32>();
124:    this->y = deserializer->Read<Int32>();
125:    this->z = deserializer->Read<Int32>();
126: }
127:
128: #ifdef __cplusplus    // If used by C++ code,
129: extern "C" {        // we need to export the C interface
130: #endif
131: // You MUST not use global variables in this shared library(DLL or SO),
132: // because it causes loader-lock deadlock at the OS kernel.
133: xThreadBase_DLL_Export void *xThreadBase_creator() {    // Don't change this function name and its
declaration (prototype),
134:                                    // since Parvicursor uses from this native function
135:                                    // to locate your exported DLL function at the runtime.
136:    Sample *s = new Sample(); // Here, You MUST call a new operator and instantiate your class to be run by
Parvicursor.
137:        return (void *)s;
138: }
139: #ifdef __cplusplus
140: }
141: #endif
```

Figure 9.7 (Continued) The DLL/SO code for the sum of two numbers is distributed on two nodes.

use the method DeSerialize(), which has an essential difference from the former method, the buffer variable is allocated by the Parvicursor platform, and it is not required to use the function MemoryCopy() (which has some overhead due to an extra copy operation) at the end of this method.

We have already created our DLL/SO file, so we will explain how to write the threads' distributor node. Figure 9.8 shows the distributor program. In lines 8 and 9, two objects of the class Sample have been instantiated; in lines 12 and 13, we add these objects to the instance xtc, of course, by specifying the DLL/SO file that previously has been compiled and created for distributed execution on the remote node. Now, we must connect to the remote xThread server and send the threads taken in

```
 1: NetworkCredential nc = NetworkCredential("user", "pass");
 2: ArrayList errors = ArrayList();
 3:
 4: int main(int argc, char *args[]) {
 5:   xThreadCollection *xtc = null;
 6:   xThreadClient *client = null;
 7:   try {
 8:     Sample s1 = Sample(10, 20);
 9:     Sample s2 = Sample(30, 40);
10:     xtc = new xThreadCollection();
11: #if defined WIN32 || WIN64
12:     xtc->AddNewThreadInstance(&s1,
"C:/Samples/xThreadAddNumbersDispatcher/Debug/xThreadSampleDLL.dll");
13:     xtc->AddNewThreadInstance(&s2,
"C:/Samples/xThreadAddNumbersDispatcher/Debug/xThreadSampleDLL.dll");
14:       // From a Windows machine we might run a remote Linux xThread thread instance!!!!
15:       //xtc->AddNewThreadInstance(&s,
"/root/projects/Samples/xThreadAddNumbersDispatcher/Debug/libxThreadSampleDLL.so");
16: #else
17:     xtc->AddNewThreadInstance(&s1,
"/root/Samples/xThreadAddNumbersDispatcher/Debug/libxThreadSampleDLL.so");
18:     xtc->AddNewThreadInstance(&s2,
"/root/Samples/xThreadAddNumbersDispatcher/Debug/libxThreadSampleDLL.so");
19: #endif
20:     client = new xThreadClient(xtc, "localhost", &nc, false, &errors);
21:     client->Run();
22:     client->WaitForSessionInitiation();
23:     while(client->get_IsAlive()) {
24:       if(client->get_AreAllThreadsCompleted()) {
25:         for(Int32 i = 0 ; i < xtc->get_Count() ; i++)
26:           client->SyncReceiveOneThread(i);
27:         client->TerminateSession();
28:         cout << "s1.x: " << s1.x << " s1.y: " << s1.y << " s1.z: " << s1.z << endl;
29:         cout << "s2.x: " << s2.x << " s2.y: " << s2.y << " s2.z: " << s2.z << endl;
30:       }
31:       Thread::Sleep(1);
32:     }
33:   }
34:   catch(Exception &e) {
35:     printf("%s\n", e.get_Message().get_BaseStream());
36:   }
37:   catch(...) {
38:     printf("An unknown error was occurred.\n");
39:   }
40:   for(register Int32 i = 0 ; i < errors.get_Count() ; i++) {
41:     Exception *e = (Exception *)errors.get_Value(i);
42:     printf("Error%d: %s\n", i + 1, e->get_Message().get_BaseStream());
43:     delete e;
44:   }
45:   if(client != null)
46:     delete client;
47:   if(xtc != null)
48:     delete xtc;
49:   return 0;
50: }
51: // LD_LIBRARY_PATH=/Parvicursor/Samples/xThreadAddNumbersDispatcher/Debug/:$LD_LIBRARY_PATH
```

Figure 9.8 The distributor program for the sum of two numbers which relies on xThread abstraction.

the xThreadCollection instance for execution; this work is done in line 20. Then, we start the execution process in line 20, and in line 22 we wait until the xThread session is completely established for the request of two remote threads' execution. In an infinite while loop, we check the completion status of all remote threads (which here just exists two threads of control in this example) as long as the object client is alive. Provided that there is completion of all remote threads, we carry out the synchronisation of the local object data in a finite for loop by invoking the method SyncReceiveOneThread() per remote thread in lines 25 through 26 (in other words, this method lets us copy the sum result stored in the variable z of the remote node into the corresponding local variable z). In line 27, by calling the method TerminateSession() of the object client, we finish the xThread session involving the two remote threads. In lines 28 and 29, the calculated values of the variable z are printed to the console. In lines 40 through 44, we print likely exceptions that occurred during the xThread session. Note that in line 43 the ArrayList elements must be freed since the memory of these elements has already been allocated by the Parvicursor platform. In lines 45 through 48, we release the allocated resources, and the program terminates.

The code of this example is located in "/Parvicursor/Parvicursor/Samples/xThreadSampleDLL" and "/Parvicursor/Parvicursor/Samples/xThreadAddNumbersDispatcher" from the companion materials of the book. It is necessary to note a point about running the executable program xThread-AddNumbersDispatcher.exe in Unix-class operating systems (this must be considered for execution of all programs that make use of the xThread abstraction). Before running the program, we need to tell the OS loader where the SO file libx-ThreadSampleDLL.so is located, because it must be loaded by the loader at first. To declare this file to the loader is done by a shell command shown in line 51 of Figure 9.8.

9.5.2 Example 2: Calculating the Value of the Number π to n Decimal Places Grounded on a Distributed P2P Master/Slave Architecture with m+1 Nodes

As the last and second example using the xThread abstraction, we will examine the design and implementation of a P2P master/slave architecture to compute the value of π to n decimal places. In the twentieth century, mathematicians and computer scientists discovered new methods to compute the number π with many digits. Scientific applications generally require no more than 40 digits of this number. Therefore, the primary motivation for these calculations is the human tendency to break records, but these vast computations have been also used to evaluate the computing power of supercomputers and high-precision multiplication algorithms. One of these algorithms to compute the nth digit of π is described in [1]. Let's consider Figure 9.9, which visualises the network topology used to calculate the number π based on a distributed P2P master/slave architecture. In this topology, the master node through the xThread abstraction distributes computational work units amongst worker nodes. To extend the expressed algorithm, we can simply compute the values of digits ith

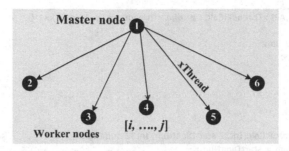

Figure 9.9 **The network topology to calculate the number π based on a distributed peer-to-peer master/slave structure using the xThread abstraction.**

to jth in each worker node. The calculation results are sent back to the master node by the Parvicursor platform.

Like Example 1, the implementation of this example also includes developing a DLL/SO file and an executable program. Figure 9.10 shows the code for the DLL/SO file. Those parts shown in dotted lines have been omitted to save space in the code. The algorithm implementation of reference [1] has been illustrated with dots as well, i.e., the method CalculatePiDigits(). The parameters startDigitNum and numDigits of the class xThreadPiCalc indicate i and j=i+numDigits, respectively. Since the constructor of line 10 executes in the client (the master node), the string result, which stores the computation result in the related interval, must be allocated with enough memory space equal to the desired number of digits in line 13. This memory allocation on the server (the worker nodes) is done inside the method DeSerialize(). The variable strLen stores the current length of the string result. Within the implementation of the method Start() in lines 36–39 with calling the function CalculatePiDigits(), which implementation has been removed from the figure, we calculate all of the needed digits of π in a loop and concatenate them to the end of the string result through the ANSI C string function strcat(). The implementation of the two methods Serialize() and DeSerialize() are very similar to Example 1, and so we avoid describing them again.

At this point, we discuss the implementation of the dispatcher program to calculate the number π as demonstrated in Figure 9.11. In this example, it is supposed that the number of worker nodes is equal to 2 and we want to compute the number π from the digit from to the digit to. The code of the parallel algorithm as seen in lines 9 through 13, first, uniformly creates the remote threads and inserts them into the array list xthreads. A small middleware is implemented in lines 24–64 in that the threads inside xthreads are equally segregated amongst worker nodes. In lines 61 through 81, we start the execution of the remote threads similar to what was presented in Example 1. Upon computation completion, the results are carried into the output per remote thread. The codes of this example are located in the directories "/Parvicursor/Parvicursor/Samples/xThreadPiCalcDLL" and "/Parvicursor/Parvicursor/Samples/xThreadPiClacDispatcher" from the companion resources of the book.

```
1: class xThreadPiCalc_API xThreadPiCalc : public xThreadBase, public Object {
2:    public:
3:        Int32 startDigitNum;
4:        Int32 numDigits;
5:        Int32 strLen;
6:        char *result;
7:        ...
8: };
9:
10: xThreadPiCalc::xThreadPiCalc(Int32 startDigitNum, Int32 numDigits) {
11:    this->startDigitNum = startDigitNum;
12:    this->numDigits = numDigits;
13:    this->result = new char[numDigits + 1];
14:    this->strLen = 0;
15:    ...
16: }
17:
18: xThreadPiCalc::xThreadPiCalc() {
19:    this->startDigitNum = 0;
20:    this->numDigits = 0;
21:    this->result = null;
22:    ...
23: }
24:
25: xThreadPiCalc::~xThreadPiCalc() {
26:    ...
27:    if(this->result != null)
28:        delete this->result;
29: }
30:
31: ...
32:
33: void xThreadPiCalc::Start() {
34:    char retStr[1024];
35:    this->result[0] = '\0';
36:    for(register Int32 i = 0; i <= Math::Ceiling(this->numDigits / 9) ; i++) {
37:        CalculatePiDigits(this->startDigitNum + (i * 9), retStr);
38:        strcat(this->result, retStr);
39:    }
40:    result[this->numDigits] = '\0';
41:    this->strLen = this->numDigits;
42: }
43:
44: void xThreadPiCalc::Serialize(char **DllBuffer, Int32 *len) {
45:    Int32 bufferSize = sizeof(this->startDigitNum) + sizeof(this->numDigits) + sizeof(this->strLen) +
this->numDigits * sizeof(char);
46:    if(this->serializer == null)
47:        this->serializer = new Serializer(bufferSize);
48:    else
49:        this->serializer->Reset(bufferSize);
50:    this->serializer->Write<Int32>(this->startDigitNum);
51:    this->serializer->Write<Int32>(this->numDigits);
52:    this->serializer->Write<Int32>(this->strLen);
```

Figure 9.10 The DLL/SO code to calculate the value of π on m nodes.

(Continued)

```
53:     if(this->strLen > 0)
54:         this->serializer->Write(this->result, this->strLen);
55:     xThreadBase::MemoryCopy(DllBuffer, len, this->serializer);
56: }
57:
58: void xThreadPiCalc::DeSerialize(char **buffer, Int32 *len) {
59:     if(this->deserializer == null)
60:         this->deserializer = new DeSerializer(*buffer, *len);
61:     else
62:         this->deserializer->Reset(*buffer, *len);
63:     this->startDigitNum = deserializer->Read<Int32>();
64:     this->numDigits = deserializer->Read<Int32>();
65:     this->strLen = deserializer->Read<Int32>();
66:     if(this->result == null)
67:         this->result = new char[numDigits + 1];
68:     if(this->strLen > 0) {
69:         deserializer->Read(this->result, this->strLen);
70:         this->result[this->strLen] = '\0';
71:     }
72: }
```

Figure 9.10 (Continued) The DLL/SO code to calculate the value of π on m nodes.

9.6 The Proof of Concept of the Philosophy behind the Parvicursor Project as a New Standard to Build the Next-Generation Distributed P2P Middleware Systems: The Design and Implementation of a Middleware Supporting Third-Party Data Transfers in xDFS Framework atop the Parvicursor Platform

In this section, we design and implement a limited middleware that relied upon the Parvicursor platform, which will be deployed and run on three nodes as a perfect P2P structure. This middleware fulfils third-party data transfers for the xDFS framework based on the combination of xDFS API features and xThread abstraction. Third-party transfers allow performing remote transmissions between two servers that in turn have been started by a local client. Such a feature does not directly exist in the xDFS protocol specification, because the protocol solely specifies direct communication between an xDFS client and server for high-throughput file transmissions and lacks a channel control concept contrary to the FTP and GridFTP protocols. In such a scenario, three entities are involved: a client, who only arranges data transfers and does not participate in it, and two servers, one of which is sending data to the other. This scenario is very common, especially in Grid and Cloud environments where we need to transfer huge data sources between two sites or two data centres for different purposes.

First, we examine existing procedures in FTP protocol for third-party transfers to better understand the strength of xThread abstraction for developing a real P2P

```
 1: int main(int argc, char *args[]) {
 2:     ArrayList *xthreads = new ArrayList();
 3:     const Int32 nodeNum = 2;
 4:     const String nodes [nodeNum] = {"localhost", "localhost"};
 5:     const Int32 xThreadPerNodeNum = 2;
 6:     const Int32 from = 1;
 7:     const Int32 to = 1000;
 8:     Int32 physicalxThreads = nodeNum * xThreadPerNodeNum;
 9:     //--- Parallel Algorithm -----------
10:     Int32 total = to - from;
11:     Int32 totalPerThread = total / physicalxThreads;
12:     Int32 totalPerThread_mod = total % physicalxThreads;
13:     Int32 i = 0, one = 0;
14:     while(from + i * totalPerThread < total) {
15:         if(i != 0)
16:             one = 1;
17:         xthreads->Add(new xThreadPiCalc(from + i * totalPerThread + one, totalPerThread));
18:         i++;
19:     }
20:     for(register Int32 i = 0 ; i < xthreads->get_Count(); i++) {
21:         xThreadPiCalc *temp = (xThreadPiCalc *)xthreads->get_Value(i);
22:         printf("startDigitNum: %d numDigits: %d\n", temp->startDigitNum, temp->numDigits);
23:     }
24:     //--- A small master-slave middleware implementation ----
25:     printf("xThreadNum: %d\n", xthreads->get_Count());
26:     ArrayList *collections = new ArrayList();
27:     register Int32 j = 0;
28:     register Int32 current = 0;
29:     while(j < xthreads->get_Count() - 1) {
30:         xThreadCollection *xtc = new xThreadCollection();
31:         for(register Int32 k = 0 ; k < xThreadPerNodeNum && current < xthreads->get_Count() ; k++) {
32:             xThreadPiCalc *temp = (xThreadPiCalc *)xthreads->get_Value(j + k);
33: #if defined WIN32 || WIN64
34:             xtc->AddNewThreadInstance(temp,
"C:/Samples/xThreadPiClacDispatcher/Debug/xThreadPiCalcDLL.dll");
35: #else
36:             xtc->AddNewThreadInstance(temp,
"/root/Samples/xThreadPiClacDispatcher/Debug/libxThreadPiCalcDLL.so");
37: #endif
38:             current++;
39:         }
40:         collections->Add(xtc);
41:         j += xThreadPerNodeNum;
42:     }
43:     Int32 remainder = xthreads->get_Count() % physicalxThreads;
44:     if(remainder != 0) {
45:         for(register Int32 i = remainder - 1 ; i >= 0 ; i--) {
46:             xThreadPiCalc *temp = (xThreadPiCalc *)xthreads->get_Value(xthreads->get_Count() - 1 - i);
47: #if defined WIN32 || WIN64
48:             ((xThreadCollection *)collections->get_Value(collections->get_Count() - 1))-
>AddNewThreadInstance(temp, "C:/Samples/xThreadPiClacDispatcher/Debug/xThreadPiCalcDLL.dll");
49: #else
50:             ((xThreadCollection *)collections->get_Value(collections->get_Count() - 1))-
```

Figure 9.11   The program for dispatching threads amongst *m* nodes depending on a peer-to-peer master/slave topology.

(*Continued*)

```
>AddNewThreadInstance(temp, "/root/Samples/xThreadPiClacDispatcher/Debug/libxThreadPiCalcDLL.so");
51: #endif
52:        }
53:    }
54:    xThreadClient **clients = new xThreadClient *[collections->get_Count()];
55:    ArrayList **errors = new ArrayList *[collections->get_Count()];
56:    for(register Int32 i = 0 ; i < collections->get_Count() ; i++) {
57:        xThreadCollection *xtc = (xThreadCollection *)collections->get_Value(i);
58:        errors[i] = new ArrayList();
59:        clients[i] = new xThreadClient(xtc, nodes[i], &nc, false, errors[i]);
60:    }
61:    //--- Execute our implemented small middleware ---
62:    try {
63:        for(register Int32 i = 0 ; i < collections->get_Count() ; i++)
64:            clients[i]->Run();
65:        for(register Int32 i = 0 ; i < collections->get_Count() ; i++)
66:            clients[i]->WaitForSessionInitiation();
67:        for(register Int32 i = 0 ; i < collections->get_Count() ; i++) {
68:            while(clients[i]->get_IsAlive()) {
69:                if(clients[i]->get_AreAllThreadsCompleted()) {
70:                    xThreadCollection *xtc = (xThreadCollection *)collections->get_Value(i);
71:                    for(Int32 j = 0 ; j < xtc->get_Count() ; j++) {
72:                        clients[i]->SyncReceiveOneThread(j);
73:                        xThreadPiCalc *calc = (xThreadPiCalc *)xtc->get_Value(j)->objInstance;
74:                        cout << "from: " << calc->startDigitNum << " to: " << calc->startDigitNum + calc-
>numDigits << " result: " << calc->result << endl;
75:                    }
76:                    clients[i]->TerminateSession();
77:                }
78:                Thread::Sleep(1);
79:            }
80:        }
81:    }
82:    ...
83: }
```

Figure 9.11 (Continued) The program for dispatching threads amongst *m* nodes depending on a peer-to-peer master/slave topology.

system when we are describing the designed middleware. In FTP or GridFTP protocol, the client must establish two control channels for both servers. The client chooses one of the servers for listening and then sends the PASV command. When the server replies with the IP address and port on which is listening, the client sends this IP address and port to the other server using the PORT command. This will cause the second server connects to the first server. To initiate the real data transmission, the client sends the RETR command (which is followed by the file name) to the server that reads data from the disc and writes it to the network (the sending server), and the STOR command (which is followed by the file name) to the other server that reads data from the network and writes to the disc (the receiving server).

Figure 9.12 depicts the P2P middleware architecture designed to realise third-party data transfers depending on two key services of xDFS and xThread in the Parvicursor platform. The client code is located at node 1 which includes a DLL/SO file and a dispatcher program. The implementation of the remote job that is executed through the xThread abstraction in node 2 is inside the DLL/SO file. Figure 9.13 illustrates the

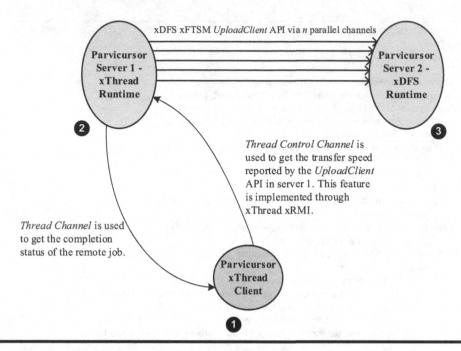

Figure 9.12 The P2P middleware architecture is designed to realise third-party data transfers in the Parvicursor platform depending on two key services of xDFS and xThread.

Start() method implementation of this DLL/SO file. As seen, one object is instantiated from the class of the xDFS framework to transfer a remote file on node 2 to node 3. The target file is uploaded to node 3 through n parallel channels when the remote thread executes at node 2. As can be seen in Figure 9.12, the Parvicursor server on node 2 executes at xThread runtime, whilst the Parvicursor server on node 3 is serviced through UploadClient API and is executing at xDFS runtime. Figure 9.14 shows the remote job distributor program which is run on node 1 (the client node). The xThread Channel is used to check the completion status of the remote job, which is located inside the method Start(). The remaining and last discussion in this chapter is devoted to how we can convey the file transfer speed from node 2 to node 1 to be reported to the user. This mechanism provides a powerful xThread feature referred to as xRMI,[6] akin to RPC and RMI functionalities (but with many differences, and more powerful and flexible), in the Parvicursor platform for distributed systems. The client code, as shown in Figure 9.14 in lines 25–31, invokes the method AuxiliaryMehtod() every 5 s (which is implemented in the DLL/SO file of Figure 9.13) and calculates the number of bytes transferred between two nodes 2 and 3, and finally reports the third-party file transfer's speed in the client (node 1).

We now describe xRMI features from xThread abstraction. As stated, the xThread abstraction over the xThread Channel allows running a remote thread based upon the method Start(), and also this channel notifies us of the status of the desired thread. The xThread Channel is simplex after starting the execution of the xThreadBase instance and only the server sends commands to the client (such as terminating the current xThread session by the server and the execution completion of remote threads). Thus, in this channel, the client has no control over the execution of the remote

```
 1: void xThreadThirdPartyTransfer::Start() {
 2:    try {
 3:        this->upc = new UploadClient(String((const char *)this->localFilename), String((const char *)this-
>remoteFilename), this->parallel, this->blockSize, this->tcpBufferSize, 100, 100, String((const char *)this-
>dest), *this->nc, false, false, this->remoteErrors, true, true);
 4:        this->upc->Run();
 5:    }
 6:    catch(Exception &e) {
 7:        this->remoteErrors->Add(new Exception(e.get_Message())));
 8:    }
 9:    ...
10: }
11:
12: void xThreadThirdPartyTransfer::AuxiliaryMehtod(In const void *input, Int32 inputLength, Out void
**output, Out Int32 *outputLength) {
13:    if(this->out == null) {
14:        this->out = new xThreadThirdPartyTransferContextOutput();
15:        this->out->transferredBytes = 0;
16:    }
17:    xThreadThirdPartyTransferContextInput *in = (xThreadThirdPartyTransferContextInput *)input;
18:    switch(in->command) {
19:        case __GetTransferredBytes__:
20:            if(this->upc != null)
21:                this->out->transferredBytes = this->upc->get_CurrentTransferredBytes();
22:            else
23:                this->out->transferredBytes = 0;
24:            *output = this->out;
25:            *outputLength = sizeof(xThreadThirdPartyTransferContextOutput);
26:            break;
27:        default:
28:            *output = null;
29:            *outputLength = 0;
30:            break;
31:    }
32: }
```

Figure 9.13   The DLL/SO code implementing the remote job that will execute on two nodes for a third-party file transfer.

thread and cannot invoke another method except for the method `Start()` on the server side (xThread client is only allowed once to call this method). To eliminate this restriction and allow the client code to invoke a variety of methods or favourite functions on the server side, we added the xRMI feature to the xThread abstraction. This extension is possible due to the existence of the xThread Control Channel concept. Consequently, xRMI enables the developer to execute different synchronous methods or to acquire full information about the execution of remote thread(s) on the server. In the implemented middleware aimed at third-party file transfers, we have used xRMI to find the number of bytes transmitted at server 2 and to calculate the transfer rate in the client node. The xRMI functionality looks like the existing mechanisms of remote procedure invocations such as Java RMI, CORBA, RPC, and WFC, but xRMI is very different from these variants that will be reviewed at the end of this section.

Figure 9.15 shows the structure and flow of the RMI that relied on xRMI. To activate xRMI in the server, we must call the method `AuxiliaryMehtodOneThread()`

```
 1: int main(int argc, char *args[]) {
 2:     const char *dest = "localhost";
 3:     const char *localFilename = "C:/test/test.pdf";
 4:     const char *remoteFilename = "C:/test/test1.pdf";
 5:     Int32 parallel = 10;
 6:     Int32 blockSize = 256*1024;
 7:     Int32 tcpBufferSize = 256*1024;
 8:     struct xThreadThirdPartyTransferContextInput input;
 9:     input.command = __GetTransferredBytes__;
10:     struct xThreadThirdPartyTransferContextOutput output;
11:     Int32 outputLength;
12:     try {
13:         xThreadThirdPartyTransfer s = xThreadThirdPartyTransfer(dest, localFilename, remoteFilename,
parallel, blockSize, tcpBufferSize);
14:         xtc = new xThreadCollection();
15: #if defined WIN32 || WIN64
16:         xtc->AddNewThreadInstance(&s,
"C:/Samples/xThreadThirdPartyTransferDispatcher/Debug/xThreadThirdPartyTransferDLL.dll");
17: #else
18:         xtc->AddNewThreadInstance(&s,
"/root/Samples/xThreadThirdPartyTransferDispatcher/Debug/libxThreadThirdPartyTransferDLL.dll");
19: #endif
20:         client = new xThreadClient(xtc, "localhost", &nc, false, &errors);
21:         client->Run();
22:         client->WaitForSessionInitiation();
23:         Int64 last = 0, current = 0;
24:         while(client->get_IsAlive()) {
25:             client->AuxiliaryMehtodOneThread(0, &input, sizeof(struct
xThreadThirdPartyTransferContextInput), &output, &outputLength);
26:             if(output.transferredBytes == (Int64)-1)
27:                 goto Terminate;
28:             current = output.transferredBytes;
29:             Thread::Sleep(5000);
30:             printf("\rspeed: %.2f MB/s\r", ((Float)(current - last))/(5 * 1024.0 * 1024.0));
31:             last = current;
32:         }
33: Terminate:
34:         client->TerminateSession();
35:         for(register Int32 i = 0 ; i < s.remoteErrors->get_Count() ; i++) {
36:             Exception *e = (Exception *)s.remoteErrors->get_Value(i);
37:             printf("RemoteError%d: %s\n", i + 1, e->get_Message().get_BaseStream());
38:         }
39:     }
40:     catch(Exception &ee) {
41:         printf("%s\n", ee.get_Message().get_BaseStream());
42:     }
43:     ...
44: }
```

Figure 9.14 The program for distributing the remote thread on two nodes to perform third-party transfers.

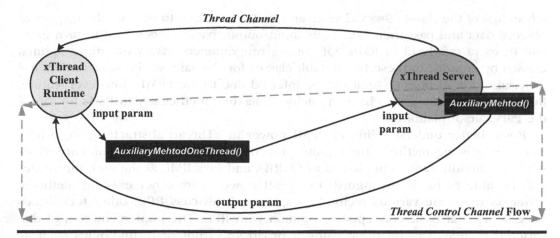

Figure 9.15 The structure and flow to perform remote method invocations in xThread abstraction which relied on xRMI.

of the class `xThreadClient` for the ith remote thread on the client. As listed in Table 9.1, this method takes the input argument's address along with its length to send to the xThread server. Having sent the complete contents of the input parameter through the xThread Control Channel over PSI, the method `AuxililaryMethod()` of the interface class `xThreadBase` is called on the server, and the result as an output parameter with its length is returned to the client code through the same open xThread Control Channel. The client code can frequently invoke the remote method `AuxiliaryMethod()`, for instance, inside an infinite loop. During this process, it seems only a remote method is called, but the programmer can pass an argument as a state machine into the method `AuxiliaryMethod()`, and then based on its value decides what code must be run on the server. This functionality is seen in lines 17–31 of Figure 9.13 for the third-party file transfer. According to the structure `xThread-ThirdPartyTransferContextInput`'s member command, we decide what code should be run in the current call. Thus, we can multiplex the implementation of any number of methods inside an `AuxililaryMethod()`'s body which depends on calling a state machine. As it is obvious when working with xRMI, we just deal with input/output parameters and there is no trace of the network communication. xRMI avoids the burden on the programmers concerned with the complexities due to network communication and instead lets them focus on their application development. One of the powerful xRMI features is its very low-level interface with no overhead. The method `AuxiliaryMehtodOneThread()` takes two input and output parameters with their length from the user and transfers them between a client and a server; therefore, xRMI exposes no overhead on a remote method call from a low-level preservative. With this point kept in mind, input/output parameters can be prepared in two ways by a programmer along with their lengths to be transferred between client and server. The first technique is to pass the address or reference of a C structure or a C++ class (the memory allocated from stack or heap) to xRMI. In this technique, since a contiguous memory space is transmitted without additional negative performance operations such as encoding or serialisation, there is no extra overhead when executing remote procedure calls. The second technique takes advantage of the classes `Serializer` and `DeSerializer` to prepare the respective objects' data and pass their buffers as input/output parameters which in turn gives rise to extra overhead in RMIs. Of course, programmers may write more optimal classes by contrast to these two default classes for the sake of the serialisation and deserialisation of objects. As it can be inferred due to the xRMI's low-level feature, the developer has a great chance to achieve maximum efficiency in RMIs on top of the Parvicursor platform.

For a better understanding of xRMI power in xThread abstraction, we briefly examine existing methods for remote procedure calls and finally compare xRMI with two middleware technologies of CORBA and Java RMI; at the end, the reader will be able to easily distinguish the xRMI power from other existing methods. Whereas there are various technologies, we only discuss RPC; other techniques have somewhat basic concepts in common with RPC. The implementation of distributed systems can be done using a broad spectrum of technologies such as pure sockets, RPC, DCOM, CORBA, WCF, Java RMI, and ICE.[7] These methods differ greatly in complexity, interoperability, standardisation, and ease of use aspects. To achieve maximum performance, pure sockets or xRMI and RPC are advisable. Overhead bottlenecks in different middleware technologies for distributed objects are caused by various factors like extra data copies, less compact encoding, and complex encoding rules.

RPC is a powerful technique for constructing distributed applications depending on clients and servers. RPC relies on the notion of extending the local or traditional procedure call so that the callee (called) procedure has not been required to be in the same address space as the caller (calling) procedure. Like a function call, when an RPC request is made, the caller arguments are passed into the remote procedure and the caller waits for the response returned from the remote callee procedure. When we write a client-server application by using sockets, we must provide a layer of code that manages the network communication. By using RPC, programmers of distributed systems avoid the interface details with the network. This allows us to focus on the details of our application rather than the details of network programming. In fact, RPC falls somewhere between the transport layer and the application layer in the OSI model. RPC includes specifications to exchange arguments and the results between a client and a server in a standard format. In other words, this format is the serialising operation of parameters into a buffer which always causes overhead; however, it improves portability amongst different systems and prevents applications to worry about low-level details like byte reordering. Figure 9.16 depicts a typical RPC flow between a client and a server.

The client calls a local stub, which initiates network communication, instead of the actual code implementation of that stub. Stubs are compiled and linked with the client-side application program. Rather than including the actual code that implements the remote procedure, the client stub code: retrieves necessary parameters from the client address space, translates the parameters into an open NDR[8] format to transfer over the network, and invokes the functions in the client RPC runtime library to send the request and its parameters to the server. The server to call the remote procedure performs the following steps: accepts the server runtime library's functions and calls the server stub, the server stub retrieves the parameters from the network buffer and converts them from NDR format to a format that the server

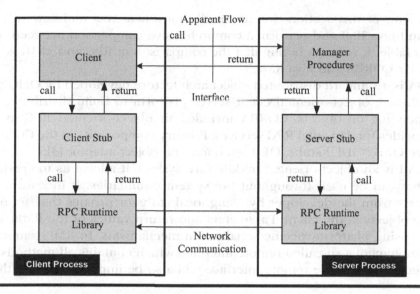

Figure 9.16   The flow of a remote procedure call between a client and a server.

requires, and the server stub calls the actual procedure on the server. Finally, the remote procedure is executed, and presumably generates output parameters and a return value. When a procedure execution completes, returns a similar sequence of data steps. To develop an RPC application, the first step is to specify a protocol for client-server communication. The communication protocol is accomplished by generated stubs. A protocol compiler is usually used to define and generate this protocol. For the protocol, we have to identify the name of service procedures, the data types of parameters, and the return arguments. The protocol compiler reads a definition and automatically generates client and server procedures.

As seen, we must carry out several steps in the development of an RPC program, and also the infrastructure supporting RPC has a complex structure itself. Furthermore, in the development cycle of programs that employ RPC, the client and server processes need to be installed separately on two different machines. In RPC for each developed function in the client, a counterpart server-side function must be implemented that services the client function. Over against these complexities, the xThread abstraction offers xRMI as a simple tool to implement such functionalities. xRMI does not require any protocol compiler and everything is performed at runtime. In xThread abstraction, there is no server-side process that must service client-side processes; the programmer writes a DLL/SO file, and its code executes in the xThread server, and the result is returned to the client code. In xMRI, there is no default serialisation operation; the programmer can decide dependent on his/her need how to use input/output parameters and occasionally develop an optimum serialisation algorithm/method. Also, concurrency and parallelism are very challenging in RPC, requests of a client are served on the server within one process, and therefore a client calls different remote procedures from just one remote process during the RPC session. In the xThread abstraction through the class `xThreadCollection`, we can define n number of remote threads for each instance of the class `xThreadClient`, so n parallel xRMI requests can be served in one xThread session.

At the end of this section, we summarily introduce two middleware platforms CORBA and Java RMI and perform a comprehensive comparison between them and xRMI in a table. It is worth noting that the comparison of RPC and xRMI is also true precisely for CORBA and Java RMI.

CORBA is a standard distributed object architecture developed by OMG.[9] CORBA is a distributed, object-oriented client/server platform to build distributed applications depending on objects. CORBA includes an object-oriented RPC mechanism which provides fundamental RPC services. Primary components in the CORBA architecture are ORB,[10] IDL[11] stubs, ORB interface, and object adaptor [3].

Java RMI is an object-oriented middleware system. It allows us to create remote objects that can be used throughout the system boundaries. It hides the distribution process from the developer by using local stubs or proxies that act on behalf of remote objects in the client. Parameters and return values of the RMIs are transmitted by using platform-specific serialisation mechanisms. In RMI, remote objects need to implement a so-called remote interface which contains all methods that can be invoked remotely. The remote interface will also be implemented via the generated stub.

Given the explanation above for CORBA and Java RMI architectures, Table 9.2 describes a brief comparison between these two technologies and the xThread xRMI.

The codes of this section are located at the folders "/Parvicursor/ Parvicursor/Samples/xThreadThirdPartyTransferDLL" and "/Parvicursor/Parvicursor/Samples/xThreadThirdPartyTransferDispatcher" from the companion resources of the book.

Table 9.2 Comparison of Different Technologies for Performing Remote Method Invocations

CORBA	Java RMI	xThread xRMI
Supports multiple inheritances at the interface level.	Supports multiple inheritances at the interface level	Supports multiple inheritances at the C++ xThreadBase class level.
Uniquely identifies an interface using the interface name and uniquely identifies a named implementation of the server object by its mapping to a name in the Implementation Repository.	Uniquely identifies an interface using the interface name and uniquely identifies a named implementation of the server object by its mapping to a URL in the Registry.	The client is responsible for distributing xThread instances over the network and managing the application.
Uses the Internet Inter-ORB Protocol (IIOP) as its underlying remoting protocol.	Uses the Java Remote Method Protocol (JRMP) as its underlying remoting protocol.	Uses PSI and PR as its underlying remoting protocol. PSI can be implemented for a vast family of transport protocols like TCP, UDT, and SCTP.

(Continued)

Table 9.2 (Continued) Comparison of Different Technologies for Performing Remote Method Invocations

CORBA	Java RMI	xThread xRMI
The mapping of Object Name to its Implementation is handled by the Implementation Repository.	The mapping of Object Name to its Implementation is handled by the RMI Registry.	The implementation of each instance must be embedded in `Start()` and `AuxiliaryMethod()`.
When passing parameters between the client and the remote server object, all interface types are passed by reference. All other objects are passed by value including highly complex data types.	When passing parameters between the client and the remote server object, all objects implementing interfaces extending `java.rmi.Remote` are passed by remote reference. All other objects are passed by value.	When passing parameters between the client and the remote server object, the client can decide which object to pass by reference or by value.
Does not attempt to perform general-purpose distributed garbage collection.	Attempts to perform distributed garbage collection of remote server objects using the mechanisms bundled in the JVM.	Does not attempt to perform general-purpose distributed garbage collection. The xThread runtime does invoke the `Deconstructor()` method at the end of each xThread session. The client code can perform any object disposition within this method.
When a client object needs to activate a server object, it binds to naming or a trader service.	When a client object needs a server object reference, it has to do a lookup() on the remote server object's URL name.	There is not any server object. A client must make use of the xThreadClient API to begin the execution of a remote thread run by `Start()` method.
The responsibility of locating an object implementation falls on the Object Adapter (OA)—either the Basic Object Adapter (BOA) or the Portable Object Adapter (POA).	The responsibility of activating an object implementation falls on the Java Virtual Machine (JVM).	The responsibility of activating an object implementation falls on the programmer implementing `Start()` and `AuxiliaryMethod()` methods.
The client-side stub is called a proxy or stub.	The client-side stub is called a proxy or stub	The client-side stub is `xThreadClient` class.
The server-side stub is called a Skeleton.	The server-side stub is called a Skeleton.	There is no server-side stub.

(Continued)

Table 9.2 (Continued) Comparison of Different Technologies for Performing Remote Method Invocations

CORBA	Java RMI	xThread xRMI
Complex types that will cross interface boundaries must be declared in the IDL.	Any Serializable Java object can be passed as a parameter across processes.	Programmer can decide how to pass objects stored within the input/output parameters, for example by using a serialisation method or passing the address of contiguous memory areas to xThread runtime.
Exception handling is taken care of by Exception Objects. When a distributed object throws an exception object, the ORB transparently serialises and marshals it across the wire.	Allows throwing exceptions which are then serialised and marshalled across the wire.	Programmer must handle exceptions that occurred within `Start()` and `AuxiliaryMethod()` methods and use proper code to serialise/deserialise exceptions.
Since this is just a specification, diverse programming languages can be used to code these objects as long as there are ORB libraries you can use to code in that language	Since it relies heavily on Java Object Serialisation, these objects can only be coded in the Java language	xThread abstraction and xRMI are simple interfaces in concept and can be easily implemented for different programming languages.
For CORBA implementation, C++ is the easiest.	RMI works only with Java.	Recently, xRMI works only with C/C++.
Best suited for enterprise-level applications.	Best suited for Internet applications.	Best suited for a broad spectrum of distributed paradigms, such as P2P systems, Cloud Computing, the Internet, and so forth.

9.7 Our Future Works to Extend the Parvicursor Platform

Over a decade of working on two projects, DotGrid and Parvicursor, and also during the writing of this book, many ideas and extensions have emerged for our future research works, and their number and descriptions are so much. As a great result, the Parvicursor project has created a good research area for upcoming years. In the following we mention a number of them. For the next versions of the xDFS protocol, we plan to extend and implement the protocol based on more novel hybrid models to achieve ultimate performance. We intend to implement some parts of the xSec protocol based on accelerators such as GPUs to increase the efficiency of cryptographic operations, particularly for Cloud platforms. Another very important part to increase the performance of the Parvicursor platform on each running node of a P2P topology will be to make full use of lock-free algorithms in critical Parvicursor services. One of the most important plans is to design a sandboxing infrastructure to achieve the features available in the CAS model of ECMA. NET standard [4] in the native Parvicursor platform; this will open new insights into the design of cloud infrastructures without the need for virtualisation platforms (like virtual machines) to increase the performance as closely as possible to the efficiency of native code. We also plan to design and implement higher-level middleware layers atop the Parvicursor APIs and services which will facilitate the construction of distributed systems.

Notes

1 Digital Signal Processor (DSP)
2 Graphics Processing Unit (GPU)
3 Application-Specific Integrated Circuit (ASIC)
4 Field-Programmable Gate Array (FPGA)
5 Instruction Set Architectures (ISA)
6 MultipleXed Remote Method Invocation (xRMI)
7 Internet Communication Engine (ICE)
8 Network Data Representation
9 Object Management Group
10 Object Request Broker
11 Interface Definition Language

References

[1] A. Poshtkohi, A.H. Abutalebi, and S. Hessabi, DotGrid: A .NET-based Cross-Platform Software for Desktop Grids. *Int. J. Web Grid Serv.*, 3(3): 313–332, 2007. https://arxiv.org/abs/1703.03904, 2022.
[2] A. Poshtkohi and M.B. Ghaznavi-Ghoushchi, DotDFS: A Grid-based High Throughput File Transfer System. *Parallel Comput.*, 37: 114–136, 2011. doi: 10.1016/j.parco.2010.12.003. https://arxiv.org/abs/1703.03905, 2022.
[3] The Common Object Request Broker: Architecture and Specification, 2022; http://www.omg.org/spec/CORBA/
[4] Code Access Security, 2022; http://msdn.microsoft.com/en-us/library/930b76w0%28v=vs.90%29.aspx

Chapter 10

xDFS: A Native Cross-Platform Framework for Efficient File Transfers in Dynamic Cloud/Internet Environments

In God we trust. All others must bring data.

W. Edwards Deming

10.1 Introduction

Despite our observation of many advances in increasing the speed of communication links between networks during the recent decades, data transmission remains a key bottleneck. Perhaps one of the major reasons is the fact that several technical and abstract factors influence the throughput delivered to the end-user from the proposal phase of a new file transport protocol to the implementation step of that protocol. The feasibility of success in a broad spectrum of distributed computing paradigms depends upon the ability to arrive at the data transmission speed as much as close to the computing power of the new generation of multi-core processors and cutting-edge system-on-chip (SoC) architectures (heterogeneous many-core CPUs will become common soon).

As we have seen in the past years, the dramatic expansion of the Internet has led to the information technology revolution. The Internet has made modern distributed infrastructures possible to emerge, such as Grid and Cloud computing. As a fundamental result of this new revolution, communication mechanisms and data transmission protocols provide an infrastructural foundation for the emergence and evolution of enormous computing paradigms and integration of data access on a worldwide scale. In the Internet industry, two protocols, Hypertext Transfer Protocol

DOI: 10.1201/9781003379041-10

(HTTP) and File Transfer Protocol (FTP), are de-facto, open standards that have provided basic file transfer functionalities [1]. To overcome the problems concerned with these two protocols that are mainly due to the overheads of the Transmission Control Protocol (TCP) protocol in its window-based congestion control mechanisms used, the GridFTP protocol was proposed [2–4]. In [5, 6], we introduced a hybrid concurrent FTP, called DotDFS, integrated with a set of event-driven and thread-based models. DotDFS was the first FTP that, in addition to proposing a new computing paradigm in the field of data transmission protocols, unveiled many architectural problems regarding the FTP and GridFTP protocols.

These major issues in the field of data transmission encouraged us to develop this key chapter of our book. In this chapter, we demonstrate the design and implementation of new xDFS protocol as a replacement for its predecessor DotDFS protocol for high-end data transports over different networks.

The TCP protocol has been used as a transport-level communication protocol on the Internet over the years. However, TCP is rather an old communication protocol designed in the 1970s. Many problems regarding the TCP have been reported such as its inability to support the increasing speeds of modern networks. One commonly used way to reduce the overheads posed by TCP is to simultaneously choose an optimum number of TCP connections and the TCP socket buffer size, which are discussed fully in [5]. This chapter tries to minimise the overheads concerned with the FTP itself as much as possible and to examine optimal software design patterns of that protocol. This goal plays a key role to reduce the problems associated with TCP overheads which decrease the throughput of file transfer systems. It increases dramatically the entire system efficiency and relieves exposed drawbacks. However, it is necessary to note that the PSI structure (refer to Section 10.5) allows the xDFS protocol to operate over more optimum transport protocols (e.g., SCTP) than TCP. PSI and xDFS framework will bring various opportunities together for research communities to implement non-TCP PSI-enabled drivers for the sake of achieving a virtually 0% overhead file transfer system currently working in userspace.

What will be presented in this chapter is not only porting an existing code base to native code, but xDFS has been designed from scratch, and this chapter explains the authors' experiences to implement optimal software systems for distributed systems in a native, cross-platform, and cross-language manner. The presented framework herein can be used for critical applications in highly concurrent environments such as data-intensive scientific applications and the Internet industry. Additionally, in this chapter, we describe the problems related to the FTP and GridFTP protocols and ultimately will propose the xDFS protocol as a suitable alternative replacement for these two protocols in dynamic Grid/Internet environments. In large parts of this chapter, we introduce different architectures of optimal server design patterns, particularly in the orientation of file transfer systems, where due to the best of our knowledge virtually no attention has been paid to them so far.

The key performance metric for a server running its workloads is the sustained throughput of client requests. Furthermore, the deployment of servers commonly happens in high compute density installations such as data centres, where supplying power and dissipating server-generated heat are very important factors in the centre's operating cost. The orientation of the xDFS framework is technology-independent due to its highly cross-platform manner and its architectural standards-based patterns and can be used to bridge with legacy systems as well.

We also believe that the main contribution of this chapter, in addition to presenting novel concepts, is to provide a complete reference and to classify all issues, in which a developer should bear in mind when implementing critical client-server programs for distributed systems.

Also, in this chapter, we investigate the rationale of the saturation speed phenomenon discussed in our previous published paper [5] and observed that such a negative phenomenon does not exist in the context of the xDFS framework. In all disc-to-disc tests in download mode for transferring a 2 GB file with or without parallelism, the xDFS throughput at a minimum of 30% and at most 53% was superior to the GridFTP. Memory-to-memory tests in upload mode showed that the xDFS protocol accessed 98.5% of the bottleneck bandwidth whilst the GridFTP protocol was reaching 95%. We will also perform a comprehensive autopsy of the xDFS anatomy that relied on communicating finite state machines.

The rest of the chapter is organised as follows. In Section 10.2, we present the next-generation requirements of Grid-based file transport protocols. Sections 10.3 and 10.4 concentrate on designing high-performance server architectures for Grid-based file transport protocols, particularly for data-intensive Grid applications and Internet services. Section 10.5 describes DotDFS and xDFS FTPs and discusses new xDFS extensions over DotDFS. Section 10.6 discusses the native and cross-platform implementation of xDFS protocol atop Parvicursor.NET Framework; moreover, making use of the concept of communicating finite state machines will help the reader better understand the presented materials throughout this section. Section 10.7 focuses on the comparison of the xDFS protocol with the GridFTP protocol in depth. The experimental studies are described in Section 10.8. Section 10.9 concludes the chapter and sketches our future research works.

10.2 The Next-Generation Requirements of Grid-Based File Transport Protocols

Many scientific applications need to stage large volumes of files from one collection of machines to another collection of machines in a wide-area network (WAN) or via the Internet. Efficient execution of such data transfers requires taking into consideration the heterogeneous disposition of the environment and dynamic availability of shared resources. This section will generally try to infer why a new file transport protocol, called xDFS, is proposed. Sections 10.3–10.8 will discuss more reasons in this regard. Globus in [3] explains the following phrase for adopting and extending the FTP protocol: "We chose the FTP protocol because it is the most commonly used protocol for bulk data transfers on the Internet and of the existing candidates from which to start (http, DPSS, HPSS, SRB, etc.) ftp comes closest to meet the needs of Grid applications" [3].

However, throughout this chapter, we will show that such a choice is somewhat troublesome. Indeed, not only has the xDFS protocol been designed from a high-level protocol view but also experiences in available development tools of server systems, advanced optimal programming techniques, and the existing hardware and software facilities have affected the specification, design method and implementation of the protocol. Noting this point is also required that a protocol specification highly dictates how to implement it at the software level. Following this section, we mention three major requirements for next-generation FTPs.

10.2.1 Towards a Low-Cost, Low-Power and Low-Overhead Data Transfer Protocol for Sensor and Ad Hoc Networks

Advances in mobile, wireless, and Internet technologies along with many of the existing smart portable devices provide pervasive access to a large amount of information. Unlimited mobility and ease in the deployment of ad hoc networks make them suitable for a broad diversity of applications such as military communications, disaster relief, and personal-area networking [7]. However, because sensors are tiny and low-cost devices, a variety of these networks have important constraints such as limited power, and limited memory and processing capacity. As implicitly expressed in these sentences, a file transfer system must consider the inherent heterogeneity of these wireless sensor networks (WSNs) [7]. The existence of an optimum, low-cost, and low-power data transfer system (or protocol) is more remarkable in the field of WSNs. DotDFS protocol attempts, about these points, to define a collection of sub-protocols that the needs of WSNs are also more considered through them. But it is necessary to note that we only remark a few insights of the xDFS protocol towards WSNs which researchers should investigate comprehensively. xDFS protocol, against FTP and GridFTP protocols, conforms itself in three aspects to the requirements of WSN networks:

a. FTP protocol (and consequently, the GridFTP protocol) requires two separate channels (control channel and data channel) which cause a client-side protocol implementation to have at least two threads of control in operating system level. Since WSNs usually use 8-bit microcontrollers, the concept of multithreading has nearly no position in them. In addition, even if a WSN could support multiple threads, then the use of them would impose large overheads, which would lead to much power dissipation in WSNs. DotDFS with merging these two channels and introducing the concept of X-Channels avoids these overheads [5, 6].

b. Fundamentally, FTP commands are sent and received as simple text strings (and follow the Telnet protocol, RFC 854 [8]) over control channels. This factor makes the WSNs need more memory and computational power to store and process strings, which unnecessarily will increase the power consumption. xDFS protocol with a fully binary model makes the problem resolved.

c. WSNs usually lack permanent storage systems due to power consumption issues, and ad hoc network devices may also have a small capacity of storage systems. For example, an ATMEL ATmega1281 8-bit microcontroller used in WSNs has 8 KB of RAM and 128 KB of ROM [9]. Therefore, the online data steaming feature plays a crucial role for WSNs. DFSM mode in DotDFS protocol can satisfy this requirement [5, 6].

10.2.2 Universality and Interoperability Issues and Scenario-Based Complexity Reduction

Two standards of HTTP [10] and FTP [1] on the Internet have been widely used for data transfers over decades. However, they have shown a series of weaknesses in the Internet industry. These issues appear as infrastructural problems in Grid environments. These shortcomings have led to suggesting several extensions in RFCs by the IETF organisation to resolve FTP problems (in Section 10.7 this issue is investigated in depth). Moreover, Grid applications and distributed environments require key features that are not supported by existing protocols used on the Internet. Of course, a few systems have been designed that provide features by special interfaces, but either only their client APIs are available or their underlying protocols and server source codes are not accessible.

Globus, with this assumption to introduce a protocol that can solve interoperability problems in such systems, proposes the GridFTP protocol for existing needs, particularly in Grid applications [2–4]. Globus makes such a claim, but only implements GridFTP protocol based on Globus Toolkit [11]. On the other hand, not only do FTP and GridFTP protocols cause interoperability issues between different implementations due to several extensions and lack of an integrated implementation, but rather GridFTP protocol as fully defined in OGF drafts can be only run in Unix-like environments. Furthermore, providing a native implementation of this protocol for other operating systems like Windows is a challenging task. Additionally, in this chapter, we will come up with structural issues in the design and implementation of the GridFTP protocol.

Globus explains two reasons for proposing GridFTP, including FTP as an IETF standard, and widely implemented and well-understood FTP protocol [2]. Of course, perhaps this Globus vision seems reasonable from this angle because Grid applications mainly assume that they have access to unlimited computing resources such as processors, storage systems, and high-bandwidth networks.

Nevertheless, what we witness in the real world represents the fact that current processing systems have different capabilities in terms of computing power and power consumption issues. Therefore, it can be concluded that the existence of a protocol that, in addition to considering a wide range of needs of various applications, requires having universality features and providing a cross-platform implementation is necessary.

Finally, it seems logically a good idea to propose a protocol that can reduce scenario-based complexities for classifying applications. The current work in this chapter is a great attempt to move towards constructing such a system. In other words, the DotDFS protocol has guided us to propose and implement another protocol called xDFS, as described in this chapter, which has been designed in native C++ with a cross-platform framework from scratch.

Furthermore, criticism is given to Globus Toolkit [11] which makes the GridFTP kernel development difficult for other researchers. It tends to require extensive experience with Grid technology and previous versions of the toolkit to understand the system design hierarchy. Then, it does require significant background reading to understand the range of software components available and the configuration required to develop significant new services. They are due to the range of issues that the toolkit addresses, and that it relies heavily upon other open-source projects and tools.

One of the difficulties with file transfer mechanisms like GridFTP is that all the unique features which they use cannot be applied outside of their architecture. This means that those who intend to use customised architectures must develop these features from scratch. The main goal of the xDFS protocol and its implementation in C++ is to solve this problem (by providing a compact, universal and cross-platform xDFS framework).

10.2.3 Towards a Service-Oriented Approach (SOA) for Secure File Transfers

To solve security problems related to FTP protocol, different methods and multiple RFCs have been suggested by IETF over the past five decades (see Table 10.6). GridFTP protocol also adds new extensions to address more security problems associated with Grid environments. These issues have led to an integration of security protocols and data transfer protocols used in the abstraction of FTP, which has made the protocol much more complex in terms of how to understand and efficiently implement it. We have separated extremely these two abstractions in the xDFS protocol. The separation of these two abstractions allows researchers to work individually to study and improve on the various parts of the xDFS protocol. In DotDFS design, we have tried to make use of service-oriented system concepts to segregate the file security abstraction from its transmission by using DotSec's Grid Security Infrastructure [5, 12].

10.3 High-Performance Server Design Architectures for Grid-Based File Transfer Protocols

High-performance server design plays a key role in satisfying the needs of different applications in a broad taxonomy of Internet services (like web servers) and Grid environments. Grid computing technologies have emerged from the heart of academic research work and also Grid applications mainly assume that they have access to unlimited computing resources (such as processors, storage systems, and high-bandwidth networks). Therefore, in this field of information technology, there has been paid less attention to the design principles of high-performance server architectures for reducing the additional overheads. Two practical examples can be pointed out to the fundamental problems discovered in the design and implementation of the GridFTP server by the Globus team [5, 6] and the Aneka Cloud Platform [13] developed on top of Alchemi [2, 14].

In this section, concerning the term *high-performance server design* in mind, a solid effort is taken to explain ways which specify a roadmap to performantly program server applications by developers in Grid and Cloud environments. It also makes the original idea behind the design and implementation of DotDFS and xDFS protocols clearer to the reader.

Whereas web servers play a vital role in delivering Web content to users for the enterprise's business in the Internet industry, they are the most critical network servers that must deal with a large number of user requests at once (in typical cases, 10,000 simultaneous requests or even more) and process them. Over the past three decades, extensive research in the design and implementation of optimised, stable, and reliable web servers has been made. This section also outlines the lessons taken from this interesting research arena [15–17].

In general, four main factors affect server application performance. Furthermore, these factors impress themselves on the classification of different server designs. They are data copies, memory allocation, context switches, and synchronisation issues. In the remainder of this section, we elaborate on these four factors in the design of server programs.

10.3.1 Data Copies

Eliminating unnecessary data copies can increase considerably the performance of most server applications. In the simplest case to prevent data copies, some primary methods like indirection and pass buffer descriptors (or chains of buffer descriptors) may be exploited rather than simply using buffer pointers. Avoiding data copies is sometimes very difficult in the development cycle of a server source code base. For instance, in some cases in which data is mapped into the user mode address space, different socket library implementations do one or more copies before delivering buffers to the network adaptor. Even in places where data copies are removed, additional overhead to read data and calculate a checksum still remains.

In fact, the main problem originating from the data copy is due to extra copies from userspace to kernel space and vice versa. Traditionally, the kernel has provided a layer of abstraction between applications and hardware, and also has been responsible to exchange data between them. This way requires two additional data transfers from an application program to the kernel and then to the hardware, compared with the scenario that an application program could have direct access to the hardware if needed. Moreover, this relationship between hardware and software allows using direct memory access (DMA) operations that will relieve the central processing unit (CPU), but such a capability does not exist between two pieces of software (i.e., between an application program and the kernel). A method called zero-copy enables such a feature. Zero-copy techniques fall into three categories as follows:

1. Data transfer optimisation between kernel and application program: This method is based on optimisation in CPU copies between kernel and userspace, where the traditional methods in classifying communications are maintained and a more flexible approach is achieved.
2. Avoidance and optimisation of in-kernel data copies: This class of techniques is going to implement new system calls or optimise traditional methods to achieve more performance in certain cases that data can be fully processed in the kernel.
3. A byway on the main data processing path: Regarding method 2, the kernel sometimes does not need to meet directly with data, and it can be avoided. On the other hand, this class of techniques allows direct data transfer between userspace memory and hardware, and the kernel just manages the transfer operation.

10.3.2 Memory Allocation

Memory allocation and de-allocation are two of the most important operations amongst long-running server programs. Two types of memory allocators exist called custom and general-purpose allocators. Many of the general-purpose memory allocators have been implemented for C and C++ languages. These allocators create a good running time and low fragmentation for a wide range of applications. However, the use of customised memory allocators can take benefit from application-specific behaviour. They can dramatically increase performance. Custom memory allocators can benefit from specific allocation patterns with many operations at the lowest level cost. For example, a programmer can make use of a region allocator to assign a number of small objects with a known lifecycle and frees all of them at a given time. This typical custom allocator returns individual objects from a range of memory, and then the whole region is de-allocated. To attain high performance, programmers often develop their own ad hoc custom allocators as macros or monolithic functions (like inline functions) to avoid function-call overhead. In fact, these methods to improve performance have been recognised as the best habits of skilled computer programmers. Generally, the requirements of a dynamic memory allocator system can be summarised as follows:

1. Stability: It is necessary to continuously keep the memory allocator system performance stable for long-running server programs. The throughput of such a system must remain stable over time.
2. Speed: Such a system must be as fast as possible in memory allocation and de-allocation. A memory block should not depend only on the thread that has allocated it. Threads must be able to operate collectively on a shared allocated memory area. This factor makes passing object references amongst different threads possible.

From other important points in the design of memory, allocators can be noted for scalability, size independency, and maximum locality.

10.3.3 Context Switching

Context switching is used as the basic mechanism to share a processor amongst multiple threads of execution. Each thread is dependent on general-purpose registers, status registers, and a processor state such as a program counter. A context switch is an operation to save the process state of a thread and load another thread, particularly in hardware-implementation context switching at the pipeline stages of a follow-on chip multi-threaded (CMT) processor (e.g., Fetch, Thread-Switch, Decode, Execute, Memory, and Writeback). If threads relate to different virtual address spaces, a context switch also contains switching the address translation maps used by the processor. Switching the address space requires that the relevant inputs in the process's address translation cache (TLB) are invalidated.

If the instruction or data caches are tagged using virtual memory addresses, they would have to be emptied as well. Context switching imposes a small performance penalty on threads in an MT environment. In addition to direct overheads concerned with a real context switching code, numerous other factors contribute to the over-head penalties. Another indirect overhead is due to disorder in branch-target buffers and CPU caches like instruction set, data, and address translation. However, another source of these indirect overheads may be attributed to the operating system memory paging. A context switch can result in an in-use memory page being moved to the disc if there is no free memory, thereby hurting the total performance.

Context switches can take place in the kernel. Kernel mode is a privileged mode of CPU, in which only kernel code is executed, and provides access to all of the memory locations and other operating system resources. Other programs, including applications that primarily are executed in user mode, can run parts of the kernel by system calls. The existence of such a structure is considered a mode switch (or mode transition) instead of a context switch because it does not change the state of the current process or running thread. So, a context switch is used as a mechanism to switch between two threads of execution. Therefore, we infer that a system call is not a context switch; indeed, it is akin to a simple function call that causes to change the state of processes from an unprivileged user mode to a privileged kernel mode. Memory mappings are not switched. Also, the return of the mode transition to user-space from the kernel during returning from a system call is similar to the return operation of a userspace function call.

In addition to context switches occurring between threads at the software level, in hardware a processor interrupt causes the state of a running task to be saved, whilst an interrupt service routine is executing. When the interrupt service routine is completed, the saved state will be restored. Whilst memory maps are not switched during interrupt servicing, it does hide the cache state and may also constitute some indirect overhead. Hence, context switching shows a substantial cost to the system in terms of CPU time for a typical operating system.

10.3.4 Synchronisation Issues

Programming complexity is an ambiguous issue in writing MT applications with shared memory regions. Although threads simplify the design logic of programs as possible, great skill and experience are required to ensure that the correct relationship amongst threads has been established. Errors for selection of appropriate synchro-nisation methods amongst a set of threads whilst accessing shared objects give rise to incorrect execution of programs. These methods are very sensitive in most cases.

In many programming languages, locks are essential synchronisation techniques to enforce limitations for having access to a resource in a computing environment in which many threads of execution exist. Two key constraints must always be consid-ered in using locks:

1. Performance: A complex trade-off often exists between programmability and performance because most programmers have to make their decisions on how to share data during the code development process using static information for dynamic runtime behaviour. Programmers usually use conservative synchroni-sation to write correct codes and keep them simple. Whilst such use can guar-antee correctness, create stable software, and lead to faster code development, it prohibits parallelism. Fine-grained locks may help improve performance,

but they make the code hard and error-prone to write. Coarse-grained locks may facilitate writing suitable code and reduce errors but hurt the key factor of efficiency. In addition to these problems, locks can impose very important overheads, serialise the execution of programs, and reduce the overall system performance.

2. Stability: If a thread acquires a lock and marks it as held, other threads acquiring this lock must wait until the lock is free. Such a wait can implicitly influence the system behaviour being designed. If the lock owner is de-scheduled by the operating system, other threads waiting for this lock cannot continue their execution since the lock is not free. If the lock owner aborts, other threads waiting for this lock will never complete; hence, this lock is never free. As seen in this scenario, the shared memory regions by an abnormal termination of a thread remain in an inconsistent state. This causes critical sections to be held in a messy granularity.

Widely-used, general-purpose locking mechanisms include mutexes, semaphores, condition variables and multiple readers and single-writer locks. Other major problems caused by locks are lock contention (due to excessively coarse granularity or inappropriate lock type), deadlock (each thread of control is waiting for a lock held by another thread of execution), lost locks, race conditions, and incomplete or buggy lock implementation. In total, the general overhead associated with locks can be summarised in the extra resources for using locks akin to the memory space allocated for locks, the time for acquiring or releasing locks, and the CPU time to initialise and destroy locks. Therefore, the more locks a program uses, the more overhead associated with the use.

10.4 Some Proposed xDFS Server Architectures in FTSM Upload Mode

With lessons taken from the four factors explained in the design of a high-performance and stable server, we can divide the existing, widely used server architectures into six main kinds including multiple-process architecture, multiple-thread architecture, single-process event-driven architecture, multiple-process event-driven architecture, multiple-thread event-driven architecture, and staged event-driven architecture (SEDA) [18]. Each of these architectures has advantages and disadvantages in designing every given application-specific server. One of the chief novel contributions of this chapter is to extend these architectures relying upon the inherent structures of the DotDFS and xDFS FTPs.

In all these models, we consider a file transfer scenario as xDFS or DotDFS FTSM Upload mode that is in progress from one client to the server using n parallel connections per each transfer session. Although these models have their own novelty suggested by the authors, it is worthwhile to note that, as stated in Section 10.6, the core of the Parvicursor server has conceptually been constructed by using a hybrid server architecture. Even though these models offer an abstraction for server-side protocol implementations, it is also required to note that all implementations of client-side APIs have benefited practically from these quasi-server-side architectures for designing a whole real-time, high-performance client-server system. Because the number of pages of this chapter is limited, we omit to describe the details of client-side implementations in this section. As follows, we suggest and explore three major models more suitable to design high-performance servers in the areas of FTPs and file servers. The first model has classically been used extensively (such as the GridFTP server), but the second and third architectures are proposed completely by the authors.

10.4.1 Multi-Processed xDFS Server Architecture

Let's start with a familiar case: a client intends to upload a large file to an xDFS server through the well-known n parallel TCP streams using FTSM mode. As shown in Figure 10.1, in the multi-processed (MP) model, a process called the *acceptor process* gets the new connections inside the body of the main() function. Each client request gets mapped into a process which manages the TCP stream. Figure 10.1 illustrates the set of n processes to represent one xDFS FTSM session. Process 1 to n may be retrieved from a process pool, or if there do not exist either enough or idle processes in the process pool, then the *acceptor process* can call the system functions, POSIX fork()/Win32 CreateProcess(), which create a new process to manage the new connection.

Synchronisation can be challenging in this MP model because each of the processes is executed in separate address spaces. This problem can be resolved by using an Inter-Process Communication (IPC) technique. This IPC mechanism, for example, may be used for passing the client socket handles to the processes, and for synchronisation amongst multiple processes, the main() function and the process pool. As it can be derived from Figure 10.1, the MP model imposes three major overheads on the system, including large open file handles, heavyweight context switches, and excessive off-chip/on-chip memory used.

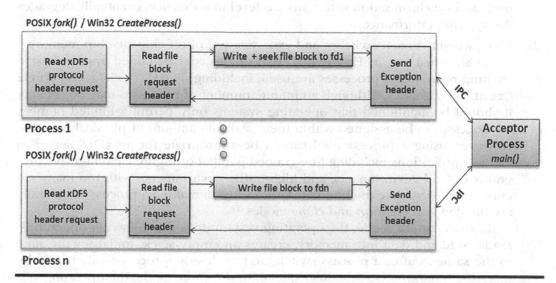

Figure 10.1   Multi-processed xDFS server architecture.

1. Large open file handles
    In the MP model, a file handle is opened per process. The set $\{fd_1, fd_2, ..., fd_n\}$ represents open file handles for n parallel connections. These n processes are concurrently receiving file blocks from the client. A single file through n separate file handles is shared to be written by the system function write() amongst multiple processes. From two perspectives, this model can significantly decrease the file transfer throughput of a single xDFS FTSM session. One negative factor on performance is the non-deterministic distribution of random disc seeks amongst n parallel processes. It is also necessary to note that each operating system according to its underlying I/O scheduling algorithms and policies usually behaves typically differently on the disc I/O throughput. Disc schedulers in current operating systems are generally work-conserving, i.e., they schedule a request as soon as the previous request has finished.

    The overhead of acquiring and releasing each lock in the OS kernel may become considerable on the overall disc I/O throughput. File system performance is often a major component of the total system performance, and, in this case, is heavily dependent on the nature of the server application operating the workload. Indeed, the use of the MP model with large open file handles can cause four major performance penalties. It increases the number of I/Os to the underlying device(s). It violates the grouping of smaller I/O requests together into larger I/Os where possible. It cannot be used to optimise the seek pattern to reduce the amount of time spent waiting for disc seeks; disc seeks are expensive head repositioning operations. Finally, it is not possible to cache as much data as realistic to reduce physical I/Os.

    Perhaps at first glance, it seems clear that these problems can be avoided in the following manner: An extra process called the *disc I/O process* has access to a single file handle, to write file blocks individually coherently to the disc, and all other processes have access to the *disc I/O process* by an IPC mechanism. However, this technique implies that the use of an extra process, an IPC mechanism and synchronisation at the process level in userspace, eventually degrades the system performance.

2. Heavyweight context switches and excessive use of off-chip/on-chip memory
    As sketched out in Figure 10.1, two of the coarse-grained approaches to creating new system processes are used, including, POSIX fork() and Win32 CreateProcess(). Although an infinite number of processes may be created, it should be mentioned that operating systems only permit a limited number of processes to be assigned within their available amount of physical memory. However, using a process pool cannot be appropriate for an xDFS server in crucial applications including fine-grained parallel or highly data-intensive programs in Grid environments, and high-traffic environments with too many clients' connections like the Internet. Approaches to making a process structurally are divided into *creation* and *clone* modes.

    In the *creation* mode, the operating system does the following operations: loads code and data into memory, creates an empty stack, initialises the state to the same as after a process switch, and makes the process ready to run by inserting it into the OS scheduler queue. In the *clone* mode, the operating system performs the following operations: stops the current process and stores its state (i.e., transiently freezing the entire application, especially in the case of a server software program), makes a copy of the current code, stack, and OS state; and makes the new-born process run.

Forks are in the *clone* mode whilst processes made by calling the system function CreateProcess() are in the *creation* mode. As can be seen in the MP model, processes impose two other important overheads, including excessive use of off-chip/ on-chip memory, and heavyweight context switches due to using n processes. Also, process context switching implies getting a new address space in place by page table and other memory mechanisms.

10.4.2 Multi-Threaded xDFS Server Architecture

Choosing an appropriate thread model for server programs is a complex decision influenced by many factors, including, performance constraints, software maintainability, and the presence of existing code. To some extent, for reducing the process-based overhead of the MP model, MT architecture is proposed for the xDFS server in FTSM mode. The MT structure is shown in Figure 10.2. In this model, processes are replaced with threads. These multiple kernel threads share a single address space and are accessible to all threads. Each thread manages one stream from the remaining

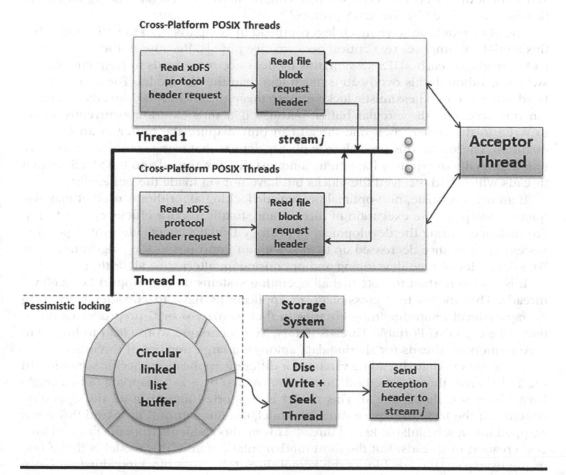

Figure 10.2   Multi-threaded xDFS server architecture.

n-1 streams. In the MT model, threads can share all public information; it makes it possible to remove the IPC mechanism used in the MP model and allows the *thread acceptor* directly to manage running threads. Threads are lightweight processes and expose much less overhead than the MP model on server applications. This model substantially reduces the total memory (physical and virtual or swap space memory) used by programs. To eliminate overheads due to large open file handles, in the proposed MT model, a thread named the *disc thread* is used to manage to write() and seek() operations for the file blocks received from the client. In Figure 10.2, the *disc thread* only opens a single file handle from the requested file.

File blocks are put into a circular buffer which contains file blocks most recently received from the client. To avoid race conditions, a pessimistic locking mechanism is used. The thread that intends to put a received file block into the circular buffer first acquires the buffer lock, and then independently takes action to fill the buffer. The *disc thread* attempts to arrive at a relative coherency and reduce the number of discs seeks through a scatter/gather I/O mechanism to contiguously write the contents stored in the circular buffer into the storage system as a whole. This buffering method can significantly decrease a lot of successive calls to the function system seek() for performance improvement. Further, the *disc thread* must inform the xDFS client of correct and errorless receiving of the file block via sending an exception header defined by the xDFS protocol.

The MT model can have much less overhead in comparison to the MP model, but this model still imposes two critical performance pitfalls. Because of the existence of n+1 threads for each xDFS session, this model once more leads to frequent context switches, although this overhead is much less than the MP model. The second overhead is the use of a pessimistic locking mechanism to synchronise threads for simultaneous access to the circular buffer, because if n threads are concurrently ready to write to the buffer, then one thread can only acquire the buffer in an OS time quantum. Therewith, this procedure explicitly depicts that many context switches are unintentionally disparately happening amongst the disc thread and the xDFS session threads which had received file blocks but have not yet made the buffer dirty.

If an inappropriate, non-optimal pessimistic locking algorithm is used, it may frequently postpone the execution of threads and, finally, reduce efficiency drastically. For instance, during the development of primary DotDFS client-side prototypes, the system performance decreased up to 50% with an improper locking algorithm used. We spent a lot of time developing and optimising an alternative algorithm.

It is also important to note that all operating systems do not support kernel-level threads. This means that cross-platform applications have to consider employing userspace-level multi-threading libraries in their C macros or C preprocessor directives, like the GNU Portable Threads library. This technique would lead to high synchronisation overheads for sharing data amongst a large number of threads.

There are multiple threading variants for different application-specific scenarios. In the 1:1 (kernel threads) method, threads are created by a 1-1 mapping onto a single kernel-level scheduled thread. This model is supported almost in all the operating systems. In the N:1 (userspace threads) model, the number of N user-land threads is mapped into a schedulable kernel thread. This method benefits from the fast and low-cost creation of threads. But the most fundamental pitfall of this model is that if one of the userspace threads blocks the kernel thread due to a blocking situation (such as in disc I/O-bound cases), then all other threads are ready to run will be blocked. In the N:M (scheduler activations) [19], equal to the number of N userspace threads are mapped to the number of M kernel threads. As a whole, the N:M model is less spread across the family of operating systems in contrast to other models, because an N:M library implementation requires extensive changes to both kernel and userspace codes.

10.4.3 Multi-Threaded Event-Driven Pipelined xDFS Server Architecture

In this section, we propose a multi-threaded event-driven pipelined (MTEDP) architecture for the xDFS server operating the FTSM mode in which multiple pipelined apartments are overlapped in execution. To increasingly enhance the performance of the xDFS server, MTEDP eliminates the synchronisation mechanisms used in the MP and MT models and reduces the number of context switches to a large extent. Figure 10.3 shows the MTEDP architecture. Due to the similarity of Figure 10.3 with pipelining techniques in computer organisation, we included the term *pipelined* in the phrase MTEDP.

These m pipelines, in which each pipeline contains n parallel connections, actually indicate m parallel file transfer sessions in FTSM mode. Each pipeline manages one transfer session. In this model, each pipeline in each thread owns n socket handles, and these handles, to asynchronously send and receive data over sockets, are managed through event-dispatching and multiplexing techniques realised as a collection of comprehensive communicating fine state machines. As it is obvious, each pipeline has an open file handle and this would lead to the avoidance of using pessimistic locking mechanisms, which reduces the performance in the MT model, and the problem associated with large open file handles in the MP model.

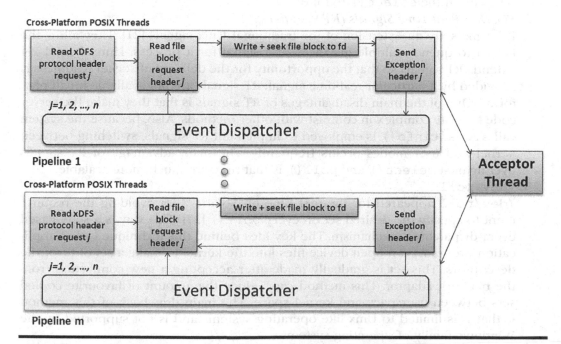

Figure 10.3   Multi-threaded event-driven pipelined xDFS server architecture.

Table 10.1   The Number of Threads

$$T_{MT} = \sum_{i=1}^{m}(n_i + 1) = \frac{m.(m+1)}{2} + \sum_{i=1}^{m} n_i$$	(10.1)
$$T_{MTEDP} = m$$	(10.2)

Now, we can derive the relationships in Table 10.1 to represent the number of threads created in an xDFS server for both the MT and MTEDP models, in which m stands for the number of FTSM transfer sessions, and each of which has n_i parallel connections.

There are different event-dispatching and multiplexing network I/O mechanisms. However, some of them are implementation-specific to some operating systems, each of which has particular advantages and disadvantages. In general, these mechanisms can be split into four major groups:

1. `select()` *and* `poll()`

   The `select()` and `poll()` system calls are stated-based event-dispatching mechanisms. They report the current status of a set of sockets as their input arguments. When there are a large number of sockets, `select()` is more suitable because less data is copied to or from the kernel. The `select()` function is available on most platforms, but `poll()` is less pervasive (e.g., `WSAPloll()` has been added to the Windows Vista operating system and its later versions [20]). For this reason, the implementation of both xDFS client and server cores relies upon the `select()` routine.

2. *POSIX.4 Real Time Signals (RT Signals)*

   RT signals are an extension of the traditional Unix signals [21]. They allow the kernel to queue multiple instances of a signal for a process. Linux kernel 2.4 extends RT signals so that the opportunity for the delivery of socket readiness is provided by a particular real-time signal. RT signals are not available on all platforms. One of the main disadvantages of RT signals is that they make the server code to write complex in contrast with other methods. Also, because the system call `sigwaitinfo()` is employed to implement RT signals, switching between kernel and user modes occurs frequently. The main advantage of RT signals over against `select()` and `poll()` is that they are much more scalable.

3. `/dev/poll`

   `/dev/poll` appeared for the first time on Solaris 7 for avoiding the requirement to specify the desired set on every `poll()` [22]. This way is a state-based event-dispatching mechanism. The key idea behind this technique is that application programs can open device files into the kernel to make a set of favourite descriptors. This set is gradually made after accepting a new connection from the network adaptor. This method can reduce the amount of favourite copied sets between userspace and kernel space. The main drawback of this method is that it is limited to Unix-like operating systems and is not supported by the Windows family of operating systems.

4. *NT Completion Ports and POSIX AIO*

NT I/O completion ports [23] supply an efficient threading model for processing multiple asynchronous I/O requests on a multiprocessor system. When a process creates an I/O completion port, the system creates an associated queue object for requests whose sole purpose is to service these requests. Processes that handle many concurrent asynchronous I/O requests can do so more quickly and efficiently by using I/O completion ports in conjunction with a preallocated thread pool than by creating threads at the time they receive an I/O request. Completion ports are only available on Windows platforms.

The POSIX AIO interface [24] allows a process or thread to start multiple simultaneous read and/or write operations to multiple file descriptors, to wait for or obtain completion notification of requested operations, and to retrieve the status of completed operations. One of the current AIO's disabling downsides is that they are not applicable to Linux kernel-mode AIO for network I/O subsystems (e.g., sockets) and also are not available on Windows platforms.

10.5 DotDFS and xDFS File Transport Protocols

DotDFS and xDFS are general-purpose network protocols to fulfil the goals of high-throughput file transfers and network file systems. DotDFS protocol was proposed based on the demands of Grid communities. xDFS investigates new objectives beyond its predecessor. xDFS adds so many new extensions to the DotDFS protocol to facilitate the use of xDFS protocol in other dynamic environments such as Cloud Computing and the Internet. xDFS protocol allows multiple clients to have simultaneous access to managed files and directories (for the large or small size of volumes with a high-throughput performance) hosted on desktop, dedicated server systems, or any other computing entity. Additionally, it makes it possible to access other services including inter-process communication, remote file streaming, and authenticated transports over all xDFS channels. Generally speaking, xDFS is a client-driven protocol in which a client requests the server and the server replies to the client. xDFS is both a stateless and a stateful protocol. It mandates several protocol-level states to maintain security contexts and cryptographic mechanisms via xSec (DotSec) protocol and file access semantics such as locking.

Furthermore, the xDFS protocol defines a set of specifications to achieve the aggregating throughput of widely used TCP protocol in WAN and MAN networks for file transfers. It enables multiple clients to simultaneously share files on server systems. It ultimately leads to facilitating collaboration, and efficiently using and centrally managing resources.

Also, we have seen in recent years, that data-intensive distributed file system frameworks are emerging as a major component of large-scale Internet services and Cloud Computing paradigms. These frameworks are designed from scratch and provide specific facilities for some applications. Three key examples of these frameworks are Google File System [25], Hadoop distributed file system [26], and Amazon S3 [27].

xDFS framework comes up with numerous high-performance services and protocols. Hence, different contemporary and ongoing projects can be facilitated in the aspects of design and implementation using the xDFS framework as a key low-level underlying file transport protocol, particularly for future data Grid and data Cloud platforms.

DotDFS protocol introduced three operating modes, including FTSM, DFSM, and PathM [5, 6, 12]. The DotDFS protocol, with three of these modes, was an attempt to accommodate the needs expressed earlier in this chapter. xDFS protocol in a new look to these three modes tries to highly extend DotDFS features in more compliance with Internet services. In this chapter, the FTSM mode is fully considered. Section 10.5.1 discusses overall xDFS features, and Sections 10.5.2 and 10.6 take a comprehensive description of the xFTSM protocol.

10.5.1 Overall xDFS Features

10.5.1.1 Transport Independence

xDFS protocol does not necessarily require the use of any specific network transport protocol. TCP is the default scheme of a connection-oriented transport protocol used to carry xDFS binary headers. As a whole, this flexibility is due to the layered model of xDFS specification. xDFS employs Parvicursor Socket Interface (PSI) architecture for underlying transport protocol in the lowest layer. For example, the highly extensible PSI architecture allows developers to implement xDFS over a variety of transport stacks such as SCTP [28], UDT [29], and RDMA [30] with the minimum changes in xDFS C++ source codes. Since the main audience of the xDFS protocol is various purposes on the Internet, a major part of this chapter discusses the implementation of xDFS over TCP-enabled PSI.

10.5.1.2 Flexible Connectivity

In xDFS protocol, a single client can connect to multiple servers, or it can establish one or more connections on each server. The activity of multiple client processes can be multiplexed over a single connection. This feature represents the support of reusable channel mechanisms in the xDFS protocol.

10.5.1.3 Feature Negotiation and Prerequisites

Because the collection of xDFS protocols during the coming years will always be evolving, the feature negotiation was added to xDFS. This feature provides the negotiation of dialect and the supported feature set of the protocol between two endpoints. For instance, before connection establishment between a client and a server the protocol version is negotiated and used for more interoperability and the support of legacy applications. As another example, the negotiation of a per-connection basis is used to choose the type of transmission channel.

10.5.1.4 Resource Access

A client can simultaneously access multiple resources shared across remote computing entities. Additionally, a client can have access to files and directories for different purposes. As a unique feature, the support of named-pipe inter-process communication was added to the set of xDFS protocols. A client can open, read, write, and close named pipes on a target server. Named pipes can be used as a communication path between client and server processes. This feature enables the possibility of using xDFS protocol in parallel computing applications based upon a concept of distributed remote file access.

10.5.1.5 Unicode File Name Support

Since xDFS protocol extends DotDFS protocol and is implemented based on native C++, it uses features of the Parvicursor.NET Framework classes for string manipulation. The class *System::String* supports the default format of Unicode strings. All the Parvicursor Framework's methods and functions make use of this primitive data type. They are redirected to the native Unicode strings before having access to call Win32 or POSIX APIs. This feature not only has no overhead but also leads to more xDFS multilingual universality.

10.5.1.6 Distributed File System Mode (DFSM)

This requested mode supports access to files and data sharing mechanisms, which have been employed in conventional distributed file systems. Additionally, this mode can be used for stripped and third-party data transfers. One good example of this mode is a situation with one or more transport streams between m network endpoints sending side and n network endpoints on the receiving side.

10.5.1.7 Path Mode (PathM)

The design goal of PathM mode is to support basic features like the creation/deletion of remote files/directories and relevant features. In the PathM mode, the xDFS server operates similar to an RPC server, but all methods requested by the client are previously defined as binary in the client-server negotiation protocol.

10.5.1.8 Authentication, Data Integrity, and Data Confidentiality

DotGrid [5, 6, 12, 14, 31] and Parvicursor projects are architectural constructs implemented as layered frameworks and are executed on top of PSI. xSec (DotSec) is the layer above PSI and provides secure communications between endpoints based on xSec (DotSec) TSI [5]. xSec is a lightweight grid security infrastructure. It is designed as a unified security model in the Parvicursor platform. xDFS protocol requires all channels shall be authenticated according to services provided by the xSec security layer. xSec, the new version of the DotSec protocol, was also implemented in native code. After authentication/authorisation steps, all channels are encrypted if the higher layers or application programs request it from the xSec layer.

10.5.2 xDFS xFTSM Protocol

The xDFS protocol is more sophisticated than the FTP and GridFTP protocols (and even the DotDFS protocol) in terms of structure and extensibility. xDFS using a fully binary protocol model and requiring the use of comprehensive finite state machines precisely defines a wide range of mechanisms and operations. This approach complicates the feasible implementations of the xDFS protocol, but ultimately significantly increases the performance and throughput of those systems that have been developed atop the xDFS framework.

Primarily, DotDFS with the introduction of the File Transfer System Mode (FTSM) sub-protocol tried to suggest a new file transfer paradigm to solve a set of problems. They were to support parallel connections and negotiate TCP window size between a client and a server [5, 12]. These two methods relieved partly the problems due to making TCP protocol the widely used transport protocol layer in the OSI model when transferring files with large sizes to increase the network throughput in high-latency WAN networks. xDFS protocol extends FTSM mode and proposes xFTSM architecture. xFTSM mode inherits all the properties of FTSM, changes the former FTSM structure, and adds new extensions to it.

Today, the design of state-of-the-art network protocols is an art of engineering. However, a standard protocol is assigned to allow different implementations to interoperate. Therefore, a standard protocol should summarise the operation of its feasible implementations. The selection of multiple implementations and many other engineering details often make the formal specification of a protocol difficult. Lack of formal specification as seen in the process of developing the IETF standards has two important negative results: The protocol accuracy is not easily verifiable, and the protocol may be ambitious in some respects. First, bugs are continuously identified and resolved in the standard protocol. Second, the protocol ambiguities can open adequate space for bugs and even attacks. These altogether are identified in an ad hoc way. Third, protocols may be used without the verification of accuracy.

According to these points and that xDFS has become more complex than its previous versions, there shall be made use of more powerful methods than common methods employed for documenting the IETF standard protocols. We widely utilise communicating finite state machines (CFSMs) to propose and design xDFS protocol. An example of CFSMs will be mentioned in Section 10.6.

The formal model of a CFSM plays an important role in three various areas of network protocol design: formal validation, protocol synthesis, and conformance testing. Protocol formal validation is a powerful technique for automatically checking that a collection of communicating processes in the CFSM is free from concurrency-related errors. Protocol synthesis is used to derive an implementation-level protocol specification from the service specification. Protocol conformance testing is a kind of testing by which an implementation of a protocol entity is tested with respect to its specification for efficiency or interoperability purposes.

To precisely understand the structure of the xDFS protocol, we present a preliminary introduction to CFSM), because we will take advantage of CFSMs to describe xDFS.

Over the past 50 years, a variety of formal models have been proposed and studied to facilitate the specification and validation of concurrent systems. One major example is communication protocols where protocol entities interact with each other under a set of rigorous rules. Designing concurrent systems is known as a significantly deep problem. One of the major sources of difficulties with concurrent systems is because the function of these systems inclines to become very complex and too large. To describe a concurrent system is difficult to the way that it operates in an environment throughout infinite time. The functional behaviour of a system is defined by a large number of ongoing system interactions with its environment, and these interactions often exhibit complex interdependencies. Therefore, it is very difficult to describe, understand and predict the behaviour of these concurrent systems, and finally to examine whether their needs are met or not.

A suitable model for describing communication protocols and concurrent systems is CFSMs. In the CFSM model, a protocol is defined as a collection of processes (i.e., protocol entities) that exchange messages over error-free simplex channels. Each process is modelled as a finite state machine (FSM) and each simplex channel is a FIFO queue. A protocol state is composed of a state for each FSM and content for each simplex channel. A state transition occurs only when the process is ready to send a message to one of its output channels or receives a message from one of its input channels. The CFSM model is an elegant and well-defined structure, and rather easy to understand. These features have made it very attractive for industry and academia. The CFSM model virtually has become a de facto standard to specify, verify, and test communication protocols in the telecommunication industry.

After this, we assume that a client intends to connect to an xDFS server through n parallel channels. A channel in xDFS protocol is an abstract concept during which the interaction of operation and data flows takes place between network endpoints. xFTSM and xPathM modes flow through these stateful channels. Furthermore, because the architecture of xDFSM and xPathM modes is beyond the scope of this chapter, we no longer discuss them fully in this section (interested readers can refer to [5] for further information).

These n parallel channels for xFTSM mode over TCP pipes are the same mechanisms of parallel TCP connections used to increase the throughput in wide-area networks. These n parallel channels for xPathM mode can denote n routes on the side that have been requested from it; they can improve the system efficiency for transferring directory trees especially in the case of a lot of small files. The implementation of xPathM mode may be taken advantage of multiple threads to handle parallel channels, which can contribute dramatically to the performance in terms of optimal use of threading concurrency. However, it is strictly recommended to limit the number of created threads equal to the number of available processor cores in xPathM mode so that additional overhead as much as possible can be avoided due to context switching. To achieve the maximum performance of the proposed protocol in xFTSM mode, xDFS requires the client-server developers to use event-dispatching and multiplexing methods for managing parallel network I/Os in which a client or a server shall create one thread per session at most. The proposed model due to compatibility with this requirement compulsorily relieves different xDFS implementations.

In the rest of this chapter, we assume that a client and a server are negotiating to upload and download files with large sizes over xFTSM channels. It must also be emphasised that whereas channels are a general concept in xDFS protocol, they can be built over different transport protocols utilising the underlying PSI stack such as TCP, SCTP [28], UDT [29] and RDMA [30].

Figure 10.4 shows the client-server xDFS protocol sequence diagram in xFTSM and xPathM modes. A client chooses the xFTSM mode after connecting to the server, selecting xDFS service and authentication in step 5. Steps 1 to 7 are repeated for all n parallel channels involved in this process. The first client channel connected to

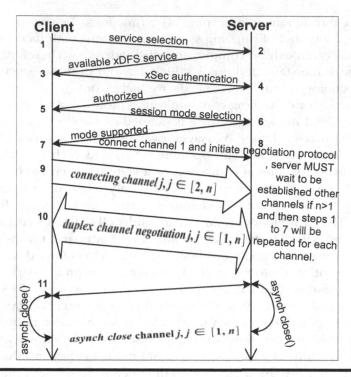

Figure 10.4 Client-server xDFS protocol sequence diagram in xFTSM and xPathM modes. n is the number of parallel channels.

Table 10.2 Parameters of the Negotiation Protocol

Local file name (to be written in download mode or to be read in upload mode).	Remote file name (to be written in upload mode or to be read in download mode).
The number of parallel channels for xFTSM and xPathM modes.	Protocol version and a unique session identifier specified by GUIDs.
TCP window size in bytes.	Desired block size of the used underlying storage system in bytes.
User credentials.	Extended mode (such as the xDFS protocol's zero-copy parameters, etc.).

the server is responsible to register a new xFTSM transmission session at the xDFS server side. This channel-based session registration shall be performed at the stage of negotiation protocol by a unique session identifier. The most important parameter passed in this step is the number of parallel channels n. Table 10.2 illustrates some parameters of the negotiation protocol. The data structure of the negotiation protocol (and any xDFS structure or object that requires to be transferred between endpoints) is transformed into a native binary format using Parvicursor Object Passing Interface (POPI) that later can be retrieved into its initial form.

In Parvicursor.NET Framework, serialisation is the low-level process of converting the state of an object into a form that can be persisted or transported. POPI can be easily implemented in many languages and platforms.

After completing the session registration step by the first client channel, the server shall wait until the remaining n-1 channel(s) are established. After getting all the channels established, there are n duplex channels between client and server which, on the demand of a client, could lead to parallel data transfer in either type of mode (upload or download). One of the new and unique extensions in the xDFS protocol is the abstraction of channel events added to the duplex channel negotiation as shown in Figure 10.4. This way in all channels the client or server can change the operating mode during the xDFS session from xFTSM to xPathM or vice versa. To further clarify this new extension, it is necessary to describe the structure of message interchange formats exchanged in the duplex channel negotiation in the form of headers between the client and server. DotDFS protocol refereed the term *data transfers* to step 10 of Figure 10.4 [5, 6]. Nevertheless, the xDFS protocol changes the term *data transfers*, refers it to as the term *duplex channel negotiation*, and provides the feasibility of operation flow, data flow, or a combination of both through the duplex channel negotiation. This evolutionary extension on xDFS highly expands the protocol in terms of functionality and extensibility for the development of future xDFS Framework versions.

An illustration of a general xDFS protocol channel binary header encapsulated in xSec TSI (transmission security interface) header appears in Figure 10.5 during step 10 of Figure 10.4. The description of the xSec TSI Header is beyond the scope of this chapter, which encrypts all xDFS channels. Channel event represents the structure of channel headers and generally describes the operation flow and data flow in step 10 of Figure 10.4. Because the channel event exhibits highly structural complexity in the xDFS specification, the pattern of xDFS channels MUST be characterised in finite state machines. Some types of channel events are shown in Table 10.3.

The structure of a channel header related to xFTSMD and xFTSMU types is shown in Figure 10.5. xFTSM header stores the information of data file blocks that are being transferred (such as the file block offset and block length). In xFTSMU and xFTSMD types, depending on the data flow, a set of operations are executed at the client-server sides as follows: reading from local storage and sending to the remote server (in the upload scenario initiated by the client) and receiving from the remote server and writing to local storage (in download scenario initiated by the client).

Implementations to satisfy the support of various types of channel events shall be considered as a collection of FSMs at the level of protocol and source codes to reduce complexities as broadly as possible.

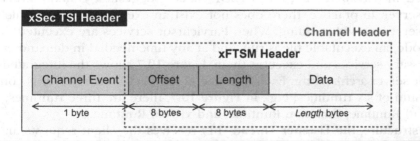

Figure 10.5   A general xDFS protocol channel binary header encapsulated in xSec TSI header.

Table 10.3   Some Types of Channel Events

Type	Description
EOFT	End of file reached and the session must be terminated by closing all channels.
EOFR	End of file reached in that channel but it must change its state to reusable channel mode.
xFTSMU	Initiate or change to xFTSM upload channel mode.
xFTSMD	Initiate or change to xFTSM download channel mode.
xPathM	Initiate or change to xPathM channel mode.
NOOP	No operation command over the channel.
CONM	Continue and maintain the previous channel event state.
ZxDFS	This channel is negotiating with a remote channel in the zero-copy version of xDFS channels.

10.6 The Native, Cross-Platform, and Cross-Language Implementation of xDFS Protocol

In this section, a concrete explanation of the new xDFS implementation in native code is given atop Parvicursor.NET Framework. Furthermore, a novel and new xDFS hybrid concurrency pattern (HCP) is proposed.

10.6.1 The Architecture of xDFS Implementation in Download and Upload Modes

The main core of the xDFS implementation is inspired by C# source codes of the DotDFS protocol. Anywhere it has been required according to the philosophy of the Parvicursor project, the C#-based DotDFS codes have been mapped into C++ codes. This sample mapping is important to prove the preliminary goal of the Parvicursor. NET Framework for an application program in the real world. Figure 10.6 portrays a simplified mapping of the C# xDfsClient class into its equivalent ISO C++ class. As seen in this figure due to innate correspondency between the structural syntax of the C++ and C# languages, Parvicursor.NET makes a suitable framework for programmers to develop software systems in native C++ environments.

As stated in Section 10.4.3, the MTEDP model suggests a general structure for the xDFS server. In practice, there does not exist an executable process file named the xDFS server notwithstanding. When Parvicursor services are executed on every network node, an executable file is run, and at any time needed in demand, it instantiates necessary services and executes them. Figure 10.7 shows the integrated hybrid Parvicursor server architecture. Each instance of the Parvicursor server is comprised of a minimum of six runtimes; e.g., in Figure 10.7, there are three runtimes, including, xThread Runtime, Common Runtime, and xFTSM Runtime.

In this structure, the Listener Thread (LT) receives the client requests and looks for what kind of service has been requested from the server through the transferred

```
// The managed CLI-based C# code
using namespace System;
using namespace System.Collections;
using namespace System.Net.Sockets;
class xDfsClient
{
    protected String host;
    protected ArrayList sockets;

    public xDfsClient(String host, Int32 port)
    {
        sockets = new ArrayList();
        Console.WriteLine(host.Trim() + port.ToString());
    }
}
```

(a)

```
// The native Parvicursor.NET CLI-based C++ code
#include <Parvicursor.h>
#pragma comment(lib, "Parvicursor.lib")
using namespace System;
using namespace System::Collections;
using namespace System::Net::Sockets;
class xDfsClient : public Object
{
protected:
    String *host;
    ArrayList *sockets;
public:
    xDfsClient(String *host, Int32 port)
    {
        sockets = new ArrayList();
        Console::WriteLine(host->Trim() + port.ToString());
        // or
        cout << host->Trim() << port << endl;
    }
    ~xDfsClient()
    {
        if(sockets != null)
            delete sockets;
        sockets = null;
    }
};
```

(b)

Figure 10.6 Direct mapping between C#-based and native C++-based DotDFS/xDFS source codes: (a) managed C# CLI code and (b) native Parvicursor.NET C++ CLI-based code.

header over the Parvicursor Socket Interface (PSI) channels. xThread is a new Parvicursor service, akin to the DotThreading model from the DotGrid platform [12, 14, 31], as discussed in Chapter 9, that allows computational threads to be distributed across Grid nodes. Common Runtime has several duties such as monitoring all running threads and the used physical memory by the clients' requests, load-balancing between the execution cycles of threads in the entire CPU cores, and eventually the complete management of a full set of Parvicursor services running at server side.

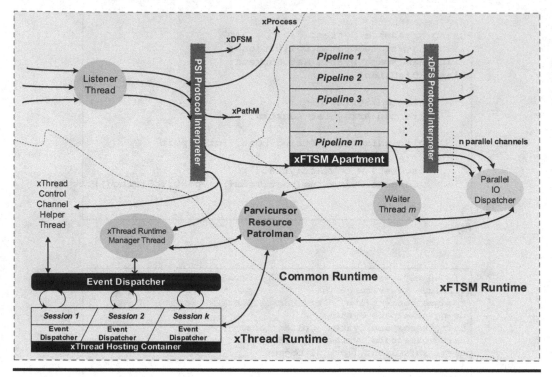

Figure 10.7   Integrated hybrid Parvicursor server architecture.

xFTSM Runtime is the same implementation of the MTEDP model for file transfers in download and upload mode. Each pipeline in xFTSM Runtime is a container for one xFTSM session which is processing n parallel channels. xFTSM Apartment also manages n parallel channels. Waiter Thread is a thread which is run by LT to manage the execution flow of every service on demand. Each collection of n parallel channels is simultaneously processed by a special module called Parallel I/O Dispatcher (PIOD). PIOD implements a C++ class interface in which one can extend its kernel relying on an extensive set of network event-dispatching mechanisms discussed in Section 10.4.3. PIOD, according to the type of upload or download mode, transfers the data packets between a client and a server through the asynchronous disc and network I/O methods. In Figure 10.7, if we assume that Session k has S_k local threads, then because Common Runtime and xThread Runtime, and xFTSM Runtime contain respectively three and m threads, so the total number of threads in a Parvicursor server's instance can be calculated from the relation 1 of Table 10.4 at any moment of time.

Table 10.4   The Number of Threads

$T_{hybrid} = 3 + m + \sum_{i=1}^{k}(S_i + 1) = 3 + m + \dfrac{k.(k+1)}{2} + \sum_{i=1}^{k} S_i$	(10.3)

To fully understand the architectural implementation of the Parvicursor server in xFTSM mode and more details on the way in which xDFS protocol functions in each either mode of client-server upload or download, we use CFSMs. Four corresponding CFSMs are illustrated in Figures 10.8–10.11. For two reasons, the first the download mode is usually used on the Internet, and the other is the page limitation of this chapter; we only describe the client-server CFSMs of the xDFS protocol in this section.

In Figure 10.8, after authenticating the client through xSec GSI, choosing the xFTSM mode by the client, and receiving the xFTSM parameters, the server checks whether the session has already been created using its GUID by the client or not. If the session already exists and the number of sockets in the hash table is not corresponding (equal) to the value of n received from the client, the server adds the new client stream to the hash table in state 8. In step 7, the server concurrently checks, so that if the number of client streams is equal to the value of n, then it moves the CFSM flow to state 9. If an error occurs during states 1 to 8, the next state will be 18.

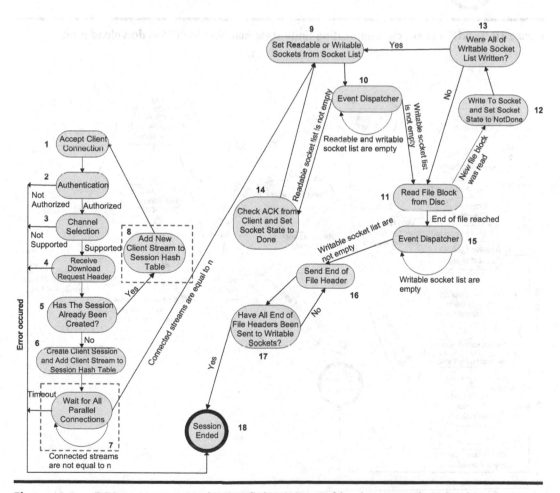

Figure 10.8   xDFS server communicating finite state machine in xFTSM download mode.

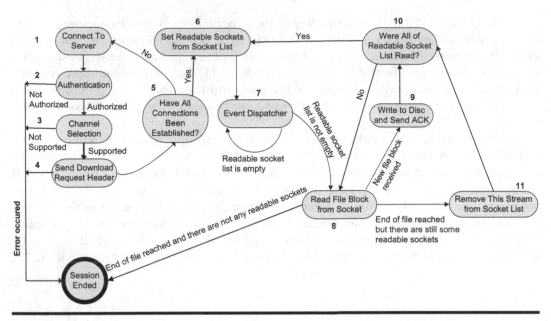

Figure 10.9   xDFS client communicating finite state machine in xFTSM download mode.

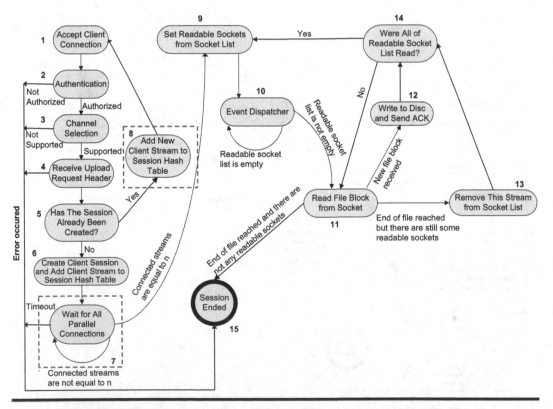

Figure 10.10   xDFS server communicating finite state machine in xFTSM upload mode.

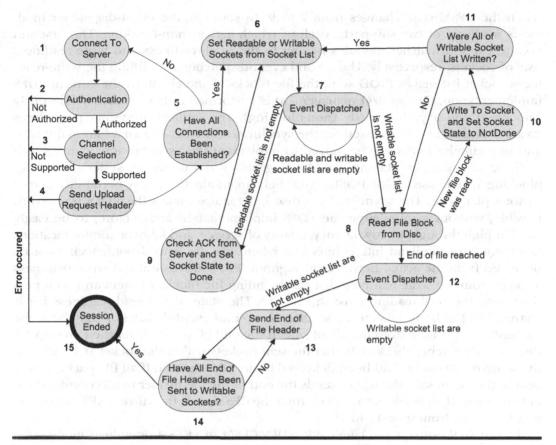

Figure 10.11 xDFS client communicating finite state machine in xFTSM upload mode.

Since the system function `select()` has been used as the event-dispatching component in the present xDFS design, these CFSMs were drawn depending on the properties of this system routine. xDFS protocol has considered an `Exception Header` packet for the response of each request at any given side; in fact, this mechanism is part of the concept of the duplex channel negotiation. If a client-side error takes place during any point of the file transfer session, then this header contains some binary details from an instance of the class `System::Exception` to be sent to the server through PSI and Parvicursor Remoting Architecture (PR), and the server decides how to deal with this error. At an erroneous point, the server either closes the current channel or terminates the entire transfer session. To preserve the state of sockets (for read-readiness and write-readiness modes), two individual array lists are used. Those sockets that are involved at the read-readiness list have three states labelled as `Done`, `NotDone`, and `FirstTime`. The state `Done` interprets that the `Exception Header` value still hasn't been received by the server, and the server in its next loop iteration, which manages the event-dispatching part, will have to receive this value from the client. The state `FirstTime` means that this socket for the first time has been used to be checked for its `Exception Header`. In Figure 10.8, both socket lists are empty when the CFSM state changes from 7 to 9. In state 10, the event-dispatcher module is made up of two sub-parts, each of which acts as non-blocking. The first and second event-dispatcher modules belong to the read-readiness and write-readiness lists of sockets, respectively. The second event-dispatcher after filling the write-readiness socket list makes PIOD send the file blocks to the client. In the current xDFS implementation, the disc I/O management is performed in two ways synchronously (blocking) and asynchronously (non-blocking). The traditional system procedures read() and write() are used for the synchronous mode, and an additional thread and one circular buffer are employed to implement the asynchronous core as well as these two routines. Making use of a ring buffer and no use of system-level non-blocking mechanisms, like POSIX AIO, help maintain the xDFS portability across various platforms. The asynchronous disc I/O feature makes the xDFS framework feasible, without manipulating the xDFS implementation architecture, to be easily used in high throughput, low latency, quality of service, and failover communications links, e.g. an InfiniBand interconnect, in where the disc speed bottleneck must be detached from the actual network throughput. PIOD drives out the write-readiness sockets from the write-readiness list after sending file blocks to them and then puts them into the read-readiness list in state 12. The state of the read-readiness list is changed to NotDone in state 12 so that the second event-dispatcher can check the Exception Header from the client side. If the end of the file is reached, in step 15, the event-dispatcher checks whether the sent packets within the socket TCP buffer of the write-readiness list had been delivered to the client or not. If all file packets were sent to the client side, the server sends the end of the file header to all connected client channels. If all headers were sent, then the CFSM ends the current xFTSM session in a transition from state 17 to 18.

Figure 10.9 portrays the client-side xDFS CFSM in xFTSM download mode. As it can be seen, the CFSM in Figure 10.9 is much simpler, and this simplicity on the client side is due to the order of data flow from the server side to the client in download mode. States 1 through 5 is performed for all n parallel channels. Each client authenticates itself to the server and sends its related session information to the server through Download Request Header over PSI after channel establishment. This header contains the information shown in Table 10.2.

The CFSM state changes from 5 to 6 after all channels were established. Since TCP sockets are normally non-blocking at every sending operation, a write-readiness socket list has not been used in the CFSM of Figure 10.9. In state 7, having chosen those sockets that infold the file blocks received from the server side, the event-dispatcher varies the CFSM state to 5. After being written the file blocks to the storage system through Parvicursor.NET Framework APIs, if all read-readiness sockets still haven't been written to the disc, state 8 is repeated for them after state 10. In step 8, if the server has already sent the end of the file header to the client, then the CFSM steps into state 12. In this state, the file transfer session in download mode terminates.

By comparing all CFSMs, it can be inferred that the right-hand side of server CFSMs in one mode has a one-to-one correspondence with the right-hand side of client CFSMs in another mode. The duality principle is referred to as such a case in mathematics and graph theory. A deep review of this concept is out of the scope of this chapter.

10.6.2 A Novel Hybrid Concurrency Pattern for xDFS POSIX-AIO-Enabled Implementation (PHCP)

The DotDFS protocol appeared for the first time in [5]. There, we argued that the protocol was the first proposal of a hybrid FTP integrating the thread-based and event-driven concurrency patterns in the area of data transmission protocols. In this section, for further clarification of this proposal, a practical implementation architecture of the xDFS protocol is introduced, which relied on the POSIX AIO [21], extending the concepts presented in Section 10.4.3. The rationale behind the theory in the xDFS protocol allowing different event-driven methods to be used is that the xDFS protocol requires the protocol implementation to process n parallel channels in a single loop of the context of execution described by a collection of FSMs, for example in the xFTSM upload mode. In this model, the implementation architecture of the xDFS protocol in xFTSM upload mode is studied on the server side. Also, we assume that the POSIX AIO standard applies to both file and socket descriptors (this assumption somewhat makes POSIX AIO similar to NT Completion Ports [23]).

The name and description of the used native functions are shown in Table 10.5. The basic idea behind the PHCP approach is that it allows the process or thread to be capable of performing many disc-based or network I/O operations without being blocked or waiting for being completed else. At some later time or the completion notification of I/O, the process or thread can retrieve the results of I/O. Figure 10.12 shows the xDFS flow of two hybrid concurrency patterns, including the PHCP, and the select-based model discussed in Section 10.6.1 (SHCP). In the SHCP model, after the blocking function `select()` chooses the favourite sockets as read-readiness, the system routines `recv()` and `write()` are used to receive the file block from the socket and to write it into the disc, respectively. In this event-driven pattern, a thread of execution is used for every n parallel channel functioning as an xDFS session because of the blocking nature of the `select()` function.

In the PHCP model, the processing and I/O overlap in execution. The read/write request returns immediately, indicating that the read/write operation completes successfully. Application programs can perform other processing whilst background I/O

Table 10.5 xDFS POSIX-AIO-Based Function List

Function Name	Description
POSIX `aio_read()`	Request an asynchronous read (from disc) or receive (from socket) operation.
POSIX `aio_write()`	Request an asynchronous write (to disc) or send (to socket) operation.
xDFS `callback_function_I()`	Implement the first xDFS FSM that is used to initiate the channel (common thread unit).
xDFS `callback_function_II()`	Implement the second xDFS FSM that is used to receive data from the socket (network I/O thread unit).
xDFS `callback_function_III()`	Implement the third xDFS FSM that is used to write data into the disc (the disc I/O thread unit).

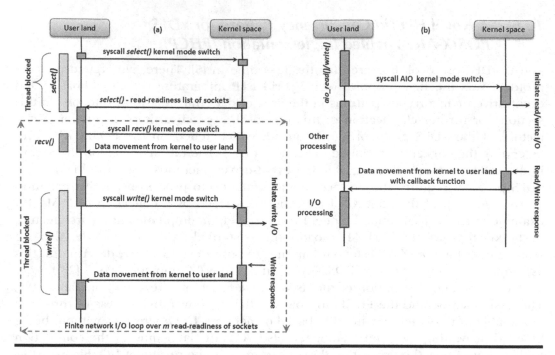

Figure 10.12   The xDFS flow of two event-driven models: (a) asynchronous blocking I/O model based on select (SHCP) and (b) the asynchronous non-blocking I/O model based on POSIX AIO (PHCP).

operation completes. One signal or a thread-based callback (as stated in Table 10.5, in this chapter the callback mechanism is used) can be generated for the completion notification of an I/O transaction. Indeed, the ability of overlapping computation and I/O processing in a single process for huge multiple I/O requests exploits the gap between the processing speed and the I/O speed.

Figure 10.13 shows the PHCP model's CFSM for the xDFS server in FTSM upload mode. There, the authentication transition has been removed for simplification. As seen in this CFSM and described in Table 10.5, each instance of the xDFS server is made up of at least four thread units of execution: acceptor thread, common thread unit, network I/O thread unit, and disc I/O thread unit. (In the most optimal situation, the number of threads in all thread units should be set to the number of this minimum value. However, also it must be noted that this value can vary depending on the available documents of every operating system or processor architecture.) Every thread unit may have any favourite number of pre-created threads, or dynamically created and added at runtime (for purposes of the resource provisioning in the integrated Parvicursor server). In this case, the xDFS server, per any number of clients and/or parallel channels, has this few specified numbers of threads. This model, due to a few worker threads used compared with the SHCP model, makes it suitable for ultra-highly scalable and concurrent server systems like Internet services. Because in the PHCP model the unnecessary context switches are completely removed, the use of synchronisation primitives is extremely avoided, and memory locality and system performance significantly improve.

One of the long-time debates over the event-driven software system development in the research community has been devoted to the subject that in these systems the

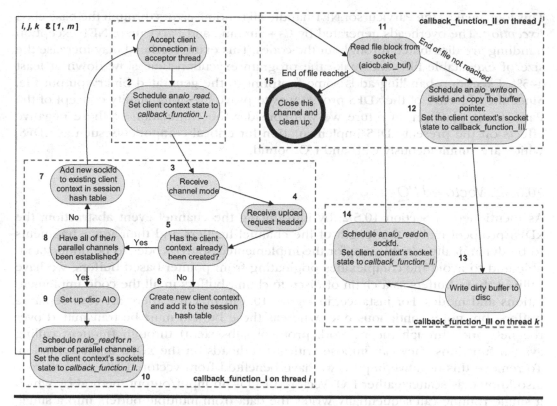

Figure 10.13 **xDFS server communicating finite state machine in xFTSM upload mode for POSIX-AIO mode (PHCP), m is the number of the created server-side worker-kernel threads (m is usually set to the total number of CPU cores).**

code is rarely modular or reusable. However, as can be seen in this CFSM, due to separating the four major components of the xDFS server into four callback thread-based functions, the code modularity extremely increases. Although the PHCP model greatly complicates the code development and maintenance, the power of such making code modular results in a standard implementation framework of the xDFS software dependent on NT Completion Ports and POSIX AIO in userspace in contrast to the complexities originating from the xDFS protocol itself.

10.6.3 Some Important Points Regarding the Implementation of the xDFS Protocol

In this section, we focus on important changes that we faced during the implementation of the xDFS framework in native code.

10.6.3.1 The Overheads of Exception Handling

Although the current version of xDFS has been implemented based on the native code, it suffers from an inherent overhead. Runtime error handling is essential in objected-oriented environments, specifically for standards similar to CLI. As stated earlier, Parvicursor.NET Framework tries to largely conform itself to the CLI-set standards.

This logic makes the Parvicursor.NET handle all runtime errors through the base class *Exception*. The overheads generated by C++ runtime and Parvicursor.NET exception handling are distributed throughout the codes. This extra overhead may increase the size of executable files and make the program execution time slow down at least 4–5%. Exception handling adds some footprint to the generated binary output file. Since the objective of the xDFS project was to prove the functionality concept of the Parvicursor platform, in future we will consider the elimination of these negative effects on the present xDFS implementation for critical components such as xDFS, which are simultaneously CPU and I/O bound.

10.6.3.2 Vectored I/O

As mentioned in Section 10.5.2, by introducing the channel event abstraction, the xDFS protocol makes the length of the channel headers and their inner fragments to be dynamically variable. So, for the implemented source codes to be understandable and to avoid the complexities originating from pointer-based buffers, we have utilised those buffers as a chain of discrete chunk buffers in all the code implementations and modes. For instance, in Figure 10.5 in practice, there are four separate buffers, but not a contiguous one. Whereas these buffers must be transmitted over the network (through the network protocol subsystem) through frequent calling system functions, they can impose critical overheads on the xDFS implementation. To remove this negative impact, we have benefited from vectored I/O mechanisms, also known as scatter/gather I/O. Vectored I/O is an input/output method by which a single routine call sequentially writes the data from multiple buffers into a single data stream or reads the data from a single data stream into multiple buffers. The chief benefits of using vectored I/O mechanisms can be noted to efficiency, splitting input, atomicity, and concatenating output.

10.6.3.3 Cross-Language, Cross-Runtime and Cross-Platform Parvicursor.NET Wrappers

In programming software components, library wrappers are composed of a thin layer of code, which transform a library's existing interface into a compatible interface. One of the key advantages of library wrappers is to enable cross-language and/ or cross-runtime interoperability across heterogeneous software components and/ or runtimes. Perhaps at first glance, it appears to the reader the main objective of the Parvicursor project is to encapsulate the operating system's APIs as a collection of C++ classes/wrappers. However, with a little inference and a good understanding of the concept of library wrappers in context, we can come to a principal point. Parvicursor was grounded on the CLI standard [32–34]. CLI, in the simplest clause, can function as the definition of a wrapper library which acts as a bridge between an application program and low-level system routines. CLI-based programs not only have cross-language benefits but also supply cross-runtime and cross-platform features. Therefore, it can be acknowledged that the Parvicursor project is the first project in distributed environments, which tries to propose itself in compliance with the CLI standard so that a move towards a standardised distributed software infrastructure begins. All Parvicursor classes are fully CLI-compliant. Because Parvicursor is a cross-platform framework, it can be interfaced with other languages/runtimes. One way is to use the system interfacing technologies such as Java Native Interface (JNI) [35] and .NET Platform Invoke [36], and the second is to directly implement the CLI standard for non-.NET-based languages like PHP, Python, Ruby, and so on. As can be concluded, the Parvicursor platform executing in the native code can function as an integrated bridge to connect distributed software components across a broad spectrum of network architectures for different languages and/or runtimes.

10.6.3.4 Parvicursor.NET Inline Expansion

Inlining is a way to replace a function site with the body of the callee. If the inlining is optimally applied to prototype and implement pure C++ classes by a framework like Parvicursor, the time and space usage improves considerably at runtime. This feature is not usually considered in software system development. Since frequent I/O procedure calls occur at the time when functioning at runtime, the role of inlining is notably visible in the implementation of protocols such as xDFS. In our experiments during the implementation of the xDFS framework, we found out that the use of appropriate inlining methods improves overall system performance by up to 10–20%.

10.6.3.5 Parvicursor.NET Runtime Profiler

Performance engineering is a critical area in any software product line over the software development or deployment life cycle. One common method in software performance engineering is to use program/software profiling as witnessed over the past decades [37]. During the development cycle of the Parvicursor.NET platform due to the lack of an integrated profiling methodology in most operating systems, a useful C++ profiler class was designed that extracts the most information about the runtime dynamics of an application program provided by the standard POSIX and Win32/64-kernel APIs. This profiler is accessible in the DotGrid platform through the managed .NET programs provided via a class component that imports the exported needed functions in a dynamically native shared object file by .NET Platform Invoke. For more simplicity in native code, we have implemented and rewritten a collection of C macro functions that eases the programmers to make use of them inside their C/C++ source codes to profile codes with minimum time spent.

10.7 Comparison of xDFS Protocol with DotDFS, FTP, GridFTP and HTTP Protocols

In this section, we compare xDFS protocol with DotDFS, FTP, GridFTP, and HTTP protocols. Some GridFTP weaknesses and structural differences between xDFS/ DotDFS and GridFTP are discussed so that the reader can understand more reasons (in addition to those considered during Sections 10.2 through 10.6) why a new concurrent FTP is proposed.

We point out some major problems associated with FTP and GridFTP protocols. These issues were considered during the process of xDFS design. Since FTP is very old from the structural design aspects, it has caused many different problems, and they are also continuing. These issues over the past years have led to recommending and standardising a lot of RFCs and protocol modifications for resolving these problems. They have made FTP very complex to be developed by implementers and caused several interoperability problems. Some of these IETF standards and drafts are shown in Table 10.6. Equally, Table 10.6 shows a comprehensive comparison of different file transfer mechanisms, including xDFS, DotDFS, FTP, GridFTP, and HTTP.

Table 10.6 Comparison of Different Widely Used File Transfer Protocols

Feature	xDFS	DotDFS	FTP	GridFTP	HTTP
Creation year	2011	2010	1971	2003	1991
Protocol standards	xDFS v.2	DotDFS v.1	20 RFCs	GFD-R-P.020 (2003), GFD.47 (2005)	38 RFCs
Protocol representation	CFSMs	CFSMs	State machines	Descriptive text	Descriptive text
Low-level transmission protocol	Multi-protocol support via Parvicursor Socket Interface (PSI)	Multi-protocol support via DotGridSocket Interface	TCP/IP only	Multi-protocol support via Globus XIO	TCP/IP only
Platforms	Cross-platform	Cross-platform	Cross-platform	Unix/Linux	Cross-platform
Execution environment	Native/ Parvicursor	CLI/.NET	Implementation-dependent	Native/ Globus	Implementation-dependent
POSIX-compliant I/O standard support	Fully	Fully	Not applicable	Partially	Not applicable
Local-area file access support (e.g., NFS)	Fully	Fully	No	No	No
Storage system interface	CLI File Stream Interface (CLIFSI)	No	No	Data Storage Interface (DSI)	No
WAN improvements (TCP window size/ parallelism)	Strong/very strong	Strong/strong	No/weak	Strong/ moderate	No/weak
Native event-driven protocol-level architecture	Fully	Fully	Not applicable	Not applicable	Not applicable

(Continued)

Table 10.6 (Continued) Comparison of Different Widely Used File Transfer Protocols

Feature	xDFS	DotDFS	FTP	GridFTP	HTTP
Stateful/stateless architecture	Fully/fully	Fully/fully	Fully/no	FullynNo	Partially/fully
NAT compliance	Strong	Strong	Weak	Weak	Strong
Firewall compliance	Strong	Strong	Weak	Weak	Strong
internationalisation	Strong	Strong	Moderate	No	Strong
Extensibility	Very strong	Strong	Weak	Moderate	Low
Protocol modularity	Strong	Moderate	Weak	Weak	Moderate
SOA architecture	Yes	Yes	Not applicable	Not applicable	Yes
Protocol message interchange exchange format	Binary	Binary	ASCII	ASCII	ASCII
Security extensions	xSec	DotSec	7 RFCs	Globus GSI, GSS-API, and FTP RFCs	10 RFCs
Scalability/large concurrent requests support	Very Strong	Strong	Weak	Weak	Moderate
File/pipe-based inter-process communication support	Strong	Strong	Not applicable	Not applicable	Not applicable
Large-size file support	Strong	Strong	Weak	Strong	Weak
Protocol-level zero-copy extensions	Yes	No	No	No	No
Distributed file systems semantics	Yes	Yes	Not applicable	Not applicable	Not applicable
Recursive directory tree transfer support	Very strong	Strong	Weak	Moderate	Not applicable

(Continued)

Table 10.6 (Continued) Comparison of Different Widely Used File Transfer Protocols

Feature	xDFS	DotDFS	FTP	GridFTP	HTTP
Operating system resource consumption	Very low	Low	High	High	Implementation-dependent
Implementation complexity	Very high	High	Medium	Medium	Low
Developer-friendly service development kit (SDK)	High	High	Implementation-dependent	Low	Implementation-dependent
Source code inline expansion	Fully	Not applicable	Implementation-dependent	No	Implementation-dependent
Built-in protocol-level runtime profiler support	Yes	Yes	No	No	No

10.7.1 Some Major Criticisms on FTP and GridFTP Protocols and xDFS/ DotDFS Protocol Alternatives over Them

a. Most FTP state machines are non-standard. Changes to the protocol can clearly cause significant changes to all FTP state machines. A modular protocol core seems that can solve these problems in future versions of the FTP. In the xDFS protocol, we considered some alternatives based on CFSMs so that the newer protocol versions would not disturb the logic of previous protocol versions and the protocol reusability would be preserved.

b. FTP is a high latency protocol due to the number of commands required for initiating a transfer. Although GridFTP protocol with the pipelining of commands and reuse of EBLOCK data channels [3, 4] tries to solve this problem in a specific area, this issue generally remains unaffected in GridFTP because it naturally relies on FTP. The binary and event-driven model of the xDFS protocol as possible can solve this problem, for instance, by multiplexing the requests.

c. Many Grid applications (like some data-intensive physics applications) require random access to partial parts of files, according to traditional POSIX I/O semantics. GridFTP protocol, to consider this need, introduces partial transfers on which a client can transfer a file with a desired offset and length [2–4]. However, what is obvious is that such a method is not scalable, and not only does it not involve all the traditional POSIX I/O semantics, but makes developers farther from their clear understanding of well-known POSIX interfaces. xDFS protocol supports conventional distributed file system mechanisms and preserves the traditional POSIX I/O semantics by xDFSM mode [5, 6]. A well-designed protocol that supports multiple Grid demands regarding storage transfers is a fundamental requirement used in the Grid. A critical necessity of Grid in data transfers is diversity issues to reign over a community as widespread and fast-moving as the Grid. xDFS provides a comprehensive protocol-set that enables wide-area file transfers, as well as a complete replacement of local-area file access protocols which are still likely to be dominated by NFS [38], AFS [39], and CIFS [40] protocols.

d. In FTP, the representation of the Ips and ports in the PORT command and PASV reply [1] poses another challenge for NAT devices [41]. NAT devices must manipulate these values so that they contain the IP of the NAT-ed client and a set of selected ports by the NAT device for data channels. Many NAT devices perform this protocol inspection and alter the PORT command without notifying the user of this modification. An important example of this scenario is to secure FTP with TLS [42, 43]. NAT devices will be unable to modify the IP and PORT of the client due to the cryptography used in the control channel. However, one may think of two practical solutions for this scenario. The first could be made use of the CCC command in RFC 2228 [44] for changing the mode of the control channel to an unencrypted mode when needed; but this seriously jeopardises the security of an FTP session for being attacked, such as port stealing and bounces attacks. The second solution could be to use the FTP active mode, but, eventually, even this method can become problematic because the active mode creates other problems related to firewalls and FTP proxies. The final solution for this problem, to some extent but not complete, is the use of application-level gateways (ALGs). ALGs are application-specific translation agents that transparently allow an application running on a host in one address realm to connect to its counterpart running on a host in a different realm. ALGs usually interact with NATs to establish a state use from state information of the NATs, modify the application-specific payload, and run anything else that enables an application program to run on distinct address realms. As can be seen, FTP and GridFTP protocols unveil many problems and more extensive complexities to be resolved concerned with NATs. We can take further knowledge about these problems by studying RFC 2663 [45]. Since all client requests in the xDFS protocol are established to the server on a default port in the mode of either xDFS over xSec TSI or xDFS over X-Channels, no IP and port are exchanged between endpoints; hence, a NAT device can easily, so close to the way that it modifies the HTTP packets, modify or filter xDFS packets in the transport layer [5].

e. FTP and particularly the GridFTP protocols are troublesome from the firewall viewpoint. These problems can mainly be discussed from several aspects. They employ a large number of dynamic arbitrary ephemeral ports over data channels. In addition, a static port number is always assigned for the control channel. Using so many random ports (even those that may be limited in a certain range) and how to configure them in client-server-side firewalls are very challenging. Only a few firewalls can handle applications that access dynamically assigned ports. Also, GridFTP in the X mode, for dynamic network resource allocation purposes, allows peers to dynamically add or remove data channels between the values of minimum-parallelism and maximum-parallelism (expressed in the format of RETR OPTS command over control channels) [3, 4]. This case used in third-party and stripped transfers can lead to critical problems in firewalled environments. Furthermore, FTP active and passive modes [1] are two other issues due to considering firewalls for network administrators and protocol developers. Finally, these two protocols require opening a large number of ports in the dynamic range in a firewall. It causes a big security hole that challenges network and security administrators. Another problem of them with firewalls is the possible disconnection of idle control or data channels. Some firewalls drop TCP connections that are idle for a long time. In the xDFS protocol due to establishing all requests from the client to the server side, we can avoid problems available in FTP and GridFTP protocols only by opening a single port in the firewall. In xDFS, the problem related to the idle TCP connections naturally is extremely eliminated because of the used event-driven model and lack of a control channel concept [5, 6].

f. In FTP, there is no standard way for transferring file system metadata. This makes the integration of file systems on Unix, Windows, and Solaris to be very difficult. These points have been considered in the design of the xDFS protocol.

g. The data structures of FTP programs are very different. An FTP kernel for the public domain should be implemented that supports cross-platform POSIX threads. The cross-platform implementation of the xDFS protocol in native C++ is opened source for public use on the Internet with this book.

h. The GridFTP specification [3, 4] states that it is not required currently considering the Internationalisation of FTP in RFC 2640 [46] for Grid environments! This fact explains that the current implementation of the GridFTP only supports ASCII pathnames, not Unicode. The default pathname mode in the xDFS protocol is Unicode strings [5, 6, 12].

10.8 Experimental Studies

The current xDFS implementation only supports xFTSM mode with types of download and upload transfers. The real execution environment of the xDFS framework is native and cross-platform, and we tested and deployed the xDFS stably on a broad spread of operating systems, including Unix, Linux, and Windows. To test and evaluate the real performance of the xDFS implementation in native code, xDFS is compared with the Globus GridFTP (explicitly the only available fully GridFTP implementation in Unix-style operating systems) in a local-area network. The experimental results presented here have the confirmation on the logic of our previous works [5, 6], but what is more, they reveal interesting insights that are analysed in this section. The test set is performed to characterise the xDFS throughput and efficiency in three categories: disc-to-disc, memory-to-memory, and CPU/physical memory usage. The tests were done in a LAN network with 0.1 milliseconds (msec) round trip time (RTT) and a 1 Gb/s bottleneck link. The machines used as the clients and servers had eight homogenous Intel Xeon Quad Core processors operating at 2.5 GHz with 6 MB cache, 8 GB RAM, and 320 GB RAID hard discs. Linux CentOS with the kernel 2.6.9.9-78, for x86_64 SMP processors, was installed on all machines. The TCP buffer size and disc block size were set to 1 MB. In GridFTP tests, its implementation of the GT4.2.1 was used [11]. The GridFTP C source codes were compiled into machine code by a makefile through the GNU GCC compiler suite.

The xDFS C++ source codes have been constructed atop the Parvicursor.NET Framework. The Parvicursor.NET codes with an extension of one static library or dynamic shared library were implemented as cross-platform using the C-language preprocessors relied upon the core of Win32 and POSIX APIs. The Parvicursor project makes extensive customised use of the comprehensive cross-platform Code::Blocks IDE. Developers and programmers can easily and quickly implement, compile, debug, and deploy their HPC/distributed applications based on the Parvicursor framework in a highly cross-platform/portable integrated environment. Finally, the C/C++ codes of the xDFS framework, through Code::Blocks and invoking the GCC compiler, are compiled and transformed into the native machine code. On the xDFS client side, the parvicursor-url-copy (PUC) utility is used. As a unique feature of the Parvicursor platform, it should be noted that we manually ported the C#-based codes of the DotDFS's PUC, which contained approximately 1,000 lines of code, into the native ISO C++ code in less than 15 minutes (the PUC itself instantiates and invokes the xDFS framework's APIs)! On the GridFTP client side, the GT4.2.1 globus-url-copy (GUC) was used. Memory-to-memory tests are performed in 15-second intervals. All test points are a mean of 15 runs.

10.8.1 Single Stream Performance in Download Mode

We carried out the first comparison between xDFS and GridFTP in a single stream test for download mode. Since there are two threads of execution for xDFS and four processes for GridFTP in the client-server sides, this experiment can give a good benchmark to compare them just at the protocol level except for how these two protocols have been implemented (e.g., using a thread-based or multiple-process implementation). Because both protocols have been implemented in native code, at first look it may hint that these protocols should have correspondent throughputs in single-stream scenarios; however, the results, as illustrated in Figures 10.14 and 10.15, promote a quite distinct fact to the reader. Figure 10.14 depicts throughputs for files of sizes ranging from 400 MB to 4000 MB. Furthermore, Figure 10.15 demonstrates the percentage of client-server CPU usage for each protocol and the mentioned files. As it is obvious, the xDFS throughput is at least 150 Mb/s better than GridFTP for files with sizes less than 1 GB. In [5], we discovered a phenomenon that was defined as the term "saturation speed". There, we concluded that the saturation speed decreases the measured throughput to very low thresholds in contrast to the actual speed of the local reads and writes in storage systems under experiment when large files were being transferred. In Figure 10.14, the saturation speed for GridFTP occurs whilst the file size is increased to greater than or equal to 2 GB. Here clearly no saturation speed occurs for xDFS, as there was no observed fall or decrease in xDFS throughput for large files. Since GridFTP forks just four processes, in this case we cannot consider the use of multiple processes as the key factor that reduces the throughput.

A GridFTP server consists of three components, including, the GridFTP protocol module, the data transform module, and the Data Storage Interface (DSI) [47]. The GridFTP protocol module is the main module that performs the network send/

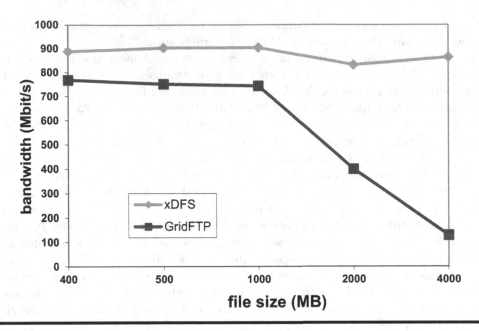

Figure 10.14   Single stream throughput in download mode.

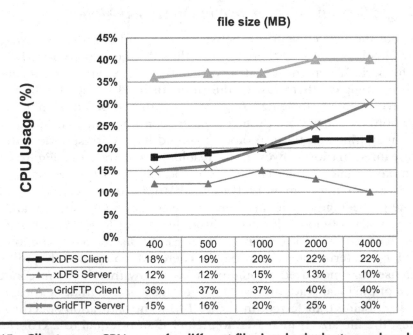

	400	500	1000	2000	4000
xDFS Client	18%	19%	20%	22%	22%
xDFS Server	12%	12%	15%	13%	10%
GridFTP Client	36%	37%	37%	40%	40%
GridFTP Server	15%	16%	20%	25%	30%

Figure 10.15   Client-server CPU usage for different file sizes in single stream download mode.

receive operations and implements the protocol. This module has been built using the Globus extensible input/output (XIO) [48, 49]. The XIO is an OCRW (open/close/read/write) abstraction layer that simplifies the development phase of transport protocols. The XIO's architecture is comprised of two abstract concepts, drivers and stacks. The specifications of a protocol are included in a driver as an abstract.

Each driver must implement a set of well-defined function interfaces based upon the C-language `typedef` (as the structure of a function pointer table) along with a collection of operations to enable dynamic runtime routine invocations. Extensively using function pointers to call functions, as XIO does, may produce a slow-down for the code on modern processors, because branch prediction may not be able to figure out where to branch to (it depends on the value of the function pointer at runtime), although this effect can be overstated as it is often amply compensated for by significantly reduced non-indexed table lookups. There are two drivers, transform drivers and transport drivers. Transport drivers are those that actually convey data inside or outside the space of a process. As seen, XIO adds an extra abstraction layer between an application program and low-level system APIs (this abstraction is not created statically at compile time; rather,it is managed and processed dynamically at runtime). Then, these additional layers can cause overheads on architected programs in terms of system characteristics and network throughput.

Globus states just extensibility aspects as the main reason for using XIO and therefore GridFTP can be leveraged to be transport protocol agnostic. Hence, in environments where they make sense, protocols much more aggressive than TCP can be utilised. To meet more specific extensibility needs, they also provide easy-to-use development libraries.

They, in [50], state that achieved respectively 990 Mb/s and 950 Mb/s of the bottleneck bandwidth for Iperf and XIOPerf implemented based on XIO in a network with a bottleneck link of 1 Gb/s. But Figure 10.14 and specifically Figure 10.15 show that GridFTP in contrast to xDFS exposes far more overheads due to using the XIO. It implies that Globus should not have used the XIO in designing very sensitive and important components such as GridFTP. In [50], they specify the overheads concerned with XIO increase linearly with incrementing the number of drivers. A GridFTP server or client is typically comprised of three TCP, GSI, and disc drivers. It is necessary to note that the overheads of a networked software system cannot be evaluated just depending on the network throughput, rather assessing a variety of system characteristics have more importance, including cache misses, CPU utilisation, interrupt handling, stalls, memory fetches, data locality, cache utilisation, thread interactions, and so on.

Moreover, GridFTP uses the DSI [47] in accessing the functionality of storage systems such as file systems accessible via standard POSIX APIs, and Storage Resource Broker. DSI abstraction provides a modular pluggable interface to the data storage systems. DSIs can be loaded and switched dynamically at runtime. When a GridFTP server is in need of a storage system, it passes a request to the loaded DSI instance. The DSI after servicing the request notifies the server of the service completion.

In contrast to the Globus XIO and Globus DSI, the xDFS framework makes use of the Parvicursor Socket Interface (PSI) and CLI FileStream Interface (CLIFSI) for integrated access to network I/O interfaces and heterogeneous storage systems. PSI and CLIFSI are two pure C++ classes that inherit from the interface (abstract/base) class `System::IO::Stream` and implement it. Virtual methods are not used to implement sensitive method stubs like the `Read()` and `Write()` methods of this base class. A virtual call requires at least an extra indexed dereference, and sometimes a fixup addition, in contrast to a non-virtual call, which is simply a jump to a compiled-in pointer. Hence, calling virtual functions is inherently slower than calling non-virtual functions. Experiments verify that approximately 6–13% of execution time is spent simply dispatching to the correct function where the overhead can be as high as 50% [51].

These two classes have been carefully engineered relying on the Parvicursor.NET inline expansion methods discussed in Section 10.6.3.4. Therefore, PSI and CLIFSI as static bindings are distributed across codes of the xDFS framework through inlining mechanisms by the compiler. Since these procedures are static, and we here avoid the use of any virtual methods, PSI and CLIFSI expose no overhead on the xDFS implementation.

The XIO internally employs several event synchronisations on the stacks to ensure the users, using the library, that are receiving events in a reasonable state. For example, a barrier is used between all data operation events. Hence, the rationale of the saturation speed phenomena can be induced to the Globus DSI and XIO, and with the mechanisms of event notifications employed in implementing both of them. Globus has considered just overheads originating from XIO over the throughput [48–50]; however, Figure 10.15 reveals other technical facts. In Figure 10.15 for this test, XIO poses at least 20% of the overhead in CPU usage as compared with xDFS, particularly, for larger files; also, this percentage linearly increases for GridFTP, as it is invariable for xDFS and even degrades in some cases.

10.8.2 Single Stream Performance in Upload Mode

The second experiment is performed for a single stream in upload mode for two protocols xDFS and GridFTP. Figure 10.16 shows the throughputs. The xDFS upload-mode profile is virtually identical to its download-mode profile, but these profiles for GridFTP differ. Because both Figures 10.14 and 10.16 relate to the single-stream

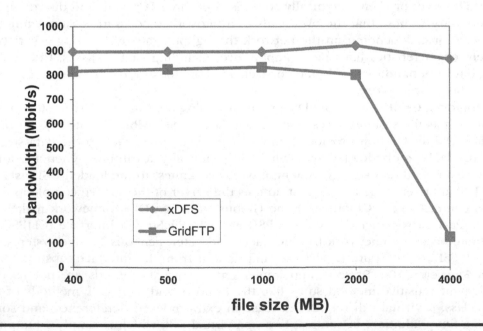

Figure 10.16   Single stream throughput in upload mode.

throughputs, the main factor for xDFS throughputs to be identical and for GridFTP throughputs to be dissimilar can be attributed to the different structure and implementation of the Globus XIO and DSI for GET/PUT modes in GridFTP [3, 4].

10.8.3 Harnessing Parallelism in Download Mode

In this section, we probe the effect of multiple streams on the overall throughput in download mode. This test is a touchstone to compare the MP model given in Section 10.4.1 for GridFTP protocol and the MTEDP model in Section 10.4.3 for xDFS protocol. Figure 10.17 depicts the obtained throughputs as a function of the number of parallel streams in download mode. This data set was carried out for three different experiments: Iperf, memory-to-memory tests (/dev/zero to /dev/null), and disc-to-disc tests. A 2 GB file is transferred between client and server in disc-to-disc tests.

In memory-to-memory tests for download mode, xDFS and GridFTP reached 97% and 95% of the bottleneck bandwidth, respectively. As it can be seen; because of using a single thread and event-driven methods, the memory-to-memory and disc-to-disc xDFS throughput are almost constant as GridFTP has very high fluctuations. Clearly, all the xDFS throughputs are better than GridFTP in all cases. Section 10.3 discussed the implementation architecture of these two protocols. As stated earlier, by increasing the number of processes in the GridFTP structure, the overhead associated with the protocol significantly increases a fact that exhibits itself in Figure 10.17. In disc-to-disc tests here, the xDFS was throughput at least 256 Mb/s and at most 432 Mb/s superior to GridFTP. An interesting point was to observe that disc-to-disc xDFS profiles followed the memory-to-memory xDFS profiles with very little difference in

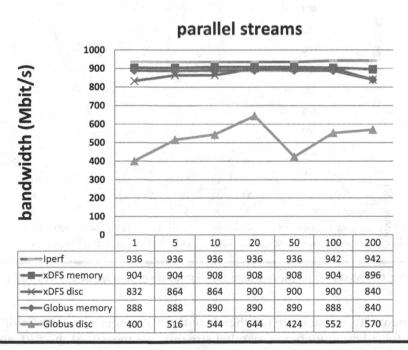

parallel streams	1	5	10	20	50	100	200
Iperf	936	936	936	936	936	942	942
xDFS memory	904	904	908	908	908	904	896
xDFS disc	832	864	864	900	900	900	840
Globus memory	888	888	890	890	890	888	840
Globus disc	400	516	544	644	424	552	570

Figure 10.17 Parallel throughput in download mode.

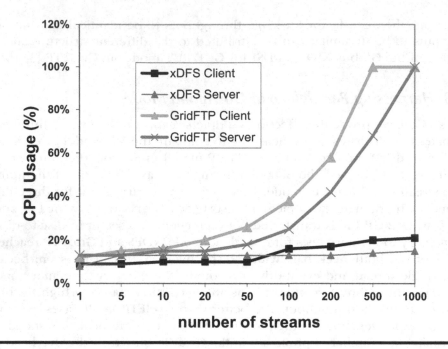

Figure 10.18   Client-server CPU usage for memory-to-memory tests in download mode.

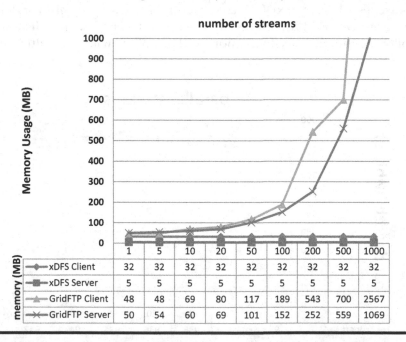

number of streams	1	5	10	20	50	100	200	500	1000
xDFS Client	32	32	32	32	32	32	32	32	32
xDFS Server	5	5	5	5	5	5	5	5	5
GridFTP Client	48	48	69	80	117	189	543	700	2567
GridFTP Server	50	54	60	69	101	152	252	559	1069

Figure 10.19   Client-server memory usage for disc-to-disc transfer of a 4 GB file in download mode.

all experiments. To reveal more overheads of the MP model upon the GridFTP implementation for a large number of parallel streams, we measured the CPU usage for a memory-to-memory test and the physical memory usage for transferring a 4 GB file. Figures 10.18 and 10.19 show the result of these two scenarios. Whilst the number of parallel streams is raised, the client-server CPU usage for the xDFS is constant and between 5 to 20%, as it is exponentially increasing for the GridFTP programs.

In this scenario, both the percentage of CPU usage and the physical memory consumption for the GridFTP client are greater than the GridFTP server. The percentage of CPU usage of both GridFTP server and client is 100% in 1,000 parallel streams over the whole 32 CPU cores! As another conspicuous issue during our experiments in download mode, the Linux machine that hosted the GridFTP client became critically unresponsive, which made us manually reboot that machine for transferring large files (greater than or equal to 4 GB) with parallel streams greater than 200. Figure 10.19 illustrates the physical memory usage in megabytes for xDFS and GridFTP programs. The profile curve of xDFS physical memory consumption is a flat line with very small values; by contrast, this profile for GridFTP increasingly consumes the physical memory whilst raising the number of parallel streams.

Based on these technical points studied in this and previous sections, GridFTP due to its intrinsic architecture and using an improper implementation (a process-based implementation, the use of Unix-based forks, and using the Globus DSI and XIO) suffers from critical overheads. Hence, GridFTP cannot be used efficiently in high-traffic and vital environments like Internet services, and data-intensive Grid and Cloud applications.

10.8.4 Harnessing Parallelism in Upload Mode

In the last experiment, we examine the effectiveness of parallel streams in upload mode for a 2 GB file transfer based on the three tests conducted in Section 10.8.3. Figures 10.20 and 10.21, for a large number of parallel streams, respectively show

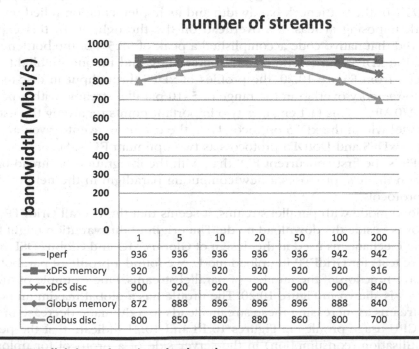

number of streams	1	5	10	20	50	100	200
Iperf	936	936	936	936	936	942	942
xDFS memory	920	920	920	920	920	920	916
xDFS disc	900	920	920	900	900	900	840
Globus memory	872	888	896	896	896	888	840
Globus disc	800	850	880	880	860	800	700

Figure 10.20   Parallel throughput in upload mode.

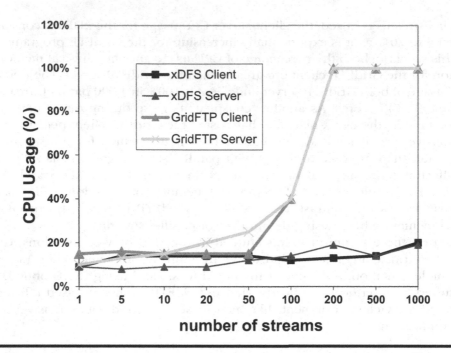

Figure 10.21 Client-server CPU usage for memory-to-memory tests in upload mode.

the parallel throughput and the percentage of CPU usage for memory-to-memory tests. xDFS and GridFTP in these experiments reached 98.5% and 95% of the bottleneck bandwidth, respectively. In [5], we stated that DotDFS in such an experiment reached 94% of the bottleneck bandwidth and its implementation relied on the .NET framework imposing at least 5% overhead on the throughput. In this experiment, we observed that native code accomplished a peak of 98.5% of the bottleneck bandwidth for the xDFS framework. Another interesting and unique highlight is that as can be seen from Figure 10.20, the profiles of xDFS throughput in disc-to-disc and memory-to-memory overlap in the range of 5–10 parallel streams with a peak bandwidth of 920 Mb/s. This fact engages two important points regarding the used event-driven model within the xDFS protocol. First, the use of an event-driven architecture is crucial in xDFS and DotDFS protocols as two optimum FTPs. Second, as stated in [5], DotDFS is the first concurrent FTP that, with the integration of thread-based and event-driven models, proposes a new computing paradigm in the field of file transmission protocols.

In upload mode with parallel streams, it seems that the overall GridFTP throughput improves beside the download mode. The origin of this variation might be attributed to the mechanisms used in the design of Globus XIO and Globus DSI. In various disc-to-disc tests for GridFTP in upload mode, we found a profile of parabolic curves as a concave function of the number of parallel streams. One example of these parabolic curves is shown in Figure 10.20. The profile has a global maximum point at 20 parallel streams as increasing these streams leads to a dramatic decrease in throughput. The CPU-usage profiles in Figures 10.18 and 10.21 indicate that the percentage of CPU utilisation (consumption) in the server side of a protocol for upload mode has a duality form in relation to its client-side for download mode and vice versa. The percentage of CPU consumption amongst all CPU cores reaches the 100% utilisation where the number of parallel streams is greater than (or equal to) 200.

10.8.5 Full xDFS/DotDFS Runtime Characterisation

As pointed out in Section 10.6.3.5, the Parvicursor.NET provides an elegant collection of C macros, C++ class APIs and P/Invoke interfaces to profile cross-platform applications developed atop Parvicursor and DotGrid platforms. In this section, we explore the results of this profiler in different case studies. Table 10.7 shows the results. The definition of some quantities in the upper horizontal column of the table is followed.

Wall clock time or wall time is a measure of how much real-time elapses from the current execution point of the program's thread (involved at the DOTGRID_RESOURCE_ PROFILER_BEGIN() macro) to the end of the running thread executing the task's thread (involved at the DOTGRID_RESOURCE_PROFILER_END() macro), including the time that passes due to programmed (artificial) delays or waiting for resources to become available. User/kernel CPU time is a representation of the elapsed time spent by the task's thread and all its children whilst executing in the user/kernel space, with or without nice priority, and collected during the interval of time. A voluntary context switch occurs when a task's thread blocks because it requires an unavailable resource. An involuntary context switch takes place when a task's thread executes for the duration of its time slice and then is forced to relinquish the processor.

For brevity, two xDFS and DotDFS protocols are only compared in upload mode but the results of the profiler for xDFS in the download mode also comes in the table without DotDFS profiles for completion purposes. The best scenario to comprehensively show the architectural overheads of the .NET Framework (as analysed in [5]) upon server programs in distributed systems is to examine the memory-to-memory transfer (MTMT) scenario in upload mode. As rows 8 and 9 of Table 10.7 promotes in MTMT mode for the DotGrid platform if we assume that the ideal base model is the native Parvicursor framework, the percentage of the overheads are the following: clock wall time—25%, user CPU time—94%, kernel CPU time—66%, voluntary/ involuntary context switches—78%/99.94%, CPU utilisation/memory—84%/65%, and speed—4%. The low and constant values related to the xDFS profiles are proof of optimal Parvicursor efficiency and the techniques used in the design of the xDFS protocol and the platform.

10.9 Conclusion and Future Works

In this chapter, we described the new xDFS FTP and its new extensions to the DotDFS protocol. In part of this chapter, we explored the fundamental requirements of next-generation data transfer protocols, which affected some parts of the chapter. In large parts of this chapter, we examined the development methods of optimal file transfer systems, and their advantages and disadvantages. Architectural differences between two protocols xDFS and GridFTP were considered, by which we proposed the xDFS protocol as a basis for high-performance and high-throughput file transfers in data-intensive Grid applications and Internet environments. By introducing

Table 10.7 Different Profiles for Various Case Studies

Row	Case Study	Platform	Clock Ticks (Wall Clock Time)	User CPU Time (Second/ Nanosecond)		Kernel CPU Time (Second/ Nanosecond)		Soft/ Hard Page Faults		Voluntary/ Involuntary Context Switches		CPU(%)/ Memory (MB)		Speed (Mb/s)
1	xFTSM, Upload, –p 1, –s 2 GB	Parvicursor	7094000	0	22396	7	393162	137	0	92365	12	33	30	768
2	FTSM, Upload, –p 1, –s 2 GB	DotGrid	6220000	1	875019	6	96073	62	0	195794	10	25	108	437
3	xFTSM, Upload, –p 5, –s 2 GB	Parvicursor	6944000	0	34794	7	34794	0	0	19658	13	37	40	900
5	FTSM, Upload, –p 5, –s 2 GB	DotGrid	6970000	1	129364	7	356359	56	0	94997	87	25	113	608
6	MTMT, Upload, –p 1	Parvicursor	1726000	0	30795	1.6	443054	0	0	63233	2	11	30	886
7	MTMT, Upload, –p 1	DotGrid	17766000	15	668570	3.2	730497	0	0	141493	5169	50	111	864
8	MTMT, Upload, –p 5	Parvicursor	13420000	0	34594	1.4	492555	0	0	32504	5	11	40	904
9	MTMT, Upload, –p 5	DotGrid	17966000	17	845902	4.2	561078	0	0	150569	8619	70	115	870
10	xFTSM, Download, –p 1, –s 2 GB	Parvicursor	4432000	0	10398	4.4	488664	37	0	3753	4.4	22	30	752
11	xFTSM, Download , –p 5, –s 2 GB	Parvicursor	4240000	0	29195	4.2	327815	0	0	15412	7	24	40	896
12	MTMT, Download , –p 1	Parvicursor	2192000	0	19197	2	174069	0	0	34103	1.6	30	14	863
13	MTMT, Download , –p 10	Parvicursor	2004000	0	8399	1.8	201617	0	0	6533	2.8	13	40	904

the implementation of the xDFS protocol on the top of Parvicursor.NET Framework, it was illustrated how we can make use of the CLI-set standards relied upon the Parvicursor platform to develop a standardised distributed software infrastructure as a general example. The presented results confirmed the accuracy of appropriate methods used in the design and implementation of the xDFS protocol. The xDFS framework is now available as a cross-platform and native-code distribution for a wide family of operating systems like Unix, Linux, and Windows. Also, in this chapter, we investigated the rationale of the saturation speed phenomenon discussed in [5] and observed that such a downside does not exist in the context of the xDFS framework. Memory-to-memory tests in upload mode showed that the xDFS protocol accessed 98.5% of the bottleneck bandwidth whilst the GridFTP protocol was reaching 95%. This outcome proves the claim that we had stated in [5], which .NET Framework exposes at least 5% overhead on the DotDFS implementation.

We believe that the main contribution of this chapter, in addition to an explanation of novel concepts, is to classify and refer to a lot of technical metrics and methodologies which must be kept in mind by developers to program critical client-server applications in distributed environments. We have determined the preliminary roadmap of our future research works based on what was presented in this chapter. Currently, we are finalising the specification drafts of the xDFSM and xPathM protocols and subsequently implementing them within the xDFS framework. At the end and after completion of the xDFS framework, we intend to extend the PIOD architecture discussed in Section 10.4.3 so that several network I/O event-dispatching approaches can be used for the sake of more optimum data transfer efficiency.

References

1. J. Postel and J. Reynolds, File Trasnfer Protocol (FTP), IETF, RFC 959, 1985; Available from: http://www.ietf.org/rfc/rfc959.txt, 2022.
2. W. Allcock, J. Bresnahan, R. Kettimuthu, M. Link, C. Dumitrescu, I. Raicu, and I. Foster, The Globus Striped GridFTP Framework and Server. In *Proceedings of Super Computing 2005, (SC'05)*, 2005. Available from: https://people.cs.uchicago.edu/~cldumitr/docs/gridftp_final.pdf, 2022.
3. W. Allcock, GridFTP: Protocol Extensions to FTP for the Grid, 2022; Available from: https://ogf.org/documents/GFD.20.pdf
4. B. Allcock, I. Mandrichenko, and T. Perelmutov, GridFTP v2 Protocol Description, 2022; Available from: https://ogf.org/documents/GFD.47.pdf
5. A. Poshtkohi and M.B. Ghaznavi-Ghoushchi, DotDFS: A Grid-based High-Throughput File Transfer System. *Parallel Comput.*, 37: 114–136, 2011. doi: 10.1016/j.parco.2010.12.003.
6. A. Poshtkohi and M.B. Ghaznavi-Ghoushchi, A Concurrent Framework for High Performance File Transfers in Grid Environments, In *Proceedings of the 3th International Conference on Computer and Electrical Engineering (ICCEE 2010)*, 16–18 November 2010, Chengdu, China.
7. J. Yick, B. Mukherjee, and D. Ghosal, Wireless Sensor Network Survey. *Comput. Netw.*, 52: 2292–2330, 2008. doi: 10.1016/j.comnet.2008.04.002.
8. J. Postel and J. Reynolds, Telnet Protocol Specification, IETF, RFC 854, 1983; Available from: http://www.ietf.org/rfc/rfc854.txt, 2022.
9. The Datasheet of the 8-bit Atmel Microcontroller with 64K/128K/256K Bytes In-System Programmable Flash, 2022; Available from: http://www.atmel.com/dyn/resources/prod_documents/doc2549.pdf , 2022.

10. J. Gettys, J. Mogul, H. Frystyk, L. Masinter, P. Leach, and T. Berners-Lee, Hypertext Transfer Protocol – HTTP/1.1, IETF, RFC 2616, 1999; Available from: http://www.ietf.org/rfc/rfc2616.txt, 2022.

11. I. Foster, Globus Toolkit Version 4: Software for Service-Oriented Systems, In *Proceedings of the IFIP International Conference on Network and Parallel Computing, LNCS, 3779*, Springer-Verlag, pp. 2–10, 2005. Available from: http://www.globus.org/alliance/publications/chapters/IFIP-2005.pdf, 2022.

12. A. Poshtkohi, A.H. Abutalebi, and S. Hessabi, DotGrid: A .NET-based Cross-Platform Software for Desktop Grids. *Int. J. Web Grid Serv.*, 3(3): 313–332, 2007. Available from: https://arxiv.org/abs/1703.03904, 2022.

13. C. Vecchiola, X. Chu, M. Mattess, and R. Buyya, Aneka – Integration of Private and Public Clouds, *Cloud Computing: Principles and Paradigms*, R. Buyya, J. Broberg, and A. Goscinski (eds), ISBN-13: 978-0470887998, Wiley Press, NY, pp. 249–274, 2011. Available from: http://www.cloudbus.org/chapters/Aneka-Cloud-Chapter2011.pdf, 2022.

14. A. Poshtkuhi, A. Abutalebi, L. Ayough, and S. Hessabi, DotGrid: A .NET-based Infrastructure for Global Grid Computing, In *Proceedings of the 6th IEEE International Symposium on Cluster Computing and the Grid*, 16–19 May 2006, (CCGrid'2006), Singapore. Available from: http://citeseerx.ist.psu.edu/viewdoc/summary?doi=10.1.1.116.3976, 2022.

15. C. Lever, M.A. Eriksen, and S.P. Molloy, An Analysis of the TUX Web Server, *CITI Technical Report 00-8*. 16 November 16 2000. Available from: http://www.citi.umich.edu/techreports/reports/citi-tr-00-8.pdf, 2022.

16. V.S. Pai, P. Druschel, and W. Zwaenepoel, Flash: An Efficient and Portable Web Server, In *Proceeding of the 1999 Annual Usenix Technical Conference*, June 1999, Monterey, CA, USA, 2022. Available from: http://www.usenix.org/event/usenix99/full_chapters/pai/pai.pdf

17. D.C. Schmidt and J.C. Hu, Developing Flexible and High-Performance Web Servers with Frameworks and Patterns. *ACM Computing Surveys*, 32(1), 2000. Available from: http://www.cse.wustl.edu/~schmidt/PDF/computing-surveys.pdf, 2022.

18. M. Welsh, D. Culler, and E. Brewer, SEDA: An Architecture for Well-Conditioned, Scalable Internet Services, In *Proceedings of the Eighteenth Symposium on Operating Systems Principles (SOSP-18)*, October 2001, Banff, Canada. Available from: http://www.eecs.harvard.edu/~mdw/chapters/seda-sosp01.pdf, 2022.

19. T.E. Anderson, B.N. Bershad, E.D. Lazowska, and H.M. Levy, Scheduler Activations: Effective Kernel Support for the User-Level Management of Parallelism. *ACM Transactions on Computer Systems*, 10(1): 53–79, 1992. Available from: http://www.cs.washington.edu/homes/bershad/Chapters/p53-anderson.pdf, 2022.

20. MSDN Library, WSAPoll Function, 2022; Available from: http://msdn.microsoft.com/en-us/library/ms741669.aspx

21. The Single UNIX ® Specification, Version 2, Realtime, 1997; Available from: http://pubs.opengroup.org/onlinepubs/007908799/xsh/realtime.html, 2022.

22. B. Chapman, Polling Made Efficient in the Solaris 7 OS, Sun Developer Network (SDN), Technical Articles, May 2002; Available from: http://developers.sun.com/solaris/articles/polling_efficient.html, 2022.

23. A. Jones and A. Deshpand, Windows Sockets 2.0: Write Scalable Winsock Apps Using Completion Ports, MSDN Magazine, October 2000; Available from: http://msdn.microsoft.com/en-us/magazine/cc302334.aspx, 2022.

24. AIO Description from POSIX Standard, The Open Group Base Specifications Issue 6 IEEE Std 1003.1, 2004 Editio,. Available from: http://pubs.opengroup.org/onlinepubs/009695399/basedefs/aio.h.html, 2022.

25. S. Ghemawat, H. Gobioff, and S. Leung, The Google File System, In *Proceedings of the 19th ACM Symposium on Operating Systems Principles*, October 2003, Lake George, NY, USA. Available from: http://labs.google.com/chapters/gfs-sosp2003.pdf, 2022.

26. K. Shvachko, H. Kuang, S. Radia, and R. Chansler, The Hadoop Distributed File System, In *Proceedings of the 27th IEEE Symposium on Massive Storage Systems and Technologies*, 28 June 2010, Incline Village, NV, USA.

27. M. Palankar, M. Ripeanu, and S. Garfinkel, Amazon S3 for Science Grids: A Viable Solution? In *Proceedings of the 2008 International Workshop on Data-aware Distributed Computing (DADC 2008)*, June 2008, Boston, MA, USA. Available from: http://www.cse.usf.edu/~anda/chapters/dadc108-palankar.pdf, 2022.

28. L. Ong and J. Yoakum, An Introduction to the Stream Control Transmission Protocol (SCTP), IETF, RFC 3286, 2002. Available from: http://www.ietf.org/rfc/rfc3286.txt, 2022.

29. Y. Gu and R.L. Grossman, UDT: UDP-based Data Transfer for High-speed Wide Area Networks. *Comput. Netw.* 51(7): 1777–1799, May 2007. Available from: http://www.cs.uic.edu/~ygu/chapter/udt-comnet-v3.pdf, 2022.

30. L. Ong and J. Yoakum, A Remote Direct Memory Access Protocol Specification, IETF, RFC 5040, October 2007. Available from: http://www.ietf.org/rfc/rfc5040.txt, 2022.

31. A. Poshtkuhi, A. Abutalebi, L. Ayough, and S. Hessabi, DotGrid: A .NET-based Cross-Platform Grid Computing Infrastructure, in: *Proceedings of the IEEE International Conference On Computing and Informatics 2006 (ICOCI'06)*, 6–8 June 2006, Malaysia. Available from: http://citeseerx.ist.psu.edu/viewdoc/summary?doi=10.1.1.110.2481, 2022.

32. ECMA-334: C# Language Specification, 2022; Available from: http://www.ecma-international.org/publications/standards/Ecma-334.htm

33. ECMA-335: Common Language Infrastructure (CLI), 2022; Available from: http://www.ecma-international.org/publications/techreports/E-TR-084.htm

34. ECMA-372: C++/CLI Language Specification, 2022; Available from: http://www.ecma-international.org/publications/standards/Ecma-372.htm

35. S. Liang, *Java(TM) Native Interface: Programmer's Guide and Specification*, First Edition, Prentice Hall, Hoboken, NJ, p. 320, 1999. ISBN 0201325772.

36. J. Clark, Calling Win32 DLLs in C# with P/Invoke, MSDN Magazine, The Microsoft Journal for Developers, July 2003. Available from: http://msdn.microsoft.com/en-us/magazine/cc164123.aspx, 2022.

37. S. Moore, Code Profiling Tools, Lecture Notes in Computer Science, University of Tennessee, 9 April 2003. Available from: http://web.eecs.utk.edu/~dongarra/WEB-PAGES/SPRING-2003/lect12a.pdf, 2022.

38. S. Shepler, B. Callaghan, D. Robinson, R. Thurlow, C. Beame, M. Eisler, and D. Noveck, Network File System (NFS) Version 4 Protocol, IETF, RFC 3530, April, 2003. Available from: http://www.ietf.org/rfc/rfc3530.txt, 2022.

39. J.H. Howard, M.L. Kazar, S.G. Nichols, D.A. Nichols, M. Satyanarayanan, R.N. Sidebotham, and M.J. West, Scale and Performance in a Distributed File System. *ACM Trans. Comput. Syst.*, 6(1): 51–81, 1988. doi: 10.1145/35037.35059.

40. P.J. Leach and D.C. Naik, A Common Internet File System (CIFS/1.0) Protocol, IETF, Internet-Draft, December 19, 1997. http://tools.ietf.org/id/draft-leach-cifs-v1-spec-01.txt, 2022.

41. K. Egevang and P. Francis, The IP Network Address Translator (NAT), IETF, RFC 1631, May, 1994. Available from: http://www.ietf.org/rfc/rfc1631.txt, 2022.

42. T. Dierks and E. Rescorla, The Transport Layer Security (TLS) Protocol Version 1.2, IETF, RFC 5246, August, 2008. Available from: http://www.ietf.org/rfc/rfc5246.txt, 2022.

43. P. Ford-Hutchinson, Securing FTP with TLS, IETF, RFC 4217, October, 2005. Available from: http://www.ietf.org/rfc/rfc4217.txt, 2022.

44. M. Horowitz and S. Lunt, FTP Security Extensions, IETF, RFC 2228, October, 1997. Available from: http://www.ietf.org/rfc/rfc2228.txt, 2022.

45. P. Srisuresh and M. Holdrege, IP Network Address Translator (NAT) Terminology and Considerations, IETF, RFC 2663, August, 1999. Available from: http://www.ietf.org/rfc/rfc2663.txt, 2022.

46. B. Curtin, Internationalization of the File Transfer Protocol, IETF, RFC 2640, July, 1999. Available from: http://www.ietf.org/rfc/rfc2640.txt, 2022.

47. R. Kettimuthu, M. Link, J. Bresnahan, and W. Allcock, Globus Data Storage Interface (DSI) – Enabling Easy Access to Grid Datasets, *First DIALOGUE Workshop: Applications-Driven Issues in Data Grids*, August 2005. http://www.mcs.anl.gov/~kettimut/publications/DSI.pdf, 2022.

48. W. Allcock, J. Bresnahan, and R. Kettimuthu, J. Link, The Globus eXtensible Input/Output System (XIO): A Protocol Independent IO System for the Grid, In *Proceedings of the Joint Workshop on High-Performance Grid Computing and High-Level Parallel Programming Models*, April 2005. http://www.globus.org/alliance/publications/chapters/hpgc05.pdf, 2022.

49. R. Kettimuthu, L. Wantao, J. Link, and J. Bresnahan, A GridFTP Transport Driver for Globus XIO, In *Proceedings of the 2008 International Conference on Parallel and Distributed Processing Techniques and Applications (PDPTA 2008)*, July 2008. http://www.globus.org/alliance/publications/chapters/gridftp_transport_driver_xio.pdf, 2022.

50. J. Bresnahan, R. Kettimuthu, and I. Foster, XIOPerf: A Tool for Evaluating Network Protocols, In *Proceedings of BROADNETS'2006*. http://www.globus.org/alliance/publications/chapters/xioperf.pdf, 2022.

51. K. Driesen and U. Hölzle, The Direct Cost of Virtual Function Calls in C++, OOPSLA 1996, USA. http://www.cs.ucsb.edu/~urs/oocsb/chapters/oopsla96.pdf, 2022.

Chapter 11

Parallel Programming Languages for High-Performance Computing

Interesting - I use a Mac to help me design the next Cray. (when he was told that Apple Inc. had recently bought a Cray supercomputer to help them design the next Mac)

Seymour Roger Cray

11.1 Introduction

Processing data and performing complex calculations at extreme speed is called high-performance computing (HPC). The HPC industry has always been evolving, particularly since 1999 when the use of commodity hardware and open-source software projects became widespread for scientific computing applications. The increasing performance of commodity processors made it possible to build large HPC clusters to aggregate performance to a more extent. That evolution today is a global standard for scientific computing and computationally intensive applications across a broad diversity of scientific disciplines such as drug discovery, artificial intelligence, and the Internet of Things (IoT). One of the ubiquitous classes of HPC is a supercomputer. Supercomputers contain many processing/storage nodes for achieving massive parallelism for parallel tasks. Despite this progress, hardware complexity, as studied during the preceding chapters, has dramatically grown mainly due to the trend in multi-core and many-core architectures. Therefore, programmers are facing new challenges for exploiting the maximum parallelism of HPC systems.

This chapter is chiefly devoted to programming HPC systems. First, a history of supercomputing is given, which outlines a brief advancement in supercomputers. Second, an overview of parallel programming models and languages developed and used in HPC platforms is presented, which acquaints the reader with the necessary

DOI: 10.1201/9781003379041-11

tools to deal with such complex systems. Third, the message passing interface (MPI) as a standard message-passing library is introduced to program supercomputers. We only examine a specific number of MPI features employed in this book to construct parallel programmes. It is necessary to note that a complete treatment of the MPI standard is beyond the scope of this book. Finally, three important examples are developed on top of MPI, which equip the reader with the necessary concepts and techniques for developing their own HPC applications.

11.2 A Brief History of Supercomputing

The emergence of supercomputers took place in 1964 when Control Data Corporation (CDC) 6600 was designed by Seymour Cray. This supercomputer had 400,000 transistors and about 100 miles of wire. It was capable of performing three million floating point operations per second (FLOPS), also known as 3 megaFLOPS, at a speed of 40MHz, so the fastest computing machine at that time. Afterwards, Cray established a company called Cray Research, which built the 80 MHz Cray 1 in 1976. Thanks to integrated circuits, the computer reached a maximum performance rate of 136 mega-FLOPS. The main success of Cray-1 was because of using shorter circuit lengths that resulted in a much faster machine, in which every component of the system was built to be as fast as possible. Cray 1 architecture benefited from vector processing, so its underlying implementation shifted to electronic chips.

The first use of transistor-based memory in supercomputers was made by Cary 1 instead of high-latency magnetic memory. The development of Cray 1 was based on a single processor by 1982 when Cray X-MP introduced four processors to the base architecture. It operated at 105 MHz and contributed more than a 200% boost in memory bandwidth compared with its predecessors. This new brand could achieve around 800 megaFLOPS in performance. The next version of Cray would arrive in 1985 as named Cray-2. This model featured eight processors, one of which managed memory, I/O, and storage, and the rest were called background processes used by applications to offload their computational tasks. A Unix-compliant operation system came with Cray 2. Before this time, supercomputers were mainly employed for nuclear explosion simulations and funded by governments. Therefore, there was no longer funding for doing such HPC tasks sponsored by them after the Cold War.

Cray systems were too expensive because of using vector architectures. At this time, markets were looking for alternative architectures using massively parallel processing (MPP) through multiple processors. MPP machines were an affordable new way of supercomputing. For example, the Connection Machine utilised a single global memory compiled with tens of thousands of very simple processors. Cray died in a car accident in 1996, and his quest for supercomputing ended very soon. However, Cray's ideas survived somewhere else in the world. In Japan, several companies started to construct vector supercomputers (including Fujitsu, Hitachi, and NEC), and there emerged the fastest computers with a performance speed of 600 gigaFLOPs.

After this period, Don Becker and Thomas Sterling at NASA created *Beowulf* taking advantage of a 10 Mbps Ethernet cable as the bus and 16 486DX processors. Today, Beowulf clusters are made up of thousands or tens of thousands of multi-core processors interconnected by high-speed fibre-optic cables and router chipset technologies such as InfiniBand and OmniPath. A parallel software program is dynamically dispatched to the cluster by a runtime system, where many processors work in tandem to solve computational problems powered by the Linux operating system. The basic concept of Beowulf systems made it possible for everyone to access HPC facilitates. Many attempted to increase the speed of supercomputers for two decades from the 1990s. A strategy to assess supercomputer performance was established in 1992, in which a set of Linpack benchmarks has been used by supercomputer vendors and the computational community.

Whilst the incremental improvement over the HPC technology has been underway for decades, software architects have also dramatically shaped the current notion of supercomputing not only to optimise the software stack of parallel programs but also to simplify the complex abstraction of supercomputers by developing new programming standards, one of the best-known types is the Message Passing Interface (MPI). The agreement for such a standard was because researchers were inventing the same wheel from scratch many times. The first version of MPI was released in 1994, whilst it took eight years until the MPI society adopted the second version of MPI called MPI-2.

Nowadays, designers use multi-core processors coupled to GPUs and other accelerators to build supercomputers. For instance, the fastest supercomputers were Tianhe-2 and MilkyWay-2 utilising Xeon Ivy Bridge and Xeon Phi (a kid of GPU) processors in 2014. The race in the construction of faster supercomputers never ends, and, currently, exaFLOPS supercomputers are sought by many countries, and they want to be the first one in this breakthrough race. In June 2020, Fugaku became the first claimed exascale computer in history. It is the first ARM-based architecture that connects 158,976 nodes, every of which consists of 52 ARM cores sustaining 32 GB high-bandwidth RAM per node, and 1.6 TB NVMe SSD and 16 nodes (L1) 150 PB shared Lustre FS (L2). Exascale computers are also a target for reaching the processing power of the human brain. After that, as of 2021, predictions say that zettascale computing will be within the reach of humans by 2035. Those imaginative supercomputers can solve problems never reached to date, ranging from forecasting the global weather and decreasing the 1,000 hours needed on exascale computers to calculating supernova simulations and to highly likely modelling the whole human brain accurately. However, other directions in massively parallel fabrics are under intense research, such as quantum and biological computers.

11.3 Parallel Programming Models and Languages for HPC

Programming parallel machines in efficient ways that can unravel the ultimate degree of parallelism from applications have been an active area of research for at least five decades. In an effort to reduce or hide the complexity of hardware from programmers, programming models have provided an abstraction of hardware features to bridge the gap between actual machine architecture and software development cycle. Therefore, parallel programming models represent a simpler abstraction of parallel machines to the programmer. On this basis, there are different variants of parallel programming models, for which a plethora of programming languages have been created, emerging from two fundamentally distinctive hardware organisations, including shared memory and message passing systems. A programming model does not depend on a specific architecture and is intended to be run by as many as possible parallel machines. In this section, we only consider those parallel programming languages that support message passing systems because of their extensive use in application development on supercomputers. Shared memory programming languages, such as Cilk, TBB, and PLINQ, are usually implemented on top of multithreading facilities of the underlying operating systems discussed in the earlier chapters of this book.

In the context of message passing programming models, they can be divided into *low-level programming models*, and *high-level programming models*, which are utilised on a trade-off between performance and ease of programming. A low-level programming language makes most of the underlying parallel architecture details explicit to the programmer by means of APIs and data structures. Since parallelism becomes explicit, one can write efficient code for tuning the best possible performance in accordance with low-level parallel metrics. For example, programmers can take control of host parallelism, problem decomposition, communication, and processor mapping. Entities have full access to communication details of the problem at best, and programmers can easily control the granularity of their programs. Maximising the performance comes at a price: decrease in programmability. In contrast, a high-level programming language removes many burdens on programmers by raising the level of abstraction and letting runtime systems and compilers do much of the work needed for parallelisation.

11.3.1 MPI

MPI supposes a collection of processes that communicate with each other only by exchanging explicit messages, so nothing is generally shared between processes. MPI is natively implemented for C and Fortran languages, which can be integrated easily into C++ programs. An MPI program is a single executable composed of individual processes, each of which runs on different address spaces. It is the programmer's responsibility to implement a diversity of functions for each process, and partition and distribute data. MPI supports a wide range of synchronous and asynchronous communication operations. Newer MPI versions include several improvements, such as one-sided communication through remote memory access, where only the sender process is involved. A rich set of collective operations are provided by MPI that can facilitate the development of parallel programs such as scatter, gather, broadcast, and reduction. These operations allow the processes within the same group to communicate. On the other hand, MPI features communicators whereby a programmer can define a group of disjoint domains of execution entities working closely together, each of which only sees its own relative collective operations. Several MPI features whose functions will be employed in this chapter to develop a number of case studies leveraging the massive parallelism of HPC clusters are given.

11.3.2 Charm++

Charm++ is an extension to the C++ programming language through a C++ library to provide parallel programming by improving programmer productivity, so it falls into high-level programming languages. A program developed in Charm++ is organised as several cooperating message-passing entities called *chars*. The Charm++ runtime system executes a whole Charm++ program and lets the programmer send a message to a remote object, which is likely to be addressed locally or remotely. Chars are asynchronously run by the runtime system. A collection of chars is assigned adaptively by the runtime system that ensures transparent scalability as required at runtime. Charm++ also features an MPI implementation on top of the core chares aiming at a more traditional programming model, which is distinguishable from an actual process-based MPI implementation in terms of performance because chars are threads of control with a much faster context switching latency between chars.

11.3.3 Partitioned Global Address Space (PGAS)

PGAS is a parallel programming model aimed to increase programmer productivity by hiding communication details through a set of conceptual shared-memory constructs implemented internally by a runtime system essentially on distributed shared memory hardware architectures. PGAS languages distinguish between access to local and remote data by providing additional programming abstractions. It means that at the hardware level the concept of shared memory from a programmer's point of view is realised such that various latencies exist for distinct memories managed by a PGAS runtime. A process, a cluster of processes, or any other arrangement can own these memories. There are plenty of PGAS languages, amongst which X10, Chapel, and Fortress have drawn wide attention.

Chapel introduces task and data parallelism without discrimination between both. Two routines `cobegin` and `coforall` are used to create and synchronise tasks in parallel. In Chapel, the responsibility of distributing irregular data structures are with the programmer by placing data objects in the intended locations. Distributed arrays in Chapel can take advantage of many memories dispersed across thousands of nodes.

X10 is a subset of Java classes that allows object-oriented programming with PGAS-based parallel constructs. All its features have been implemented by the notion of partitioned global address space. A programmer cannot migrate the main thread of control, called an activity, of an X10 program; instead, an activity can spawn activities in other places asynchronously (whether locally or remotely) with the `async` keyword. Distributed partitions of PGAS are called `places` in X10; therefore, regular data can be allocated throughout places. The programmer must move the computation to where data resides.

11.4 A Concise Introduction to the MPI Standard in C Language

MPI is a comprehensive parallel programming standard that presents the best features of existing message-passing programming models and includes new extensions unavailable in previous models whenever necessary. Here, we introduce four basic classes of widely used MPI routines (with bindings to C language) to develop parallel programs. Interested readers can refer to the MPI standard or other texts for a complete description of further MPI functions.

11.4.1 MPI Setup Routines

This collection of routines provides means of obtaining from or setting an MPI execution. For example, they can be used to initialise, terminate, and query the MPI execution environment operating inside an MPI program. An essential list of these widely used routines is as follows:

int MPI_Init(int *argc, char ***argv)
Initialises an MPI execution environment. Each MPI program must invoke this routine before issuing any parallel execution through MPI routines. The program's environmental variables can be passed into the MPI runtime through this function, i.e., `argc` and `argv` variables.
int MPI_Finalize(void)
Causes termination of an MPI program, and thereafter no code or other MPI routine will run after reaching this routine.
int MPI_Comm_size(MPI_Comm comm, int *size)
Returns the total number of processes participating in a specified communicator. The default communicator type `MPI_COMM_WORLD` is used throughout this chapter.
int MPI_Comm_rank(MPI_Comm comm, int *rank)
Returns the identifier of the calling MPI process by the specified communicator. MPI processes are ranked from zero to the total number of processes minus one within the current communicator.

11.4.2 MPI Blocking Point-to-Point Communication Routines

In message-passing systems, such as the MPI programming model, a region of a process's address space is transparently copied to another process which is usually instructed by the programmer. The sender must specify which portion of its memory and to what size will be transferred to which destination process's address space. The data type and usually the number of bytes for transmission must also be specified. For the receiver, the address and length of the intended memory region for copy operations in conjunction with the sender identity must be provided. It is a typical scenario in which point-to-point communication happens within an MPI program. The most basic type of this communication is to use a blocking communication, in which the code that calls it returns its control to the MPI runtime. The MPI executable will inform the calling process when the requested data becomes available and is copied into an appropriate calling MPI routine. A downside of this approach occurs when data is unavailable, and the program is blocked incapable of performing any useful task. However, it avoids the burden on the programmer to write proper code to handle this situation. Two commonly used routines for blocking point-to-point communication are as given below:

int MPI_Send(const void *buf, int count, MPI_Datatype datatype, int dest, int tag, MPI_Comm comm)
Sends the contents from buffer with the number of data elements specified as `count` to a destination process. Four fundamental data types specified by datatype includes `MPI_INT`, `MPI_FLOAT`, `MPI_DOUBLE`, `MPI_LONG_DOUBLE`, and `MPI_BYTE`, which are equivalents to `int`, `float`, `double`, `long double`, and `char` data types in C language, respectively.

int MPI_Recv(void *buf, int count, MPI_Datatype datatype, int source, int tag, MPI_Comm comm, MPI_Status *status)
Fills the buffer with the contents specified by the length of data elements and their data type received from a source process. status is a useful variable that can be accompanied by other MPI routines to interrogate information about the data (e.g., the actual bytes received from the sender). Unless specified, a value of MPI_STATUS_IGNORE is used for status in this chapter.

11.4.3 MPI Non-Blocking Point-to-Point Communication Routines

An alternative approach to point-to-point communication is non-blocking send/ receive routines that complete I/O asynchronously in the background of an MPI program. This method is beneficial to the programmer in terms of performance in contrast to blocking communication because every MPI process can perform useful computations, as the MPI runtime system completes send/receive operations on behalf of an executable. A call to asynchronous MPI routines returns immediately and gives control to the application, whose responsibility is to manage the completion of I/O requests. It implies that additional programming is required to keep track of open communication channels. Four non-blocking MPI routines to initiate and manage requests asynchronously are as follows:

int MPI_Isend(const void *buf, int count, MPI_Datatype datatype, int dest, int tag, MPI_Comm comm, MPI_Request *request)
Immediately sends a buffer. Many of the parameters of this routine resemble MPI_Send function except the request variable. Because a non-blocking operation may not complete before the MPI system informs the calling process of completion, the MPI runtime issues a unique number accessible to the process as a request context. The programmer must use this context by calling MPI wait routines in order to determine the status of a non-blocking send/receive operation.
int MPI_Irecv(void *buf, int count, MPI_Datatype datatype, int source, int tag, MPI_Comm comm, MPI_Request *request)
Begins an asynchronous receive in the background. Similar to MPI_Isend, a request can be registered by this routine to take care of non-blocking I/O progress.
int MPI_Wait(MPI_Request *request, MPI_Status *status)
Waits on a non-blocking request to complete. This routine should be used immediately after a non-blocking MPI operation to check the underlying transport status. Of course, the programmer can write extra code after a call to any non-blocking routine and before MPI_Wait, of course, to exploit more parallelism by overlapping computation with communication.
int MPI_Waitall(int count, MPI_Request array_of_requests[], MPI_Status *array_of_statuses)
This routine is an extension of MPI_Wait to monitor the status of multiple requests represented as an array. The size of the request array must be specified by count.

11.4.4 MPI Collective Operation Routines

The operations introduced in the previous two sections are known as a point-to-point message passing system in which a sender directly addresses a destination process by exchanging explicit messages. What happens if a task intends to send a message to many others is to use basic point-to-point messages to imitate a one-to-many message delivery system; however, this kind of implementation has two disadvantages. On the one side of the coin, it becomes cumbersome for the programmer who is forced to write extra code for issuing send calls. On the other hand, this naïve implementation suffers from critical scalability problems because it dramatically increases communication time in an inefficient manner as discussed in Section 11.5.2. An alternative approach is using MPI collective operations that avail of efficient implementations internally for a wide diversity of HPC interconnect architectures.

Figure 11.1 a conceptual interpretation of four basic MPI collective communication routines. It is essential to point out that these operations are meant to establish global synchronisation points amongst all processes of an MPI communicator. As a result, when these routines are used within an MPI program, all processes must reach these points before the MPI runtime environment can allow all the involved processes to continue their execution. A broadcast operation is when a process sends the same data to all other processes within a specified communicator. All processes must wait until this operation completes (an internal MPI implementation may use an MPI_Barrier to ensure this property). A reduce operation is a classic conceptual mechanism borrowed from functional programming languages in that a collection of data items are integrated into a single data or value. The most useful operations

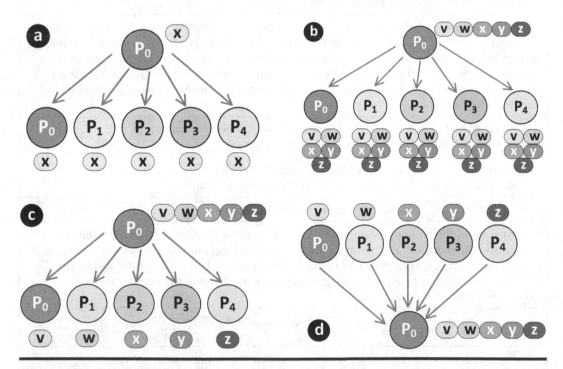

Figure 11.1 Conceptual illustration of MPI collective operations: (a) MPI_Bcast routine, (b) MPI_Reduce routine, (c) MPI_Scatter routine, and (d) MPI_Gather routine.

are summation and multiplication across all data items. The result of this operation returns to a single process (usually the root MPI process). Contrary to a broadcast operation is the transmission of different values from a root process to all processes. A scatter operation sends chunks of data items to different processes. On the opposite side, a gather operation takes many data items and delivers them as contiguous data to a single process. These two operations are beneficial to many parallel algorithms (e.g., sorting algorithms). Note that an MPI implementation may likewise present non-blocking collective operations in a similar approach to what was discussed for non-blocking communication routines.

An essential list of these widely used routines is as follows:

`int MPI_Barrier(MPI_Comm comm)`
Suspends all MPI processes specified within a communicator until all of them reach this routine.
`int MPI_Bcast(void *buffer, int count, MPI_Datatype datatype, int root, MPI_Comm comm)`
Broadcasts a message specified by `buffer` to all processes participating in the collective operation.
`int MPI_Reduce(const void *sendbuf, void *recvbuf, int count, MPI_Datatype datatype, MPI_Op op, int root, MPI_Comm comm)`
Collects all the data specified as `sendbuf` defined by a mathematical operation `op` within a single value and delivers it to the `root` process declared by `recvbuf`.
`int MPI_Allreduce(const void *sendbuf, void *recvbuf, int count, MPI_Datatype datatype, MPI_Op op, MPI_Comm comm)`
Collects all the data specified as `sendbuf` defined by a mathematical operation `op` within a single value and broadcasts it to all participating processes declared by `recvbuf`.
`int MPI_Scatter(const void *sendbuf, int sendcount, MPI_Datatype sendtype, void *recvbuf, int recvcount, MPI_Datatype recvtype, int root, MPI_Comm comm)`
Propagates chunks of data to all processes specified by `sendbuf`. Note that either `sendbuf` or `recvbuf` can be null at a time; for instance, if a root process sends only data to other processes, then its `recvbuf` can be set to null whilst other processes must set their `sendbuf` to null.
`int MPI_Gather(const void *sendbuf, int sendcount, MPI_Datatype sendtype, void *recvbuf, int recvcount, MPI_Datatype recvtype, int root, MPI_Comm comm)`
Collects chunks of data from all processes of a given communicator and delivers a single concatenated data to the `root` process.

11.5 Case Studies

In this section, we consider a collection of examples to illustrate how a parallel MPI program is developed in practice. Simplicity is an important issue when it comes to programming highly complicated MPI applications. For this purpose, the examples given provide sufficient basic routines needed in such situations. To make the overall examples manageable in terms of complexity and ease of understanding, all abide by a master/slave paradigm given in Figure 11.2(a). A controller is spawned at the beginning of every application whose role is to create and distribute worker MPI

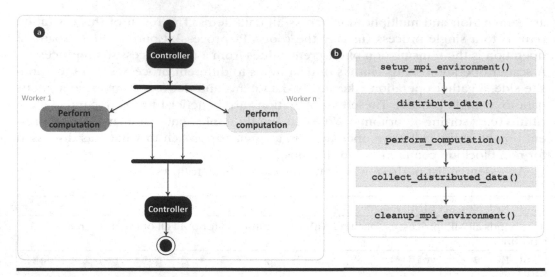

Figure 11.2 **Typical parallelisation implementation for the examples of this chapter: (a) a controller setups and manages a number of workers, each of which performs necessary divided computation, and (b) the implementation of every example takes five consecutive steps in terms of C functions to complete.**

processes across a network of HPC nodes. Every worker will then take the responsibility to execute part of their workload in parallel. It is worth noting that workers with each other or the controller begin a globally coordinated synchronisation point if the underlying parallel computation requires it for a sound completion. This deployment eventually gathers the result of all distributed computations on the controller. Figure 11.2(a) depicts the flow of developed routines used in all examples. First, an MPI environment is configured and created, which is compulsory for each MPI program. Then, the controller distributes data via calling distribute_data(). Every example implements a customised perform_computation() function that performs a fine/coarse grain computation on data per worker. When a global computation completes, the generated data is collected through different MPI communication primitives (this is the case in which distribute_data() routine is implemented similarly). Finally, before every example termination, the MPI execution environment is cleaned up by invoking clean_up_mpi_environment(). Due to lack of space, we present all the examples merely with the help of pseudocodes. Developed MPI codes are written in a mixture of C and C++ languages and can be found in the path "/Supercomputing/Examples" in the companion materials of the book.

11.5.1 A Warm-Up MPI Example

The first example is a perfect parallel program to compute the natural logarithm of a decimal number. We avail of numerical integration herein as illustrated in Figure 11.3 and expressed below:

$$lna = \int_{1}^{a} \frac{1}{x} dx$$

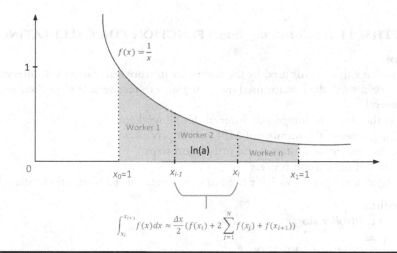

$$\int_{x_i}^{x_{i+1}} f(x)dx \approx \frac{\Delta x}{2}\left(f(x_i) + 2\sum_{j=1}^{N} f(x_j) + f(x_{i+1})\right)$$

Figure 11.3 A parallel algorithm for calculating `ln(a)` based on the definite integral of homographic function.

The entire integration interval is divided into n segments, each of which is integrated locally by a worker MPI process. Because the numerical integration of each region is independent of others, each worker can numerically integrate its assigned subinterval, and, finally, the calculated integrals are collected by the controller. Note that, due to this perfect parallel nature, the only synchronisation point is introduced into the computation after all workers complete their execution to which a reduction is performed to add all partial local sums into the final integration value. The trapezoidal rule, which is a simple technique for approximation of definite integrals using a trapezoid as shown in Figure 11.3, is exploited in each subinterval.

Algorithm 11.1 explains an implementation of `distribute_data()` function. A rank is used to distinguish between a controller and a worker. Since the information of each subinterval is simple and its structure is similar to all workers, one can allocate a contagious area of memory such as an array of a simple data structure and spread it to all workers through MPI collective operations. Although it may raise code complexity, performance is not sacrificed. In this way, a lot of processing information or data can be shared with many processes; however, it is not a concern in this simple example because `distribute_data()` function is called once before the actual execution begins. The controller prepares the information array in lines 10 through 16 and then calls the `MPI_Scatter` routine to scatter the array whose every three elements correspond to a single worker process. Carefully look at the calling convention used in line 17. The controller is playing the role of a data distributor, so it sends data out, and when the first argument is a buffer to be sent and the receiver buffer is ignored (by setting it to null). On the other side, which is a worker, receiving task data is more than simply just by calling `MPI_Scatter` in line 19, but this time by nulling the sender buffer.

ALGORITHM 11.1: *distribute_data()* **FUNCTION FOR CALCULATING** *ln (a)*

Definitions:

1 *works*: a large data vector used by the controller to store integration sub-intervals
2 *my_work*: a small data vector used by the workers to receive and store their integration
3 sub-interval
4 *step_x*: the length of integration intervals for all workers
5 *num_of_wokers*: the number of MPI worker processes
6 $[x_0 \; x_1]$, Δx: integration interval and integration steps
7 *rank*: rank of the current process
8 *current_x*: a temporary variable used to store points of the integration interval

The Algorithm:

9 **if** *rank = controller* **do**
10   $step\_x \leftarrow \dfrac{x_1 - x_0}{num\_of\_workers}$
11   $current\_x \leftarrow x_0$
12   **for all** element $\in$ works **do**
13    $element.x_0 \leftarrow current\_x$
14    $current\_x \leftarrow current\_x + step\_x$
15    $element.x_1 \leftarrow current\_x$
16    $element.\Delta x \leftarrow \Delta x$
17   **MPI_Scatter(&works[0], 3, …)**
18 **else do**
19   **MPI_Scatter(…, &my_work[0], 3, …)**
20 **MPI_Barrier()**

Until now, our worker processes have received their local information and can start their actual execution. As earlier stated, this example does not require any particular synchronisation point during parallel execution; therefore, every process will perform a locally sequential version of the trapezoidal rule as detailed in Algorithm 11.2.

ALGORITHM 11.2: *perform_computation()* **FUNCTION FOR CALCULATING** *ln (a)*

Definitions:

1 *local_sum*: the area under $f(x) = \dfrac{1}{x}$ in the sub-interval of a worker
2 *x*: a variable used to advance the numerical integration for every iteration of the trapezoidal rule
3 x_0, x_1: initial and final points for which the local numerical integration is performed by every worker

The Algorithm:

4 $local\_sum \leftarrow \dfrac{1}{x_0} + \dfrac{1}{x_1}$
5 $x \leftarrow x_0$
6 **while** $x < x_1$ **do**
7   $x \leftarrow x + \Delta x$
8   $local\_sum \leftarrow local\_sum + \dfrac{2}{x}$

Ultimately, it is needed to add all local sums together to find the composite value of our natural logarithm. It is realised by Algorithm 11.3, which has just a single line of code by calling the `MPI_Reduce` procedure. All processes will receive the summation of local values inside a globally defined sum variable.

ALGORITHM 11.3: *COLLECT_DISTRIBUTED_DATA()* **FUNCTION FOR CALCULATING** *LN(A)*

Definitions:
1 *local_sum*: the area under f(x) in the sub-interval of a worker
2 *global_sum*: a variable that is used to sum all local areas into a global one

The Algorithm:
3 **MPI_Reduce(&local_sum, &global_sum, 1, MPI_LONG_DOUBLE, MPI_SUM,...)**

After compiling the MPI code of this example, the user can run it via several similar syntaxes as follows:

```
mpirun -np 4 ParallelLn.exe
```

where np stands for the number of MPI processes followed by an MPI executable file. Another way can be as given below:

```
mpiexec -np 4 ParallelLn.exe
```

11.5.2 Scalability of MPI Programs

After our simple journey to MPI programming's world, we are going to delve into a non-trivial MPI program but very useful to illustrate the strength of MPI primitives. Scalability is the ability of a computer system to perform more computational work when the capacity of a computer is raised (e.g., the number of processing elements). Therefore, scalability importantly is indicative of how well a high-end computer (particularly, HPC clusters) can reach more processing capacity when available resources increase. From a software's point of view, scalability emphasises how much a parallel application can reach an actual speed-up (which is the ratio of sequential execution of the original program to parallelised one). The difficult task of parallel programming is how to efficiently decide to break a computation in such a way that maximum scalability is accomplished through an MPI-based implementation.

A parallel application may exhibit one of the two scaling types: Strong and weak scaling. Strong scaling happens when a computational problem size stays constant whilst it can complete quicker by increasing the number of cores. This type usually refers to those applications that are CPU-bound with long runs. The best case is when all processors almost stay busy to achieve the maximum speed-up. In contrast, an application operates under weak scaling to reach a reasonable performance when both the problem size and the number of processes increase simultaneously. This type usually is used for constructing memory-bound applications where a single program with its data is not able to reside in a limited amount of physical memory. Some several metrics and rules affect the final scaling and should be contemplated during algorithm design and program implementation using MPI. As there is no definite best practice for writing efficient parallel MPI code because it is highly application specific, here we lay three steps that are supposed to bear in mind.

As applications are developed mainly for sequential runs and then incrementally are changed to adopt parallelism, programmers should write codes in such a way that it is affordable for improvement and maintenance. If the final goal is to develop a high-performance application, sequential and parallel code shall be implemented in tandem.

Due to the complex nature of parallel programming and unexpected outcomes of a developed program, the developer should initially write a first version of the program and then try to tune those parts that require more attention for optimal execution and peak efficiency.

Code optimisation can begin basically from tuning compilation flags followed by testing it with extensive parallel setup arrangements, for example profiling the code on a single multi-core node and afterwards on an HPC cluster. Manual screening and leveraging existing profiling tools help the programmer identify which parts of the code are time-consuming and likely a source of suspicion for degrading the perfor-mance and scalability of the software.

The first phase in parallel application development is to change the underlying algorithms to be able to run in parallel. However, the next step shall be identifying parallelisation opportunities for every software component implemented in favour of ultimate performance. For example, some components can be implemented using threads, some others using MPI routines or even GPUs. Of course, choosing an appropriate programming library beyond MPI as a basis of the development can be also taken into consideration. One can find these opportunities at different levels of the code. For example, inner loops of an MPI process may be well suited to harness vectorisation features.

After the initial implementation of a program, multiple opportunities exist to opti-mise it. One can think of improving data locality when accessing data in memory. An extremely powerful criterion in performance optimisation is when the programmer pays closer attention to overlapping communication with computation. It can give rise to much lower latencies, exploiting the hardware as fully as possible, and higher throughputs. For example, inter-node communication using shared and conditional variables, and in the case of MPI level using non-blocking communication primitives (and reusing the existing collective operations or designing new ones), all can sig-nificantly contribute to better performance.

Last but not least, an important guideline in parallel programming is to validate the correctness of parallel programs in which the results must entirely match the sequential version of it. The program must be free of any kind of race condition and be deterministic (i.e., the final numerical results of each run ought to be identical).

In this section, we intend to implement different variants of MPI_Bcast that will show efficient use of MPI primitives, or most importantly, proper dealing with communication scalability can deliver better concurrency. Let's suppose that in our main framework of Figure 11.2, the controller becomes in charge of broadcasting a time value in performing a physical phenomenon by utilising numerical simulation. This time is broadcast in time steps (which may be dynamic) repeatedly until a final time reaches. A typical implementation can be to use a while loop whose iterations involve a call to the MPI_Bcast routine as given in Algorithm 11.4. Note that the controller only updates its local simulation time where workers only receive it.

ALGORITHM 11.4: *test_mpi_broadcast()* **FUNCTION USING NATIVE MPI BROADCAST**

Definitions:
1 *t*: time
2 *time_step*: a value by which time increments
3 *simulation_until*: the execution terminated when *t* reaches this variable

The Algorithm:
4 $t \leftarrow 0, time\_step \leftarrow 10^{-6}, simulation\_until \leftarrow 1 \Leftarrow$ Initialise variables
5 Initialise MPI environment
6 **while** $t \leq simulation\_until$ **do** $\Leftarrow$ Simulation loop
7   **if** *rank* = *controller* **do**
8     $t \leftarrow t + time\_step$
9   MPI_Bcast(&t, 1, MPI_DOUBLE, controller,...)
10   **else do**
11   MPI_Bcast(&t, 1, MPI_DOUBLE, controller,...)
12   MPI_Barrier()
13 Finalise MPI environment

If we were wanted to replace MPI_Bcast with our own variant, there would be many different alternatives. A naïve realisation (causing the worst performance) is when the controller sends its local simulation time to all workers through a loop in which every iteration calls the blocking MPI_Send primitive, and each worker issues the blocking MPI_Recv routine on the opposite side. This model is explained in Algorithm 11.5. One might think of modifying this code to be accompanied by a non-blocking send and receive; although it can improve the performance a little, there is not so much gain obtained because when the controller singly sends packets of data network, congestion may occur in the sending side. Network resources are usually limited; for instance, when a network node sends more data than it can handle, congestion may happen from the node side to the nearest router (which has a constrained amount of processing time and throughput).

ALGORITHM 11.5: *test_blocking_broadcast()* **FUNCTION TO EMULATE** MPI_Bcast

Definitions:
1 *t*: time
2 *time_step*: a value by which time increments
3 *simulation_until*: the execution terminates when *t* reaches this variable

The Algorithm:
4 $t \leftarrow 0, time\_step \leftarrow 10^{-6}, simulation\_until \leftarrow 1 \Leftarrow$ Initialise variables
5 Initialise MPI environment
6 **while** $t \leq simulation\_until$ **do** $\Leftarrow$ Simulation loop
7   **if** *rank* = *controller* **do**
8     $t \leftarrow t + time\_step$
6   **for all** $w \in workers$ **do**

```
9        Send the value of t to w by calling MPI_Send
10   else do
11       MPI_Recv(&t, 1, MPI_DOUBLE, controller,...)
12 MPI_Barrier()
13 Finalise MPI environment
```

To tackle this dilemma, a hierarchical model of communication can be developed whereby every node shares its packet processing capability and link throughput in a critical attempt to prevent congestion problems and any performance bottleneck through a collective operation. Tree data structures are perfect examples for facilitating collective communications, which are scalable and highly used in supercomputers. Here, we choose balanced binary trees (BBTs), also known as height-balanced binary trees, to implement our customised MPI broadcast operation. A BBT is a type of tree in which the height of the right and left subtrees of any node cannot differ by more than one. Note that a node's height in the tree terminology is defined as the number of edges to its farthest leaf node. The C++ code of a typical BBT implementation is accessible from the book's companion materials for this example. The execution of the code for a total of 16 MPI processes gives rise to the tree deployment in Figure 11.4, which is also well balanced.

Let's focus on our BBT-based broadcast operation using non-blocking MPI primitives. Algorithm 11.6 shows the whole flows needed to implement our example rather than using the MPI_Bcast routine. The first stage is to set up a distributed BBT by which all processes are informed of their corresponding node information in lines 10–15 by calling MPI_Send and MPI_Recv routines. Note that for a large-scale supercomputer with millions of processor cores, such a setup procedure could be performed by a more comprehensive mechanism, even outside the MPI environment. Then, this information can be accessed by all nodes before executing MPI applications. In this example, we have integrated the controller code with the workers; nevertheless, in lines 17–19, the simulation time is only updated on the controller. Each

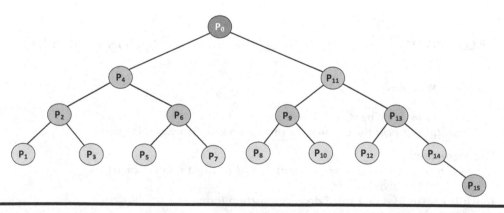

Figure 11.4   A typical example of a balanced binary tree structure formed to implement a customised MPI broadcast using non-blocking communication operations comprising 16 MPI processes.

node first receives a message from its parent in lines 19–21 by invoking the non-blocking `MPI_Irecv` function; consequently, the controller has no parent, and these lines do not execute for it. Since the function MPI_Irecv in line 20 asynchronously returns immediately, we need to wait until the receive operation completes. If the current process (either controller or worker) has a left or/and right leaf, `MPI_Isend` is called with the corresponding child identifier to asynchronously send the value of t in lines 22 through 25. By taking how many children a node has into account, a convenient MPI wait routine is issued in lines 26–31, in which `MPI_Wait` and `MPI_Waitall` routines stand for single and double leaf(s), respectively.

ALGORITHM 11.6: *test_broadcast_balanced_binary_tree* **FUNCTION USING TO EMULATE** `MPI_Bcast` **USING A HIERARCHICAL STRUCTURE AND NON-BLOCKING MPI COMMUNICATION OPERATIONS**

Definitions:
1 *t*: time
2 *time _ step*: a value by which time increments
3 *simulation _ until*: the execution terminated when *t* reaches this variable
4 *request, status*: Two variables are used when calling non-blocking MPI routines for an asynchronous receipt from a parent three node
5 *requests, statuses*: Two arrays, each of which is composed of two elements representing left/right children of a tree node, that are used when calling non-blocking MPI routines for asynchronous dispatch to the children of a tree node
6 *workers*: the list of worker MPI processes
7 (*parent, left, right*): stores the current node information made up of parent and left/right children

The Algorithm:
8   $t \leftarrow 0, time \_ step \leftarrow 10^{-6}, simulation \_ until \leftarrow 1 \Leftarrow$ Initialise variables
9   Initialise MPI environment
10 **if** *rank = controller* **do** $\Leftarrow$ Set up a distributed binary tree
11   Create a balanced binary tree in which every node stands for a single MPI process in the broadcast
       hierarchy
12 **for all** *w* ∈ *workers* **do**
13   Send the node information corresponding to w by calling **MPI_Send**
14 **else do**
15   Receive the node information for the current worker by calling **MPI_Recv**
16 **while** *t* ≤ *simulation _ until* **do** $\Leftarrow$ Simulation loop
17   **if** *rank = controller* **do** $\Leftarrow$ Increment *t* on the controller
18        $t \leftarrow t + time \_ step$
19   **if** *the current process **has** a parent* **do** $\Leftarrow$ Asynchronously receive *t* from a parent
20   **MPI_Irecv(&t, 1, MPI_DOUBLE, parent,..., &request)**
21   **MPI_Wait(&request, &status)**
22   **if** *the current process **has** a left child* **do** $\Leftarrow$ Asynchronously send *t to* a left child
23   **MPI_Isend(&t, 1, MPI_DOUBLE, left,..., &request[0])**
24   **if** *the current process **has** a right child* **do** $\Leftarrow$ Asynchronously send *t to* a right child
25   **MPI_Isend(&t, 1, MPI_DOUBLE, right,..., &request[1])**

```
26    if the current process has two children do
      ⇐ Asynchronously wait on requests already set ups
27        MPI_Waitall(2, requests, statuses)
28    else if the current process only has a left child do
      ⇐ Asynchronously wait on the left child
29        MPI_Wait(&requests[0], &statuses[0])
30    else if the current process only has a right child do
      ⇐ Asynchronously wait on the right child
31        MPI_Wait(&requests[1], &statuses[1])
32 MPI_Barrier()
33 Finalise MPI environment
```

11.5.3 Parallel Sparse Matrix-Vector Multiplication

In this and the next example, we deal with parallel MPI algorithms on sparse matrices. In a sparse matrix, the majority of entries are zero compared to dense matrices whose entries are mainly non-zero. One can find many different ways (data structures) to store and retrieve sparse matrices. In any possible way, storing zero elements must be avoided, which will make the algorithms to work with this type of matrices difficult.

A beneficial kind of sparse matrix representation is the *compressed column storage* (CCS) form, which we will use in this chapter. In the CCS format, the columns of a sparse matrix are stored instead of rows. This data structure is expressed by three arrays p, i and x (we take advantage of array indexing in C language by which the first entry of an array begins at position 0). If our matrix is m by n, the size of p is n+1. The array i stores row indices of the matrix in which the row indices of column j are stored in i[y] to i[z], where y=p[j] and z=p[j+1]-1. Note that the first entry of p is always set to be zero, and the k'th entry p is always the sum of all non-zero elements of all columns up to the current column. Figure 11.5 represents the sparse matrix A with three arrays (p, i, x). It is necessary to note that the elements of each row stored in i and x can be either sorted or unsorted. Because the results in matrix operations are unknown before actually performing any operation, we do not want to be strict in sorting every entry of each column stored in i and x. Every algorithm of this chapter processes each column without assuming ordered entry elements of every column. It is advantageous in terms of efficiency because sorting a large sparse matrix in every column-wise operation can cause critical overhead. It is worth noting that most CCS algorithms access a sparse matrix column by column.

$$A = \begin{bmatrix} 0 & 0 & 0 & 2 \\ 0 & 0 & 2 & 0 \\ 1 & 1 & -1 & 0 \\ 1 & 0 & 0 & 0 \end{bmatrix} \implies \begin{array}{l} p = [0\ 2\ 3\ 5\ 6] \\ i = [2\ 3\ 2\ 1\ 2\ 0] \\ x = [1\ 1\ 1\ 2\ -1\ 2] \end{array}$$

Figure 11.5   An example sparse matrix with its *compressed column storage* representation.

The simplest form of sequential sparse matrix operation is matrix-vector multiplication (even easier than matrix-matrix addition because in sparse matrices locating the corresponding column entries in two matrices A and B is non-trivial, and in most cases an out-of-order search to find pairs in two columns of both matrices must be made). We first develop a simple algorithm for sequential sparse matrix-vector multiplication (SPMV) and then extend it to support parallelism. Since our sequential algorithm requires accessing columns of a sparse matrix A, the multiplication of A by v vector is expanded for a general 3-by-3 matrix below

$$
A.v = \begin{bmatrix} a_{11} & a_{12} & a_{13} \\ a_{21} & a_{22} & a_{23} \\ a_{31} & a_{32} & a_{33} \end{bmatrix} \begin{bmatrix} v_1 \\ v_2 \\ v_3 \end{bmatrix} = \begin{bmatrix} a_{11}v_1 + a_{12}v_2 + a_{13}v_3 \\ a_{21}v_1 + a_{22}v_2 + a_{23}v_3 \\ a_{31}v_1 + a_{32}v_2 + a_{33}v_3 \end{bmatrix}
$$

As seen, there is a pattern in the expansion, and it appears that the resultant vector is a sum over every column j by its corresponding entry in v_j. Therefore, we can write this interpretation as given below:

$$
A.v = \begin{bmatrix} a_{11} \\ a_{21} \\ a_{31} \end{bmatrix} v_1 + \begin{bmatrix} a_{12} \\ a_{22} \\ a_{32} \end{bmatrix} v_2 + \begin{bmatrix} a_{13} \\ a_{23} \\ a_{33} \end{bmatrix} v_3 = \begin{bmatrix} A_{*1} & A_{*2} & A_{*3} \end{bmatrix} \begin{bmatrix} v_1 \\ v_2 \\ v_3 \end{bmatrix}
$$

Where A_{*j} is short for all the three row-wise entries of column j of the A matrix. This straightforward formula can be generalised to n-by-n matrices easily. In our sequential algorithm, the resultant vector is pre-allocated and then overwritten within a loop whose every iteration multiplies a single column by its corresponding entry in v.

Let's now turn our attention to the parallelisation of the basic sparse matrix-vector multiplication algorithm. Consider a sparse 5-by-5 matrix shown in Figure 11.6 multiplied with a vector of length 5. Given two worker processes, we intend to perform this multiplication in parallel. Worker 1 receives two columns of A, as the rest of the columns of A are assigned to Worker 2. Note that this task division on the A matrix is carried out vertically, but it is rather horizontal for the v vector (mainly due

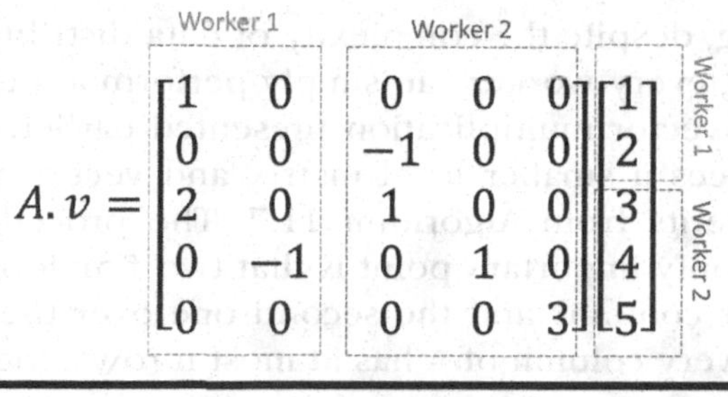

Figure 11.6 A typical parallel example of a matrix-vector multiplication over two workers.

to the necessity for every worker to access its corresponding range of rows in A). The parallelisation algorithm is a bit messy because of the sparsity nature of the A matrix; therefore, we give only a big picture of parallel algorithms for this and the next example due to space limitation and miss the details out. We leave them with the reader to take a careful look at the source codes of both examples, which are available in the companion materials of the book.

The data distribution phase of parallel matrix-vector multiplication is shown in Algorithm 11.7. The controller needs to divide the data structure of the A matrix into individual sparse submatrices and sends them out to workers. From a controller's perspective, these are submatrices, but workers must treat them as complete sparse matrices. Hence, the main duty of the controller is to nicely break both A matrix and v vector down to submatrices and sub-vectors, and then every worker itself builds a new sparse matrix and a new vector.

ALGORITHM 11.7: *distribute_data()* **FUNCTION FOR SPARSE MATRIX-VECTOR MULTIPLICATION**

Definitions:
1 p, i, x: elements to store the matrix A or a sub-matrix of A
2 v: the matrix A is multiplied by vector v or a sub-vector of v
3 w: An MPI worker process
4 *workers*: the list of worker MPI processes

The Algorithm:
5 **if** *rank = controller* **do**
6   **for all** $w \in$ workers **do**
7   Create a column-wise sparse sub-matrix from A from p, i and x
8   Create a sub-vector from v
9   Send the newly created sub-matrix and sub-vector to w by consecutive calling to **MPI_Send**
10 **else do**
11   Receive the size of p, i, x and v for the current worker from the controller process by consecutive calling to **MPI_Recv** and creating a sub-matrix A and sub-vector v
12 **MPI_Barrier()**

For the time being, despite the complexity of data distribution for our recently developed algorithm, every worker can simply perform a local sequential version of the sparse matrix-vector multiplication presented earlier. It is mainly because every worker only sees a smaller local matrix and vector as long as the distribution structure inherits from Algorithm 11.7. The procedure is elaborated in Algorithm 11.8. The only important point is that two for loops are used in which the first iterates over columns and the second one over the rows of the current column of A. Since every column of A has at most n rows, the size of the resultant vector r is n.

ALGORITHM 11.8: *perform_computation()* **FUNCTION FOR SPARSE MATRIX-VECTOR MULTIPLICATION**

Definitions:
1 A: a sub-matrix on each worker
2 v: a sub-vector on each worker
3 r: a vector that is used to store the result of multiplication on each worker

The Algorithm:
4 *columns* ← the column pointers of A stored in $A.p$
5 **for all** column ∈ *columns* **do**
6   *rows* ← the row pointers of A stored in $A.i$ located in the current column
7   **for all** row ∈ *rows* **do**
8   *val* ← the value of the matrix A in the current pair of (*row, column*) stored in $A.x$
9        $r[row]$ ← $r[row] + val.v[column]$

In Algorithm 11.8, every worker has computed a resultant local vector r so far; hence, all these local vectors (that have the same length) must be added together to produce the final result. This is depicted in Algorithm 11.9 in a single line of 3 by calling MPI_Allreduce. The MPI_IN_PLACE constant is a flag to let this MPI routine know that this call should involve both send and receive operations.

ALGORITHM 11.9: *collect_distributed_data()* **FUNCTION FOR SPARSE MATRIX-VECTOR MULTIPLICATION**

Definitions:
1 r: a vector that is used to store the result of multiplication on each MPI process
2 *size*: denotes how many elements the vector r has, which is equal to the number of A's rows

The Algorithm:
3 MPI_Allreduce(MPI_IN_PLACE, &r[0], size, MPI_DOUBLE, MPI_SUM,...)

11.5.4 Parallel Sparse Matrix-Matrix Multiplication

As the last MPI example in this chapter, a parallel implementation of sparse matrix-matrix multiplication (SPMM) is considered. SPMM has important applications in graph algorithms and scientific computing, such as multi-grid linear solvers, graph analysis, and shortest path finding, and is widely used in HPC. Hence, a parallel SPMM can have potential impacts on numerous applications. First, we devise a sparse SPMM algorithm that directly accesses the entries of multiplicand and multiplier matrices column by column. Then, it is parallelised akin to our developed parallel SPMV algorithm. Let's assume that we are going to multiply two sparse 4-by-4 matrices

$$C = A \times B = \overbrace{\begin{bmatrix} a_{11} & a_{12} & a_{13} & a_{14} \\ a_{21} & a_{22} & a_{23} & a_{24} \\ a_{31} & a_{32} & a_{33} & a_{34} \\ a_{41} & a_{42} & a_{43} & a_{44} \end{bmatrix}}^{\text{All workers}} \times \begin{bmatrix} \overbrace{\begin{matrix} b_{11} & b_{12} \\ b_{21} & b_{22} \\ b_{31} & b_{32} \\ b_{41} & b_{42} \end{matrix}}^{\text{Worker 1}} & \overbrace{\begin{matrix} b_{13} & b_{14} \\ b_{23} & b_{24} \\ b_{33} & b_{34} \\ b_{43} & b_{44} \end{matrix}}^{\text{Worker 2}} \end{bmatrix} = \begin{bmatrix} \overbrace{\begin{matrix} c_{11} & c_{12} \\ c_{21} & c_{22} \\ c_{31} & c_{32} \\ c_{41} & c_{42} \end{matrix}}^{\text{Worker 1}} & \overbrace{\begin{matrix} c_{13} & c_{14} \\ c_{23} & c_{24} \\ c_{33} & c_{34} \\ c_{43} & c_{44} \end{matrix}}^{\text{Worker 2}} \end{bmatrix}$$

Figure 11.7 A typical parallel example of a matrix-matrix multiplication over two workers.

A and B, and store the result in a C matrix shown in Figure 11.7. All three of the matrices are denoted symbolically.

As far as a sparse matrix is concerned in the CCS form and must be accessed by its columns, we can derive the symbolic expression of the first column of C matrix by expanding C=A×B in Figure 11.7 as follows:

$$\begin{bmatrix} c_{11} \\ c_{21} \\ c_{31} \\ c_{41} \end{bmatrix} = \begin{bmatrix} a_{11}b_{11} + a_{12}b_{21} + a_{13}b_{31} + a_{14}b_{41} \\ a_{21}b_{11} + a_{22}b_{21} + a_{23}b_{31} + a_{24}b_{41} \\ a_{31}b_{11} + a_{32}b_{21} + a_{33}b_{31} + a_{34}b_{41} \\ a_{41}b_{11} + a_{42}b_{21} + a_{43}b_{31} + a_{44}b_{41} \end{bmatrix} = \begin{bmatrix} a_{11} \\ a_{21} \\ a_{31} \\ a_{41} \end{bmatrix} b_{11} + \begin{bmatrix} a_{12} \\ a_{22} \\ a_{32} \\ a_{42} \end{bmatrix} b_{21} + \begin{bmatrix} a_{13} \\ a_{23} \\ a_{33} \\ a_{43} \end{bmatrix} b_{31} + \begin{bmatrix} a_{14} \\ a_{24} \\ a_{34} \\ a_{44} \end{bmatrix} b_{41}$$

As it can be seen, the first column of C is obtained by multiplying every column of A by individual row entries of the corresponding column in B. We can generalise this observation to conclude that, in SPMM for the CCS representation, every column j of the C matrix is a matrix-vector multiplication of the A matrix over B_{*j}.

By establishing our sequential SPMM algorithm, we can now dive into its parallelisation. The overall view of the parallelisation is depicted in Figure 11.7 with two workers. To avoid excessive complexity and for educational purposes, only the B matrix is broken into submatrices, each of which is sent to a single worker process which resembles what was done for the parallel SPMV algorithm. Therefore, matrix A is copied into the physical memory of all worker nodes without any division as exactly as it is. These steps are explained by Algorithm 11.10.

ALGORITHM 11.10: *distribute_data()* FUNCTION FOR SPARSE MATRIX-VECTOR MULTIPLICATION

Definitions:

A, *B*: two sparse n-by-n matrices to get multiplied
p, *i*, *x*: elements to store the sparse matrix *A*
v: the matrix A get multiplied by vector *v* or a sub-vector of *v*
w: An MPI worker process
workers: the list of worker MPI processes

The Algorithm:

if *rank* = *controller* **do**

```
 7   for all w ∈ workers do
 8       Send the data structure (p, i, x) associated with A to w via MPI_Send
 9       Send the matrix B to w by performing lines 7 to 9 of Algorithm 11.7
10   else do
11       Receive (p, i, x) for the current worker from the controller process and reconstruct
     the matrix A via
     MPI_Recv
12   Receive B matrix for the current worker by performing line 11 of Algorithm 11.7
13   MPI_Barrier()
```

In accordance with our parallel SPMV algorithm, a bare minimum of change to the sequential SPMM is required for its parallelisation in the `perform_computation()` phase, mainly thanks to the local view of the distributed B and C submatrices. Algorithm 11.11 details the computation phase of SPMM, which is too complex with respect to its dense matrix-matrix multiplication counterpart. The operation progresses over each column of the B matrix in line 15. We keep track of how many non-zero entries per iteration exist that will be used to reconstruct the matrix C. In each column of B, rows of both A and B matrices are fetched and multiplication over them is performed in lines 17–33. Because we are dealing with sparse rows of a column (i.e., we are not aware exactly which rows are non-zero), two helper vectors are used, including ws and x. The workspace vector provides the ability to check if there is a non-zero entry in the kth row of the multiplication of two corresponding columns of the A and B matrix. In addition, the variable x stores the actual multiplication of two columns in compliance with entries in ws. If an entry exists at a location of ws, the current value of x at that position will be incremented by the multiplication values fetched from both columns (i.e., valA and valB in lines 21 and 22) during the iterations in lines 23 and 24; otherwise, it is just an ordinary multiplication of valA by valB. When a new entry insertion into the C matrix is required, and the underlying vectors of C.i and C.x have no sufficient space, they must be resized in lines 26 to 28 to accept the new entry. Finally, for each column of the C matrix and after performing all operations, the results of the multiplication of the A matrix by the column of the B matrix, which have been saved in x vector, are copied into the end of C.x. Note that the positions in x that have entries for this operation are fetched from C.i, which beforehand had been inserted into C.i in line 30. Moreover, the column pointer of the next column is updated in line 35 to include the recent number of non-zero elements in the C matrix.

ALGORITHM 11.11: *perform_computation()* **FUNCTION FOR SPARSE MATRIX-MATRIX MULTIPLICATION**

Definitions:
```
1  A: the matrix A on all workers
2  B,C: A sub-matrix from B and C on every worker
3  columns_B: the column pointers B matrix
```

4 *column$_B$*: a column pointer in the current column of *the B* matrix

5 *nz$_{total}$*: the total number of nonzero entries in the *C* matrix

6 *nz*: the number of nonzero entries in the current column of the *C* matrix

7 *rows$_A$, rows$_B$*: the row pointers in the current column of *A* and *B* matrix

8 *row$_A$, row$_B$*: a row pointer in the current column of *A* and *B* matrix

9 *value$_A$, value$_B$*: the value of two entries of *the A* and *B* matrix in their current row and column

10 *nzmax*: the maximum nonzero entries that a sparse matrix can have

11 *ws*: a workspace vector used to keep track of a given row index if it is already in the set

12 *x*: a dense vector that is used to store the outcome of multiplication of the matrix *A* by the submatrix *B* on each worker represents the rows of the current column of *the C* matrix

The Algorithm:

13 $nz_{total} \leftarrow 0$

14 $columns_B \leftarrow$ the column pointers of B stored in $B.p$

15 **for all** $column_B \in columns_B$ **do**

16      $nz \leftarrow 0$

17      $rows_B \leftarrow$ the row pointers of B stored in $B.i$ located in the current *column*

18   **for all** $row_B \in rows_B$ **do**

19          $rows_A \leftarrow$ the row pointers of A stored in $A.i$ located in the current *column*

20   **for all** $row_A \in rows_A$ **do**

21              $value_B \leftarrow B[row_B][column_B]$

22              $value_A \leftarrow B[row_A][column_B]$

23   **if** $ws[row_A] = column_B + 1$ **do**

24                  $x[row_A] \leftarrow x[row_A] + value_A.value_B$

25   **else do**

26   **if** $C.nzmax < nz_{total} + 1$ **do**

27                      $C.nzmax \leftarrow C.nzmax + 2(nz_{total} + 1)$

28   Resize $C.i$ and $C.x$ to the size of $C.nzmax$

29                  $ws[row_A] \leftarrow column + 1$

30                  $C.i[nz\_total] \leftarrow row_A$

31                  $x[row_A] \leftarrow value_A.value_B$

32                  $nz \leftarrow nz + 1$

33                  $nz_{total} \leftarrow nz_{total} + 1$

34   Copy the results saved in x to appropriate entries in $C.x$

35      $C.p[column_B + 1] \leftarrow nz_{total}$

The function `collect_distributed_data()` for our parallel SPMM illustrated in Algorithm 11.12 considerably differs from our parallel SPMV because we must transfer the whole submatrices from workers, which contain triplets of (p, i, x), to the controller process. The chief role of the controller is to integrate all the results into a resultant matrix C in lines 4 through 6.

ALGORITHM 11.12: *collect_distributed_data()* **FUNCTION FOR SPARSE MATRIX-MATRIX MULTIPLICATION**

Definitions:
1 C: A resultant sparse n-by-n matrices after distributed multiplication
2 w: An MPI worker process
3 *workers*: the list of worker MPI processes

The Algorithm:
4 **if** *rank* = *controller* **do**
5   **for all** $w \in$ workers **do**
6   Receive submatrix $w.C$ and copy it to appropriate places in the allocated matrix C on the controller (if the size of the internal data structure of C changes, resize the C matrix) via consecutive call to **MPI_Recv**
7 **else do**
8   Send the data structure of the submatrix C on the current worker to the controller by consecutive calling to **MPI_Send**

Finally, we leave it as an exercise to the reader to improve the performance of the parallel SPMM algorithm such that the A matrix is also evenly distributed between workers. It is expected that this improvement outperforms the current algorithm in terms of locality of reference (spatial/data locality) and the most efficient use of processor caches of every node on an HPC cluster.

Index